D0899297

BALKAN SMOKE

TOBACCO AND THE MAKING OF MODERN BULGARIA

MARY C. NEUBURGER

CORNELL UNIVERSITY PRESS
Ithaca and London

Copyright © 2013 by Cornell University

All rights reserved. Except for brief quotations in a review,
this book, or parts thereof, must not be reproduced in
any form without permission in writing from the publisher. For information, address Cornell University Press,
Sage House, 512 East State Street, Ithaca, New York 14850.

First published 2013 by Cornell University Press
First printing, Cornell Paperbacks, 2016

Library of Congress Cataloging-in-Publication Data

Neuburger, Mary, 1966–
Balkan smoke : tobacco and the making of modern
Bulgaria / Mary Neuburger.
    p. cm.
  Includes bibliographical references and index.
  ISBN 978-0-8014-5084-6 (cloth : alk. paper)
  ISBN 978-1-5017-0572-4 (pbk. : alk. paper)
  1. Tobacco industry—Bulgaria—History—19th century.
2. Tobacco industry—Bulgaria—History—20th century.
3. Smoking—Social aspects—Bulgaria—History—19th
century.   4. Smoking—Social aspects—Bulgaria—
History—20th century. I. Title.
  HD9145.B9N48   2013
  338.4'76797309499—dc23   2012018011

Cornell University Press strives to use environmentally
responsible suppliers and materials to the fullest extent
possible in the publishing of its books. Such materials
include vegetable-based, low-VOC inks and acid-free
papers that are recycled, totally chlorine-free, or partly
composed of nonwood fibers. For further information,
visit our website at www.cornellpress.cornell.edu.

Dedicated to my loving parents, Sandy and Jerry,
whose unrelenting belief in me made me who I am

Contents

Acknowledgments

I would like to thank a number of people and institutions that extended the support and resources that made the writing of this book possible. First and foremost, the University of Texas granted me the supported leave-time to pursue this research and fill these many pages with my findings. My colleagues in the University of Texas history department offered encouragement, helpful commentary, and pointed critique. In particular I thank Anne Martinez, Madeline Hsu, Ginny Burnett, Nancy Stalker, Joan Neuberger, David Crew, Bob Abzug, Tatiana Lichtenstein, Karl Miller, Ruramisai Charumbira, Mark Metzler, James Vaughn, and anyone else who listened to my ramblings on tobacco. I also thank the chair of the history department, Alan Tully. Among the more recent sounding boards, Doug Biow was a particularly valuable colleague and friend who helped me weather the transition to being an administrator while the book was still in process. I also warmly thank my graduate students—Emily Hillhouse, Zachary Doleshal, Karl Brown, and Mehmet Celik—who listened, commented, and in the cases of Emily and Zach, helped to edit the rough manuscript. I thank the Center for Russian, East European and Eurasian Studies that not only granted me research support and an interdisciplinary home, but also adopted me—or perhaps I adopted it—as fearless leader in 2010.

In addition to the University of Texas, I also received financial support for this project at various stages from the National Council for Eurasian and East European Research, the American Council of Learned Societies, and the International Research and Exchanges Board. Without their support the research and writing of this work would simply not have been possible.

I am also grateful to a number of friends and colleagues outside of the University of Texas who listened to my ranting or who read and commented on my work over the years. I am sure I am forgetting many of you but to name a few I thank Paulina Bren, Kate Brown, Artan Hoxha, Ali Igmen, James Felak, Hillel Kieval, Kristen Ghodsee, Patrick Patterson, Maria Bucur, Melissa Bokovoy, Keith Brown, Irina Gigova, and Theodora Dragostinova. A special thanks to my friends and colleagues in Bulgaria, especially Mariana

Stamova, Kostadin Grozev, Rumen Daskalov, Rossitza Guencheva, and all the archivists and librarians who were so patient and helped me find my way through the enormous maze of sources.

Finally, I am grateful for the help of my family. A thank you to my children—Sophie, Bella, and Dean—for their patience and support while I was a slave to the documents and computer for all those years. Thank you Ann Marie, my ever faithful sister. Thank you Mom and Dad! You are the best and I dedicate this book to you for all you have given to me and endured from me over the years. Thank you Jeff, for giving me a second wind in life.

Some material from chapter 3 originally appeared, in altered form, as "The *Krŭchma*, the *Kafene*, and the Orient Express: Tobacco, Alcohol, and the Gender of Sacred and Secular Restraint in Bulgaria, 1856–1939," *Aspasia: International Yearbook of Central, Eastern, and Southeastern European Women's and Gender History* 5, no. 1 (2011): 70–91. Parts of chapter 6 were first published in "The Taste of Smoke: *Bulgartabak* and the Manufacturing of Cigarettes and Satisfaction," in *Communism Unwrapped: Consumption in Postwar Eastern Europe*, ed. Paulina Bren and Mary Neuburger (Oxford: Oxford University Press, 2012); and will be incorporated into "Smoke and Beers: Touristic Escapes and Places to Party in Communist Bulgaria, 1956–1976," in *Socialist Escapes: Breaking Away from Ideology and Everyday Routine in Eastern Europe, 1945–1989*, ed. Cathleen Giustino, Catherine Plum, and Alexander Vari (New York: Berghahn Press, 2013). The material is reused here, in revised form, with the permission of the publishers. Parts of chapters 6 and 7 were drawn from "Inhaling Luxury: Smoking and Anti-Smoking in Socialist Bulgaria 1947–1989," in *Pleasures in Socialism: Leisure and Luxury in the Eastern Bloc*, ed. David Crowley and Susan Reid (Evanston, IL: Northwestern University Press, 2010), and are used by permission. Other sections of chapter 7 were adapted from "Smokes for Big Brother: Bulgaria, the USSR and the Politics of Tobacco in the Cold War," in *Tobacco in Russian History and Culture*, ed. Tricia Starks and Matt Romaniello (New York: Routledge, 2009).

BALKAN
SMOKE

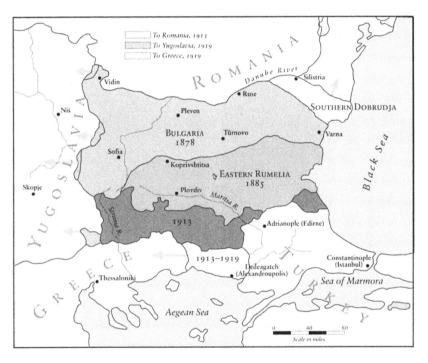

The changing borders of Bulgaria, 1878–1945

Introduction

"People smoke, from the poles to the equator, the civilized and the savage. As one wise observer from the Orient answered to the enigmatic question of why; the sick smoke—to improve their health, the dreamer—to improve his mood, the happy—to heighten his joy in life, the rich man—out of boredom, the poor man—to forget his horrible fate."

—*Bŭlgarski tiutiun* (Bulgarian Tobacco) July 7, 1935, 2.

There is something about tobacco that drew me in; it was as if I were being deeply inhaled. Perhaps it was the picturesque garlands of lush green tobacco leaves that hung drying in the eaves of houses in the Rhodope and Pirin Mountains of southern Bulgaria. These leaves seemed to call me to explore the lives spent gathering them and hanging them to dry, sorting, packing, rolling them into cigarettes, trading them in distant smoke-filled rooms. I wanted to follow tobacco from these mountain plots to the smoky cafés, bars, and restaurants of Sofia—not the ones I inhabited between long days in the archives but the establishments of bygone days. My fascination, though, was also rooted in today's Sofia, a world of sociability that still requires a cigarette in hand. I wished I could partake, but I felt unequipped—unable, or perhaps simply unwilling, to inhale. Still, I was and am continually seduced by the grace, the repose, the sensual aura of passionate smokers and the era they evoke, an era when people either didn't know about or didn't fear the effects of so many things that bring pleasure into our lives.

Today tobacco is a bogeyman, most starkly in North America, and perhaps rightfully so, though it was only a generation ago that North Americans smoked in restaurants, café, on planes and buses, and even in classrooms, while our favorite heroes and ingenues puffed away on the silver screen. Smoke's path from delectable to devilish was a long and complicated one, but for better or worse we have arrived in a new world. The question is, how did we get here? And why are Bulgarians, like many others across the globe, still "behind" us in this regard?

The global story of tobacco has been told in splendid and enlightening detail.[1] It has drawn in historians, who have explored the economic, political, and social implications of the commodity in various national contexts, most notably in the United States.[2] But what about other contexts, peripheries, or, more accurately, other *centers* of the tobacco world? As other work on tobacco production, commerce, and consumption has shown, outside the United States the tobacco narrative is radically different.[3] Tobacco was experienced, lived, and filtered in entirely different ways, driving or accompanying different kinds of transformations. This book explores the ways in which the social life of tobacco in Bulgaria was shaped by local mores and experiences and mitigated Bulgaria's place on the periphery of other centers of political and economic influence. By 1966 Bulgaria had become the largest exporter of cigarettes in the world. I explore the path to that place of preeminence, focusing on the attendant social and cultural transformations, as well as the politics and geopolitics of Bulgarian tobacco.

Tobacco provides a valuable lens through which one can gainfully study and even rethink the parameters of Bulgarian history. As Dimitŭr Iadkov, director of the state-run Bulgarian tobacco industry from 1970 to 1991, observed, "I am certain that there is no other economic branch whose history has more analogy and organic connection with the history of Bulgaria than does tobacco. In its 'biography,' as in a mirror, one sees Bulgaria's economic, social, and political condition."[4] This book is essentially the biography that Iadkov suggests. It traces the commodification, patterns of production and commerce, and modes of consumption of tobacco in Bulgarian history. It illuminates the ways in which tobacco was woven into local social, cultural, and political dynamics as well as into Bulgaria's shifting relationships to the outside world. Tobacco did not just reflect—like Iadkov's mirror—changes in Bulgarian society. Its commodification was a critical factor in *driving* those changes. Pushing further, I maintain that smoking itself was implicated in Bulgarian social change. The pharamacological and sociological impacts of smoking were instrumental in the arrival of *modernity* to the Bulgarian lands. As elusive as such a prospect may be, smoking seems to have driven transformation, accompanying and even propelling a coming of age for various social groups. At the same time, tobacco consumption, like the tobacco trade, was always linked to global consumption patterns. The story of Bulgarian tobacco is at once deeply local and profoundly transnational.

This history of Bulgarian tobacco explores the plant as a source of pleasure and toxicity, promise and violence, entrepreneurship and exploitation. I make every effort to understand the cultural mores and complicated politics of the age in which tobacco became first acceptable and then desirable. I juxtapose the achievements of tobacconists and merchants to the deplorable conditions of tobacco workers and peasant growers in the pre-communist period. I trace the fall of Bulgaria's great tobacco moguls as well as the greatly improved conditions of the tobacco workers and peasant growers in the communist period. Throughout, I embrace the pleasure of smokers and the fragrant quality of a Bulgarian cigarette while giving due respect to the heartfelt campaigns against smoking that punctuate the modern age.

More pointedly, I show how conflict tied to tobacco production, commerce, and consumption is grounded in Bulgarian history and extends well beyond. Tobacco, like other commodities, inevitably crosses borders. So too does this story. It moves in caravans to Ottoman Istanbul, on ships up the Danube to Austria-Hungary and later Nazi Germany, across the Black Sea to Soviet Russia, and across oceans to the New World, Africa, and Asia. Bulgarian tobacco promises a journey that takes us not only into the hamlets of the Rhodope Mountains or the smoky recesses of Sofia café life but also to the fields and factories of R. J. Reynolds in North Carolina. The hero of my story is Bulgarian tobacco itself; a substance whose aroma infused so many lives in and outside Bulgaria, from the pickers and sorters to traders and merchants, politicians, armies, and terrorists, and finally to smokers who wanted simply to enjoy a cigarette. These lives were at once separate yet entwined by the "godly and devilish" weed that bewitched not just Bulgarians but the entire modern world.[5]

The Social Life of Tobacco

Every commodity has a "social life" that can be defined through its value and modes of consumption, production, and exchange—in short, through its social meanings and impact over time.[6] For tobacco, as for other "intoxicants," these meanings are particularly complicated because of the physical and moral implications of bodily inebriation. A prodigious literature has focused on tobacco, which along with alcohol and coffee was one of the modern era's preeminent chemical palliatives.[7] The circulation and consumption of these mind-altering substances have always been subject to public scrutiny and debate. Yet they have thrived precisely because their addictive nature as stimulants or depressants made them a "necessity" for increasing numbers of consumers, and as a result their value grew exponentially. Alcohol and tobacco profits and taxes, in fact, provided the fiscal foundation for many states and empires. The value of tobacco, like that of any commodity, was not inherent but provisional, created by a variety of social forces and conditions.[8] For whatever reason, tobacco, along with its preferred accompaniments coffee and alcohol, was consistently the twentieth-century drug of choice.

Tobacco became king in the United States during that century, but it also thrived in other regions that had particularly hospitable climates and networks of exchange. Bulgaria was one of those places. Tobacco seeds had germinated in its soils since the seventeenth century, brought from the Americas and introduced as a curiosity to Europe, Asia, and other parts of the Old World.[9] The soils of the western Balkans, then a core province of the Ottoman Empire, were ideal for the plant, which underwent a significant transformation as it adjusted to the mountainous region's sandy, alkaline soils. The result was the emergence of a number of varieties that fell under the subgenus of "Turkish" or, more properly, "Oriental tobacco." In the Americas, the tobacco plant also evolved into a few common varieties— primarily Virginia and Burley—with stable, recognizable properties. These commercially grown American tobaccos tended to be higher in nicotine but decidedly less flavorful than the Oriental types. Such differences assured that both varietal groups had a place in the nineteenth and twentieth centuries' global marketplace.

The market for American and Oriental-type tobaccos did not emerge overnight, even on a regional level. When it was first introduced in the Old World, in fact, the American plant provoked a strongly negative response in many quarters. In the Ottoman lands as well as Britain, Russia, and elsewhere, tobacco was debated, rejected, and periodically banned as religiously unorthodox or seditious.[10] Its novelty bred suspicion, compounded by uncertainty about its chemical properties and social implications. In spite of such complications, by the late seventeenth century tobacco enjoyed a wide measure of social, political, and religious acceptability. In the Balkans, tobacco's compatibility with the local Ottoman Muslim coffeehouse culture facilitated its acceptance. Since alcohol was prohibited by Islamic law, tobacco and coffee provided the needed lubricants for public male sociability. Though the coffeehouse remained primarily a Muslim institution well into the nineteenth century, Christians and Jews were exposed to and increasingly intimate with local Ottoman coffeehouse culture. Smoke was in the air, so to speak, and since tobacco was grown locally, it was widely available to broad segments of the population.[11] In contrast, tobacco was integrated into early modern Western European culture always as an imported and hence borrowed luxury good.[12]

Whereas tobacco itself arrived from the New World, the West's smoking *rituals* were borrowed from the East. Oriental-style smoking became an escapist symbol of wealth and excess for the West to emulate, succeeding where American "savage" smoking rites had not.[13] Like many other practices and institutions long seen as integral to the birth of the *modern* in the West, smoking, like coffee and the coffeehouse, was the product of Eurasian cultural interaction and exchange.[14] In time, the coffeehouse was transformed in its various local contexts, giving us the British and German bourgeois commercial institutions and the French cafés notorious for middle-class oriented intellectual life and proletarian sedition.[15] In turn, as travel abroad increased during the nineteenth century, these now distinctively "European" coffeehouses would play a role in the making of modern Bulgaria. Still, it was the Ottoman coffeehouse where Bulgarians first *learned* to smoke and Ottoman markets that drove tobacco (and other) commercial networks and practices.[16] In and outside the world of tobacco, the West was not the only point on the Bulgarian compass when it came to the making of modernity.

Smoking was the quintessential twentieth-century habit, a necessary accoutrement of the modern man and woman. The century witnessed a palpable acceleration of consumption, production, and commerce not only in Europe and Bulgaria but around the world. There was something about tobacco—perhaps its pharmacological effects—that both drove forward and calmed, both accelerated and paced the makers of modernity. At the same time, the "modern condition" was brought into tobacco-growing regions through the weed's production and commodification, the steep rise in value, the resultant credit-cash economies, and the influx of merchants and processing plants. The unparalleled pace and scope of change in the modern period brought new modes of living, thinking, and consuming, as well as social and political mobilization.[17] From the city to the village, tobacco facilitated the transformation of minds and bodies, economies and societies. It was a boon to those regions that were well equipped to provide the world with the wondrous weed. But tobacco also brought exploitation, economic ruin, social and ethnic conflict, even war and death. In short, as Bulgaria began to supply tobacco to the world, tobacco brought the promise and predicaments of the modern world to Bulgarian soil.

Producing Histories

The prolific Soviet author Ilya Ehrenburg was said to have claimed, "Capitalism in Bulgaria smells of tobacco."[18] Without a doubt capitalism followed the tobacco seed, scattered far and wide and planted deep in Bulgarian soil. Histories of tobacco elsewhere tend to trace the social life of the plant either through trajectories of production and commerce or through consumer phenomena, the expansion of smoking and its discontents. But this separation is largely artificial as these producer and consumer histories inevitably overlap; demand drives production, while production is linked to demand through marketing and trade.

In the Bulgarian case, wool and wheat dominated nineteenth-century trade, spurring the commercial revival of that period. But tobacco slowly gained ground at the end of the century, its value enormously higher, its transportation costs lower. Local and regional demand crept upward as new segments of Ottoman and post-Ottoman Bulgarian society began to partake in the pleasures of smoking. But ultimately it was Anglo-American and Central European fascination with "Turkish" tobaccos that brought about the surge in prices for Balkan tobaccos. Demand accelerated exponentially during and after World War I and especially World War II, for both wars made smokers out of large segments of the population—particularly the troops who returned from the front accustomed to cigarette rations as well as the "emancipated" women who worked on the home front. Bulgaria supplied tobacco to the Central Powers during the Great War, thereby stoking a taste for Bulgarian tobaccos across Central Europe. Demand grew in the interwar years, making "Bulgarian gold" the country's most valuable and marketable commodity. The especially lucrative tobacco trade with Germany drew Bulgaria into World War II, after which the Soviets emerged as the primary consumers of Bulgarian leaf. Trains that had once headed northwest were redirected eastward as the Soviet Bloc became an all-but-captive market for Bulgaria's most valuable export.

The communist years were the heyday of "Bulgarian gold," which now attracted worldwide attention. More than ever, tobacco was a conduit for Bulgaria's ever-shifting connections to the outside world, East and West. The postwar transition to a communist system witnessed the greatest expansion and success the tobacco industry had seen. The tobacco-growing and -processing and cigarette-manufacturing industries were integrated under the umbrella of the state monopoly Bulgartabak, and Bulgaria became the key supplier of cigarettes to the Soviet Union and the Bloc. Contrary to what one might expect of a communist enterprise, by the 1960s, Bulgartabak began to pay ever-closer attention to the issue of product quality, branding, and the desires of the Bloc consumer. By 1966 Bulgaria was the largest producer of tobacco per capita in the world.[19] The transformation in the lives of workers and tobacco growers was as impressive as the production statistics. Tobacco truly became Bulgarian gold for more than a privileged few. One-eighth of the Bulgarian population was now involved in a far safer, more humane and streamlined industry that financed much of the infrastructure and many of the social services that brought Bulgaria firmly into the twentieth century.

Global engagement was central to Bloc producer and *consumer* experiences in this period. Though the Soviets and the core Bloc states were its main market, Bulgartabak enjoyed carte blanche to carry out technological exchanges and sign licensing agreements with American and other Western tobacco companies. A wide range of Western aesthetic and technological forms were selectively amalgamated into a system that allowed a surprising degree of creativity and flexibility.[20] The tobacco industry illustrates this elasticity even as it reveals the challenges and pitfalls of economic development under communism.

Consuming Thoughts

Capturing a history of smoking in Bulgaria with paper and pen—or less romantically, in an electronic document—has been one of this project's driving impulses. Certainly I was fascinated by the story of camel caravans carrying tobacco, wily merchants, tobacco plants clinging to mountainsides, and dust-choked tobacco factories. But somehow the story of smoking itself was more enticing, in part because it eludes documentation, dissipating like smoke. As much as smoking has been maligned, it has also been celebrated as a cultural phenomenon worthy of description and analysis.[21] At the same time a spate of scholars now argue that consumption was the engine of the Industrial Revolution and of modernity itself.[22] Consumption has also been linked to self-expression, subjectivity, resistance, morality and social identities—gender, class, and race.[23] Coupling consumption with intoxication brings forth a number of discrete and especially intriguing issues— propriety and social boundaries, morality, deviance, health and longevity, pleasure and escapism.[24] Such issues were key to mapping a history of tobacco consumption in uncharted Bulgarian waters.

Much of this world has been lost or hidden in bits and pieces, passing references that dot a vast quantity of materials. Still, as I stumbled across many such sources, a detailed and colorful picture emerged, not only of smoking in Bulgaria but also of its feisty discontents. Individuals and movements opposed to smoking voiced their opinions in editorials, letters, and morality tales devoted to the spread and evils of smoking. In contrast, the memoirs of smokers are replete with celebratory odes to the muse of smoke and imagery of a time when smoke saturated the air. In a sea of memoirs I found scattered islands of lush description of Bulgarian smoke and sociability. While archival sources and tobacco industry periodicals revealed trends and aesthetic shifts in Bulgarian (and global) tobacco consumption, these memoirs closed the circle, cementing the inherent link between production and consumption.

Tobacco consumption in Bulgaria, I found, was best explored from the vantage point of the *kafene* (coffeehouse or café) and to a lesser extent the *krŭchma* (tavern). These leisure venues, as I call them, are by no means the sum and substance of the smoking story. Rather, they form a primary point of reference, a place to begin and return. They were, I argue, a central and important trope in practices and understandings of smoking because they were so public and functioned, in certain periods, as central sites of Bulgarian political and cultural exchange.[25] I explore the smoke-filled kafene (and krŭchma) in Bulgarian culture from the late Ottoman period to World War I within an archipelago of urban sites—in the Ottoman Empire and abroad—where a new Bulgarian elite gathered. Muslims in the Ottoman Balkans, as elsewhere in the empire, had smoked in the coffeehouse environment for centuries. But for Balkan Christians the move to the sober kafene marked a transition from the drunken forms of male social interaction that had characterized the traditional krŭchma. By the nineteenth century, expanded legal parameters and new social roles accompanied the entrance of non-Muslims into the world of tobacco consumption, as well as its production and commerce. The Bulgarian national revival and the country's cultural and political coming of age blossomed in both the smoke-filled environment of the Ottoman coffeehouse and the European café.[26]

The kafene, then, was profoundly local but also became a context for Europeanization, that is, the appropriation of a variety of new modes of cultural production and political debate. In the interwar period, the kafene was at the heart of intellectual life. Significantly, the kafene and the krŭchma remained primarily male spaces for smoking and sociability, though a select group of intellectual women did make inroads into kafene life. In the same years, women from various social groups were present at some of the newer establishments of the period. Still, the notion of the "fallen" smoking woman remained prevalent in that period, revealing the double standard inherent in gendered patterns of smoking and propriety.

The unprecedented consumption of tobacco in interwar Bulgaria also provoked a robust abstinence movement that proclaimed the evils of the weed, often linking them to the desultory charms of the city with its Western influences. Abstinence impulses in Bulgaria flowed from two rather disparate sources, American (and Bulgarian convert) Protestants and the primarily communist Bulgarian Left. These groups shared a penetrating social critique and a radical vision for moral uplift and social reform, which nourished various utopian visions of the future, in heaven or on earth. The resonance of these visions among various segments of the population was understandable given the sense of moral free fall that accompanied World War I, a total war in which Bulgaria was defeated and humiliated. But the sources of both abstinence movements were, in a sense, foreign, and both were doomed to repression by right-wing political forces that dominated interwar and war-time Bulgaria. Though Bulgaria's Nazi German ally was strongly opposed to smoking as "polluting" the national body, the Bulgarian state viewed abstinence movements as a threat to the body politic. Moreover, as the main beneficiary of tobacco industry revenues and consumption taxes, the state could hardly have been expected to welcome the antismoking message.

In the decades after World War II, the communist takeover posed an entirely new set of practical and theoretical concerns about smoking and society. As the state-run Bulgarian tobacco industry produced ever-greater numbers of increasingly luxurious cigarettes, official anti-smoking campaigns were inherently contradictory. Yet by the 1960s and 1970s communist abstinence efforts had reemerged even as the state provided cigarettes and places to smoke them as never before. In the later decades of the period there was a veritable explosion of state-built and -run restaurants, cafés, hotels, and seaside resorts. As elsewhere in the Bloc, the post-Stalinist Bulgarian communist regime openly attempted to provide the "good life" to the "workers" but also to new elites and technocrats—an urbanized and educated segment of the population with novel consumer expectations.[27] Paradoxically, as state ministries provided more luxurious places to rest and cigarettes to smoke, the regime also funded a reinvigorated abstinence movement. In particular, heightened concerns over the growing numbers of female and young smokers sparked more directed campaigns—with exhibits, meetings, plays, periodicals, and books that explored the health as well as the social and moral implications of smoking. This literature linked smoking to Western moral profligacy and remnants of the capitalist past, a presumed threat to the building of socialism. But in spite of the regime's efforts, Bulgarian smoking rates skyrocketed under communism. For Bulgarian smokers the voice of abstinence was just another form of state propaganda.

Nothing in these chapters is meant to imply that smoking was the most central issue in Bulgarian public life or the primary engine of Bulgarian history. On the contrary, smoking was more often than not a given. It was literally the air people breathed, not to be questioned or wrangled with. Undoubtedly its pharmacological effects did provide a kind of mental fuel to important figures and social groups and hence to developments in Bulgarian history. This, though, is mere speculation and hard to trace precisely. Yet smoking as a phenomenon—and particularly life in Bulgaria's smoke-filled rooms—not only intrigues but enlightens, revealing deeper issues in each period of the country's history. Tobacco consumption in Bulgaria helps fill in a global picture in which consumption was always profoundly local and culturally determined. Bulgarians loved and hated smoking as they saw fit; the smoking West (and world) was at times an alluring model and at other times a decadent foil.

I would venture to guess that few in Bulgaria, including the smokers who still frequent the ubiquitous local cafés and new "cocktail bars," know the extent to which tobacco has permeated their history. Exploring the history of tobacco from seed to cigarette has added an entirely new dimension to my understanding of Bulgarian history. So many people have stories to tell—the tobacco-growing peasants in their mountain hamlets, the factory workers mired in dust, the specialists and the merchants in their smoke-filled rooms, and the ordinary and extraordinary Bulgarians in their gritty rural taverns or their gleaming Sofia cafés. I only hope that the publication of this book will set me free from my five-year obsession with Bulgarian tobacco. Perhaps whatever has drawn me in so deeply will finally exhale.

CHAPTER 1

Coffeehouse Babble

Smoking and Sociability in the Long Nineteenth Century

> Ganko's *kafene* was, as usual, filled with noise and
> smoke. It was the meeting place of old and young
> alike, where public matters were discussed, and the
> Eastern Question too, as well as all the domestic and
> foreign policy of Europe. A miniature parliament one
> might say.
>
> —Ivan Vazov, *Under the Yoke*

Awash in smoke and sociability, Ganko's kafene
is the fictional social hub and main setting for the most widely read Bulgarian novel, Ivan Vazov's *Under the Yoke (Pod Igoto)*. With Vazov as guide, the
reader experiences Ganko's social panorama, its parade of archetypal characters from a Balkan mountain town in Ottoman Bulgaria who drink bitter coffee, ruminate and debate, laugh and observe, within a "dense fog
of tobacco smoke."[1] Set in the period before Bulgarian political autonomy,
Ganko's has an air of political excitement. On the canvas of the kafene Vazov
skillfully paints a late Ottoman landscape—the months leading up to the
April Uprising of 1876—rife with social change. Indeed, in *Under the Yoke*
Vazov portrays a time of upheaval in which generations, ways of life, and
political objectives collide head on, noticeably between the kafene walls. Yet
in spite of this ferment, the kafene and the surrounding Balkan towns strike
the reader as somehow timeless; stagnation is the subtext to the impulse for
change.

The social life of tobacco in Bulgaria's long nineteenth century is virtually
inseparable from the life and times of the kafene. Slavic-speaking Christian, or "Bulgarian,"[2] men had traditionally gathered in the alcohol-imbibed
krŭchma (tavern), but over the course of the century they began to enter
the "sober" social life of the kafene. Already a centuries-old Balkan Muslim tradition, the kafene was a new phenomenon for Balkan Christians, a

Bulgarian men at a traditional krŭchma in the Plovdiv region, date unknown. Courtesy of the Regional State Archive in Plovdiv.

portal to a new world. Facilitated by the ritualized consumption of coffee and tobacco, the discovery and invention of "Bulgarianness" took place, at least in part, amid kafene conviviality. Smoking and sipping coffee in the kafene (and later in the European café) became intimately connected to Bulgarian upward mobility; to their increased authority in Ottoman villages, towns, and cities; and for many, to a national and political awakening.[3] The changing clientele of the Balkan kafene to a large degree mirrored the dramatic changes in Bulgarian society in the long nineteenth century.[4]

Patterns of tobacco consumption both reflected and drove new modes of political organization and cultural identification, particularly inside privileged smoking venues like the kafene. Smoking, in a sense, was connected to Bulgarians' initiation into a broader world of commerce, politics, and urban culture that took on a decidedly European hue over the course of the century. It is tempting to map this story through the familiar paradigm of "Europeanization," which so often shapes understandings of this period in both Bulgarian and Ottoman-Balkan history.[5] Certainly the penetration of European ideas, material culture, social mores, and a range of institutions was an important aspect of change in the nineteenth-century Balkans. This was especially true after the Crimean War (1853–56) and the momentous Russo-Turkish War (1877–78), in which Bulgaria gained autonomy and de facto independence from the Ottomans. Western commerce, consular and missionary activity, and the travels and studies of Bulgarians abroad brought an avalanche of influences, and the kafene was an important conduit. But an emphasis on Europeanization offers a rather false and value-laden teleology of change that belies the complexity of the Bulgarian introduction into a world of smoking and sociability. For many Bulgarians, their entrance into kafene culture was entirely local or connected to work and travel to Ottoman towns or cosmopolitan port cities. Of course, Bulgarian merchant colonies abroad were also exposed to European café culture, but Ottoman kafene culture in Istanbul and the Bulgarian provinces was the most readily available coffeehouse experience.

Significantly, the Ottoman coffeehouse was the original model for ritualistic coffee and tobacco consumption in Europe, imported and appropriated into early modern culture along with other Eastern "pleasures."[6] Over the centuries its shape and aesthetics evolved in various contexts, subjected to a range of both laudatory and critical appraisals.[7] And while the café drew scrutiny, European observers also projected onto the Ottoman kafene their own doubts and anxieties about idleness and lax morality at home. Western visitors seemed preoccupied with the coffeehouse and Ottoman smoking habits. For most, the patterns of Ottoman Muslim leisure were emblematic of idleness, decadence, and degeneration. Yet others viewed the Bulgarian shift from the drunken krŭchma to the sober kafene as a positive phenomenon. Idle as it may have seemed, the kafene was a presumed improvement for drunken and "subjugated" Christian men.

Western appraisals of local vices were voiced just as increasingly decadent forms of Western leisure culture were making their way into the Ottoman and post-Ottoman realm. These both seduced and repelled Bulgarians, who saw them as either pleasurable or as a perceived threat to Balkan national cultures and mores. Some were attracted to Western impulses of "moral uplift," while others saw such notions as fundamentally foreign and patronizing, attached to invasive Protestant missionary efforts. In short, Bulgarian kafene and smoking culture evolved in the midst of a simultaneous embrace and rejection of various elements of Western leisure culture and normative values. In addition, because smoking and kafene culture were both local and broadly cosmopolitan, they could be embraced as intimately native or rejected as deeply foreign.

By the late nineteenth century, Bulgarian smoking had become a constant in a rapidly transforming world of commerce, politics, leisure, and sociability. Whether associated with sobriety in the kafene, or inebriation in the krŭchma, Bulgarians learned to smoke amid profound shifts in Ottoman and Western smoking practices. As Bulgarian smoking increased, so too did anti–Ottoman and anti-western sentiments influence newly articulated critiques of smoking and leisure, and the broader project of defining boundaries of national culture and public morality. Embraced or reviled, smoking had carved a permanent place for itself in the Bulgarian social world while undeniably playing a role in the rapid transformation of that world.

Aghast and Titillated: The Western Gaze

The history of nineteenth-century Bulgarian smoking is difficult to unearth. Given the paucity of sources, the voluminous writings of the travelers, missionaries, and other Westerners who crisscrossed or settled in the region are worth exploring. Here they are employed not just as empirical supplements but as a reminder that the Bulgarian kafene and smoking culture did not unfold in a vacuum. By the nineteenth century, the Bulgarian coming of age—embedded in a world of smoke and social interchange—was taking place in a highly fluid late-Ottoman world, amid foreign observers and participants. It goes without saying that these memoirs and travel writings were deeply biased, though such biases are far from uniform. Instead they reveal significant contradictions and shifts in Western attitudes toward Ottoman and especially Bulgarian leisure and consumption practices.

Competing narratives of fascination, revulsion, condescension, and criticism have left behind a rather mixed legacy. The layers, inconsistencies, and significance of such writings have only begun to be untangled.[8] On the one hand, Western observers most often defined the Balkans or "European Turkey" as part of the Orient. But the presence of separate Christian and Muslim populations complicated this picture.[9] An analysis of nineteenth-century Anglo-American observations of leisure and consumption in the Ottoman lands seriously muddies the clarity of dichotomous constructions of the "Orient" and "Occident," or any notion of a distinct "Balkanness."[10]

As one might expect, the smoking "Turk"[11] perpetually titillated Anglo-American observers as a central trope in their exotic image of the Ottoman East. For example, in her memoirs, Fanny Blunt, the British consul's daughter (and later wife of another consul), says of the perpetually smoking Turk, "his cup of coffee and his chibouk contain for him all the sweets of existence." She speaks wistfully of the kiosks along the Bosporus, in which a "range of sofas runs all around the walls on which the Turk loves to sit for hours together lost in meditation and in the fumes of his indispensable companion the *narghile* [hookah]."[12] In the Ottoman lands, the *chibouk* (a long pipe) and narghile were the preferred forms of smoking paraphernalia until later in the century, when they were gradually displaced by the cigarette. The narghile in particular was an object of Western fascination, a central prop in European images of nineteenth-century Ottoman life. Its supple, curvy, almost womanly form—and its long (vaguely phallic) tube for sucking—undoubtedly seduced Western consumers. Numerous photographs and paintings from the period featured men posed in a coffeehouse or in front of mosques, next to a narghile or the long, slender chibouk.[13] "Harem" women—probably paid prostitutes or lower-class women—were also posed against the narghile for maximum effect.[14] The market for pictures of the "real" Orient, however, coincided with a period when numerous travelers complained that Ottoman authenticity was presumably being spoiled by "foreign" influence. Indeed, by the 1860s the narghile was already on its way out, eclipsed by the hand-rolled cigarette, though the chibouk proved more persistent.

At the same time "authentic" Eastern pleasures continued to be packaged and appropriated for consumption in Europe (and the United States), even as they became the subject of pointed critique. A recurrent theme in virtually all European travel writings in the nineteenth-century Ottoman Empire was the image of the Oriental as a "sensual and lazy being 'doing nothing.'"[15] In a variety of works, Western travelers were seemingly baffled by the presumed immobility of Balkan Muslims, "whose only delight was to sit day after day in a coffee house sipping his coffee, smoking his pipe and fiddling with the beads of the *tesheh* [worry beads]."[16] The Turk's seemingly prevalent forays into Eastern *kayf* (pleasure seeking) appeared to many the polar opposite of the reputed industriousness of the West.[17] This image of the decadent smoking Turk was to a large degree a reaction to changes within economically and militarily ascendant Western society, with its relatively newfound cult of sobriety and industriousness.

Certainly by the early nineteenth century, Western assessments of leisure and consumption had become normative if not explicitly political. The Oriental penchant for pleasure and idleness, while seductive, was ultimately seen as indicative of Ottoman decay and decline.[18] As the Scottish-British novelist and trader John Galt (1779–1839) argued, if one kept in mind Ottoman "idleness and constant use of the pipe," then it was "not absurd to argue that tobacco brought down the Ottoman Empire in the same way that gun powder maintained it."[19] The image of the idle Turk in a cloud of smoke in fact, seemed to explain the Turkish inability to bring order to the increasingly violent and disorderly Balkan world. As the British diplomats and travelmates Stanislas St. Clair and Charles Brophy described in their *Residence in Bulgaria,* based on observations from the late 1860s, "the Zaptiehs [Ottoman police] prefer their coffee and cigarettes at their guard house to scouring the countryside in search of brigands."[20] In the same vein, they maintained that "at the Sublime Porte functionaries give you a cup of coffee, a chibouque, and an evasive answer," further lamenting that they don't seem to want to "civilize," which would mean they would have to "trade in their cafés for prisons."[21]

Yet St. Clair and Brophy employed such imagery not to demonize but to undermine the image of the "terrible Turk" lording over the "innocent" Balkan Christian. American and British Protestants, among others, had propagated the latter image, intent upon drawing support for their missions among the reputedly innocent and industrious Bulgarians. In contrast, St. Clair and Brophy maintained that the Balkan Christian peasant was "morally and physically degraded and idly lies dead drunk upon a dung-heap" and hence was better off under Ottoman rule.[22] St. Clair and Brophy's image of the drunken Bulgarian was one of many images that resonated in the pantheon of Western travel writings and memoirs on European Turkey.[23] Prevailing assumptions about alcohol and Christian moral degradation seemed to offer an explanation for the Balkan political and cultural predicament. The Bulgarians were, after all, Christian and technically a European people, yet they had been subject to Muslim Asiatic rule for five centuries. The idle Turk was at least sober.

Christian drunkenness, in fact, was a driving force behind the nineteenth-century civilizing missions undertaken by Anglo-American missionaries in the eastern Balkans. By midcentury the explicit focus of American and closely associated British Protestant missions to the Ottoman lands was on the "nominal Christians" or "degenerate churches" of Eastern Orthodoxy who seemed most in need of "moral renovation."[24] Concurrent with the rise of British and, more slowly, American commercial and diplomatic interests in the region, missionaries flooded the Ottoman lands with the desire to import morality, education, a work ethic, and, when possible, the Protestant faith. Muslims, Jews, and to a certain extent Greeks, proved hostile to such efforts from their inception. Faced with this reality, Western missionaries focused on Bulgarians, along with Armenians and Syrian Christians.

Using Istanbul as a base, Anglo-American Protestant missionaries established schools—for local boys and girls—throughout the region, contributing to early Bulgarian educational and cultural life.[25] With carefully delineated turf, the Methodist Board began operating north of the Balkan Mountain chain in 1857, while the non-denominational American Board set up in 1858 in the southern districts.[26] The 1863 establishment in Istanbul of what was later called Robert College, the very first American missionary school abroad, was indicative of the American commitment to the region.[27] Not only did more Bulgarians graduated from Robert College than did any other ethnic group, five of its graduates went on to become prime ministers, while others became ambassadors, industrialists, and prominent personages in post-1878 autonomous Bulgaria.[28] Robert College, as well as an associated women's college, was a central institution in the Protestant engagement with Bulgarians in the midst of Istanbul's "labyrinth of temptation."[29] As Cyrus Hamlin, Robert College's founder and president until 1877 bemoaned, "Steam made Constantinople a commercial city and brought civilization, the arts, and the vices of the West and the East together in the Ottoman capital."[30] Although he had arrived on a "rum and missionary vessel," Hamlin was decidedly an active believer in abstinence.[31] But "morality," as Hamlin himself implied, was defined as Christian rather than explicitly Western. To a large degree the Protestant project in Bulgaria sought to battle both local moral ills and newly proliferating immoral pursuits associated with the West, such as gambling and prostitution. Indeed, the West was the home front and also a central battleground for the Protestant civilizing mission. The export of Protestant values, though varied and in flux, was critical to the missionary project in the Ottoman Empire.

Hamlin himself, like his successor George Washburn, was an unequivocal advocate of sobriety from the moment he set foot on Ottoman soil. Alcohol was strictly forbidden at Robert College, and numerous students were "publicly thrashed" or expelled for coming back to the college dormitories drunk. For Washburn, as for Hamlin, temperance was critical to the overriding goals of inculcating moral strength and industry in the student body and in the region more broadly. To that end, physical activity, labor, and even handicraft production were part of the college curriculum. This inculcation of the Protestant work ethic was part of a more general assault on Balkan drunkenness and idleness.[32] Literacy and education, though, were the primary tools of moral uplift, and Protestant missionaries were responsible for translating the Bible into modern Bulgarian, as well as publishing one of the first and longest-running Bulgarian-language newspapers, *Zornitsa (Morning Star)*.[33] As early as 1848 they had also translated into Bulgarian a tract on temperance, which was only the beginning of their active temperance efforts. Until the first decades of the twentieth century, however, the struggle against alcohol remained the central focus of the temperance movement at home and abroad.

In fact, many British and American writings actually celebrated the coffeehouse and even smoking as acceptable and regenerative forms of leisure, a sober foil to the drunken Balkan krŭchma. As Washburn remarked in his memoirs, "There was restfulness in the life of Constantinople in those days which was refreshing to an American. No Turk was ever in a hurry. Time was of no account. If a Turk moved it was with deliberation and dignity. If he smoked it was a *tchibouk* or *nargileh,* and it was the business of the hour." For Washburn, Turkish smoking was restful, dignified, and even "business." Hamlin also found "Oriental etiquette" so agreeable that he appropriated its rituals in his own home in Rumeli Hisari, the small town outside Istanbul (now a suburb) where Robert College was founded. Hamlin admitted to having gone native, sporting a beard and fez, and offering coffee and the chibouk to visiting guests, as was the Ottoman custom.[34] A variety of other nineteenth-century Anglo-American sources also depict the Ottoman coffeehouse less as a haven for Eastern pleasures and more as a sanctuary for sobriety. This, of course, required turning a blind eye to opium and hashish, which were also consumed in the coffeehouse setting. But with their quest for Ottoman-Christian sobriety and civilizing mission in mind, Protestant observers began to view the coffeehouse with new eyes. Washburn, for example was impressed by the "freedom of speech" he encountered in Istanbul coffeehouses, where "anything might be discussed" and there were "no class distinctions."[35] Fanny Blunt also recognized that coffee and tobacco were "sober" pursuits. She described with approval the coffeehouse culture that had developed among Bulgarian shopkeepers and guilds, who met before and after work for coffee and a chibouk. Hence, she claimed, "Bulgarians are not all drunks as most assume."[36] Recast as sober and positive, the smoking Turk became a veritable role model for the Bulgarian Christian as a variety of Westerners recast the coffeehouse as a temple of sobriety and productive interchange.

At the same time, however, it became increasingly clear that smoking was by no means a guarantee of sobriety among Balkan Christians. In fact, just as Bulgarians began to enter the kafene (as discussed below) the line between kafene, krŭchma, and *bakal* (store that also functioned as a krŭchma) became increasingly blurred, especially in small towns. In the Ottoman context the krŭchma and the bakal had long been rural and urban social institutions for Balkan Christians, existing alongside the primarily Muslim kafene. In the krŭchma and bakal context, drinking was not traditionally accompanied by smoking, but tobacco began to quickly penetrate the tavern walls once smoking spread from the kafene. As St. Clair and Brophy describe in this typical scene in front of a Bulgarian village bakal from 1869:

Before the door of each is a knot of men, sitting cross-legged on the ground, occupied in drinking, smoking, and discussing their own and their neighbors' affairs, very much as if they were Englishmen in

England, except that, as the drugged wine produces its effect, a dispute arises, and they start to their feet abusing one another with all the facile eloquence of Slavonic vituperation.[37]

As is described here, smoking had quickly moved from the sober world of the kafene to the drunken bakal, the unseemly world of Bulgarian revelry. In some cases the same bakal would be a kafene by day and a krŭchma by night; as the sun went down, the coffee would be replaced with *rakia* (plum brandy).[38] Far from assuring sobriety, tobacco became a kind of bridge between sober and intoxicated leisure. It became an almost required accompaniment of both coffee and alcohol, mired in the rapidly developing world of new and unsavory Bulgarian leisure pursuits—connected to Eastern and Western pleasures.

Just as Bulgarians were entering the sober world of the café, Ottoman Muslims were becoming more visible in the immoral and drunken Christian social world. Turcophile British sources explicitly blamed Greek immorality for infecting the sober Turk, noting the increased presence of urban Turks in Greek-owned taverns.[39] But for many, the West was also to blame as the gateway to Turkish moral degradation. As St. Clair and Brophy observed with derision, the young Turkish elite whose destiny was to "become a Pasha" were sent to study in Paris, where they "assiduously attended a course of lectures at the Café Anglais and the Bal Valentino."[40] Although St. Clair and Brophy did not deem Turks immoral as a race, they questioned their judgment as guardians of the next generation: "[I]f you, an Osmanli, send your son to acquire European polish and civilization amongst the moral sewers of Paris, what can you expect?"[41] In many respects, the distinctions between East and West became hopelessly muddied as Western commentators disparaged the morality and leisure consumption practices of both imagined worlds.

Eastern and Western consumption had long been intertwined, but this phenomenon accelerated in the nineteenth century as a result of unmediated and prolonged contact. As Western observers and Ottoman peoples began to encounter each other more directly, several factors complicated notions of the idle and sensuous East as opposed to the industrious, moral West. In particular, Anglo-American Protestant influence had a marked legacy. Though few Bulgarians actually converted to Protestantism, Robert College and other Protestant institutions and messages inculcated a significant segment of both influential and ordinary Bulgarians with a new sense of the importance of morality, education, work, and *sobriety*. There were, of course, other sources for such values. However, the sobriety message, which would eventually be broadened to include an antitobacco message, came almost exclusively from the Protestant wellspring. And this spring both attracted and repelled the Bulgarian population, whose nineteenth-century world was rocked by dramatic social and political change. New forms of leisure consumption were not only part of that change, they were driving forces in its realization.

Inside the Kafene

The Ottoman origins of the coffeehouse are too often forgotten. Even if remembered, the Ottoman coffeehouse is often portrayed as an idle and decadent foil to the more "productive" coffeehouse that played an important role in the making of Western modernity. Historians have argued that in the West the coffeehouse spawned a "public sphere," in which the dueling pharmacological effects of coffee and tobacco drove commerce and modern modes of productivity.[42] Glaringly absent, though, in such accounts is a counterexplanation of why coffee and tobacco in the sober Muslim East did not drive a competing industrial revolution or civil society. A growing literature on non-European societies, however, has gone far to revise this notion of the productive coffeehouse as a uniquely European phenomenon.[43] Works on the Ottoman Empire in particular have helped to complicate the simplistic idea of a productive and dynamic West in contrast to an idle and decadent East.[44]

As smoking and coffeehouse culture entered into seventeenth-century Ottoman practice, both were initially reviled by Muslim religious elites as foreign innovations. Unlike alcohol, neither substance was explicitly prohibited by the Koran, but their pharmacological qualities made them the subject of critique and interpretation. In the early years, influential Muslim leaders connected tobacco imports to a potential plot against Islam, voicing fears that tobacco bales were "soaked in wine or pig lard."[45] But tobacco was also politicized because it entered into Ottoman social life via heterodox Sufi practices and their perpetually suspect "spectacle of idleness."[46] In addition, as Ottoman coffeehouses mushroomed, they tended to be located next to mosques and so functioned as waiting rooms and postprayer gathering spaces, representing a potential rival center for Muslim male sociability, which beckoned believers.[47] Ottoman authorities perpetually viewed coffeehouses as "breeding grounds for gossip," idleness, and sedition, a place of mixing and undermining of social hierarchies.[48] These early Ottoman-Muslim religious objections were mired in anxieties about the immoral influences of the Christian or heterodox Muslim world or of a *new* world of secular socialization and social mixing.[49] For even when smoking in the Ottoman coffeehouse was a purely leisure pursuit, this itself was arguably a modern (or early modern) phenomenon, a sign of change rather than stagnation.[50] As strong as such elite Ottoman objections were, their advocates ultimately lost out. Tobacco seduced the Muslim populations of the empire, and its place was quickly established in the Ottoman-Muslim social world.

Even after religious objections quieted, however, the coffeehouse continued to have political significance for Ottoman authorities. Because of perceived threats of rebellion, coffeehouses had been periodically closed since the seventeenth century, under Ahmed I (1603–17) and Murad IV (1623–40). In Istanbul and elsewhere, the unruly elite Janissary corps had become a dominant force among the *kavecis* (coffeehouse owners) by the early nineteenth century. Their coffeehouses became centers of political influence, organization, and in many cases, outright rebellion. Most tellingly, Mahmud II (1808–39) temporarily closed all coffeehouses when he abolished the Janissary corp in 1826.[51] But Janissaries were not the only concern by this period, as coffeehouses were important sites of sociability where "assembled crowds" confronted state power.[52] By the nineteenth century, all Ottoman sultans— Abdul Aziz, Abdul Mejid, and Abdul Hamid—hired spies to monitor the activities of coffeehouse patrons and so keep them abreast of public opinion in the capital and provinces. And although contemporaries interpreted such activity as signs of "Oriental despotism," it paralleled similar consolidations of state power and fears of coffeehouse sedition in the West. By the 1840s coffeehouse spying had gone from sporadic to a consistent feature of Ottoman urban life, and the informers tended to be coffeehouse owners, patrons, or other civilians of mixed religious affiliation.[53]

In general, coffeehouse clientele were engaged in more than just hours of idle chatting, as Western observers presumed. Studies have shown that "intense literary activity" in the Ottoman café predated a similar phenomenon in the European context. For the illiterate the coffeehouse was also a conduit for information. Newspapers, pamphlets and other materials were often read aloud by the literate few and then discussed by all present. In addition, the coffeehouse was a place where commercial transactions, guild meetings, and other kinds of productive activities took place.[54] In many parts of the empire, especially rural areas, it functioned as a bank, a barbershop, a post office, a store, and even a dentist's office. It acted as a hub for village or *mahalle* (urban neighborhood or quarter) elders to make important administrative decisions. In short, the notion of Muslim men sitting and idly babbling for hours comes from a very narrow understanding of Ottoman coffeehouse culture, a culture that was gradually extended from Muslims to the Christians and Jews of the empire.

It is exceedingly difficult to trace a starting point for the entrance of Bulgarians and other Christians and Jews into the coffeehouse milieu and by extension into the world of smoking and sociability.[55] Ottoman Greek and Armenian merchants had participated in coffee-drinking (and presumably smoking) rituals in elite Ottoman circles before the nineteenth century.[56] It would make sense that non-Muslims who participated in Ottoman urban life would have been exposed to and participated in social rituals over coffee and tobacco in the commercial contexts of the *caravanserai* or *han* (roadside or urban inns) or *çarşı* (market). But there seems to be no evidence of the participation of self-described Bulgarians and other Balkan Slavs in such modes of consumption before the nineteenth century. Prior to that time, Slavic Christians were primarily rural peasantry and animal herders. Certainly Slavs who converted to Islam or became part of the Hellenized commercial elite would have joined the world of Ottoman urban and town sociability much earlier.[57] Yet by the early decades of the nineteenth century, a critical mass of Slavs became part of the Ottoman urban commercial and artisan culture without assimilating into Greek (or Ottoman-Turkish) culture. It was in this period that they discovered their Bulgarianness and began to smoke as Bulgarians.

Learning to Smoke

Late-eighteenth-century commercial revival and nineteenth-century Ottoman reform created the conditions for the rise of a new urban Bulgarian-speaking merchant and artisan stratum. Cities large and small within the empire attracted Bulgarian peasants and artisans to ethnically mixed urban (or urbanizing) centers such as Istanbul, Salonika, Plovdiv, Ruse, Skopje, and Varna. At the same time, in majority Slavic-Christian regions such as the central Balkan Mountains, new "Bulgarian revival towns"—like Gabrovo, Koprivshtitsa, and Veliko Turnovo—mushroomed around centers of protoindustrial and commercial activity. In addition, by the mid-nineteenth century, scores of Bulgarian speakers left the empire as merchants, students, laborers, or (nationalist) political exiles. These Bulgarians, who maintained significant contacts and activities within the empire, were to be found across Central and Western Europe, most notably in the relatively nearby cities of Vienna, Bucharest, Odessa, and Braila (in Russian Bessarabia). This new Bulgarian urban diaspora, inside and outside the empire, became schooled in both Ottoman and European cosmopolitan cultures—themselves entwined—especially in the Ottoman capital.

For Christians the krŭchma and bakal had been traditional sites for social gathering and group consumption of intoxicants. These contexts, like the Muslim coffeehouse, served a number of functions (e.g., dry goods supply, post office). Especially in rural regions, the line between krŭchma, bakal, and kafene was increasingly blurred as alcohol, tobacco, and food crossed the boundaries of these consumer venues. The line between sober and intoxicating consumption was often obscured, just as the consumption habits that distinguished Muslims from non-Muslims began to change. Ottoman urban culture had always brought Muslim, Christian, and Jew into intimate contact. But a shared culture of consumption within the coffeehouse seems to have been a particularly nineteenth-century phenomenon. In part this was surely a consequence of late eighteenth and nineteenth century Ottoman reform era, which brought commercial revival and new administrative roles to non-Muslims, while promoting an integrated "Ottoman" identity. Along with increased contact, however, the dramatic social changes of that period also made the coffeehouse a context for ethnic polarization and separation as exclusive-ethnic cafés were opened. Whether uniting or dividing, the coffeehouse (and the transformed tavern) played a central role in Ottoman Balkan politics and ethnonational identity formation within the cities of the empire.

Perhaps not surprisingly, coffeehouse culture decidedly excluded women in this period. That is not to say that women did not smoke in nineteenth-century Ottoman society. In fact, Muslim women had been tobacco enthusiasts since the seventeenth century, though generally not in the coffeehouse setting. Tobacco consumption spread to non-Muslim women in roughly the same period that it spread to non-Muslim men. By the mid-nineteenth century, numerous travelers and diplomats commented on the prevalence of smoking among women of all religions, but again not in the coffeehouse.[58] Smoking was a relatively common practice for Ottoman elite women of all religions, occurring primarily in private homes and gardens, in the baths, at fashionable parties, or in the salons of elite Ottoman or foreign homes.[59] In fact, in their smoking habits, as in the wearing of bloomerlike pants, Ottoman women were a veritable model (or at least a subject of fascination) for elite Western women, accustomed to more restrictive Victorian mores.[60] Mary Patrick Mills, the longtime head of the Protestant missionary American Women's College, marveled, for example, that "during the whole period of Turkish history good tobacco was one of the luxuries of life, enjoyed equally by men and women alike."[61] This speaks to the fact that a separate but significant (and largely unexplored) world of female sociability—one that also included smoking—existed outside the male-dominated coffeehouse.[62] We have only glimpses of this world, in part from women travelers such as Fanny Blunt, who, like other English women before her, was routinely invited into the harems of Turkish women for a ritual smoke. And though Blunt seemed to have enjoyed such rituals, she was less impressed by the cigarette-smoking non-Muslim new rich, whom she encountered during her social fêtes in the provinces. In one instance she reported on one of her own parties in Salonika, where she was disgusted to discover a "fat Armenian lady covered with jewels comfortably ensconced in the corner of a sofa smoking a cigarette."[63] Apparently, Oriental smoking rituals held more charm than the *modern* smoking practices of new Christian elites at the end of the century.

When Bulgarian women smoked, they generally did so behind closed doors or high garden walls. One of the most famous women of the Bulgarian national revival, Baba (grandmother, but here a title of respect) Nedelia Petkova, was known to have scandalized Bulgarian sensibilities with her public smoking habit. Baba Nedelia, famous as the founder of women's education in Sofia, was one of the first Bulgarian women teachers. A widow with five children, she tirelessly pursued her career, which took her from city to city, mostly in Ottoman Macedonia. In many of the places she taught, Baba Nedelia was treated with open hostility, both as an "emancipated and independent woman" and as a Bulgarianizer of women amid the intensifying Bulgarian-Greek cultural struggle. According to one source, she was fired from her job in the city of Prilep, "because of her extremely free behavior, clothing, and her smoking."[64] It is telling that one of the most famous of the "emancipated" female figures from the revival was also a known smoker. Clearly, though, the habit among women was subjected to a different kind of scrutiny and hence was more connected to private modes of urban sociability.[65] For men, however, smoking was increasingly connected to their place in new forms of public urban culture.

Perhaps most critical to this culture was Istanbul itself, where a large Bulgarian population of thirty to forty thousand had coalesced by the mid-nineteenth century. This was easily the largest concentration of Bulgarians in any urban environment in this period.[66] The coffeehouse was central to Istanbul urban life, with at least one in every neighborhood. Istanbul was a highly mixed city in terms of language and religion, and by the nineteenth century there were some 2,500 coffee houses, compared with a mere 600 taverns. In fact "kafeci" was the largest subgroup in the overall guild registry for the city by that time. Though predominantly Muslim, a few Greek, Jewish, and Armenian coffeehouse owners had also appeared by this time, indicative of the shift in consumption habits among non-Muslims.[67] Confessional lines of ownership, however, were not necessarily indicative of ethnic segregation among the clientele of the coffeehouse or tavern.[68] Some scholarship on the Ottoman city has pointed to the blurred lines of mahalle residential segregation and emphasized points of confessional interaction in places such as the çarşı[69] caravanserai or han, and town squares, where coffeehouses tended to be concentrated.[70] Christians as well as Jews had always interacted with Muslims in these contexts, but the nineteenth century ushered in a period of much greater participation in trade and mahalle administration for Slavic Christians and non-Muslims as a whole; this was coupled with a greater engagement in public smoking and gathering in the kafenes of the capital and provinces.

By the nineteenth century, a significant Christian (and Jewish) elite penetration of Istanbul coffeehouse culture was well established. By the 1840s non-Muslims already made up about 28 percent of Istanbul's coffeehouse clientele, though half of these were "foreigners."[71] Eventually Christian- and Jewish-owned coffeehouses proliferated and began to specialize, especially within urban areas. Coffeehouses served not only ethnoreligious groups but also various interest groups based on age, social status, language, place of origin (for migrants), or political leanings. As Bulgarian urban colonies spread across and outside the empire, Bulgarians abroad coalesced around ethnic (though also multiethnic *political*) coffeehouses, where shared interests warranted a site for social exchange.

In Istanbul, the most notable of such early Bulgarian meeting places was the Balkapan Han (Balkapan Inn). Bulgarian-speaking Christians, primarily itinerant men, had migrated to Istanbul in significant numbers by the early nineteenth century, and this inn became a residential, commercial, and social hub.[72] In the Bulgarian-inhabited eastern Balkans, as in the empire as a whole, an intricate web of caravanserai and hans was the cornerstone of overland Ottoman trade.[73] While Ottoman Greeks made their commercial fortunes at sea, Bulgarian merchants were more entrenched in this land-based trade network. The han was a critical context (and later nationalist trope) for Bulgarian commercial and national cultural revival. The Balkapan Han itself was located in the famous Fener (Phanar in Greek) district of Istanbul—the quarter inhabited by the elite Greek Phanariotes, who played an important role in Ottoman administration in the Balkans. Within this mixed but primarily Christian milieu, the Balkapan Han functioned as a center of Bulgarian trade and manufacture (primarily tailoring). It also housed the first Bulgarian-language printing press, set up in 1849, and became a center for Bulgarian-oriented (as opposed to Grekoman—or Hellenized Slavic) merchants.[74] The Balkapan with its centrally positioned kafene became a kind of Bulgarian "consulate"—a point of entry for migrant Bulgarian men. Balkapan merchants and artisans would gather in the main kafene, where "they smoked tobacco and sometimes played cards or backgammon, telling over and over of their years in Istanbul; they read the newspapers, discussed politics, education, and regional affairs."[75] For Bulgarians, the Balkapan was central to community life in the capital, where they were rapidly developing a national identity as well as economic and political power. The Balkapan was also associated with cultural change and innovation as a result of contact with the outside world through the lively portal of Istanbul.

But as the Bulgarian community in the capital grew larger and more diversified, the Balkapan did not remain the only or even the primary site of sociability. In 1866, Istanbul Bulgarians set up a *chitalishte* (reading room) with its own kafene not far from Balkapan. This became a rival gathering place for the younger Bulgarian elite, who also "smoked and drank bitter coffee discussing the daily news." The chitalishte had its own printing press and soon evolved into the more dominant "spiritual center of Bulgarians in Istanbul."[76] Its location in the Greek Fener, however, had important political implications by the 1860s. While Bulgarian-Greek mixing within Christian quarters of the empire was common, in the past these Christian mahalle had been essentially Hellenizing contexts where Bulgarians adopted the Greek language, to be employed in trade and Orthodox administration. As a result, early Bulgarian nationalist demands focused on throwing off the "Greek yoke" of religious and secular cultural dominance. By the 1860s the famous Bulgarian-Greek "church struggle" over the Bulgarian right to be administered separately from the Greek Orthodox Church was in full swing.[77] Even after Bulgarians were granted church autonomy through their own exarchate in 1871, the Bulgarian-Greek battle over Orthodox souls continued to spread from the Christian quarters of Istanbul and Plovdiv to the provinces of Macedonia. Within Istanbul and elsewhere, young and politically engaged self-proclaimed Bulgarians pursued their social, linguistic, and spiritual separation from Greeks in part by setting up their own kafenes in the Fener. Because these were in close proximity to and so invited mixing with the Greek community, there was widespread suspicion that the Greeks were spying on their activities.[78] The fact that in Istanbul, as in other cities of the empire, the urban tavern was owned and frequented primarily by Greeks, most likely made new spaces for cultural interaction necessary for self-proclaimed Bulgarian nationalists. For a variety of reasons, not least of which was its mercantile function, the kafene fulfilled this need. In spite of Bulgarian-Greek and mounting Bulgarian-Turkish cultural and political tensions, however, interaction and social mixing in the kafene and elsewhere were still prevalent and in many places the rule.

Perhaps no one celebrates the rich cultural life of Bulgarians in Istanbul better than Khristo Brŭzitsov in his *Niakoga v Tsarigrad (Once in Istanbul)*. Brŭzitsov skillfully mixes ethnography with memoir in a vivid portrait of the Bulgarian community in Istanbul, which celebrates the city's intense mixing of cultures and influences.[79] Smoking Muslim men on the streets of Istanbul are described as an almost organic and inseparable part of the Istanbul land-scape, significantly without any negative assessment of Oriental repose: "In front of Akhmed Topal's kafene, hidden from a red ribbon of baking sun, sat the Turks in their holiday clothes....They sipped steaming coffee out of large *fildzhans* [a type of cup], filling the entire pot with coffee, and the narghiles were well-supplied."[80] In the imagery of Brŭzitsov, the world of the smoking Turk and his coffeehouse was tightly woven into the tapestry of the city in such a way that non-Muslims lived and breathed it, walking the streets onto which it spilled. During Ramadam Bairam (the festivities at the end of the Ramadan month of fasting), people of *all* confessional backgrounds and ages gathered in Muslim coffeehouses to watch the playful Karagöz shadow puppetry.[81] As Brŭzitsov describes it, the show was staged in the center of the coffeehouse amid billows of smoke. "In front of every audi-ence member—a pipe, long amber cigarette holders, tobacco/cigarette cases, tobacco pouches with golden tobacco—a whole tobacco arsenal."[82] Here, as in various commercial and mahalle settings, tobacco consumption was a shared social ritual for Istanbul's nineteenth century polymorphous society, and the coffeehouse provided a place for public indulgence.

But Istanbul was only one island in an archipelago of concentrated sites of Bulgarian commercial and cultural ferment that followed the trade routes from Istanbul through Plovdiv to the port cities of the Danube (Ruse, Lom, Svishtov) and abroad to Vienna, Odessa, St. Petersburg, and cities of the Danubian principalities such as Bucharest and Braila. All these cities and their coffeehouses nourished the growth of a Bulgarian cosmopolitan smoking culture within webs of interethnic contact. As newcomers to these locations, Bulgarians learned to smoke under the tutelage of Ottoman-Muslims, other non-Muslims, and various Western Europeans. The small but burgeoning port town of Lom provides an example of this process. In Lom local Muslim men had traditionally gathered in coffeehouses, which functioned like politi-cal clubs for administering the *reaya* (peasantry) of the region. By the 1830s, prominent Jews and Christians were occasional guests in the coffeehouses, where one could rent a chibouk with tobacco for five *para* (an Ottoman coin) and a narghlie for ten.[83] By the 1840s Armenians, Greeks, and Slavs begin to appear on the kafeci guild registry for Lom and other cities, while Jews also entered the ranks of the kafeci at various times.[84] As Bulgarian migrants moved into the city, they established their own residential mahalle, which by 1876 housed some twelve kafenes, differentiated by class and status.[85] In Danubian port cities like Lom and Ruse (much like Black Sea posts such as Varna), kafenes also served foreign (as well as Ottoman) merchants and trad-ers, even functioning as inns, restaurants, bars, opium dens, and brothels. Here, as in Istanbul, the kafene became the center of male itinerant merchant and artisan life but also a conduit for cultural influence.[86]

After Istanbul, Plovdiv was unquestionably the most influential city at the heart of this kafene life. The road from Istanbul to the central Balkan Mountains region—the heartland of Bulgarian proto-industrial development—passed through Plovdiv, which was later called the spiritual center of the Bulgarian national revival. Unlike the towns of the central Balkans that were relatively new and heavily Slavic well into the late nineteenth century, Plovdiv was in many ways a typical Ottoman-Balkan city. It had the largest urban density in the inland western Balkans, and its estimated thirty to fifty thousand inhabitants (by midcentury) were of mixed ethnic origin—Turks, Jews, Gypsies, Armenians, Greeks, and Slavs. There had always been a trickle of Bulgaro-Slavic populations into Plovdiv, but in the past the bulk of these had become "Grekomans," melting into the Greek community of Plovdiv's prominent Christian merchant and artisan quarter that occupied its lovely "three hills."[87] By the mid-nineteenth century, though, a much greater influx of Slavs into Plovdiv was proceeding apace, and a growing number of self-proclaimed Bulgarians lived there.[88] Whether "Bulgarians" or more fluidly "Ottoman" in orientation the city's new Slavic populations were privy to a shared Ottoman urban culture.[89]

In post-1839 Plovdiv, a time of deepening Ottoman reform, urban life had an increased vibrancy for Bulgarians with the opening and frequenting of coffeehouses, as well as Bulgarian schools, presses and other urban services. Nouveau riche Orthodox merchants set the tone for revival culture throughout the region, which was still wholly Ottoman in form and substance. As upwardly mobile Ottoman citizens, the new Bulgarian merchant class wore the fez and other Ottoman accoutrements, furnished their houses in an Ottoman urban style, and took part in Turco-Ottoman leisure practices.[90] For Bulgarian merchants and artisans, predominantly of peasant stock, these practices were indicative of their new elite status.[91] Part of this status was having both the time and social necessity for the coffeehouse, which first the "çorbacıs" (notables) and then a broader Bulgarian-speaking population began to enter in the midcentury.[92] In addition, in conformity with Ottoman elite practice, Bulgarians began to engage in smoking at home, where the chibouk or narghile and coffee were offered as a sign of Ottoman hospitality and refinement.[93] Most elite Bulgarian households in Plovdiv had a receiving room where a collection of smoking paraphernalia was displayed for the benefit and choice of the guest.

But in the course of the century, slowly and unevenly, European accoutrements and leisure practices began to bear more and more normative cultural and political weight. For many, *a la franga* (literally, in the French way) things and practices remained just a part of the synthesis and borrowings that filtered through Ottoman elite culture. For others, however, they came to be associated with a burgeoning European cultural orientation, an embracing of modernity and the discovery of Bulgarianness. As the merchant elite began to define and shape the parameters of Bulgarian identity, they discovered, explored, and displayed their Europeanness on their bodies, in their homes, and through their leisure practices.[94] The Christian quarter of Plovdiv and the revival towns of the central Balkans played a prominent role in this flowering. Bulgarians merchants and artisans in these areas had the resources to educate their young sons and daughters, and many chose to forgo the traditional Greek schools for the now expanding Bulgarian ones. Even more significantly, many sent their sons abroad to Vienna, Odessa, St. Petersburg, and Paris, as well as to the American College in Istanbul. Interactions with other—many nationalist—citizens abroad took place in the smoky recesses of the European café, where Bulgarians learned to drink coffee and smoke a la franga. In practice, such changes in consumption were primarily aesthetic. As the century wore on, enlightened Ottomans chose to smoke the cigarette or the shorter European pipe (instead of the narghile or chibouk) and drink coffee from cups with handles (rather than from the handleless filzhan). This is not to say that the cigarette was a European invention. The modern cigarette seems to be an amalgam of Mayan rolling practices transmitted via the Spanish and Egyptian rolling practices popularized during the Crimean War (1853–56).[95] Though the cigarette and its technologies spread faster in the West, its diffusion was still perennially tied to notions of Eastern pleasure. From the turn-of-the-century Anglo-American craze for "Turkish" cigarettes to the famous Camel cigarette brand and advertising campaign launched by American Tobacco in 1913, the cigarette was sold in the West as an imagined Eastern product. However, for Ottoman Muslims, Jews, and Christians, dressing *a la franga* or smoking a cigarette instead of a chibouk was an emblem of civilization and the West. In the late Ottoman milieu, the *form* of smoking itself, as with clothing furniture and other aesthetic changes, came to represent a western orientation.

The Crimean War hastened the aesthetic Europeanization of Balkan life as European products penetrated the Ottoman Near East. With the increasing realization—or more accurately, *invention*—of a European pedigree, Bulgarians and other Balkan peoples began a long and uneven process of Europeanization that was economic, social, and political. The spread of the Europeanized coffeehouse was part of this process, as was jettisoning the chibouk and narghile for a European pipe and cigarette. But even (if not especially) among nationalists, who were arguably more predisposed to European influence, European material culture and leisure practices also provoked a strong current of criticism toward Bulgarians who were "aping foreign ways."[96] After all, by definition, modern European culture potentially threatened what was authentically national—still a fragile category in the making.

Western contact increased markedly in the second half of the nineteenth century. The Bulgarian new rich of Plovdiv, Ruse, and elsewhere became hosts for Western merchants and consular representatives, whose scruples often were dramatically different from those of the familiar local missionaries. The new Bulgarian urban elite with larger homes and sumptuous salons hosted and attended soirées, dances, and other events where, among other things, people smoked. This excerpt from the 1866 memoir of Rada Kirkova describes one such event: "We used to have parties every now and then in the houses of Plovdiv notables and communal leaders. There the gentlemen spent time mostly in conversations among themselves and smoking cigarettes, and the women, chatted, flirted and played cards...interrupted only by the singing of old or rebellious [nationalist] songs."[97] Such overtly Bulgarian displays would not have been possible in the more public venues of the coffeehouse, the marketplace, or even the church. In the urban home a new field and style of social interaction emerged, less restricted by the surveillance of other ethnic groups or the Grekoman and Turcophile Bulgarians. At the same time, Bulgarian *public* smoking, drinking, and other forms of leisure abounded as Bulgarian artisans and merchants began to build their own kafene and taverns in an ever-increasing number.[98]

Plovdiv, a hub of Ottoman-Bulgarian manufacturing and development in the mid-nineteenth century, became the model for Bulgarian urban culture in the central Balkan mountain region where a concentration of Bulgarian-speakers resided in villages and growing towns. Nourished by the Tanzimat reforms (1839–76) and especially by the rigorous reforms of Midhat Pasha (1864–69) in the adjacent Tuna Vilayet (Danube region), the region flourished. Nestled between two mountain ranges, with trade routes through Plovdiv to Istanbul and north to the Danubian port city of Ruse, the towns of Kotel, Sliven, Gabrovo, Koprivshitsa, Veliko Turnovo, and Karlovo became major centers for Bulgarian commercial and cultural revival.[99] By the mid-nineteenth century every mahalle in the primarily Bulgarian town of Gabrovo had its own kafene, and many of them also functioned as barbershops and stores. Men would gather at the neighborhood kafene in the mornings and after work to smoke and drink coffee.[100]

The kafene was so well established by the second half of the century that it secured a place as an organically *Bulgarian* institution in the fiction from

the period, which offers a window into nineteenth-century smoking culture. In *Under the Yoke,* for example, Vazov shows how smoking aesthetics,
in and outside Ganko's kafene, reflected social status and cultural orientation.[101] Vazov's Bai Marko, a Bulgarian çorbacı, luxuriates in his parlor and
garden with his guests and family, smoking his chibouk in the old Ottoman
fashion.[102] Embodying the older generation of Bulgaro–Ottoman elites, Bai
Marko proudly displays his chibouk collection on his wall even though they
"are no longer in fashion."[103] Marko is also a fixture in Ganko's kafene, where
the kafeci provides shaves and haircuts as the town's dramas unfold. Although
decidedly against an armed uprising, Marko is the one çorbacı who is at least
marginally sympathetic as he openly debates the future of Bulgaria with the
more radicalized younger generation. Hence Ganko's kafene in its small-
town setting offers a forum for interaction and debate among the various
social strands of the revival period.

Ethnic interaction, even intimacy, is also revealed in the novel in relation
to the kafene setting. Through the character of the young revolutionary hero,
Ivan Kralich, the reader is invited to experience the inside of a Turkish coffeehouse in a neighboring village. Kralich, a character based on the Bulgarian
nationalist hero Vasil Levski, is wanted by the Ottoman authorities for his
seditious activities. In one scene he journeys incognito as a "common Turk"
through a snowy winter evening, when he is forced by inclement weather to
stop for the night at a small inn in a Turkish-populated village. Kralich enters
through the inn's kafene and is taken aback to see that it is crowded with *agas*
(Ottoman-Turkish officers):

> To leave immediately was awkward. He decided to sit down, and made
> his salaam [hello], which they politely returned. As he had lived long
> among the Turks he knew their customs and their language very well.
> They were squatting on straw-mats, their shoes off, pipes in hand. A
> dense fog of smoke filled the room.
> "A coffee!" he said sternly to the host.
> And he started filling his pipe, bending low over it to hide his fea-
> tures as much as possible.[104]

Kralich does his best to remain invisible, "furiously sipping his third cup
of coffee, while at every other moment he blew out a cloud of smoke."[105]
Although the Ottoman-Turks are depicted as "phlegmatic" and ultimately
out for blood, Kralich's intimacy with their "habits and language" is striking.
His ability to pass for Ottoman-Turkish hinges on his willingness to consume
large amounts of coffee and tobacco, the rituals of which he has learned from
"living among the Turks." As part of his disguise as a common "Turk," Kralich

wears a pipe tucked into his "greasy belt" along with a pistol and a dagger. In fact, it seems as if he smokes in this scene *only* in order to pass. Indeed, he is neither a smoker nor a drinker; this fact and his mastery of disguise are key hints to the reader that his character is based on the revered Vasil Levski.

Levski, to this day the most legendary of all Bulgarian nationalist revolutionaries, was well known as a proponent of abstinence from both drink and tobacco.[106] As one of his biographers explained,

> Levsky himself rigorously abstained from both alcohol and tobacco, both of which he considered to be harmful to the individual and society. He was a firm believer in personal as well as organizational discipline. People who were slaves to habit and desire made unreliable revolutionaries, and were a potential danger to their comrades. "Crave nothing in life except bread and water," he told the boys from Tŭrnovo who wanted to become members of the [underground revolutionary nationalist] Committee.[107]

Similar statements about the "purity" of Levski, while prone to hero-worship and mythmaking, permeate sources from his contemporaries.[108] As Nikola Obretenov, a revolutionary comrade in arms, asserts in his memoirs, Levski "would not touch alcoholic drinks of any kind, and did not smoke; he drank only tea. He did not like luxury."[109] Not only Levski but other notable revolutionary leaders—Georgi Rakovski, Georgi Benkovski, Todor Kableshkov—were famously abstinent. That their abstinence was noteworthy, however, points to the pervasiveness of drinking and smoking in the life of Bulgarian society, including its revolutionaries. New recruits to Levski's secret revolutionary committee took a "moral" oath of abstinence, which prohibited drunkenness, along with lying and stealing.[110] Nevertheless, the Bulgarian revolutionaries of 1860—most notably Khristo Botev—were known for spreading their message through urban and rural kafenes.[111] The true Bulgarian revolutionary was viewed as akin to the ethos of the "freedom-loving" *haidut* (mountain brigand), whose highly romanticized image was often linked to his ubiquitous pipe, tobacco pouch, and jug of wine by the campfire. These two competing myths of the nationalist revolutionary pervade Bulgarian sources. The monklike ascetic who sacrifices all for the good of the nation and sets a moral tone for the Bulgarian future competes with the freed world of the freedom-fighting bandit, which allows the pleasures of alcohol and tobacco to this otherwise self-sacrificing hero. The latter, it seems, was the more realistic model for Bulgarian men of the nineteenth century and those who would follow in their footsteps as twentieth-century revolutionaries, partisans, or citizens. Levski, after all, was

mythologized to such a degree that his moralistic practices could be justifi-
ably ignored by mere mortals. He was the monklike—even saintlike—figure
to respect and worship. Very few could actually follow in his footsteps.
Indeed, by the time of the 1876 April Uprising, smoking would have been
a fairly pervasive practice in both the Bulgarian krŭchma (and bakal) and
the kafene. It would complement both the drunken revelries and the sober
musings of the new Bulgarian intelligentsia.

Independent Smoking

In the spring of 1876, Bulgarian nationalist revolutionaries—operating out
of the kafene and krŭchmas of Ottoman Bulgaria and abroad—launched
the famous April Uprising. In the town of Panagyurishte, Muslim civilians
were murdered by Bulgarian rebel leaders, and the Ottomans responded with
reprisals. An estimated ten to twenty-five thousand Bulgarian civilians there
and in neighboring towns were slaughtered. When news of these events
arrived in London, Benjamin Disraeli, the Turcophile British prime minister,
cast doubt on the accuracy of the reports and contemptuously described
them as "mere coffee-house babble."[112] Disraeli's view of events was eventually discredited by reports that confirmed the massacres and prompted William Gladstone, Disraeli's political rival, to publish his famous pamphlet "The
Bulgarian Atrocities" as a corrective and to heighten public awareness of the
Bulgarian cause. It was Russia, however, and not Britain that finally intervened on behalf of Bulgarian Christians in 1877 and secured their autonomy
in 1878. By this time, Bulgarian coffeehouse conversations had evolved into
coherent nationalist politics, which moved from the kafene to administrative
circles within the new principality.

But far from replacing kafene politics, the expanded possibilities of the
new de facto state allowed for the proliferation of Bulgarian political ideas
and movements, which took place amid a mushrooming kafene culture.
Nineteenth-century processes that had begun to shape Bulgarian urban culture gained momentum after 1878 as Bulgarians flocked to the cities of
the new principality to fill jobs and space left by the emigration of urban
Muslims. In the last decades of the nineteenth and first decades of the twentieth century, a vital new Bulgarian urban culture was spawned, and European influence brought many changes to Bulgarian political institutions, city
planning, building practices, and education. A greater influx of foreigners
brought material changes to Bulgaria's doorstep from many directions. At
the same time, Bulgarians traveled and studied abroad more than ever, and
an urban cosmopolitan culture continued to develop under the conditions

of intensified interaction. As the normative values of European superiority swept in at a torrential pace, Bulgarians were enticed but also wary about trading one set of "foreign" forms (Ottoman) for another (European).

Not surprisingly, the Europeanization of cultural and aesthetic life in Bulgaria heightened soul-searching about what was truly Bulgarian. Untangling the Bulgarian simultaneously from the Ottoman and the European was exceedingly complicated, even as the latter was theoretically rejected and the former embraced. Moreover, this process was slow and uneven. In Sofia, for example, a more brisk Europeanization led to a rapid influx of European-style cafés and other leisure venues and aesthetic forms in the last decade of the nineteenth century.[113] This was in marked contrast to the provinces and even larger provincial cities like Plovdiv, where more traditional coffee-houses and Ottoman-style cosmopolitanism had a longer life span. In general, the Europeanization of architecture, clothing, and other visual markers of European belonging were accompanied by the increased dominance of the cigarette—though hand-rolled—or the *lula* (a shorter European pipe) over the traditional chibouk and narghile. The chibouk and narghile, like the fez and other Ottoman accoutrements, persisted primarily among Muslims and became associated with Ottoman allegiances. In larger cities in particular, like Sofia and Plovdiv, the large-scale exodus of Muslims meant that only a small elderly Muslim population remained, which slowly died out. As was the case in virtually all postempire Eastern European cities, the triumph of nation over empire meant the increased ethnic homogenization of the city on the heels of exile and assimilation.[114] The Bulgarianization of the principality's cities, though, proceeded gradually as urbanizing Bulgarians replaced Muslims, then Greeks after the Balkan Wars (1912–13), Armenians after World War I, and Jews after World War II. In the last decades of the nineteenth century the rich world of commercial and consumer practices arguably connected, rather than divided, these populations. As this world slipped away, it provoked a strong sense of nostalgia among Bulgarians who had grown up among the zesty smells and tastes of Ottoman and early post-Ottoman Bulgaria. The loss of such a world in some respects was tantamount to losing something vitally native if not essentially Bulgarian.

This nostalgia can be traced in the richly textured work of Nikola Alvadzhiev, which takes the reader on an ethnographic tour of the dying Ottoman world. As he walks the streets of early-twentieth-century Plovdiv, Alvadzhiev explores the city quarter by quarter, detailing its kafene and taverns, its colorful characters, its notable people and places. He also intimately depicts Plovdiv's aromas and *kefove* (pleasures, from the Arabic *kaif*) conjuring a clear picture of an early post-Ottoman world that was palpably fading from view. The reader experiences a city crisscrossed by ethnic neighbor-hoods, whose boundaries were frequently and easily crossed for the sake of business and sociability. Admittedly, numerous ethnic establishments existed, such as the Greek-dominated kafenes at the Hotel Acropolis or the Moralita, a krŭchma with "Czech ashtrays full of cigarettes."[115] But even in the Greek establishments, prominent Bulgarians, such as the famed Petko Slaveikov, were known regulars.[116] Each Plovdiv establishment, as described by Alvadzhiev, had its own reputation, specialties, and clientele and tended to be at least partially ethnically mixed. A Bulgarian tavern in the Marasha neighborhood, for example, was known for its cleanliness; "God save anyone who threw cigarettes on the floor." In contrast, a Bulgarian *mekhana* (tavern/restaurant), was known for its rowdy male gatherings, with wine, rakia, gypsy music, and *skara* (grilled food) as well as a "Greek known for smoking."[117] It was not uncommon for these places to have a cast of characters, like the drunken Turk, Mustafa Aga, who frequented Iovchoglu's tavern on Miuselle Street and whose wife had to come looking for him, dragging him home after his late-night carousing.[118] And then there was Arlin, the Armenian who cut off his ear in a fit of rage when the cook at a local establishment claimed there were no *meze* (appetizers) left; he handed his ear to the cook, shouting "Here, cook this."[119]

But whether in the kafene, tavern, mekhana, or çarşı, smoking was a con-stant. Smoking in the Plovdiv market, for example—always with coffee—was an integral part of a day of commerce. As Alvadzhiev details, each day would begin with the unlocking of stalls, a hello to one's neighbors, a spritzing down of the dusty streets. Then merchants would move on to the coffee and smoking: "They tell one or two funny stories, they laugh and then go into their stores, they sit on the wide bench, cross their legs in the Turkish style and start to noisily sip coffee. The morning coffee! A habit, an unwritten rule, honored by all in the marketplace. Afterward, the master artisan rolls a cigarette, grasps a flint and steel, lights up and waits for his journeymen."[120] Commerce by its very nature encouraged, even required, interethnic sociabil-ity, but mixing was common even beyond the market. Alvadzhiev describes the scene in the kafenes on Dzhumaia Street in Plovdiv: "In the summer all the tables were full on the little square and even on the street. For hours the Bulgarians, Turks, Greeks, Armenians, drank coffee, smoked, and chatted about everything imaginable."[121]

Though they were certainly part of the life at the çarşı, Alvadzhiev claims that Plovdiv's Jews lived concentrated in the Jewish quarter, Ortamezar, and gathered primarily at home and not in the kafenes or taverns of the city. In other cities, however, Jews were known to frequent kafenes or have their own haunts, such as the "kafene of Feizi" in the town of Shumen near the synagogue, where they gathered and drank coffee or Chinese and Russian teas.[122] In Plovdiv, however, the Jewish population was made up primarily of small-scale merchants and peddlers who sold their wares throughout the city. It was not uncommon, according to Alvadzhiev, for Jews to stop at the kafene and ask smoking Bulgarians or Turks to light their cigarettes, always a gesture of familiarity.[123] Smoking by its very nature bred such intimacy among the male populace of Ottoman and post-liberation cities.

The coffeehouse and to a certain extent also the tavern, continued to have a number of social functions, which were decidedly in flux in this period. Kafene owners, for example, continued to practice as barbers and even dentists until the end of the nineteenth century, when the "sanitary officials" put an end to their pulling teeth.[124] One Plovdiv kafene was known for hosting an agency that facilitated emigration to the United States and Latin America, with prices posted and opportunities to buy passage detailed.[125] The kafene also became a context for intellectual and political ferment, in particular among the New Left. Apparently the first socialist congress in Bulgaria, lorded over by the father of Bulgarian Socialism, Dimitŭr Blagoev, was held in a kafene. And as Alvadzhiev elaborates, the kafenes of Plovdiv's Bunardzhik quarter were filled with educated and politically engaged youth, who "oiled back their long hair, dressed in black, and sported beards in imitation of the Russian nihilists. They read Gorky, Tolstoy, and Bakunin as they drank coffee and smoked into the night."[126] In Plovdiv, as in Sofia and elsewhere, certain kafenes became known for allegiance to a particular intellectual orientation or political party, and many even functioned as party headquarters. At the same time, in periods when ethnic tensions flared, ethnic-based kafenes were prone to becoming sites for clashes. In 1905–6, for example, the first major anti-Greek riots in Plovdiv began with the breaking of the windows of the Greek kafene, the Acropolis, in reaction to Bulgaria-Greek diplomatic tensions over Macedonia.[127]

Still, such explosive moments are overshadowed in Alvadzhiev's account by nostalgia for the ethnic richness that marked fin de siècle Plovdiv. His Turkish figures, far from abhorrent, are colorful and beloved, the last Muslim generation to live and die in the kafenes, shops, and streets of Plovdiv. They go out, so to speak, in the clouds of smoke that permeate their existence, in imagery that is at once alluring and comforting. There is Sherif, for example, the "old Turk" who sold all kinds of tobacco and cigarette papers at an old *vakf* store.[128] With his white turban and white beard, "like a prophet" he was "beloved by all of the Bulgarians."[129] And then there is Mustafa Aga (not the drunken one), a seventy-year-old cobbler in the Kapana neighborhood who set up business on a wobbly old table on the street. Although his family had left for the Ottoman lands in 1877–78, he had stayed in "his native Filibe" (Turkish for Plovdiv), sporting a "white beard with a mustache yellowed from tobacco smoking, with a little fez wrapped in something like a turban." As Alvadzhiev lovingly details, he had "skin as if out of cigarette paper" and when he smoked, "he pulled out of his belt a colorful bag, in which there were, here and there, some tobacco crumbs, he slowly rolled a cigarette, lit it off of flint and steel. . . . The old man took long, deep drags on the cigarette holder until his cheeks were hollowed, and out of his nose flowed two small streams of smoke. And he thought, and thought. . . . One Spring the place of Mustafa was empty."[130] Though a stereo-typical contemplative Turk, Mustafa Aga was beloved, his absence lamented. In fact, Alvadzhiev seems to revel in the image of the smoking Turk in the café, the çarşı, in front of the mosque, and at the "famous Adzhensko café" run by "Persian bank robbers." These are not the images of a despised "other" but rather a rendering of Turks and others as integral strands in the tapestry of Bulgarian life, one in which Turks were arguably more connected to native Bulgaria than to the new European (and also nationalist) ways that hastened their death and exile.

In Sofia, the Ottoman tapestry unraveled even more quickly than Plovdiv.[131] In a matter of decades, Sofia was transformed from a provincial Ottoman town to a minor European capital. The razing of mosques and other Islamic structures in this process enabled the transformation of Sofia's urban vistas from a sea of minarets to a dense collection of European architectural forms. The winding streets of the Ottoman cityscape were considered an Oriental hindrance, and wide boulevards became a hallmark of Sofia's new urban planning.[132] Because Sofia was the capital and hence the flagship city for Bulgarian progress, planners initiated a destructive "Haussmannization" that wiped out hundreds of mosques, coffeehouses, and Ottoman monuments.[133] Old hans with their dark cavernous kafenes were gradually replaced by more luxurious European cafés and eventually beer halls, cabarets, restaurants, and other European urban institutions. Before and after Bulgarian independence was recognized in 1908, the West, with all its contradictory vices and moralistic judgments, penetrated Sofia with vigor unknown elsewhere in the country.

As part of such developments, by the 1880s and 1890s Sofia had developed a lively and assertive café set, its own social life as well as political and intellectual ferment. Public smoking and drinking proliferated in Bulgaria as the kafene and krŭchma were accessible to ever-broader segments of the population by early twentieth century.[134] The Sofia kafene and krŭchma offered a range of goods, services, clientele, and atmospheres, from chic to seedy.[135]

Opened in 1906, for example, the Bŭlgariia was among the most famous kafenes of the capital; luxurious and "Vienna-style," it graced the central and fashionable Tsar Osvoboditel Boulevard. Its smoky environs were the meeting grounds for Bulgaria's most elite actors, artists, and writers, including Elin Pelin and Iordan Iovkov.[136] In the decades after liberation, noted for their scant political liberties, kafenes functioned as political clubs and continued to play the role of a "public sphere."[137] At the same time, they spawned some of the earliest critiques of smoking, that accompanied the complex soul searching of Bulgarian intellectuals.

Roots of Antismoking

One of the most visible commentaries on the kafene and Bulgarian smoking from the period came from Aleko Konstantinov, a famous kafene regular (and smoker) from fin de siècle Sofia. Konstantinov, who compares only with Vazov in the pantheon of Bulgarian literary and intellectual figures, was admittedly a "passionate smoker." Interestingly, in the Bulgarian language there is no such thing as a "heavy smoker," only a "passionate" (*strasten*) one. In Konstantinov's famous feuilleton, "Strast" ("Passion"), the author desperately seeks out a free source of tobacco, as he lacks the "forty-five *stotinki* [cents] necessary to buy it." In an almost delusional state he wanders the streets of Sofia, haunted by hallucinations that all the rich people on the streets had transformed into "the ashes of my cigarette from last night.'"[138] In the throes of nicotine withdrawal, the author curses his own "stupid" passion, "Goddam it! I want to smoke, I really want to smoke!"[139] Returning home, he tries to write some meaningful prose but is unable to do so without his tobacco—his muse. Finally he heads to a kafene, where the owner sells him coffee on credit, but his lack of tobacco makes it virtually unpalatable. "But what now? How can I sip down that first gulp of coffee, when I can't fill my lips with tobacco smoke?" Finally, after borrowing two *lev* (Bulgarian equivalent of a dollar) from a friend on the street, he buys tobacco and at long last lights up, exclaiming, "Is there anyone happier than me?" "Strast," with the subtitle "an idler with the pretensions of an artist," is extremely tongue-in-cheek, a lampoon of the author himself and his odious passion.

Kostantinov, along with a select a few of his generation, went further than mere lampoon in critiquing the habit. He became famous for founding the "tourism" movement in Bulgaria, which promoted healthy and productive alternatives to idle kafene life.[140] This movement—and the term tourism at that time referred to hiking and mountaineering—focused on inculcating "love of the homeland" and nature into broad segments of the urban population. To do this, Konstantinov used the genre of the feuilleton (in 1895) to admonish the urban population for their idleness and unhealthy ways: "You worked six days and you secured plenty of bread for the week. On the seventh day don't be diverted to the kafene or krŭchma. Don't you hate the horrible monotony: the smoke of the cigarettes, the stupid clinking of the dice and the billiard balls, the vulgar buffoons, the yawn, and the perpetual feel of frustration, this inertia, and this musty apathy—aren't you bored with it?"[141] As an antidote, Konstantinov issued "invitations" in the newspaper to "Sofia lovers of nature" to join his "club for Bulgarian tourists" for mass climbs to the highest peaks of adjacent Mount Vitosha and other such natural wonders:

> Brothers, set aside for now your thirst for gold, your thirst for power, your vain drive for status, your poisonous pen, leave behind your soft beds, crawl out of your smoky cafés, leave behind the dusty streets and the city and come here for a few days, to this height of 2,500 meters, experience for at least a small amount of time real, pure pleasure and you will transform, you will become better, more healthy, and more well-balanced and more enamored with life.[142]

In another essay he rants, "picturesque nature cannot be experienced in a cafe or tavern, amid the suffocating smoke, under the influence of narcotics and intoxicating drinks... where cynicism and self-deprecating talk prevail."[143]

Konstantinov was not the only nineteenth-century voice that critiqued Bulgarian idleness and indulgence in the kafene and krŭchma settings. Khristo Danov (1828–1911), a well-known publisher from Plovdiv, wrote a treatise for the nation, *Za teb mili rode* (*For You My Dear Homeland*), in which he chastises Bulgarian men who, "smoke their cigarettes one after the other, while others rumble on their nargiles and all impatiently wait for the sun to set so they can move on to plum brandy."[144] Danov, himself a known regular of the kafenes of Plovdiv's three hills, was increasingly impatient with what he saw as a waste of Bulgarian energies in this setting. Echoing the Western critique of Oriental kafene idleness, Danov lamented that so much time was "spent smoking" in these venues instead of reading in the newly established chitalishte.[145] This was in subtle contrast to Konstantinov, who also linked the ills of urban life to the kafene and krŭchma but found a connection between idleness and Western-cosmopolitan vices such as vanity and the pursuit of money. Danov and Konstantinov, looking east and west to assign blame, were practically voices in the wilderness in a period when tobacco, accompanied by coffee and alcohol, was gaining greater social acceptance.

Their message found an echo primarily in the American-led Protestant abstinence movement in Bulgaria that had greatly intensified by the 1880s but was still more focused on alcohol. By the 1880s, "special efforts" had led to the production and distribution of some hundred thousand tracts and seven posters.[146] According to missionary observers of Bulgarian religious and social life, there was a great need for temperance in a society where "the village priest was commonly accorded the privilege of acting as the local liquor dealer." Missionary reports tended to describe a rather positive response to temperance efforts in the region. Branch societies were formed, especially strong in out-stations north of the Balkans, which "met fortnightly and held public meetings," and in at least one case, an 1884 temperance rally attracted more than four hundred people.[147] But in spite of noted successes in the provinces, evidence of Bulgarian hostility to the temperance movement is overwhelming. There are numerous stories, for example, of local hostility to the Protestant presence by Bulgarians who saw the Protestant message as foreign and even threatening to the "national" faith. And while Protestant educational and other efforts were sometimes welcomed, it is important to note the stoning of local missionaries, the ostracism of cooperating or converted Bulgarians, and even the kidnapping of American missionaries.[148] As temperance began to take root in Bulgarian soil, the missionary message and its messengers also spawned deeply moored resistances that would later have significant repercussions. And while such messages were almost exclusively directed against spirits, smoking began to be increasingly associated with drinking.

By the early twentieth century the scope of the Protestant message gradually broadened as did vigorous initiatives by a growing number of native abstinence advocates. These advocates, under the influence of the international temperance movement, began to organize abstinence associations on Bulgarian soil. A colony of left-leaning Bulgarian students studying in Geneva in the period, whose ringleader was Khristo Dimchev, became the core of an abstinence movement that began to proliferate through student and teacher organizations beginning in 1906. Their primary inspiration was the well-known Swiss psychologist and outspoken socialist and temperance advocate August Forel. During the same period, Bulgarian Protestants under James Clark began to aggressively organize Protestant-based abstinence movements throughout the country.[149] With the cooperation of the Bulgarian Ministry of Education, Clark had abstinence pamphlets distributed throughout Bulgarian schools in the early decades of the century. From 1907 to 1910 his temperance society published and distributed 350,000 temperance tracts.[150] Increasingly these movements, whether Protestant or socialist, began to target smoking, along with gambling, prostitution, and other elements of urban vice.

This interesting convergence of purpose from the Bulgarian far Left and the evangelist Right became a permanent feature of the temperance movement as it gained strength in the decades that followed. As strange as it seems, there was a certain symbiosis between the activities and paradigms of these two very different sets of social actors. Dimitŭr Blagoev, the founder of Bulgarian socialism, was, after all, the product of a Protestant upbringing. In a sense Protestantism was the first step to radical socialism, representing a break from Bulgarian religious (and hence national) tradition. In fact, at least some American Protestants in Bulgaria were quite approving of the "essentially Christian virtues" of the early Bulgarian socialists in this period.[151] For Protestants, temperance was a defining feature of their community—missionaries and Bulgarian converts. For socialists, however, only a segment of the movement rejected alcohol and tobacco as capitalist vices. The rest were mired in smoke at the kafene Sredets and cafés across Europe, or drinking at the working-class local krŭchma. In a sense both socialists and Protestants laid deep roots in nineteenth-century Bulgarian soil. Protestants had wielded influence through their role in the Bulgarian national revival, particularly in publishing and educational activities. Many revival figures were inspired by socialism's message, and Bulgaria came to have the largest socialist movement in the Balkans in the twentieth century. It is important to note, however, that both Protestants and socialists provoked strong negative reactions, being viewed as "foreign," or traitorous to the *national* cause. Their messages of abstinence, which were brought forward at a time of widespread acceptability of drinking and smoking, were inevitably unwelcome to most who partook of such consumables.

Over the course of the nineteenth century, smoking betokened a new era of leisure and sociability in Balkan male society, one that echoed and underpinned commercial revival, urbanization, and Bulgaria's political and social coming of age. The kafene was not the only context for the rise and spread of the smoking phenomenon in Bulgaria, but it certainly was the most powerful engine for its spread and for new modes of social interaction. This process, though, did not occur in a vacuum. The Ottoman coffeehouse tradition offered a ready model for sober male sociability, while the European café and other leisure venues tuned and expanded that model. From Istanbul to Vienna Bulgarians learned to smoke in the multifaceted and dynamic environment of East-West interaction, commercial exchange, and cosmopolitan urban leisure. At home and abroad, foreign models of morality, sobriety, and leisure both attracted and repelled Bulgarians, who were groping for a place in a nineteenth-century world that was becoming both modern and increasingly national. Smoking had helped create such a world among the Bulgarian population of the eastern Balkans. But its very diffusion and acceptability—its penetration into the fabric of society by this time—also made it alarming to various segments of the population. Yet for those concerned with the proliferation of tobacco in the early twentieth century, unraveling what had been so intricately woven into Bulgarian social life would not be an easy task.

CHAPTER 2

No Smoke without Fire

Tobacco and Transformation, 1878–1914

In 1892 the young Bulgarian principality staged an International Agricultural and Trade Exhibition in Plovdiv, its second-largest city, with the idea of drawing crowds of international and domestic participants and spectators.[1] The fair's organizers saw the event as fulfilling a number of important functions, prime among them the stimulation of trade and local industry. As in other fairs of the period, displays of Bulgaria's rich resources, handicrafts, and manufactured goods shared the stage with entertainment and displays of folk and high culture, carefully ensconced in an ensemble of specially commissioned works of architectural and landscape design.[2] The resulting assembly of people, buildings, and goods was meant to display and sell the glories of "free Bulgaria" to foreign visitors as well as its own population—both urban dwellers and peasant delegations from the provinces. In addition, Bulgarian planners encouraged legions of Slavic peasants to attend from the adjacent Ottoman provinces of Thrace and Macedonia, offering cheap train fares and accommodation. From the earliest planning stages of the fair organizers wistfully asked, "and who of those Bulgarians who live outside our borders does not want to see the happiness and delight, the life force, riches and successes of their free brothers, which reflect the prosperous future of the whole nation?"[3] With broadly defined goals and a diverse audience in mind, they presented an interesting amalgam of exhibits that combined informational displays with pure entertainment, artifacts of progress with quaint folksiness, and the modern European with the exotic and Oriental.

Undotubtedly this event was a veritable coming out for the nation, albeit with sufficiently ambiguous messages and often contradictory goals. Bulgarian statesmen were keen on displaying national culture and progress to the citizens of the principality, as well as to visiting Bulgarian nationals from neighboring regions and to foreigners. But the fair was also meant to drive (rather than express) economic and social advances. With its display of agricultural and industrial technologies, the fair had clearly stated "instructional" functions for the Bulgarian populations.[4] Foreigners, on the other hand, were meant to bear witness to Bulgaria's potential for development as well as its exotic desirability. From the moment they walked through the Oriental-style entrance gate visitors were invited to immerse themselves in the pleasures within, from the Turkish sweets to the colorful panoply of peasants in national garb. Along these lines, one of the central buildings in the center of the fairgrounds was the tobacco pavilion of Dimitŭr Stavrides, a Greek and one of Bulgaria's most prominent tobacconists of the period. Beyond its evocative Oriental-Mughul style exterior, spectators observed demonstrations of sorting and cutting the rich and flavorful Oriental tobaccos grown in the Bulgarian provinces.[5] Oriental or Turkish tobaccos had already attained a degree of international renown in this period for their exceptional quality and unique aroma and flavor. Generally these tobaccos tended to be associated with other Balkan provinces, Thrace and Macedonia, still under the direct control of the Ottoman Empire—or with Egypt, through which many of them were re-exported. In Plovdiv, however, Turkish tobacco was explicitly displayed as Bulgarian, in and among the other products of newly autonomous Bulgaria.

In 1892 the Bulgarian nation was still an amalgam of elements, not yet untangled from the Ottoman past and still trying to negoti ate a future within Europe. This was a process that would unfold, among other ways, through internal and international economic relationships and commodity exchange. By the 1890s tobacco was a central player in such interactions as one of the few highly valuable and marketable Bulgarian commodities with an immediate potential for export growth. Although other products were sold and displayed at the fair, tobacco was the only commodity with its own pavilion, and its centrality marked the beginning of the tobacco era in Bulgarian history. The Stavrides pavilion was visited and experienced by Bulgarians and foreign spectators at a historical moment when tobacco was becoming a pervasive palliative for Bulgarians. The rapid expansion of tobacco cultivation, processing, and commerce by the late nineteenth century reflected a domestic and growing global tobacco addiction. As with other nondurable addictive goods, consumers required ever large quantities of tobacco in order to achieve its desired effect. Bulgarian statesmen and merchants had begun to recognize that the expanding domestic and international market for this cash crop offered an opportunity to mitigate the extreme economic hardship that loomed over the principality.

But if tobacco was the future, it was also entangled with a past that could not easily be discarded. In the 1890s the Bulgarian economy was in critical condition. The post-1878 transition to autonomy had been disruptive, especially given the large scale emigration of Muslims from urban areas.[6] The loss of population from these centers of local consumption and the substantial loss of Ottoman markets, especially for Balkan textiles, was ruinous to local proto-industry.[7] Even more damaging was the massive influx of European manufactured goods, which rapidly displaced local goods, sending Bulgarian proto-industry into a free fall from the late 1850s and devastating the guild-based urban economy.[8] Even as the young Bulgarian principality sought to detach itself politically, economically, and culturally from the Ottoman East, the West quickly loomed as a far greater and more immediate threat.[9] Though freedom from the Ottoman Yoke was an explicit subtext to the 1892 fair, organizers also warned that Bulgaria was "threatened with something worse than political slavery."[10] The notion of a Western threat was pervasive in various sources from the period, which tended to agree that "Europe has deemed to give us independence but has saved for itself the right to exploit us.... Political slavery is bad but economic slavery is worse."[11] Perhaps paradoxically, the Bulgarian prime minister from 1886 to 1895, Stefan Stambolov—whose power far exceeded that of the reigning Prince Ferdinand—decided to address this threat through a further *opening* to the West.[12] Stambolov, one of the biggest supporters of and a frequent visitor to the fair, believed in both the appropriation of Western technologies and the *selling* of goods to the West for the good of Bulgarian trade.[13] In practice this meant the packaging of at least some Bulgarian wares as Oriental. Still, given Bulgarians' observations of increased Western economic penetration of the Ottoman Empire across the border, protectionism as opposed to free trade was the order of the day.[14] In fact, Western trade partners—European and American—operated with fewer hindrances in the Ottoman Empire than in Bulgaria in the decades leading up to World War I. As a result, the Bulgarian tobacco trade with the West was often conducted across the Ottoman border, which remained exceedingly porous. To a large extent the

Bulgarian economy remained dependent on old Ottoman trade networks and institutions within and across newly placed borders, as well as traditional (though ever-changing) ethnic divisions of labor and interdependencies. As exemplified in the Stavrides pavilion, the rise and shape of the early Bulgarian tobacco industry was grounded in local patterns of economic exchange and the desire, albeit cautious, to seduce Western buyers.

In the years following the exhibition Bulgarian tobacco was rapidly commodified as a result of local and growing international demand in the years leading up to World War I. In many respects tobacco was a kind of fiscal savior, a boon to the state economy. Social actors of various nationalities—merchants, factory owners, middlemen, and even peasants—met with marked economic success in the tobacco world. But the tobacco boom was also an intensely destabilizing factor. It deepened social and, in some cases, ethnic divisions within a complex and shifting web of labor patterns and resource control. In addition the presence of valuable tobacco reserves in the coveted territories of Ottoman Thrace and Macedonia undoubtedly intensified competing Bulgarian, Greek, Serbian, and local "Macedonian" claims to lands that held far more than just ethnic constituencies. As Bulgaria was flooded with massive waves of Macedo-Slavic refugees in the period following 1878, so too did tobacco dreams and grievances permeate the cities and rural areas of "free Bulgaria." As Bulgaria expanded south into the tobacco-growing regions of Eastern Rumelia (1885) and parts of Macedonia and Thrace (1912–14), tobacco moved into an even more central role in the Bulgarian economy and social life. It was increasingly vital to Bulgaria's penetration and control of its own periphery—a process that was also fraught with social and ethnic conflict. At the same time, as tobacco became more export-oriented, prosperity was coupled with increased dependency on and hence vulnerability to fickle Western markets.

Tobacco Roads

Of course Bulgaria was by no means a newcomer to the world of tobacco in the late nineteenth century. Introduced in the late sixteenth century, the New World variety had adjusted and transformed into a more flavorful and lower-nicotine plant in the rich alkaline soils of the Ottoman Balkans. These soils, especially those on the terraced bases of surrounding mountains, were not suitable for cultivation of much else, but were ideal for growing Oriental tobaccos, which especially thrived in the dry Mediterranean climate of Ottoman Thrace and Macedonia. Initially only Muslim populations grew tobacco for consumption and trade, and Christians grew it in rare cases for medicinal purposes, such as treating sheep with scabies.[15] As has been widely noted, however, non-Muslim merchants seemed to be the biggest beneficiaries of the Ottoman commercial revival of the late eighteenth century, which surged with the increased regional stability of the 1830s and 1840s and increased export trade after the Crimean War (1853–56).[16]

By the nineteenth century, expanded legal parameters and new social roles accompanied the entrance of non-Muslims into the world of tobacco production and commerce, though tobacco itself was but one of the many goods transported and sold by established and newly mobile non-Muslim merchants. Until the last decades of the nineteenth century, ships and caravans that carried goods within and beyond the Balkans were more likely to be carrying cotton, wool, or grains than tobacco. This new class of self-described Bulgarian merchants tended to stick to Balkan land routes, in contrast to Greek merchants, who tended to dominate (along with Salonika's Jews) the much more lucrative trade on the Black and Aegean Seas.[17] Some went as far as Vienna in the west, Egypt to the south, and India to the east with hundreds of horses, mules, camels, or buffalo laden with a variety of raw materials and native handicrafts.[18] By the 1830s these merchants began to use their newfound prosperity to fund commercial and educational associations with an explicitly Bulgarian cast while establishing colonies in Vienna,

Camels with tobacco bales on their backs, circa 1914. Courtesy of the Regional State Archive in Plovdiv.

Odessa, Bucharest, and elsewhere. The newly burgeoning Danubian port cities hosted a robust mix of Bulgarians, Turks, Armenians, Jews, and European nationals, who eclipsed the shipping and trade power of Greeks. Proto-industrial development and commerce were boosted by improvements in land security, infrastructure, and credit, especially in the 1864–67 period, when the well-known Ottoman reformer Midhat Pasha governed the Danube *vilayet* (province) of northern Bulgaria. Under his administration, the core Bulgarian lands became one of the most industrialized regions of the empire besides Istanbul and its environs.[19] Until 1878, raw and manufactured goods from Bulgarian districts were used primarily to provide Ottoman cities with grain and the reformed standing army with wool and braid for uniforms. These paths of exchange, traditional and newly forged, later provided ready conduits for the surge in tobacco commerce both in Bulgaria and in adjacent Ottoman Macedonia and Thrace. In this period the increased export of cash crops, primarily wheat and cotton, to Western Europe also paved the way for the eventual shift to a tobacco-based economy.

The European trade advantage was heightened by the increased use of so-called capitulations, a series of trade concessions made with European powers in various treaties, many of which were centuries old. According to treaty provisions, European merchants had considerable extraterritorial rights—such as duty-free exports from the Ottoman lands and low tariffs on imports into these territories—which they routinely extended to local non-Muslim Ottoman subjects. These conditions had stimulated a lively European commercial advance into the Ottoman environs by the late nineteenth century.[20] The Habsburg Empire, France, and the United Kingdom in particular were engaged in trade with port cities surrounding Ottoman Bulgaria.[21] The Austro-Hungarian Steamship Company Austrian Lloyd, was by far the most vigorous commercial presence on the lower Danube by midcentury, as the river was "internationalized" after the Crimean War.[22] Ottoman-Habsburg land routes were increasingly directed to Danubian ports—Lom, Svishtov, Ruse, and Vidin—from which steamships took people and goods up and down the river, out to the Black Sea, and on to Istanbul or the Mediterranean.[23] The United Kingdom and France, though also present on the Danube, generally bought goods at Black Sea ports such as Varna and Burgas but also at Aegean ports such as Salonika and Kavala.

In this period an unequal balance of trade, in addition to war loans for the Crimean and Russo-Turkish Wars, contributed to the Ottoman Empire's first accrual of a rapidly expanding debt to Western banks.[24] Massive debt was exacerbated by the so-called Long Depression of 1873 and the reappearance of American cotton and grain on the global market after the American Civil

War, causing the collapse of grain and cotton prices in the 1860s and 1870s.[25] This influx of market forces, far from simply devastating the region, forced a certain resiliency in local economies, many of which responded relatively quickly to changes in price and demand. Though the majority of Ottoman (and Balkan) export goods were agricultural, most required some local processing or manufacture before they could be shipped to cities or foreign markets.[26] As prices for grain, cotton, and manufactured textiles fell in the late century, demand for Ottoman tobaccos consistently expanded.[27] Consumed in ever-greater quantities both globally and locally, tobacco was a needed palliative to late-nineteenth-century Balkan ills under and after Ottoman rule.

When Bulgaria gained autonomy as a result of the Russo-Turkish War of 1877–78, it was heir to both the promise and the predicament of the late-Ottoman economic transformation. It inherited a portion of Ottoman debt as well as a region devastated by war and the displacement of peoples.[28] The young principality was held to the Ottoman trade capitulations until more favorable trade agreements were negotiated by the 1890s.[29] In spite of such conditions, the Bulgarian nationalist dream seemed to be realized in the expansive new state encoded in the Peace of San Stefano (1878), which granted Bulgaria Thrace and Macedonia, regions with some of the empire's most well-developed manufacture and trade. In the subsequent Treaty of Berlin, however, the new principality lost these ethnically mixed regions with their large Macedonian-Bulgarian populations and economic potential, including the empire's best tobacco. The treaty also detached the more immediate southern districts of San Stefano Bulgaria, creating Eastern Rumelia, an autonomous and multinational province on the Thracian plain with its capital in Plovdiv. This region, which merged with Bulgaria in 1885, shared with Macedonia (and the rest of Thrace) a burgeoning tobacco economy in the last decades of the century as tobacco demand began to rise.[30]

For Bulgaria, no city was more central to the new tobacco economy than Plovdiv, the site of the Stavrides tobacco pavilion at the aforementioned 1892 fair. It was a central commercial center on the Thracian plain and one of the largest and most prosperous cities in the region even before it benefited from Ottoman reforms in the Tanzimat period (1839–76).[31] It adjoined the central Balkan Mountain region, where both early- and mid-nineteenth-century Bulgarian-proto-industrial development and the national revival were centered. It was also adjacent to the tobacco fields of Thrace and the foothills of the Rhodope Mountains, which facilitated the success of tobacco trade processing in the city in the latter half of the century. As tobacco production began to gain traction in the Ottoman, Eastern Rumelian, and Bulgarian economies, Plovdiv became a central entrepôt for tobacco

Stringing tobacco leaves for drying. Leaves hung to dry in background. http://www.lostbulgaria. com.

processing and commerce.[32] The city was ideal both because of its central location along traditional and new—the Orient Express (as of 1885)—trade and travel routes and because of its commercial and handicraft traditions and relatively large and diverse population. As of 1830, Plovdiv's estimated thirty to fifty thousand inhabitants were of mixed ethnic origin—Muslim, Greek, Armenian, Roma, and Slav—though the ethnic balance of the city was slowly tipping toward Bulgarians, particularly after 1885.[33]

The rapidly developing tobacco industry in Plovdiv was as multiethnic as the city itself. The first Plovdiv workshop, Tomasian and Sons Inc. was established by a prominent Armenian tobacconist, Magurdich Tomasian, who is considered by many the founding father of the industry in Bulgaria.[34] Tomasian had sailed the Danube as a tobacco trader under the protection of the Austrian flag before settling in Ottoman Plovdiv in the 1870s. After 1878 he established numerous tobacco warehouses (for sorting and fermenting) and workshops (for cutting and packing). Not content with only Bulgarian and Ottoman tobaccos, Tomasian traveled as far as Odessa and the Caucasus in the 1880s looking for other fine varieties to mix into his flavorful loose-leaf tobacco bouquets. A merchant and industrialist in one, he expanded his business, integrating the latest tobacco-cutting (1895) and cigarette-rolling (1905) machines into a highly profitable venture. Tomasian was a key player in the development of the Bulgarian tobacco industry, which by 1908 employed 9,450 people in Plovdiv alone.[35] Tobacco, even in its rawest form, was labor-intensive at all stages of production. In addition to cultivation and harvesting it also required fairly elaborate processing—drying, fermenting, sorting, and packing—to be ready for sales, storage, transport, and/or export. Though Plovdiv had other factories, which produced soap, beer, perfume, and ink, tobacco was the most visible industry by the end of the century. In addition to Tomasian, there were the prominent Greek tobacconists and partners Dimitri Madras and the aforementioned Dimitŭr Stavrides—benefactor of the tobacco pavilion in 1892.[36] Like Tomasian's, the tobacco workshops and products of Madras and Stavrides were renowned among Plovdiv residents, who relished their hand-rolled cigarettes "in pretty metal boxes...made from the more rare tobaccos—local and Turkish."[37] Alongside local ethnic "minority" figures in the industry, another key figure was K. Vakaro, a Habsburg Italian, who purchased Stavrides's business in the 1890s and ran it with great success in the ensuing years.[38] This pantheon of non-Bulgarian tobacconists fueled the perception that Bulgarian tobacco profits were being drained by foreigners, though most came from ethnic communities who had lived in Plovdiv for centuries. Certainly, given the traditional urban cast, commercial experience, and contacts of Greeks, Armenians, and (for certain cities) Jews in the region, these groups were well placed to succeed in tobacco enterprise.

At the same time, a number of Bulgarians were also pioneers in the industry, though more conspicuously so outside the confines of Plovdiv. By the 1880s all Bulgarian cities, both those that were in tobacco-producing districts and those that were major entry points for domestic trade and export, had at least one tobacco-processing facility. Bulgarian names are prominent among tobacco factory and workshop owners in many mixed towns of the period, like Sliven, Shumen, Stara Zagora, Razgrad, Pleven, and Ruse.[39] In general, a more intensive concentration of Turkish-owned workshops could be found in the tobacco-growing and heavily Turkish-populated regions in the South, which were incorporated into Bulgaria only after the first Balkan War.[40] In the Gorna Djumaya (now Blagoevgrad or Pirin Macedonia) region, for example, a landowner named Osman Bei encouraged his peasant tenants to grow tobacco and then hired Vlach-run caravans of 1,400 pack animals to take his tobaccos to Danubian port cities like Vidin, Lom, Ruse, and the Aegean port of Salonika.[41] In Rhodope towns like Kirdzhali, all the big tobacconists were Turkish, as were the *tiutiundzhi* and *havandzhi* guilds (tobacco shops and cutting houses, respectively).[42] But the emigration of Turks during the Russo-Turkish War (1877–1878) and later the Balkan Wars (1912–13) greatly curtailed the Turkish role in such endeavors in regions that fell within the new principality. In larger post-Ottoman Bulgarian cities, like Plovdiv, significant populations of non-Slavic Christians (Armenians and Greeks) meant that Bulgarians were overshadowed within the upper ranks of the industry. Even in Plovdiv, though, a number of Bulgarian tobacconists—for example, Stavri Stamov and Nikola Libenov and sons—played an important role in the industry's early development. In practice, such ethnic divisions had little impact on the functioning of the industry, and tobacconists worked comfortably across ethnic lines. For example, as early as 1909, Plovdiv tobacconists—under the leadership of Vakaro—organized a statewide tobacco monopoly, the so called Kartel (cartel) that processed about 76 percent of all Bulgarian tobaccos after 1909.[43]

In the years that followed, ethnic cooperation was the rule; it was primarily those outside the industry who were critical of its "foreign" nature.[44] Even as Bulgarians entered the world of commerce in the eighteenth and nineteenth centuries, they were at a severe disadvantage in relation to other non-Muslim merchant groups who had well-established commercial networks at home and abroad. During the nineteenth century, Bulgarian merchants tended to join Turks or Vlachs in large trade caravans, but they were far less visible, though a growing factor, in most port-city commerce, where

Tobacco hanging to dry over a street in a village in Bulgaria. http://www.lostbulgaria.com.

Greek, Vlach, and Armenian merchants were predominant.[45] Jews tended to be visible as tobacco merchants primarily in Salonika, though they often played roles as smaller-scale middlemen in other Macedonian cities and had a significant commercial presence in Ruse.[46] Only a few notable Bulgarian tobacco merchants emerged before World War I, all based outside the principality in Ottoman Macedonia. Gorna Djumaya's Georgi Chaprashikov, for example, became rich and well known through his activities in the tobacco trade. Also famous were Mitko Kutsev (or Kutsolgu) and later his son Vasil; they were based in the tobacco-rich Rhodope environs of Smolian, which (like Gorna Djumaya) came under Bulgarian rule only in 1912.

The Kutsev story offers a window into the incredible social mobility that commercial success in tobacco could offer in the latter half of the century. Mitko Kutsev was born sometime in the mid-nineteenth century into a Slavic Christian peasant family in the village of Raikovo (now a suburb of Smolian). The family business was animal husbandry, and Kutsev expanded his herds to nearly ten thousand sheep during the lucrative wool boom in the region.[47] As with other merchants of the region, he was on the road for much of the year, returning only in the winter to see his wife and ten children. While trading animals and wool, Kutsev also began to buy tobacco from the adjacent Aegean Macedonia region for sale across the Ottoman Empire. By the last decades of the century, he became a man of status who could afford an opulent home and premium educations (in Istanbul and abroad) for his sons, who were groomed to take over the business. By the early twentieth century the family wool interests were rapidly eclipsed by involvement in the tobacco trade, primarily out of the Aegean ports of Salonika and Kavala.[48] For Rhodope tobacco merchants, the importance of Aegean ports and Ottoman markets was as critical as access to the superior leaf of the districts of Ksanti and Drama as well as the minor valleys of the southern Rhodopes. Arguably the "best tobaccos in the world" were grown within the confines of connected districts of Ksanti and the port city Kavala, where three quarters of all Ottoman-Balkan tobaccos were produced.[49] The Ottoman lands, with their large internal market, well-worn trade paths, excellent supplies of leaf, and openness to European trade were a boon to Bulgarian merchants, who were among the major beneficiaries of the tobacco boom as it gained momentum. Indeed, Kutsev had assumed the name Kutsolgu (using the Turkish instead of the Slavic ending) around the turn of the century, perhaps as a way of foregrounding his Ottoman loyalties.[50]

In spite of such successes, Bulgarian statesmen harbored anxieties about a preponderance of foreign merchants in the tobacco trade, which compounded larger concerns about Bulgarian vulnerability to the West. Grigor Nachovich, the then minister of finance, published a tract in 1883 entitled *The Tobacco Indus-try in the Bulgarian Principality* that articulated a contradictory approach toward the future of the industry. On the one hand, Nachovich recognized the impor-tance of tobacco for the Bulgarian economy and advocated the rapid expansion of its cultivation and processing. Nachovich, in fact, was one of the primary engineers of the Plovdiv fair of 1892, which after all was set in Bulgaria's most productive tobacco-processing town and aimed to seduce Western buyers with Bulgarian leaf. On the other hand, Nachovich was keenly aware of the dangers of free capitalist exchange and openly articulated the need to keep profits from falling into the hands of foreign merchants such as Greeks, Vlachs, and other middlemen who were purportedly milking profits from the Bulgarian peasant.[51]

Even more emphatically he counseled Bulgarians to avoid the unfavorable situation in the rest of the Ottoman Empire.[52] Specifically, he wanted to avoid Bulgarian subordination to the so-called Ottoman Régie. The Régie was a European consortium established in 1883 under the umbrella of the Otto-man Public Debt Commission (OPDC). Because Ottoman debt to Western European banks was so high, the Régie began to directly collect revenues to service the debt by 1884. More pointedly, the Régie had taken over the regulation and collection of the *miumurie,* or banderol, the lucrative Ottoman tax on internal tobacco consumption originally imposed in 1872. Though the Ottomans still made a substantial sum on export duties, the loss of lucra-tive banderol profits, which were steeply on the rise in the late 1880s, was a huge blow to the already beleaguered economy. The Régie, which had a French, Austrian, and German board of directors and a preponderance of Brit-ish employees, was charged with closely regulating tobacco production and commerce in the Ottoman Balkan provinces to stop contraband production and consumption and hence tax evasion. This regulation accompanied gradu-ally increasing Great Power control of Ottoman finances as well as pressure for, and direct participation in, reform on the ground, particularly in Macedo-nia. This foreign intervention, along with the sapping of the Ottoman econ-omy by the Régie, was one of many factors that encouraged Bulgarians to limit and direct Western control over Bulgarian tobacco, as well as other resources. And although this stunted the industry in certain respects, the Bulgarian prin-cipality was also able to maintain more control over its commercial contacts than was the empire, of which it was still nominally a part.

Tobacco Inroads

By the early years of the twentieth century, Balkan tobaccos were in high demand. From 1899 to 1909 there was a huge jump in sales of Oriental tobaccos that were used in Turkish and Egyptian cigarettes. In the United States, for example, wooden Turks in turbans and Oriental pants replaced Indians in front of tobacco stores, and Oriental names and designs such as Mecca and Fatima were all the rage.[53] It was in this period that American Tobacco, the cartel that controlled American tobacco production, made serious commercial inroads into the Balkans.[54] It built warehouses and created bases of operations in Ottoman Macedonia and Thrace, where the ample tobacco supply flanked readily available seaports. Processing facilities mushroomed in inland tobacco entrepôts like Serres, Ksanti, and Prilep, while Kavala became the primary Aegean port, with Salonika a close second. The shift to tobacco cultivation in these districts was dramatic. In the case of the Serres district, for example, only 240,000 okka (1 okka = 1.2 kilograms) of tobacco were produced in 1902, compared with 3.5 million in 1917.[55] American as well as Habsburg, German, and French companies began to set up branch offices in Plovdiv and other Bulgarian cities, and Bulgarian tobacco production also increased, though not on the same scale as in the Ottoman lands. Still, the Bulgarian-Ottoman border was fairly porous, and Bulgarian tobacco often made its way to Ottoman ports, where it was exported to other countries.

Significantly, this period of intensive commodification of Balkan tobacco coincides with one of the most violent periods (1900–1908) in Macedonian (and to a lesser extent Thracian) history. This raises the obvious question as to whether there was a connection between the steep rise in violence and the construction of value around Turkish tobaccos that characterized these years. Certainly, the competing claims of the surrounding Balkan principalities and states—Greek, Bulgarian, and Serbian—and the local competition for ethnic loyalties to justify those claims were paramount in the rise of violence. The diverse ethnic mosaic, as well as the indistinct nature of most of these identities, Christian and Muslim, made attempts to ethnographically map and hence politically claim these mountainous swaths of territory quite a challenge.[56] But contrary to common assumptions, nationalist struggles were by no means the only driving forces behind violence in this region.[57] Conflicts over land, resources, and sovereignty in Macedonia took place in the shadow of the rapidly accelerating international and local tobacco trade. The uneven prosperity that tobacco commerce brought to the region surely exacerbated local ethnic, social, and political tensions.

The machinations of the tobacco economy greatly undermined the Ottoman Empire's bid to bring order and reform to the region and to stem the tide of violence. The bulk of tobacco revenues went to service the foreign debt via the Régie or into the hands of a relatively small but visible coterie of merchants and industrialists, while the restless local peasantry and growing working class experienced far more limited gain. Initially, with the arrival of Régie officials into the Ottoman Balkans in the mid-1880s, tobacco production was stunted by the dizzying web of regulations and taxes associated with the banderol. But by the 1890s many growers and traders had learned to avoid or otherwise navigate the Régie system, and tobacco production, official and unofficial, was steeply on the rise. Although it is impossible to obtain exact figures, contraband production and trade appear to have taken off by the turn of the century as a way of evading the banderol. According to John Foster Fraser, a British reporter who traveled through Kavala in 1905,

> Cigarettes! The only cigarettes you are supposed to smoke in Turkey are Régie, the Government monopoly. But nobody in Kavala ever smokes Régie cigarettes. Every cigarette in Kavala is contraband and is good. The best tobacco in the world is grown on the plains at the back of Kavala. Egypt, though it sends us [the UK] cigarettes, does not grow an ounce of tobacco. It imports the best from Kavala. In 1905 about one thousand tons were exported from this port, and the value was about one million pounds sterling. The Government takes a clear ten percent royalty. Only the dust and scrapings go to the making of Régie cigarettes.[58]

Smuggling, he observed, was an everyday occurrence across Macedonia and the region in general. In fact, it was so pervasive that the Régie was able to procure, tax, and sell only tobacco of markedly lower quality, making contraband trade that much more profitable and desirable. It was not only in Kavala but in other towns like Elbasan (today in Albania) where the Régie was defied. As Foster narrated,

> [Contraband] Tobacco is openly sold. The soldiers of my escort did a little trade in it. Their bread-bags they loaded with tobacco, stuffed their pockets with it, even their pistol holsters, so that they might take it back to Macedonia and sell it at a profit. I know that they went on short commons in the matter of food so that their bags could be used in this illicit trade. The captain of the guard knew what they were doing. They grinned when they saw that I realized it also.[59]

Tobacco apparently moved across the region in pockets and pistol holders, and as in this case, local gendarmes and officials were deeply implicated.[60] Although the Albanian lands had a special reputation in this regard,[61] the lack of Régie control was also reported in the Skopje environs, as in Kavala and elsewhere.[62] Though hard to precisely track, it was apparently common for Balkan merchants to ship tobacco outside the empire—for example, to Malta or even London—and then re-export into Ottoman Egypt in order to avoid the banderol.[63]

Smuggling, though, was hardly the result of some sort of Balkan propensity for lawlessness. On the contrary, it arose in response to a rather byzantine web of controls put in place and theoretically enforced by the foreign representatives of the Régie. They and their local minions apparently harvested tidy profits for turning a blind eye to the "second" tobacco economy that they themselves had created. As Foster explained, "the humor of the situation is that most of the Kavala officials are steeped to the eyes in smuggling. Ostensibly they do their best to check it, but manage to secure a considerable profit by failing."[64] Of course, not all officials were implicated in such activities. Tremendous efforts were made to enforce the Régie monopoly on internal sales.[65] But certainly, Régie officials were also heavily implicated in contraband trade. Foster gives an example of an official—citizenship and nationality unstated—who purposefully requested a position in a district where tobacco smuggling was rife. After a few years he was able to retire, having saved four hundred Turkish lira, though his salary was only thirteen lira a month.[66] Foreign travelers also regularly enjoyed contraband tobacco. George Abbott, a British folklorist traveling through the region in 1903, positively wallowed in the guilty pleasure of smoking it with every possible local character. In an incident in a hotel in the town of Drama, he reported, "All of these gentlemen . . . though officials of the *Régie*, or perhaps because of that, smoked contraband tobacco, which is cheaper and better than the monopoly stuff."[67] Whether consuming confiscated or purchased contraband tobaccos, this perfect "Concert of Europe" flaunted their violation of the Régie both to each other and in an exceedingly public space.

At the same time Régie and other Western interests were undoubtedly behind the *stimulation* of official tobacco production and trade. They were increasingly present on the ground in the Ottoman provinces, offering generous advances to peasant farmers to grow tobacco. This model, quite similar to the British practices with opium in India, meant that the peasants of Ottoman Thrace and Macedonia got into a cycle of cash exchange and debt that could be alleviated only by further tobacco cultivation. In some cases local merchants, such as Mitko Kutsev in the Rhodope region, began to emulate the model of cash advance with crop yields for collateral. But the Régie was the apparent pioneer in this method, which brought large profits to its foreign holders. At the same time, the development of a lively export trade—also not subject to the banderol—posed serious competition for suppliers to the Régie. Austro-Hungarian export companies, particularly the Hungarian company Herzog and Co., rapidly expanded business into the region in the first decades of the century.[68] Even more prominent was American Tobacco via its international wing British American Tobacco (BAT), which became one of the biggest exporters from Ottoman Balkan ports by the early twentieth century.[69] In fact, witnesses to the phenomenon called 1903 the "American year" and 1908–11 the period of the American "rain of gold," when American Tobacco offered the highest advances to tobacco-producing peasants.[70] American companies under the aegis of the American Tobacco cartel at first produced pure Turkish cigarettes for the niche market at home. But these were precursors to the Camel—the newly perfected blend of American and Turkish tobaccos—which exploded in popularity after its introduction in 1913. By 1911, American Tobacco and Herzog and Co. alone were exporting some 10–12 million kilograms a year, compared with Régie purchases of only 2–4 million kilograms.

In spite of Bulgarian protectionism, the principality also played a part in the Turkish tobacco boom of the early twentieth century. The tobacco trade blossomed as caravans, now heavily laden with bales of tobacco, made the trek to Salonika and especially Kavala on the Aegean coast. As mentioned before, Bulgarian, like other Balkan tobaccos, tended to be exported, packaged, and marketed as Turkish or even Egyptian. Both designations carried a certain seductive Oriental caché, which the term "Bulgarian" (still off the mental map of most) could not confer. Bulgarian tobaccos were generally exported and blended into Turkish cigarettes, often by Greek and other former Ottoman expatriate communities. In fact, Greeks with their expanding shipping networks and Balkan as well as Western contacts (in London, New York, and other cities) were well placed to make fortunes on the Balkan-Egyptian global tobacco trade. Though a modest Bulgarian cigarette industry developed in this period, it was mostly for local consumption, with only minuscule exports.[71] The Egyptian industry, in contrast, successfully developed and branded widely popular Egyptian cigarettes, filled with superior Balkan tobaccos, for export and internal consumption.[72] From 1897 to 1900 the two largest importers of Bulgarian leaf were consistently the Ottoman Empire and Greece, a statistic that reflects both domestic Ottoman consumption and re-export. By 1900–1901, however, the Austro-Hungarian Empire had jumped into the position of number one, importing 621,000 kilograms in 1901 and 1,458,000 in 1902.[73]

But as foreign interests in Bulgarian tobacco were on the rise, so too was Bulgarian debt. Perhaps inevitably, as in the Ottoman case, Bulgarian tobaccos were extremely desirable as collateral for foreign loans that the state was compelled to secure by the turn of the century. A small 1901 loan from the French-dominated consortium Paribas (Banque de Paris et de Pays Bas), for example, required the state to earmark revenues from the bande-rol for debt repayment.[74] By this time the tobacco banderol provided some 10 percent of the state budget of Bulgaria.[75] Politicians fought the initially proposed terms tooth and nail to keep French control over tobacco revenues to a minimum, and in the final agreement tobacco revenues were earmarked only from 1901 until 1904.[76] In terms of debt, commerce, and penetration of foreign corporate interests, Bulgaria still remained relatively closed in the years leading up to World War I. As one British consular report from 1908 complained, the opportunities for expanding British trade were bleak because of the "laudable ambition of the Bulgarians to keep Bulgaria for themselves, and to supply everything which they can for themselves."[77] This protec-tionism both stunted the tobacco industry and kept it under relatively local control. Though foreign companies set up offices and engaged in commerce, these enterprises were nothing like the large-scale warehouses and factories across the border in Ottoman Macedonia. Therefore, in Bulgaria, unlike the Ottoman lands, burgeoning local demand and accompanying urbanization, as well as immigration and shifts in leisure consumption behaviors, drove the tobacco industry's development as much as foreign demand.

In the same period, Ottoman instability as well as the lure of the newly autonomous Bulgarian Principality brought a steady flow of refugees— some thirty thousand between 1904 and 1908—from the tobacco-growing regions of Ottoman Thrace and Macedonia.[78] The rain of American gold, it seems, was not enough to keep these settlers in the last European provinces of the Ottoman Empire, which were fraught with ever-greater violence. Since the 1878 Treaty of Berlin, Greek, Serbian, and Bulgarian armed bands had been asserting their presence in the region. From committed revolu-tionaries to hired guns, these bands rose and fell in the final decades of the century. None were more powerful, brutal, and organized, though notori-ously fractious, than the Internal Macedonian Revolutionary Organization (IMRO). IMRO fought against Ottoman rule on behalf of "Macedonia for Macedonians"—its dream was a multiethnic Macedonia free of Otto-man rule. In practice, however, it was a predominantly Slavic organization with close ties to Bulgaria. Curiously, some of the most flagrant IMRO-initiated violence was not ethnic but rather was between factions of its own organization—the local (the so-called Internal Organization) and the Bulgaria-based leadership (External Organization, EO). Divisions were based on broader goals of annexation to Bulgaria versus autonomy, but also the Internal Organization tended to be more influenced by socialist and anarchist ideas than the EO, which had close ties to the Bulgarian military and more right-wing nationalist thinkers. This complex nature of IMRO and its fractured historical legacy—was it Macedonian, Bulgarian, or truly multiethnic?—has been well documented.[79] But the role of tobacco in the rise, maintenance, and concrete activities of IMRO has been rarely mentioned, if at all.

Given the increasingly prominent place of tobacco in the local economy of Macedonia in this period, this omission is particularly glaring. Tobacco played an important role in funding and shaping IMRO activities. A number of well-known tobacco merchants, such as Georgi Chaprashnikov from the Gorna Djumaya region of Macedonia, donated large sums of money to the IMRO cause.[80] In addition, IMRO broadcast a primarily *social* message to peasants of the region, with clear implications for the local tobacco economy.[81] In the largest of all IMRO-organized actions—the 1903 Illinden Uprising, which mobilized some thirty thousand rebels—the seizing of Turkish land was generally among the first orders of business.[82] According to the Austro-Hungarian consul in Bitola, the "Bulgarian rebels" primarily burned farm-houses, the "so-called 'bulwarks' of the Turkish oppressors."[83] This is significant, given that Turks still owned the bulk of the prime land in the region, upon which tobacco and other cash crops were grown.[84] As one rebel leader noted, "everyone was glad that we will burn out every Turk and the *chorbadzhis* [wealthy Christian notables] of Resen who had for so long enslaved the peasantry economically." Significantly, this rebel leader presented Turks as a clear target, but also included *chorbadzhis*, which generally denoted "Turkophile" Bulgarian, Greek, Vlach, or other Christian notables.

Similarly, the 350,000 Ottoman troops and irregular forces responding to the rebellion settled social scores in addition to unleashing a more general violence against the Slavic Christian collective. As they crushed the rebel movement, they burned numerous Bulgarian villages to the ground in retribution and some 4,694 noncombatants were killed along with 994 rebels.[85] In addition to committing atrocities against Slavic villagers, however, the troops—who themselves lost 5,328—also massacred Greeks and plundered their largely urban properties.[86] In fact, in the case of Krushevo, a town that rebels held for ten days, an American consul reported that Ottoman soldiers looted and massacred Greek and Vlach populations but left the (much poorer) Bulgarian population untouched.[87] Ottoman Muslims used the opportunity to vent social grievances against well-to-do "Greeks" (some assimilated Vlachs and Bulgarians) and Vlachs, who were both major beneficiaries of urban tobacco entrepôt commerce. In the complicated case of Illinden alone, the tangle of ethnic and social identities is hard to unravel.

Generally, however, violence was directed against those who had something to lose—Muslims and Greeks—by those who had nothing to lose, mostly Slavic rebels and peasants as well as many Ottoman soldiers.

Though the uprising ultimately failed, it did manage to attract international attention, but not with the desired outcome of Macedonian autonomy. Instead, much to the chagrin of IMRO, the Great Powers pressured the Ottomans to enact even more reforms and allow a more pervasive Great Power presence in the region. The Murtzeg Program of 1903 required the increased presence of Western advisers and gendarmes on the ground. Among other things, the reforms demanded a greater enforcement of the Régie monopoly and so more revenue for the involved Great Powers. As H. N. Brailsford, an agent for a British relief agent in the region, described it in 1903–4, European interests were able to "wring steady revenue" from the bankrupt and anarchic Ottoman polity through railroads, the public debt administration, and the tobacco monopoly.[88] The reforms, though far from successful, also brought a greatly increased commercial penetration of the region, including that by American tobacco interests. Great Power designs, as well as Régie and other commercial tobacco interests, were generally anathema for IMRO, which was also known for smuggling contraband tobacco and collecting its own taxes from the local populations under its shifting jurisdictions.[89]

The outcome of Illinden sharpened IMRO's already imbedded anti-Great Power bent, inherent in its intended goal of Macedonia for Macedonians. The IMRO leadership, itself very ideologically fragmented, had generally agreed that the West was ruinous to Macedonia. In a typical 1901 letter that Gotse Delchev, one of the most prominent figures in the movement, sent to another IMRO leader, he spoke of "internal armed resistance on the part of the population against the cruelties of the Sultan's butchers" and the "favorable disposition of his fellow tyrants—the European Masters."[90] Even before 1903, representatives of the Great Powers—as well as the United States—were frequent targets of IMRO attacks, including a spate of kidnappings from 1880 to 1908. The most famous of these was the well-publicized kidnapping in 1901 of the Protestant missionary Ellen Stone, which brought IMRO its largest ransom ever, $65,000.[91] These attacks were only partially motivated by the immediate revenue potential of ransoms and theft.

European assets and institutions were also targeted for wanton destruction just prior to and during the 1903 uprising. The most famous of such incidents was the bombing of the Ottoman Bank in Salonika and the related bombings of numerous foreign ships and railroad lines—all newly constructed by Western European companies and consortiums. The Ottoman Bank, a

French-controlled but multinational financial concern, also happened to be intimately connected to the Ottoman Public Debt Commission and the revenue collection of the Régie. After purchasing a grocery store across the street, a number of radical IMRO members tunneled under the street and set off explosives that left only the outer walls of the bank standing.[92] In the years that followed Illinden, IMRO also directly targeted tobacco-connected Westerners. In 1905, for example, its members kidnapped Martin Wills, a British subject working for the Régie who was stationed in the tobacco-growing district around Monastir (today Bitola).[93] In July of 1905, Wills was caught off guard and captured in the town of Ohrid, where he was investigating tobacco and firearms smuggling across Lake Ohrid.[94] Unfortunately for him, one of his ears was cut off because his ransom was too slow in coming. He managed to escape, almost intact, while his two guards slept, exhausted from the forced marches that moved them and their hostage through the Macedonian mountains by night. Though weak from hunger and exhaustion, Wills was able to find friends to help him, tobacco-growing peasants in a neighboring village, who sent for the proper authorities.[95]

Clearly the Ottoman Empire was by no means the only sworn enemy of the Macedonian movement. Great Power representatives, inside and outside the Régie, who tried to control the flows and profits of the local tobacco economy were also at risk. They provided fodder to the socialist and anarchist elements of Macedonia-based IMRO members with close ties to the tobacco proletariat and its rising labor organizations. As one of the most famous socialist IMRO activists, Dimitŭr Vlakhov, would later claim, from the establishment of the Régie (1883) until 1913, fifty thousand people died in clashes between contrabandists and the Régie authorities—though this figure is surely an exaggeration.[96] Even if only a fraction of this number is correct, the Régie was still implicated in the atmosphere of violence that marked the period. There is undeniable evidence that a certain amount of bloodshed was associated with the imposition of and resistance to informal empire on the part of the competing (and at times cooperating) Great Powers. But many IMRO spokesmen were also keenly aware and critical of bourgeois Bulgarian, Greek, and Serbian designs on the region that were both economic and political.

The issue of the present and future role of Bulgaria in the region was one of the major divisive factors within the movement. Certainly there was the perception among many IMRO operatives that Bulgaria had "the need of acquisition of new territories for political and economic exploitation."[97] Such suspicions were behind the increasingly socialist orientation of the internal movement and the cooperation of IMRO with the Committee for Union and Progress that organized an uprising and brought the reformist Young Turk regime to power in 1908.[98] In support of the Young Turk program, IMRO vowed to "fight against the attempts for guardianship by the Great Powers in our country, against the 'reformatory' intrigues of the die Kulturträger, which by their notorious 'reforms' helped the [Sultan's] monarchy in its crimes and along with it were engaged in our spiritual and economic subjugation."[99] Such cooperation against the larger enemy of the West and Ottoman despotism was short-lived, however, given the Young Turks' efforts to disarm and quell the still-extensive local power of IMRO. Nevertheless, it is clear that perceptions of political and economic threats to the very vague idea of Macedonia for Macedonians were fractious and fluid. Social questions and the closely related penetration of Western interests—both closely tied to the fin de siècle tobacco bubble—were clearly paramount.

Tobacco Politics

The intensification of the Macedonian question within Bulgaria itself was concurrent with the mass migration of Macedonian Slavs into Bulgaria and the attendant shift toward a tobacco-based economy. The 1903 Illinden Uprising brought masses of Slavic refugees across the border, many with tobacco-growing and -processing skills and even seeds, which they spread across the provinces. In the countryside, the influx of Slavs from Macedonia aggravated the parceling of arable land, which meant that rural families had only tiny plots—some suitable mainly, if not only, for tobacco production.[100] But Bulgarian-Macedonians also moved into urban areas, where they came to play a disproportionate role in politics and were among the most radical nationalist voices, adamant advocates of expansion into Macedonia. In Plovdiv, for example, Macedonian refugees organized the notorious Rodoliubets (patriot) association that was behind the radical anti-Greek actions in the city (and nationwide) that peaked in 1906. Along with Greek schools and church properties, Greek businesses were also targeted, boycotted, and looted. Unquestionably, the anti-Greek actions on the street, which precipitated the migration of thirty thousand Greeks from Bulgaria, threatened Greek tobacco interests.[101] Stavrides, for example, sold his factory to the Italian entrepreneur Vakaro within a year. At the same time, Plovdiv tobacconists reportedly took over abandoned Greek houses and other properties and turned them into processing workshops to fill the growing demand for tobacco. Like the Turks, the Greeks of Plovdiv were a dying breed, and the Macedonian question remained a major source of tension in the city between them and the nationalist Bulgarians (especially those from Macedonia).[102]

As mentioned before, the multiethnic masses in Bulgaria and Macedonia still lacked clear national identities, and ethnic tensions to date had been largely spurred by social mobilization against Greeks and Turks. Even as national identities began to harden with the spread of education, national presses, and other cultural institutions, ethnic tensions were severely complicated by the fact that new social divisions often chafed against ethnonational tensions. Social interests as well as ethnic interdependencies competed with ethnic-identity based interests and alliances. In the countryside, where the emigration of Muslim landlords had left only Muslim peasants behind, as well as in Bulgarian urban areas, where tobacco-processing facilities employed a budding and ethnically mixed tobacco proletariat, ethnic violence was not as acute as social strife. In Bulgaria, as in Ottoman Macedonia, tobacco workers became the largest and most mobilized segments of the working class in the early twentieth century.[103] By 1908 Plovdiv had the largest concentration of tobacco workers, mostly former peasants who had flocked to the city from the impoverished Bulgarian (or Ottoman) countryside.[104] As described in the memoirs of the tobacco labor organizer Nikola Abadzhiev, by the beginning of the twentieth century "the city on the Maritsa was transformed into a workers' city," with all that implied. According to Abadzhiev, mass unemployment, some of it driven by the seasonal nature of tobacco processing, made Plovdiv home to "hungry crowds" of workers, whose idleness and dissatisfaction were a potent combination.[105] Former peasants and tobacco workers from Macedonia were a visible and vocal part of these crowds, and they formed a large and rapidly radicalizing contingency. From early in the century spontaneous tobacco workers' strikes, some with as many as a thousand participants, had shaken the industry in Haskovo, Dupnitsa, and Plovdiv.[106] By 1908 tobacco unions had formed in Plovdiv as well as Ottoman Kavala and Salonika, with local branches and periodic strikes mushrooming across the region.[107] In the short term, the political changes following the 1908 Young Turk revolution and Bulgarian independence made the flowering of the new labor organizations possible, while in the longer term expectations for change, disillusionment with results, and the ensuing tobacco boom provoked a frenzy of strikes in both the Ottoman and Bulgarian lands.[108]

Although various stripes of Bulgarian socialists were involved in labor organization among Bulgaria's tobacco workers, none were as proactive as the so-called Narrows. The Narrows were the break-off segment of the Bulgarian Social Democrats that conformed to the Russian Bolsheviks' break with the Mensheviks in 1903. Key members of this party, which after 1919 came to be known as the Bulgarian Communist Party, spent some of their formative years working among Plovdiv's tobacco workers. Dimitur Blagoev, Vasil Kolarov, and Georgi Dimitrov agitated among these workers, though the less-known Nikola Gospodinov was the most important socialist organizer in the city before World War I. By 1908 Gospodinov had risen through the party ranks to become a critical player in Plovdiv's tobacco worker politics as strike organizer and editor of *Tiutiunopabotnik zashtitnik* (*Tobacco-Worker Protector*), a Narrows publication.

Gospodinov's path was in many ways a common one for the tobacco proletariat or socialist agitator in turn-of-the-century Plovdiv. Raised in the town of Harmanli in Thrace, Gospodinov was exposed to socialist ideas when his father's tavern was turned into a socialist political club by a new set of tenants. Though his father heartily disapproved of the "atheists" in residence, Gospodinov befriended the owner, Beliu Bakalov, and was inspired by his ideas about social inequality within the Ottoman Empire and Bulgaria. Such tendencies blossomed when he was sent to a gymnasium in Plovdiv in 1905, where his Russian language teacher was none other than the father of Bulgarian socialism, Dimitŭr Blagoev.[109] Blagoev was himself from Macedonia and was the head of the Plovdiv Macedonian Society, which had connections to revolutionaries in Ottoman Macedonia.[110] Under Blagoev's influence, Gospodinov became a key organizer in Plovdiv, organizing lectures, conferences, and social events, which after 1906 centered around the *naroden dom* (people's house) on Saxat Tepe (one of the three hills of the old Christian quarter). Tobacco workers were the central focus of Gospodinov's efforts, which he described as quite difficult in the early years. "Workers would come to meetings with bottles of *mastika* [Bulgarian ouzo] in their pockets and sit crossed legged—in the Turkish manner—heckling during the talks and conversations."[111] But after 1910, Gospodinov's tireless efforts brought more and more workers to actively participate in the struggle against the Bulgarian tobacco industry and its organized cartel, formed in 1909.

Bulgarian tobacco workers were of mixed (or undetermined) ethnicity, though the labor movement itself did have a decidedly Bulgarian cast. Indeed, the socialist tobacco workers' press frequently felt compelled to respond to accusations of the "Bulgarian character" of the worker's movement in Plovdiv.[112] They countered such accusations by periodically highlighting the movement's multiethnic character in the workers' press, which sought to orchestrate a class consciousness that crossed the boundaries of nationality.[113] A degree of participation by non-Bulgarians was certainly evident in Plovdiv as elsewhere in Bulgaria. According to *Tiutiunopabotnik zashtitnik,* for example, some 1,300 workers "speaking in five languages" participated in the various May Day events of 1910. Plovdiv's workers, though, were predominantly Bulgarian as a result of the urbanization of Bulgarians and the influx of Slavo-Bulgarian populations from Ottoman Thrace and Macedonia. But there were also significant Turkish, Greek, Armenian Jewish, and Roma elements—longtime inhabitants of the city—many of whom participated in newly established workers' associations.[114] In addition to Bulgarian, only the Turkish language appears to have been used in speeches at a 1910 May Day event, though workers speaking in Greek, Armenian, and Ladino (the language of Bulgaria's Sephardic Jews) were reportedly present.[115] Turkish was used to rally people at strikes, in Ottoman-Turkish language columns (in Arabic script), and in the communist Turkish language periodical *Ziya* (light).[116] Still, workers' associations were led by a preponderance of Bulgarians, with only limited and lower-rank participation of Jews, Turks, or Greeks. Greeks in particular seem to have been alienated from the Bulgarian tobacco workers' associations and are rarely mentioned in their accounts. This silence was the result of growing tensions between Bulgarians and Greeks following the eruption of riots against Greeks in Plovdiv in 1906.[117]

The role of Bulgarian-Macedonian refugees—many of whom were tobacco workers—in directing such violence points to an ethnically based fissure among socialist organizers of the day. In a feature article of *Tiutiunopabotnik zashtitnik* from 1910, for example, the "nationalism of workers" came under fire. In spite of social mixing and the commonality of interests among workers, there were also residential segregation and ethnic tensions based on nationalist narratives of past and present injustices.[118] In truth, these nationalist tendencies had a variety of sources, internal and external, economic and cultural. In the eyes of *Tiutiunopabotnik zashtitnik,* however, "the clever masters [the bourgeois industrialists] use national differences to their advantage." They and their "agents" were accused of provoking the 1906 "anti-Greek movement" as well as driving the various nationalities to see each other as occupational competition. With its simple and oft-repeated appeal, "factory owners and not other workers are your enemy," the paper made clear that nationalism was viewed as one of many obstacles to development of the movement. This is not to say that national affiliations were necessarily stronger than social ones in Plovdiv or other tobacco towns, but rather, to point out how national and social affiliations competed in a field that was complicated by new social divisions wrought by tobacco production. In many contexts—especially in the countryside and smaller entrepôts of Macedonia—divisions of labor in the web of tobacco production and commerce seemed to heighten religious–ethnic tensions. But in the larger cities, such as Plovdiv, Salonika, and Kavala, social divisions associated with tobacco production tended to soften such divisions.

Still, the dynamic between ethnic and social demands was exceedingly delicate, especially within Ottoman Macedonian cities. In these cities not only was the tobacco proletariat much larger—some twenty thousand tobacco workers in Macedonia alone—but loyalty to Ottoman pluralism competed with a myriad of other identities: religious, ethnic, regional, and political. After the Young Turk revolution of 1908, trade unions and strikes were legalized, and by 1909 the Socialist Federation had been organized as an umbrella for a large number of trade unions, many of which were ethnically delimited. Its model of organization mirrored the ethnic federative approach of Austro-socialism, and its leadership was avowedly multiethnic. The key organizers were Abraham Benaroya (a Sephardic Jew from Bulgaria) and Dimitŭr Vlakhov (a Bulgarian), while other important figures included Mehmed Nazimi (a Turk) and Istiryo Nikopoulo (a Greek). The federation, at least temporarily, published a journal in four languages (Ladino, Bulgarian, Ottoman-Turkish, and Greek) and mobilized multi-ethnic crowds into strikes of tens of thousands of workers. In the federation's first organized strike in Salonika in 1909, approximately 10,000 tobacco workers participated, compared with only 2,000–3,000 workers from all other trades combined.[119] Of the 3,200 members of the tobacco workers' union in Salonika, 200 were Jews, 500 Greeks, 400 Turks, and 200 Bulgarians.[120] But the federation leadership and organization, particularly in Salonika, was also increasingly Jewish in organization and orientation. An exodus of Bulgarian socialists opposed to the federative organization had resulted in a weakened Bulgarian representation in this period. No doubt tensions over the Young Turk treatment of IMRO were also a factor, as the defecting Bulgarian socialists accused the federation of being a tool of the Young Turk regime.[121] The federation did initially cooperate with the Young Turks, and Dimitŭr Vlakhov became a member of the Ottoman parliament. But Young Turk relations with organized labor broke down as early as the end of 1909, and open confrontation ensued after the regime enacted antilabor legislation, strike limitations, and the ultimate banning of the tobacco syndicate in 1910. Tensions with Young Turks brought Bulgarian radicals back into the organization, and the federation staged unprecedented demonstrations in Salonika in 1911, during which Vlahov gave a speech to twenty thousand workers on the Place de la Liberté square. Ultimately ethnic divisions haunted Balkan tobacco labor, but they were not enough to tear its organization asunder.

Tobacco factory owners, by comparison, seemed to work together in enviable unity.[122] By 1909, eighty of Bulgaria's tobacco interests merged under the direction of Vakaro (the Habsburg Italian tobacco factory owner) to form the Kartel, a tobacco trust that encompassed fifty-two factories.[123]

As the Kartel had a large capital base, it was able to purchase more machines, which led to the layoffs of at least two thousand workers.[124] In response, socialist newspapers vilified all tobacco factory owners, regardless of ethnicity, as shameless exploiters who made women and children work for less than a lev a day for twelve hours of work. Stavrides was described as the "worst offender," accused in one instance of hiding sickly, tubercular children workers in a locked room when a doctor inspector visited the factory. Since 1900 workers had organized boycotts and other actions against Stavrides's business interests, such as a 1905 appeal sent out to workers of Bulgaria urging, "Don't smoke Stavrides Cigarettes or Tobacco!"[125] Vakaro was similarly described as a "bloodsucker" and a "murderer," his factory as a "tomb."[126] Interestingly, however, Tomasian (an Armenian) was accused only of hiring a "strict" manager who would "not let the workers have even one cigarette."[127] Whatever its scale, labor oppression was generally not described or understood in national terms. For example, the factory Zheleznitsa (Railroad), owned by Stamatov (a Bulgarian), was also described with fierce criticism: "The floor was covered with water and girls from ten to eighteen sat on the floor quickly moving their hands [working]; they had incredibly poor and inadequate clothing—but the worst was the smell of tobacco—it suffocated and irreparably damaged the human chest. The misery left its stamp on the faces, which were a pale blue, emaciated and suffering."[128] Likewise, Libenov and other Bulgarian factory owners were attacked for the horrible conditions in their factories, where women and children bore the brunt of the suffering. As an article in the periodical *Rabotnicheska borba* (*Worker's Struggle*) asserted, factory owners' solidarity had led them to "divide and conquer" by plying men against women, and young against old to break the spontaneous strikes in the city.[129] Though filled with hyperbole, socialist criticism was an on-the-ground response to the gradual feminization of the workforce.

Undoubtedly, the tobacco workers' movement gained significant momentum from 1903 to 1908 because of the replacement of adult male workers by women and children.[130] Because many phases of tobacco processing and cigarette rolling were considered light work, women and children made up an ever-larger percentage of the workforce in these years of industry expansion. According to *Tiutiunopabotnik zashtitnik,* in 1900 only 10 percent of tobacco workers were women, which by 1908 had grown to an average of 70 percent. The paper's detailed "factory inspections" gave exact figures on gender and age configurations of labor, as in the Madras factory, where of 184 workers in 1908, 34 were men and 150 were women.[131] For the country as a whole, in 1910 only 21.6 percent of tobacco workers were men, and 56.4 percent of all workers were under eighteen.[132] More damning, these women and children were paid a fraction of what men had formerly made in the same jobs.[133] Now greater profits came to the industry, but tobacco worker families were devastated as many of the men were compelled to migrate, primarily to Germany or the United States, or were unemployed and shiftless on the streets of Plovdiv. Workers' associations—in which women were newly active participants[134]—brought this critical situation to the attention of the authorities in Sofia in 1906, and a law for "women and children's labor" was passed limiting the workday to ten hours for women and eight hours for children. According to the pages of *Tiutiunopabotnik zashtitnik* and other socialist papers, however, these laws as well as regulations on working conditions were summarily ignored by factory owners, who were subject to only periodic small fines.[135] As a result, strikes and open confrontations between workers and the tobacco industry became regular occurrences in Bulgaria as well as the Ottoman Empire in the years leading up to the Balkan Wars.[136]

In spite of any gains made by the economy, rising social tensions plagued the Bulgarian regime in these years. Indeed, the regime may have launched the first Balkan War as a way of diverting explosive social issues into a war of nationalist unity—a rationale, it has been argued, that is linked to the origins of World War I. By all accounts nationalist fervor did erupt during this brief and bloody war of 1912–13. But what is more significant is the extent to which Bulgarian nationalist purpose was also summarily and abruptly redirected in light of the shifting enemies and alliances in the Second Balkan War (1913) and World War I (1914–18). These wars by no means can be read as indicative of deep-seated ethnic tensions in the region. On the contrary, the shifting designation of enemies and allies makes it clear that in Macedonia, as in the surrounding Ottoman successor states, ethnic and social categories were still exceedingly malleable, with the potential to reinforce or undermine each other. The machinations of the tobacco economy, I argue, worked against a clear crystallization of ethnic horizons or hatreds. Social mobility and social interests—though far from representative of coherent social classes—kept national identities at least partially in check, allowing for their pliability in the years to come.

Tobacco and War

World War I has been clearly recognized as a watershed in European, U.S., and indeed world history because of the dramatic political, social, and geopolitical transformations that accompanied and followed it. In the history of global tobacco, the war was also a critical turning point. Both during and after the war, tobacco production and consumption grew by an unprecedented measure.[137] Bulgaria fit into this global process in a specific and, by some measures, more direct and intimate way, given the role of tobacco production in the region. As in other Balkan states, the meteoric rise in production and consumption associated with World War I, had begun several years earlier with the eruption of the first Balkan War in October of 1912. During three consecutive but very different wars—the First and Second Balkan Wars and World War I. the Bulgarian tobacco industry decidedly expanded. Territorial expansion and wartime mobilization had far-reaching and permanent impacts on tobacco production and commerce. At the same time, under the extreme conditions of war, the depth and complexity of overlapping or competing social and ethnic tensions came to the fore around and outside the world of Balkan tobacco.

The First Balkan War was waged by the Balkan League (Bulgaria, Serbia, Greece, and Montenegro) against the Ottoman Empire between October 1912 and May 1913 over its remaining European territories. As the league invaded the Ottoman Empire—against the express wishes of the Great Powers—they waged a so-called crusade of the cross against the crescent. This state-formulated crusade built upon existing notions of the "Turkish Yoke" and summarily ignored the reality of Bulgarian-Greek-Serbian tensions on the ground in Macedonia. Although only six months long, the First Balkan War had a dramatic effect on Bulgaria as one-seventh of the total population—six hundred thousand men—were mobilized, and 21 percent of these were killed in battle.[138] To justify such carnage, Bulgarian (as well as Greek and Serbian) elites and armies created a narrative of liberation of their own conationals to accompany their advance into Ottoman territories. Bulgarian Orthodox priests accompanied the advancing troops, forcibly converting to Christianity some 250,000 Bulgarian-speaking Muslims (Pomaks), who were given Bulgarian names, Bibles and "Christian" clothing.[139] In contrast, Turkish-speaking Muslim populations—military and civilian—were targeted for massacre by Bulgarian and other advancing Christian armies. European and U.S. observers were shocked by the barbarism of the carnage, rape, and mutilation that characterized military and civilian Christian and Muslim interaction across the region. The scale of civilian violence in the First Balkan War was commonly viewed as indicative of accumulated Christian hatred of Muslims from five centuries of Ottoman rule.[140] But the Second Balkan War, which broke out on June 1, 1913, seemed to belie such a formulation. For two months the Christian allies turned on one another, waging equally bloody warfare over the spoils of the First Balkan War, specifically the division of Macedonia. Not only were Bulgarians fighting against Greeks and Serbs, who were not allied with the Ottomans, but all sides enlisted ready and willing local Muslims to massacre the opposing Christian forces and civilians. As Muslim irregulars and new recruits joined Bulgarians in sacking predominantly Greek towns, the narrative of an all-Balkan holy war was suddenly moot.

The scale of violence was massive as villages were burned, women were raped, and bodies were mutilated across the region in indescribable brutality. These events were later characterized by George Kennan as "savage and violent" and remarkably similar to the events in Bosnia in 1992–95.[141] But the widely held notion reflected in Kennan's analysis of a kind of timeless Balkan violence rooted in ancient enmities has not held up to academic scrutiny.[142] Indeed, if anything, the Balkan Wars clarify the fact that social and cultural tensions in the region could be directed in various ways. From the perspective of the "Bulgarian" peasant recruit, grievances could be against "Turkish" or Muslim landlords or against "Greek" merchants and urban dwellers. Ethnic terms appear in quotes here because of the extreme malleability of the terms and affiliations in this period. By many accounts most Slavic Christian peasants had traditionally referred to themselves as "Christian" and had referred to all Slavs in towns as "Greeks," while Greeks called all peasants "Bulgars," and Turk" generally meant Ottoman official or landlord.[143] Such designations, though, were clearly complicated by the changing social landscape of Macedonia in which there were increasingly more Bulgarian merchants and urban dwellers.

It was both the continued power of traditional social divisions and their contemporary upset that spurred such multivalent violence during the Balkan Wars. The situation in which non-Muslims had ever more socioeconomic but no institutionalized political power has been widely noted as a source of late-Ottoman tensions. Equally important for late-Ottoman Macedonia, though, was the conflict between traditional Greek urban and commercial power and newly mobilized urban (and militant rural) self-identified Bulgarians who sought control over Macedonian resources and territory. IMRO local bands and even the unaffiliated masses defined their social and political enemies not only as Ottoman administrators and the West but also as Greeks and Bulgarian "Grekomen"—Slavs who claimed to be Greek. Here "Greekness" was based on the social or political decision to speak Greek and patronize Greek schools and churches. Greeks, broadly defined, were also known to cooperate with Ottoman officials in denouncing and ferreting out IMRO members.[144] In addition, in the decades leading up to the Balkan Wars, the influx of Muslim refugees from Bosnia, Serbia, Bulgaria, and other lost territories only served to heighten tensions within Thrace and Macedonia.

During both Balkan Wars, in the midst of seemingly wild and wanton violence, social scores were settled or opportunities for material gain were seized. During the First Balkan War, rich Muslim landlords were driven off their land, which was taken over by eager Christian populations. In addition, urban Muslims from across the region were targets of Christian violence that had a clear economic motivation. As one British observer of the aftermath of the Bulgarian occupation of Ksanti noted, "[T]here was no general massacre by Bulgarians at Ksanti, but a very large number of isolated acts of violence and murder for the purpose of robbery."[145] Similarly, in the Second Balkan War, in Bulgarian-occupied territories, massacres of Greeks by Bulgarian and Turkish mobs also took the general form of an economic rather than an ethnic pogrom, in which tobacco merchants were prime targets. According to the testimony of an observer in Doxato, "a man with distorted features, dashed towards us like a madman and asked for piece of bread...he was a millionaire tobacco merchant, whose family had been massacred and his properties destroyed. We took him with us in our carriage to Drama."[146] Some of the most egregious examples of economic pogroms took place in the visibly prosperous tobacco entrepôts of Serres and Doxato.[147]

But local tobacco merchants were not the only explicit targets in the reckless destruction. In Serres, for example, Bulgarian forces burned down virtually all the warehouses of Herzog and Co. and American Tobacco, whose representatives fled to Salonika.[148] Without question, a fair amount of destruction was wrought on all sides to the tobacco industry during the war. As the British vice consul, H. E. W. Young, complained, "[B]usiness was at a standstill and thousands of peasants who might have been manipulating tobacco for the American and other companies, were kept in idleness while the stock was in imminent danger of perishing."[149] As Bulgaria and other Balkan Christian states advanced into Ottoman Thrace and Macedonia, they were now in possession of tobacco-rich territories, and it was to their benefit to unseat foreign control of this resource.

The Balkan Wars were ultimately a boon to the Bulgarian tobacco industry. In part this was because Bulgaria temporarily held the coveted port of Kavala and wide swaths of rich tobacco territories in Aegean Macedonia and Thrace. Although soldiers had smoked in past wars, the Balkan Wars were the first Bulgarian wars in which there was a widespread belief in the need to provision the soldiers with tobacco as critical to the war effort. Even in the socialist press Nikola Gospodinov exclaimed, "The Army of thousands on the battlefield need to stave off hunger and inexpressible suffering with tobacco smoke." Tobacco factories were kept running during the war, with an even greater dependence on female and child labor. But the industry was deemed so important that it also requisitioned forced labor or labor from the military itself. According to British documents from the period, the "bulk of able bodied Pomak males were deported to Plovdiv and other places in Bulgaria" for forced labor, primarily in tobacco warehouses. As a British consul who visited the Vakaro tobacco factory in Plovdiv confirmed, some 983 Pomak "prisoners of war" were working there.[150] But such use of Pomak labor was temporary. By the Second Balkan War Pomaks were mobilized as loyal allies of the regime against Bulgaria's Christian neighbors. When Bulgaria was defeated in this war, it lost the best tobacco districts and the tobacco port of Kavala.

But Bulgaria's ultimate territorial adjustments as a result of the Balkan Wars still boosted the tobacco-based economy. The loss of grain-rich southern Dobrudja to Romania and the gain of the tobacco-rich regions of Pirin Macedonia and the Rhodope mountains further shifted the country's commercial focus from grains to a tobacco export-based economy. Yet in spite of ultimate territorial gain, the Bulgarian narrative of *loss* as a result of the Second Balkan War was pinned to the greater dream of annexation of all of Macedonia and Thrace. More pointedly, the loss of the briefly held port of Kavala loomed large in the atmosphere of defeat. Bulgaria's lust for Kavala was widely known during the negotiation of the Treaty of Bucharest in August of 1913. As Leon Trotsky, a reporter and witness to the peace process, noted,

> In the forefront of their [the Bulgarians'] minds all the time was Kavalla, the most important port on the Aegean after Salonika, the center of the export of tobacco: ten million rubles worth of tobacco passes through Kavalla every year. In the face of tobacco plantations and tobacco exports, questions of the culture and conscience of the 200,000 Bulgars in Southern Romania seemed very unimportant. Nevertheless Bulgaria did not get Kavalla and all that is left to her is the chimerical hopes of aid from Austria-Hungary when the treaty goes to the Great Powers for ratification.[151]

The concession of the lesser port of Degedatach did little to assuage the feeling of national catastrophe that made Bulgaria's entrance into World War I almost inevitable.[152] Bulgaria was an attractive ally to the Central Powers, not just because of its revanchism but also because of its newly acquired tobacco-producing potential. After it secured promises of gaining Thrace and (the rest of) Macedonia, its alliance with Austro-Hungary and Germany was sealed by 1914. Bulgaria's entrance into war on the side of the Central Powers, in fact, was predicated on a large Austro-German loan with Bulgarian tobacco as collateral.

Clearly the alliance was mutually beneficial at the time—for Bulgaria it promised the desired territorial expansion and a new expanded market, and for Austria and Germany it fulfilled a desire to dominate the Danube and "expand trade with the Orient."[153] For Bulgaria, World War I also meant the rapid expansion of its tobacco output, from 3 to roughly 15 million kilograms a year in the course of the war years.[154] During World War I Bulgaria held much of Macedonia (including Kavala) and Thrace for three consecutive years. After the initial conquest, there was little actual warfare conducted in the region, and Bulgarian authorities were able to concentrate on economic development. On the ground much was done to improve agricultural production in Macedonia, a region that one Bulgarian report to Berlin described as "the most fertile in Europe...an immeasurable treasure trove, in which there is tobacco, opium, cotton, and sesame." Well aware of Macedonia's potential, Germany sent advisers to counsel Bulgarian occupational forces in agrarian technologies.[155] Bulgarian authorities, though accepting of such help, also asked Germans to keep a low profile in order to allay local fears that Germany was the dominant political force or economic beneficiary in the region. Issues of authority aside, expanded Bulgaria now became the major supplier of tobacco (along with other agricultural goods) to Germany and Austria-Hungary, their troops and home fronts alike. As a direct result there was an explosion of tobacco cultivation and processing, though cigarette production still remained mostly for domestic consumption.

As Bulgaria advanced into Thrace and Macedonia, it proved its loyalty to Germany by expelling American Tobacco, which still had a virtual monopoly over leaf buying and processing. American Tobacco had weathered the havoc of the Balkan Wars, though large revenues and in many cases employees were lost in the destruction of people and property.[156] But as World War I broke out American Tobacco was virtually expelled from the region.[157] Now Bulgaria was in control of procuring premium leaf for the German cigarette industry.[158] Politics prevailed over a diversified market, and the Allies were virtually cut off from Oriental tobacco supplies during the war. Supplying tobacco to Germany and Austria more than sufficed to stimulate the rapid expansion of production as tobacco prices soared and production went up by 100–200 percent, even though most men of working age had been mobilized.[159] According to one wartime report, the huge demand for tobacco during the war "opened the eyes of the population" to the possibilities of tobacco as a commodity while also creating new and viable transportation arteries.[160] The primary improvement was access to Kavala, which served the Kavala-Trieste sea-trade route to the back door of Central Europe. Of course Danubian trade also improved, but Kavala had the advantage of a well-established processing infrastructure and proximity to the best tobacco fields in the region. In 1916, for example, Germany exported some 5–6 million kilograms of tobacco (and 120 kilograms of opium) via the port of Kavala alone.[161] By 1917, Bulgaria was exporting a total of 13 million kilograms of tobacco to Germany and Austria and only a few hundred thousand to other countries in the alliance.[162] As the war raged on, however, the Allied presence in the Aegean created extreme difficulties for transport routes, and supply tensions began to rock the alliance.

The advantages of the Bulgarian-Austro-German relationship faded as tensions over tight supplies and severe social unrest distressed the tobacco industry. There was a growing perception that the bulk of Bulgarian goods, including tobacco, were being shipped off to Germany and Austria, especially as the Central Powers' position in the war became more tenuous and the scarcity of goods across the region increased.[163] Tensions within the Central Powers' camp had begun to increase as early as 1916, when German consular officials began to complain that Bulgaria was raising tobacco tariffs and holding back supplies.[164] Bulgarian officials countered that difficulties in transport as well as "opposition to exports among the population" were behind the declining deliveries of leaf.[165] In response to such opposition, the Bulgarian government began to sequester 25 percent of all tobacco produced for Bulgarian troops and civilian domestic consumption. This shift in policy raised concerns among its German trade partners, who claimed that "our interests will be most directly harmed by this," given the need to "supply the troops with cigarettes."[166] Bulgarian opposition to tobacco exports was inspired less by Bulgarian nationalism vis-à-vis Germany than by the social unrest that increased in intensity as the war progressed. For the wartime tobacco boom did not translate into better conditions for tobacco workers, who were expected to perform for lower rations and pay. In the war years, some forty thousand workers were employed in processing warehouses and factories, 75 percent of whom were women and children.[167] Organized labor within old Bulgaria was enlivened by the migration of about one thousand workers from Drama, Serres, Kavala, and Ksanti to Plovdiv, as well as by intensified contacts with workers in the new territories who had strong organization and strike traditions.[168]

Though the industry was drawing a huge profit from wartime sales, workers continued to operate under extreme conditions, and the scarcity of food became a critical problem. In Bulgaria food shortages were greatly exacerbated by the major shift from grain to tobacco cultivation that had taken place during the war to supply the Central Powers. Given mass inflation and shortages, thousands of deaths by starvation were reported in Bulgarian cities, and children begging for food at taverns and other establishments became a regular feature of late-war city life.[169] As the war dragged on, and in the shadow of the Russian Revolution, spontaneous social unrest was also building in Bulgarian cities. Tobacco workers were incited to violence in cities like Plovdiv, where hunger and desperation drove hundreds (some argue thousands) of women from the tobacco factories to march the city streets in the spring of 1917.[170] This was part of a general "women's revolt" that shook much of the country and was echoed in similar revolts across Europe.[171] By December, around ten thousand workers, many tobacco workers among them, swarmed the streets calling for peace and revolution. The upheavals rapidly snowballed into antiwar protests across the country and on the front and led to mass desertions.[172] As the Entente marched into Macedonia, the Bulgarian military's collapse was the final undoing of the old regime. World War I ended amid social upheaval and another national catastrophe—the loss again of occupied Thrace and Macedonia.

The Balkan Wars and World War I brought Bulgaria headlong into the wider web of the modern global economy and all the changes that entailed. Isolationism and protectionism became increasingly untenable as Bulgaria groped for national footing beyond its borders and entered into an active alliance with the Central European powers. But as much as foreign demand played a role in the expansion of its tobacco economy, Bulgaria was also an organic part of global shifts in production and leisure consumption that were by no means simply imported from the West. Many of the changes that laid the groundwork for the commodification of Bulgarian tobacco were intimately local, tied to Ottoman trade routes, consumption models, and patterns of urban provisioning. Until the Balkan Wars, increases in production were primarily for local consumption, which relied upon an urbanizing and more educated population and more cash-based and luxury-seeking rural economies.

Tobacco became an agent, ushering in new economic conditions and increased contact with the outside world. On the one hand, tobacco was a kind of economic savior for a region in severe economic trouble and with little hope for other kinds of domestic and export revenue. But the rise of tobacco production, in spite of its successes, was also a destabilizing factor. The commodification of tobacco seemed to invite violence, upheaval, and a complex, respun web of social and ethnic struggles for resources. In a period when ethnic identities were crystallizing, new social divisions alternately reinforced and undermined ethnic categories, underpinning a range of violent encounters. Macedonia became the central object of local, regional, and international ambitions and its fragrant tobacco fields became one of the grounds for conflict. Tobacco was behind the forging of new networks of foreign dependency, accompanied by intensified social and ethnic domestic interdependencies, all carrying the potential for clash or coalition. In the decades that followed World War I, though, tobacco would bring even greater changes to Bulgarian (and global) society, for the cigarette century was just beginning to dawn.

CHAPTER 3

From the Orient Express to the Sofia Café
Smoke and Propriety in the Interwar Years

In the early years of the twentieth century a young Bulgarian woman traveling alone on the Orient Express nearly set the train on fire. Raina Kostentseva later related this tale proudly in her memoirs, recording neither her age nor the exact year of the incident. At a prolonged stop, Kostentseva stepped out of her compartment and onto the platform for a breath of fresh air. As passengers milled about, two foreigners engaged her in conversation and offered her a cigarette. Ready and willing to smoke, Kostentseva suggested that they adjourn to her compartment, where she had special Bulgarian cigarettes and, more exotically, a special lighting kit involving flint, steel, and tinder that would have been "completely unknown to them." As Kostentseva related, she lit a fire in front of the curious foreigners, and they lit up her Bulgarian cigarettes while she smoked one of theirs. After smoking and engaging in lively conversation, they parted with warm good-byes. Kostentseva extinguished the fire and put the paraphernalia back in her bag. She lay down to sleep but soon smelled smoke, the odor rapidly growing in intensity. Her quick wits about her, Kostentseva jumped out of bed and noticed that her bag was on fire. She tossed it out the window, saving the train and herself from catastrophe.[1]

As the burning bag fell next to the tracks, Kostentseva's train continued to head north and west, not to but rather away from the Orient. Bulgaria, in fact, was a stop on the Orient Express, one that was already *in* the Orient, from the perspective of many travelers. Even Kostentseva herself, with her Bulgarian cigarettes and lighting kit—perhaps meant as presents for someone at her European destination—served up a bit of the exotic to the foreigners, who were presumably on their way home. Yet in her behavior, traveling alone and smoking with foreigners, Kostentseva was breaking out of many of the behavioral conventions for a Bulgarian woman of the period. While such conventions were in gradual flux at the turn of the century, and more rapidly after World War I, Kostentseva, a woman from a rather "modern" family in Sofia, was surely ahead of her time. And she was also headed westward, both literally and figuratively. Smoking, even by women, was not Western in and of itself; it was the public (or semipublic) display, the image of a woman with a cigarette in her mouth that broke new social ground. In fact, the incident on the Orient Express was one of the few moments of relative social abandon in Kostentseva's memoirs, which detail her life in Sofia from the turn of the century through the interwar years. For even in Sofia, a rapidly growing and rather cosmopolitan city by this time, the social world of this relatively modern girl was deeply embedded in a matrix of intertwined social conventions, in which gendered patterns of sociability and consumption were tightly circumscribed.[2]

Still, these social conventions were unstable in this period, especially after the momentous changes that accompanied and followed World War I. During the war itself, women, along with the peasantry and workers, were mobilized on the front and home front in unprecedented ways. Their newfound roles in the military or in wartime production brought new kinds of social and political mobilization as the war came to a close, and their increased assertiveness in the public sphere was a harbinger of a new era. New leisure venues and an increased consumption of tobacco (along with alcohol) by both women and men penetrated Bulgarian social life.[3] Indeed, in post–World War I Bulgaria, the most dramatic change in the culture of smoking, particularly in its public incarnations, was the partial inclusion of women in a rapidly changing world of public leisure consumption. This pattern was also a general European, if not global, one, but there was something very specific about the Bulgarian experience. Women's emergence into a world of public smoking and sociability took place in the shadow of the Europeanization of leisure establishments, a kind of boarding of the Orient Express on its return to Europe. The new culture was most evident in Bulgarian cities, where it was inspired by the influx of people, ideas, media, goods, and new modes of thinking. Sofia itself was at the epicenter of an explosion of leisure consumption, cultural production, and political ferment, in which smoking took a visible and unshakable role.

To be sure, the interwar period was a like a second coming of age for Bulgarian men, and a first for Bulgarian women, in which the smoke-filled kafene functioned as a site of intensified productive cultural and political interchange. As many have noted, the interwar period produced an active cultural ferment, with more outstanding original works of Bulgarian literature, drama, and art than in any other period in Bulgarian history. This cultural upheaval fomented in the smoky halls of Sofia kafenes, where men and a handful of modern women exchanged ideas over coffee and a smoke. As never before, tobacco smoke permeated the social and cultural centers of Bulgarian life, lubricating, if not propelling, a quickening of Bulgarian letters—which for the first time included serious and highly respected writings of women. As in the past, intellectuals continued to play critical roles as producers of a uniquely Bulgarian high culture but also as "mediators of European and world culture."[4] In this process the smoke-filled kafene was imbued with significance and, at least for some establishments, acted as a liminal space in which Bulgarianness and Europeanness, along with men and women, commingled as in no prior period.

As smoking increased, so too did more articulate and organized forces of abstinence, which attacked smoking—along with drinking, gambling, and sexual depravity—as a ruinous Western vice. In Bulgaria these voices of restraint were not entirely new, but they grew louder after the First World War, especially as women smokers became more visible. For the leaders and organizers of these movements, increased drinking and smoking represented a portent of the downward slide of Bulgarian society and the exploitive and destructive aspects of the new age. As an article in the abstinence newspaper *Trezvenost* (*Abstinence*) lamented: "Thanks to the ruinous influence of the recently concluded war, we see today a large part of society, regardless of social standing, sex, etc. giving themselves over with a rapacious ferocity to various things that are destructive to individual and social life; alcoholism, nicotinism, gambling, and promiscuity. These vices are suffocating all that is 'human' which is left in people...leading society to a very sad end."[5] Bulgarian Protestants under American missionary influence continued to be strong voices of abstinence in this period. But an even stronger, more organized abstinence movement also rapidly expanded after World War I under Bulgarian communist leadership. Though ideologically opposed, both movements shared certain moralistic assessments of the new life of pleasure in interwar Bulgaria and tried to mobilize the population around the notion of a higher good or a brighter future. The communists' commitment to abstinence, however, was always tempered by the love of drink and smoking among party members. While some communists devoted their lives to abstinence efforts and avowedly ascetic lifestyles, others sought solace and intellectual inspiration in tobacco and the café environs, where the bulk of the Bulgarian Left came of age.

Inside and outside the abstinence movement, Bulgarians were shocked and alarmed by the profound changes in social mores coupled with the extreme politics of the post–World War I period. The fact that many of these changes were inspired by Western examples only heightened such anxieties. The seeming onslaught of Western cultural norms at the expense of authentic national ones was a perennial issue in Bulgarian national soul searching, but it reached a fever pitch in the interwar period. Not all the changes, including the avalanche of leisure consumption, were attributed to Western influence, however. On the contrary, the loss of World War I was like a dark cloud hanging over the Bulgarian psyche. Seen as the cause of moral devastation, inertia, and also new modes of pleasure seeking, the national disaster of the war inspired both individualistic pleasure seeking and collectivist movements of national renewal. At the same time, under the influence of self-congratulatory and self-critical Western voices, Bulgarians embraced as well as rejected presumably Western forms—including a new culture of leisure and pleasure seeking. And as never before, women joined the exploding number of pleasure seekers, soul-searchers, and revolutionaries, smokers and antismokers in the vibrant if unstable interwar Bulgarian milieu.

The New Sofia

World War I, for Bulgaria as elsewhere, had a cataclysmic effect on public life. Mobilization on the front and home front of a new range of social actors—namely peasants, workers, and women—heightened expectations for political and social change in the wake of war. Europe was shaken by the Russian Revolution and leftist revolts in Germany and Hungary as Bulgaria ended the war in a near revolutionary situation that swept the Bulgarian Agrarian National Union (BANU) into power. The Bulgarian Communist Party was also at its peak of popularity in the immediate postwar years, garnering the second-highest number of votes in the national assembly and taking power in several municipalities. Along with such political changes, Bulgarian social life changed rapidly with a number of new outside influences—namely, the occupying Allied troops and large numbers of Russian "Whites" (anticommunists) fleeing the revolution. An array of new clubs, cabarets, cafés, and other consumption venues expanded, and public smoking and drinking became more widespread among both men and women.[6]

Since becoming the capital in 1879, Sofia had always been at the heart of Bulgarian historical change, but it was also somehow a transplant—foreign and even rejected by the hinterland it ruled. An incredibly diverse Ottoman city in 1878, Sofia had rapidly Bulgarianized, even as it became host to numerous colonies of Russian and Central European migrants (Czechs, Austro-Germans, and Hungarians but also Serbs) seeking opportunities in the Bulgarian "El Dorado."[7] This, in addition to foreign legations and traders as well Bulgarians returning from study in Europe, gave Sofia an increasingly European cast. The pulse of the city had gradually accelerated since 1878, and by the turn of the century a lively café set, beer halls, and cabarets were regular features of city life. This set Sofia apart from most of the country, where change was more gradual and traditional Ottoman leisure institutions more unwavering. But even in Sofia, old institutions continued to coexist with new ones, and the bohemian café life and elite high life shared the city with old-fashioned krŭchmas on every corner and old-style kafenes with coffee *a la turca* (in the Turkish style).[8] As sober cafés—in the old or new style—persisted and expanded in Sofia, so too did the drunken krŭchmas, beer halls, and *mekhanas* (wine houses), where intoxication mixed with smoke and sociability. Abstinence advocates tracked this "unstoppable march of the krŭchma" with considerable alarm: As one article in *Trezvenost* noted, the war took 100,000 lives, injured 220,000, called for 20 million lev in reparations, and caused the number of taverns in Bulgaria to mushroom to twenty thousand.[9] Mirroring the rapid expansion of such establishments, abstinence movements also expanded, focused on both alcohol and tobacco as signs of moral degeneracy. Admittedly, rural alcoholism was a central concern of the abstinence movement, but the idle consumers of the city also drew its attention. Sofia was viewed as the consuming head of the Bulgarian national body, afflicted with foreign vice as was no other place in Bulgaria.[10]

Such rhetoric emerged in the shadow of the post-1878 and particularly post-World War I replacement or commingling of traditional Balkan establishments with foreign-owned or -styled establishments. Kostentseva, our intrepid traveler from the Orient Express, described this process of Europeanization with some irony: "Time flew, 'Western civilization' penetrated quickly into our life, seducing us."[11] For Kostentseva, this "civilization" seemed to have sprouted quickly out of a Sofia of snake-ridden open spaces and wolves howling at night, a city where an Oriental kafene was in every neighborhood and Turks sat all day smoking their narghiles on the city streets.[12] Over the decades, Sofia was remade into a virtual playground of leisure establishments, from brothels to billiard halls, casinos to cabarets with "half-naked" women.[13] Kostentseva viewed this flood of changes with some skepticism in spite of her relatively modern ways. As she offered with a touch of sarcasm, "*Sofiantsi* [residents of Sofia] quickly began to become modern."[14] But

Kostentseva hardly embraced a vague or idealized past. On the contrary, she abhorred the "superstitions" and "religious fanaticism" that had historically kept women in subordinate roles and the socially prescribed sense of "shame" that made them walk behind men on the street and dictated that they not cut their hair, smoke or go into a café or tavern unaccompanied by a man. Like her contemporaries, she blamed this backwardness on the practices from "Turkish times," a presumably infectious stagnation from the Muslim East.[15]

But just as Kostentseva and her generation rejected the Ottoman past, so too did writers across the political spectrum scrutinize the penetration of the West. Some contemporary observers—for example, Naiden Sheimanov—lamented the fact that "[s]trong currents of foreignness are flowing into all arenas of our life. Europe has gone East. The curse of becoming West Europeans hangs over us."[16] This "curse" and the general "transformation of Bulgaria" Sheimanov located firmly in Sofia, a city lit up by the "red lights of cabarets."[17] From the very beginning of the post-war period, numerous observers noted the "degradation of morals," the gold seekers, and the parasitic habits that characterized Sofia. Among others, this view was shared by the leader of BANU, Alexander Stamboliski, who refused to live in Sofia during his four years in office (1919–23). He and the Agrarian Party saw Sofia as the "Sodom and Gomorrah," of Bulgaria, the consuming leech on the productive peasant body of the nation. On the other end of the political spectrum, right-wing nationalist journals like *Rodliubets* also lashed out against "European morals" and "café dandies" that sullied the purity of the Bulgarian nation.[18] Various incarnations of the Right and Left deemed the unfettered penetration of the West the culprit in fueling Bulgaria's major social ills, and Europeanized Sofia was central to such perceptions.

Kostentseva, though, also described the brighter side of the changes. Far more family-friendly (meaning open to women) venues appeared in this period, including *biraria* (beer halls), social and professional clubs, dance halls, restaurants, and *kafene-sladkarnitsi* (café sweet shops). The latter were a more Europeanized—mostly Viennese—take on the traditional male kafene, relatively open to the female customer though admittedly still male-dominated.[19] Interwar Sofia allowed new social spaces for Bulgarian women, but generally a woman would still earn a reputation as "fallen" if she went to any of these places unaccompanied by a man. Only the brave few ventured into such establishments without their husbands or fathers or at least in mixed gender groups, such as newly formed literary circles. Even Kostentseva, well positioned in a prominent family and certainly modern with her self-described short hair and occasional cigarette, viewed Sofia high life and low life not from the confinement of her home but rather from the streets, on walks to the market, the public baths, or an evening promenade.

The *new* Sofia, then, was still largely a field of pleasure and sociability for Bulgarian men, who were its primary customers. Men were still generally arbiters of women's participation and by extension women's smoking in public spaces. Kostentseva spoke frankly about the Orthodox Christian notion of shame and sin that kept Bulgarian women from smoking or drinking in public or going alone to cafés or taverns.[20] Kostentseva continually described walking by cafés and taverns full of men; she looked on or in as they looked out. She mentioned wistfully at one point, a biraria that she never got to visit because "no one would accompany her."[21] Instead, as Kostentseva described, women tended to socialize primarily at home, at the public baths or at church, which was above all a women's space. As far as tobacco was concerned, Kostentseva noted that only the "Jewish" and "Gypsy" women of Sofia could be seen smoking outside on their stoops and that even this level of public consumption was considered shameful to Orthodox Christian women. Only women with a "certain past" could be seen smoking in public or appearing in traditionally male establishments.[22] Some of the first women to appear in public establishments in postliberation Bulgaria were prostitutes, singers, or dancers—most of them foreign or local women of questionable morals.[23] At the same time, newly educated and engaged women intellectuals also now appeared in the gleaming European-style cafés, clubs, and cabarets of Sofia. The city—its anonymity, chaos, and for many a loss of religious or ethnic-family strictures—meant a new freedom of movement, modes of sociability, and intoxicating escape.

Bulgarian observers often explained such changes as a reaction to the devastation and humiliation of war. Some social critics viewed smoking and drinking, especially among women, as part and parcel of a larger moral free fall caused by the effects of war and the rapid influx of Western material culture and vice.[24] But for Bulgaria as elsewhere, providing men with cigarettes at the front and new social roles for women on the home front were surely also responsible. After all, smoking and drinking in ever-greater amounts was a phenomenon in countries on both sides of the Great War.[25] In addition, as the Bulgarian journalist and keen observer of interwar Sofia Khristo Brŭzitsov posited, "[M]aybe those who were saved from the war just wanted to live…a second life!" With tens of thousands of unemployed after the war, Brŭzitsov noted that the cafés of Sofia were full of people, Bulgaria's "lost generation."[26] And Khristo, like other Bulgarian men with or without means, seemed to spend a good portion of his life in the café setting. If Kostentseva was on the outside looking in, Brŭzitsov was decidedly on the inside looking out.

In stark contrast to the memoirs of Kostentseva, Brŭzitsov's memoirs are a virtual tour of interwar Bulgarian café life: a who's who of the cultural scene almost exclusively set within smoky Sofia cafés and to a lesser extent taverns. His *Niakoga v Sofia* (*Once in Sofia*) is less a memoir of his own life than a chronicle of Sofia's kafene life, for which he is a self-appointed flaneur. Kostentseva's and Brŭzitsov's memoirs offer quite a contrast, given the kafene and krŭchma walls that separate their two worlds. While Kostentseva is also a flaneur of the Sofia streets, she rarely mentions the *inside* of any establishments and even then only family venues to which she is accompanied by males. Brŭzitsov, in contrast, seems to have spent almost every waking hour trolling the kafenes and (to a lesser extent) krŭchmas of Sofia. For him as for many of his peers and contemporaries, these spaces were the virtual center of intellectual, cultural, and professional life. This explains why the smoke-filled kafene is so central in Brŭzitsov's memoirs and those of other men.[27] Brŭzitsov, though, documents the kafene habits of his generation, including their smoking habits, with a thoroughness that tops that of his peers.

For Brŭzitsov the kafene scene, was a seductive and highly textured world of intellectual contemplation and political interchange where smoking among regulars with "saved" tables was integral. In the kafene Moskva, for example,

A kafene and biraria (beer hall) with all-male clientele. Courtesy of the Regional State Archive in Plovdiv, http://www.lostbulgaria.com.

he described how Ivan Andreichin (writer and literary critic) was "always with a pipe in his lips as if it were part of his face" near the *mangal*—the old-fashioned stove where pipes could be lit.[28] Andreichin was also famous for holding court at the well-known kafene Armensko (Armenian)—so called because of its Armenian proprietor, Chausja.[29] As described in another memoir of the period, "the cramped place was always stuffy and full of thick smoke, especially in winter when the cruel Sofia cold didn't allow for the opening of a door which served as the window."[30] In the summer, however, it opened its doors wide and, like other kafenes in the capital, moved its tables onto the sidewalk; its clientele was a bohemian mixture of "Argonauts" of the new world, "enthusiastic dreamers, feisty anarchists, and extreme individuals."[31] The Armensko, like other kafenes, had its own peculiar flavor. Sofia literati (and other intellectuals) chose their venues according to literary taste as well as political or social leanings. Konstantin Gulubov, for example, notes in his memoirs that upon meeting Pencho Slaveikov, the latter immediately judged him to be of a certain bohemian nature. Because of Gulubov's "long hair," Slaveikov assumed that he was a regular at the Armensko. Slaveikov openly berated the Armensko crowd as "literary maniacs" who gathered around the figure of Ivan Andreichin, whose "goal is to lead literature along a path which leads it to the cabaret and establishments for smoking hashish." As Slaveikov noted, the atmosphere of the Armensko was not conducive to literary production that was "better rooted in the wild folk song that comes down from the serene heights of the Balkan Mountains rather than stench-filled Parisian haunts."[32] Ironically, since before the war Slaveikov himself had been a known regular at the kafene Bŭlgariia, the meeting place of the famous *Misul* (Thought) circle that was the center of his intellectual orbit.[33]

Much of the new Bulgarian literature of the period, most of which described Bulgarian folk and village life, was written or at least conceived in the stench-filled halls of the Sofia kafene. It is interesting that neither these halls nor the Bulgarian urban experience inspired the works of the best minds of new Bulgarian letters. The only exception was the genre of memoir, which contained thick ethnographies of kafene and krŭchma conversations and ashtrays brimming with cigarettes. In such memoirs all of interwar Sofia could be mapped, the habits of every famous personage cataloged. Interwar Sofia comes alive in such chronicles, with their descriptions of the gritty holes in the wall like the "classic" kafene Makedoniia, which was the center of life for Macedonian revolutionaries, old and young. Veterans of the 1903 uprising in Ilinden or *komitadzhi* (rebels) of the still-active Macedonian revolutionary movement would gather at the Makedoniia, sometimes firing off rounds into the air. It was the Makedoniia that Kostentseva remembered walking by on her way to and from the public baths, the place of ritual hygiene and sociability for Sofia women. The men at the Makedoniia, as she remembered, would sip coffee a la turca and from their sidewalk perches watch the women walking home from the baths, still clutching their towels. Their voyeurism, as Kostentseva recalled, was somehow inappropriately intimate. But Kostentseva's only route home was past the Makedoniia and down one of Sofia's central streets, Vitosha, lined with kafenes that spilled their male customers onto the streets when the weather was mild.[34] Though on the outside looking in, Kostentseva still had ample knowledge of the Sofia establishments. Her view from the streets was enough for her to know who or what kinds of men went where, as they were visible through windows, at sidewalk tables, or entering doors.[35]

Still, Kostentseva's stolen glances could not compare with Brŭzitsov's penetrating knowledge of the ins and outs of the kafene and krŭchma scene. Much like Nikola Alvadzhiev's *Plovdivska khronika,*[36] Khristo Brŭzitsov's *Niakoga v Sofiia* takes us through virtually every neighborhood, described as inseparable from its most central or characteristic establishments. For example, there was the elegant street and central promenade destination for Sofia high life, the Lege (Legation) Street, where the kafene Kontinental was the center of "spiritual life." There the famous Bulgarian opera composer Georgi "Maestro" Atanasov routinely "built up in front of him 10 cups of coffee and lit his cigarettes one after another; two ashtrays were not enough." His colleague, the composer Petko Naumov, was reported to have told him, "You could carry the holy fire from Preslav to Sofia with your cigarette."[37] Brŭzitsov also takes the reader down the streets of Iuchbunar, the Jewish and proletarian quarter of Sofia. As he describes, "this city within a city" was the well-feathered nest of leftist intellectuals and revolutionaries like Georgi Dimitrov, the future first communist leader of Bulgaria, and the leftist poet Khristo Smirnenski. In Iuchbunar the streets were filled with people in the evening but not the "dandies of the 'Lege'"; rather, they were "workers with yellow faces from their labor in tobacco factories."[38] Reflecting Brŭzitsov's characteristic ability to see all sides of Sofia, including its gritty underbelly, the sallow faces of tobacco laborers were in stark contrast to the smoking dandies on the other side of town. Iuchbunar, though, did have its bohemian, even "snobbish," niche on Pozitano Street, where "artistic types" gathered in the mekhanas.[39] Far worse off were the quarters on the outskirts of Sofia where in the immediate postwar years Brŭzitsov caught a glimpse of the lives of some of the twenty-five thousand registered unemployed in Bulgaria. The men spent their empty days at the corner kafene: "[T]he kafene was full, but no one drank! And it was good they didn't drink, because they would not be able to pay."[40] The kafene (along with the krŭchma) was the only solace for these unemployed workers and offered an escape from their decrepit living conditions.

But although he visited this world, Brŭzitsov was by no means a citizen of it or an organic part of its squalid desperation. Instead he was a regular at numerous more upscale establishments across town, where he made his rounds, meeting, visiting, and exchanging news and opinions with the who's who of the various intellectual, artistic and political elite of the period. Among the most famous of his kafene companions was Elin Pelin, one of the biggest names in Bulgarian interwar literary life. A famous writer of prose, Pelin was known for his smoking but especially for using smoke as his muse, a necessary creative lubricant. In one interwar memoir he was reported to have "begged his wife" for cigarette money, as he was barely able to afford his daily smokes.[41] In another, Pelin is described as a contemplative fixture at the kafene Bŭlgariia: "In front of him on the marble table there was a heavy ashtray full of cigarette butts and ash. Pelinko [Elin Pelin] was not a *strasten* [passionate] smoker, but he would focus on the ashtray for inspiration." Not surprisingly, Pelin named one of his collections of short stories "The Ash of My Cigarettes."[42] Brŭzitsov spoke of Pelin as "keeping a priestly eternal fire" when he first met him at the house of Ivan Vazov, the father of Bulgarian literature. The house had become a museum sometime after Vazov's death in 1921, a year that marked the end of the older generation of Bulgarian literati, who had sought a direct grounding in European literary forms.[43] Pelin and his cohort were much more concerned with creating a specifically *Bulgarian* literature that drew deeply on Bulgarian dialects and rural life. And though it arose in the urban halls of the kafene, much of this new and rich work in Bulgarian literature sought inspiration in rural authenticity.

The other major literary figure who contributed to the creation of a canon in the genre of rural fiction was Iordan Iovkov, who was known—even more so than Pelin—for his addiction to tobacco and Sofia kafene life.[44] As noted in the memoirs of Petŭr Mirchev, Iovkov was "never at parties, or taverns, only at kafenes." But his favorite was undoubtedly the Tsar Osvoboditel.[45] The kafene was in effect Iovkov's office, where he sat "unapproachable" most of the time, writing with an unlit cigarette in front of him. Apparently he wrote most of his famous short stories amid the haze to which he amply contributed.[46] Iovkov was said to have been unable to "last more than 2–3 days" without going into a kafene. Spending mornings at the Tsar Osvoboditel, where he was known for bumming cigarettes,[47] in the afternoons he migrated to the Viensko or the Bŭlgariia—where Ivan Vazov had been a morning regular before his death.[48] According to Dimo Kazasov, a noted intellectual and keen observer of the period, the Bŭlgariia was the main seat of Sofia's political bourse. It was here that, among other things, the boundaries of greater Bulgaria had been drawn, only to be foiled by the Bulgarian defeat in 1918, which understandably sent shock waves over kafene regulars. The tsar's *slukhari* (listeners or spies) were always present, tracking public opinion within the kafene walls.[49] The phenomenon of café surveillance, which had been common to the region since Ottoman times, was particularly vigilant at the more politically oriented kafenes like the Bŭlgariia and the leftist Sredets. The Sredets was said to have a characteristic "cocktail of old tobacco smoke, floor oil, and burnt coffee," but also an "agent's corner" where state spies would watch over the activities and listen to the conversations of the radical regulars.[50] It was owned by left-leaning Macedonians, and many called it the Jacobin Club, noting that it was under constant state supervision.[51] In short, politics as well as literary production were born out of Sofia's kafene scene.

Still, it was literary figures who were most likely to publicly embrace smoking, to extol its virtues as intellectual muse. One such devotee was Georgi Tsanov (Gogo), a Bulgarian poet from Vidin, who broke the world's record for smoking at a Sofia kafene on May 24, 1930.[52] According to the newspaper *Sofiia,* the session began at the kafene Feniks under the direct observation of a control commission. At nine in the morning Gogo— Tsanov's pseudonym—opened his first packet of Tomasian cigarettes; "he took out a cigarette knocked it against the table and put it between his lips." After 15 hours and 47 minutes, Gogo had smoked 144 cigarettes, breaking the previous world record of 121 smoked in 24 hours. To give the event a Bulgarian spin, it was purposely timed to coincide with Cyril and Methodius Day, in honor of the two "Bulgarians" who had devised the Cyrillic alphabet.[53] Before popping the first cigarette in his mouth, Gogo reportedly pronounced, "We gave something to the world!" Here he was referring to both the Cyrillic alphabet and "quality Bulgarian cigarettes," the presumed enablers of the Sofia record. It was the excellence and "refinement of the Tomasian cigarette," Gogo claimed, that had allowed him to light up cigarette after cigarette, smoking without pause except to drink coffee and eat chocolate.[54] In the afternoon the "nicotine ace" relocated to Borisova Gradina, Sofia's largest park and the "lungs of the city," continuing to smoke as he strolled. Gogo, like many of his contemporaries, was said to have "built a bridge between tobacco and literature." As he himself claimed, "the bluish strands of smoke connected him to his muse." The classic writers all "inhaled heartily," Gogo argued, from Khristo Botev in his Wallachian taverns to Ivan Vazov, who never went without tobacco; "when he worked he always smoked. It [tobacco] inspired his creative imagination."[55] As for Gogo, he never became famous for his exploits, as the *Guinness Book of Records* did not begin its publication until 1955, and his poetry was never among Bulgaria's best known.[56]

Most of interwar Bulgaria's kafene regulars, writers or aspirants, politicized or indifferent, have also irretrievably fallen out of Bulgarian history. Even the voluminous memoirs drop names only of the more well known. But among that relatively small literary cohort, there is a dizzying web of names, clever pseudonyms, and literary circles woven through interwar Sofia establishments.[57] Undoubtedly the most important circle from the period was the Zlatorog (Golden Horn). It published a journal of the same name whose prominent editor was Vasil Vasiliev. Zlatorog met regularly in the aforementioned Tsar Osvoboditel, arguably the most famous and important kafene in Bulgarian history.[58] It was one of Sofia's most Europeanized, modern establishments and the most described of any kafene in memoirs of the period.[59] The Tsar Osvoboditel has been described as a liminal space, a "sojourn in parallel realities of Bŭlgarskoto and Evropeĭskoto [Bulgarianness and Europeanness]."[60] It was a place that reminded many Bulgarian elites of their youth in European universities and cities, a place that evoked dreams and desires of the European high life. Unlike other kafenes, it did not cater to a clientele that was differentiated along political or literary-aesthetic lines, but was rather a "tolerant port for every aesthetic and political ship."[61]

Its famous proprietor, Kosta Stoianov, was a Macedonian-Bulgarian who had made good in the United States and come to Bulgaria to open a first-rate European-style, kafene-sladkarnitsa. Kosta, as the urban legend went, did not require his poorer literary clientele to pay and would let them loiter all day in their "second home" for free.[62] Many intellectuals also served as social servants in some form, but the global economic crises of the 1930s meant a generalized poverty among most of the Bulgarian intelligentsia.[63] Brŭzitsov summed up the Tsar Osvoboditel in the following way:

> On boulevard Tsar Osvoboditel, there where it crosses with Rakovski [Street], the café of the artistic world flowered. From there radiated the warm heart of numerous Bulgarian poets, writers, artists, scholars, philosophers, actors, journalists, and their admirers, peering into the café just to see their beloved. The happiest was the waiter, Kosta, who had the honor of being on familiar terms with all the great spiritual greats of Bulgaria.[64]

It was his honor apparently to tolerate clients who stayed all day "without consumption." Kosta never made such clients feel shame. On the contrary, he gave them glasses of water. The well-worn trope of the poor starving artist who could scarcely afford his coffee or cigarettes is carved deep into the romance of interwar Bulgarian artistic life.[65]

Hence, regardless of resources, there was a broad spectrum of people associated with Bulgarian intellectual or spiritual endeavors at the Tsar Osvoboditel.[66] According to one contemporary, if the walls of this kafene were mirrors, they would "reflect completely all political and cultural events in the country."[67] And certainly its clientele amply reflected the changing political landscape of the period.[68] Mirrored walls would also have revealed a tangled web of producers of Bulgarian culture over the twenty-five interwar years, which one contemporary described as Bulgaria's "peak of native expression of self."[69] Yet as Brŭzitsov enumerates the names of the great minds of interwar Bulgaria at the Tsar Osvoboditel, the reader is struck by the absence of women. Was this a kafene inhabited exclusively by men?

The New Woman

In the period following World War I, smoking became an increasingly common social practice among Bulgarian women, an indicator of emancipation, glamour, and cosmopolitan urban culture. American films that featured and popularized glamorous smoking ingénues—for example, Greta Garbo and Marlene Dietrich—began to be widely shown in Bulgaria. Smoking women seduced the world and the Bulgarian cigarette industry openly marketed women's cigarettes, like the brand Zora. Zora, with an image of a glamorous smoking woman on the front, was packaged with collectible pictures of Hollywood stars or of Miss Bulgaria and other beauty pageant women.[70] These new cigarettes were produced in reaction to a growing demand. But though public smoking was on the rise among women, scores of observers believed smoking among women (and youth) to be a specter of rebellion, of communism, of prostitution, and a clear threat to traditional values. Nevertheless, as Sofia was the center of new social forms in Bulgaria and a rapidly growing center for bourgeois high-life the newly liberated woman began smoking in public as never before.

After the war, more women made their way into a few of the more respectable kafenes, and the Tsar Osvoboditel topped the list. This type of upscale place, a spacious, Europeanized kafene-sladkarnitsa was steeped in propriety, unlike the grittier male-dominated krǔchmas and kafenes that still dotted the city. Establishments like the Tsar Osvoboditel became an extension of the growing promenade culture of Sofia, in which women and men commingled on the streets without the intimacy and judgment of private venues. But these kafenes, and smoking in particular, were also vital to

ТЮТ. Ф-КА

ЗОРА

ПАП.II К.
Ц. *12* ЛВ.
ОБЕЗПРАШЕНИ

Д.Г.СПАСОВЪ
ПЛОВДИВЪ

A pack of Zora cigarettes from the interwar period. Author's own collection.

intellectual labor, in which Bulgarian women played an ever more vital and visible part. As is apparent in the memoirs of Khristo Brŭzitsov and others, a number of well-known Bulgarian women intellectuals and/or performance artists, generally associated with the political Left, frequented many of the newly opened Europeanized cafes and clubs of Sofia in the first decade of the century.[71] But Brŭzitsov fails to mention the most famous and culturally significant women kafene regulars of the period, the women of the Zlatorog circle. Fortunately, other writings from the period have left us with at least a partial account of their lives and social world.

By far the most important female members of this group were the poets Elizaveta Bagriana and Dora Gabe, who frequented the Tsar Osvoboditel along with other writers from the journal *Zlatorog*.[72] Dora Gabe made a place for herself in the history of Bulgarian letters, not only as a highly respected poet but as the founder of the local chapter of the prestigious PEN club (an international writers association founded in London) in 1927.[73] Bagriana is known as one of the best poets in interwar Bulgaria, male or female.[74] Although many claimed that Bagriana was, among other things a Tolstoyan—by implication a believer in abstinence and antismoking—she was quite at home at the Tsar Osvoboditel.[75] Gabe and Bagriana frequented the kafenes but not unattended. Rather, they were always in the company of their fellow *Zlatorozhi* (members of the Zlatorog circle), most of them men but also the well-known writer Fani Mutafova-Popova, who shared the window table with them almost every evening.[76] These women were immortalized in Alexandŭr Dobrinov's famous 1935 caricature painting of the Tsar Osvoboditel. Yet they were three of only four women who appeared in the entire painting out of a total of 106 figures; all the women were at the same table and two of them were smoking.[77] But of course, not all women at the Tsar Osvoboditel would have been considered regulars, let alone been worthy of a place in Dobrinov's painting. The ballerina Maria Dimova was an occasional guest, according to the memoirs of Konstantin Konstantinov.[78] And some high-life Sofia women also came in as admirers[79] or to be admired.[80] As Dimo Kazasov asserted, the Tsar Osvoboditel was the *only* café where women could go, and even then it was decidedly *muzhko* (male) in the morning; women made their appearance only in the afternoon and evening.[81] This was surely an exaggeration, as other sources mention the presence of women in other kafenes—for example, the Café Royale and the Sredets. Bagriana was also known to frequent the Armensko, where she hung out with other left-leaning intellectuals.[82] Still, women remained relatively rare within these specialized spaces of male sociability. On the other hand, given their closed nature, it is perhaps more surprising that women appeared at all.

Of course, not all socially engaged women (or men) were part of the café scene. As Kazasov notes, a mere hundred Sofia families had the free time and money for such leisure, the men spending their days in kafenes and birarias while women strolled the streets in their best clothes."[83] At the same time, many women participated in cultural networks outside the café setting; a women's press emerged and salons continued to function, many of them hosted by women.[84] For many, like Gabe, Bagriana, and Evgenia Mars, the patronage of men secured by kafene networking helped them establish a place in Bulgarian literary and social life. But it also gave them a unique degree of independence. By 1930 Bulgarian women had formed their own writers' union with thirty-six members, many of whom became household names in the period and well after.[85]

There was also an explosion of new venues where respectable ordinary women were present as regular consumers, though generally accompanied by spouses or male family members. Not just Kostentseva but even the most progressive Bulgarians tended to bow to such norms.[86] With men in tow, women were now frequenting the birarias on the Austro-Hungarian model, such as the Cherven Rak (Red Crab), in ever-greater numbers.[87] They also very occasionally went to the krŭchmas when popular entertainment beckoned. As Kostentseva describes, in the 1930s there was a very popular krŭchma on the edge of Sofia where a Gypsy woman, Keva, filled the place night after night, singing songs in Romani and Serbian.[88] According to Kostentseva and many of her contemporaries, "all of Sofia" went to see Keva, husbands with wives on their arms pulling up constantly in their *faitoni* (horse-drawn coaches).[89] Kostentseva also depicts the crowds of men and women that frequented new postwar cabarets, like the Nova Amerika (New America) cabaret, where one could also see "fallen women" amid the show artists and crowds.[90] Though appalled by Bulgarian "attitudes towards women," she was clearly also judgmental toward fallen woman; more pointedly, she feared being placed in the same category.

Even the most progressive or left-radical women of the period seem to have shared many of Kostentseva's assessments. Tsola Dragoicheva, one of the most involved communist women from the period, wrote of the increased presence of "half-naked" dancing women in cabarets or prostitutes in taverns. Dragoicheva, who lived and operated mostly underground after 1923, was in and out of prison because of her communist activities. It was there among Sofia's female criminal elements that she noticed all the "pretty women in prison," prostitutes who were the victims of "roundups" in krŭchmas. Although these prostitutes were nice to Dragoicheva, she also assumed that they were employed as spies against her and other communist women; she suspected them, among other reasons, because of their "vices."[91] It's hard to say how many of these women were actual prostitutes and how many were simply of loose morals by the standard of the day. But she was judgmental toward women who lived this kind of life. Dragoicheva, however, was by no means representative of all members of the Bulgarian Left, many of whom retained a visible place at the krŭchmas and kafenes of Sofia. Café culture, in fact, continued to be central to leftist intellectual labor and social networking.

At the same time, for much of the Communist Party this kind of public visibility would have been impossible, especially after the party was made illegal after the rightist political turn in 1923. For Dragoicheva and others, a life of daily smokes and conversation at the Tsar Osvoboditel would have been out of the question.[92] Dragoicheva was hidden and unregistered, with a variety of pseudonyms, squatting in apartments arranged by the party. In the early postwar years, Dragoicheva had frequented the rather modest party club in the so-called Red Iuchbunar (communist, Jewish quarter) of Sofia.[93] It was there, she noted, that she gained her political education among the most dynamic minds in the party. After 1923, however, the new right-leaning political leadership under the umbrella of Naroden Sgovor (People's Accord) took this space over, and party members had to meet on the street and in secret apartments in order to avoid arrest and even murder.[94] Hence, for most of the interwar years the Sofia kafene scene was far too dangerous. Dragoicheva was much more fulfilled in her capacity as underground organizer and devoted political orator, traveling about the country incognito with her pseudonyms and rotating secret apartments.

But she, like other leftists of the period, was also openly critical of Sofia's high life and the snobbery of the rich elite on their way to the Union Club, while "unseen plebeians with empty pockets" filled the city.[95] For Dragoicheva, as for many other communists (male and female), such decadent—even capitalist behavior—seemed to conflict with their deep commitment to social change and political revolution. Indeed, she spoke periodically at leftist abstinence congresses, such as the one in Vratsa in 1934.[96] She was also cognizant, however, of the need to tolerate smoking and drinking because it was so prevalent among many communist thinkers, supporters, and leadership.[97] With that in mind, she was not openly critical of leftist intellectuals or party elites, like Georgi Dimitrov, who met primarily in the cafés and restaurants of Sofia or abroad.[98]

At home, as in the kafene, Bulgarian communists had smoked since the early days of party organization. Vela Blagoeva (1858–1921), the wife of Dimitur Blagoev, was a well-known smoker and one of Bulgaria's first "modern girls."[99] Abstinence was not pushed on members, and communist workers who ended up in prison were even supplied cigarettes by communist women's clubs.[100] Drinking and smoking were by no means taboo among party operatives. Dragoicheva narrates her party past, describing comrades lighting up at meetings or in moments of work or intimacy, as when she and Traicho Kostov listened to Radio Moscow; "over clouds of tobacco smoke, the voice on the speaker vibrated."[101] In one case, she describes meeting in a secret apartment, where one corner was dirty with evidence of cigarette butts and hence "work done by men" from the party.[102] Even as the communist abstinence movement gained momentum, Georgi Dimitrov, the head of the party was still a well-known public smoker and a passionate one.[103] Though Dragoicheva claimed that Dimitrov hated restaurants and cafés, this was mostly because public places "had ears." Dimitrov, in fact, was arrested in a Berlin café in 1933, before he was put on trial by the Nazis for his purported role in the famous Reichstag fire.[104] Still, communist men's smoking practices hardly marked a departure from established traditions of Bulgarian male sociability. In contrast, smoking marked women as radicals, indicative of their embrace of a radical ideology of emancipation and release from convention. Hence it is no surprise that politically left-leaning women were among the few who braved the still male-dominated public spaces of the interwar period.

As women, communist or not, slowly began to enter into spaces of public leisure consumption, they became vulnerable to stinging social criticism. As mentioned, many saw such women as fallen and as shirking domestic responsibilities. Some viewed the change as an alarming transgression of traditional gender boundaries of public sociability. Among those ensconced in tradition or part of the newly burgeoning political Right, such attitudes were perhaps quite understandable. But even for those on the Left, the smoking woman was seen as a threat to their new world, as yet unborn.

A New World?

Interwar changes in Bulgarian leisure and sociability were in no way limited to Sofia. In the summer, Bulgarian high life also spilled over to Varna and other Black Sea and Danubian port cities where a similar, though less extensive, infrastructure of pleasure and sociability became well established.[105] There were also changes, though generally slower, in inland commercial cities, like Plovdiv, and in other provincial capitals. Local cafés and taverns, as in Sofia, became gathering places for new modes of leisure consumption as well as radicalized political organization. What had been a rather quiet kafene with coffee and smoke from the narghile became full of "beer, wine, and cigarettes" as well as dancing women. This penetration of new forms was alarming for many, not just the more traditional local Bulgarian and non-Bulgarian populations but also the local (and rapidly growing) Left.[106] Significantly, such changes entered the provinces in tandem with a cash-based economy, associated with the commodification of tobacco and other products. For some, this meant more liquid income, however paltry, that could be spent in the rural krŭchmas and kafenes. Though rural poverty and rural debt remained the rule rather than the exception, these changes heightened alarm, especially among socially and nationally concerned parties worried about rural moral degradation.

Through the initial postwar boom to the Great Depression of 1929–33 and during the roller coaster of crises in between, the mass expansion of new leisure venues meant the increase of drinking and smoking among the entire Bulgarian population. Smoking was the palliative of the age, increasingly spreading across gender, class, age, and geographic expanse.[107] And as in the cities, many blamed this new rural blight not only on the devastation of war but also on the commodification of rural products and the penetration of capitalist relations. To a large degree, of course, Bulgarian rural poverty and the wasting of time and money in the exploitative local tavern were also prewar practices. What was different in this period was an intensified concern for alcohol also smoking in the village by a Bulgarian communist—as well as the still functioning American Protestant—grassroots abstinence movement.

The explosion of abstinence organizations in interwar Bulgaria built upon Protestant and (admittedly shallower) socialist roots in the prewar period. By 1927 there were some eighty thousand members in various abstinence groups across Bulgaria.[108] Since the mid-nineteenth century, abstinence (or temperance) movements in Bulgaria had developed primarily under the influence of American Protestant missionaries.[109] By the early twentieth century the scope of the Protestant message had gradually broadened from anti-alcohol to a war against tobacco, gambling, and other vices. In the same period, Bulgarian socialist activists, under the influence of select European socialists, were also increasingly focused on Western vices. One important inspiration for the prewar and postwar abstinent Left was Lev Tolstoy and the Tolstoyan movement. Tolstoyanism had motivated one of early leftist founders of Bulgarian abstinence, Ivan Pavlov, which was indicative of the strand of rural utopianism behind the movement. Pavlov was from a small village and had been educated in an agricultural-cooperative school. Pavlov linked cooperativism and abstinence as cure-alls for the misery of the rural population.[110]

But in spite of this connection with the Left and agrarianism, for most Bulgarians Protestantism and abstinence were synonymous. As Khristo Dimchev, one of the socialist founders of the movement, lamented, before World War I it would have been "incomprehensible for a healthy person to abstain if they were not an evangelist."[111] Though Dimchev himself was not Protestant, he was influenced by Protestant abstinent thought. His primary inspiration, however, was the well-known Swiss psychologist and outspoken socialist and temperance advocate August Forel, whose ideas were central to the Bulgarian socialist (later communist) abstinence movement.[112] Forel was a former Protestant who had turned away from religion and toward socialism in the course of his intellectual and political development. This was also the case for such well-known interwar abstinence advocates as Nikola Vaptsarov (also a famous poet), whose Protestant youth seemed to meld well with an abstinence-oriented socialist adulthood, where utopian visions of a bright future simply shifted from heaven to earth.[113] Protestantism—a radical break from Orthodox Christianity—formed an odd kind of philosophical jumping-off point for Bulgarians on their way to socialism in the late nineteenth century.[114] Protestantism was the first step to radical socialism, representing as it did a break from Bulgarian religious (and hence even national) tradition. Kostentseva concurred: "There is something revolutionary in the activities of the Protestants that attracts many people."[115] By the early twentieth century, at least a segment of Bulgarian socialists seemed to echo Protestants in their call for a revolutionary change in Bulgarian consumption habits, that is, the advocacy of total abstinence. Incidentally, in the newly established Soviet Union alcohol and tobacco were vilified and came under at least temporary attack. But they were also hotly debated issues within changing visions of socialist propriety and consumption.[116] In fact, by the time Stalin—a well-known pipe smoker—had taken the helm of the Soviet Union in 1928, revolutionary zeal against these intoxicants had been jettisoned in favor of an ideologically awkward embrace of what some saw as bourgeois consumption practices.[117] This resulted in a changing and ambiguous model for the Bulgarian Left, opening the door for much of its leadership to remain mired in smoke at Sofia's kafenes or rural krŭchmas.[118] The krŭchma, in fact, became a major organizational point for socialist men in some rural areas,[119] just as the urban kafene was both a meeting place and a workshop for leftist intellectuals in Bulgaria and abroad.[120]

It was precisely this tendency that abstinence-minded socialists sought to counter on the local level, choosing instead the local chitalishte as an organizational center for the movement. The reading room, they claimed, had been connected to abstinence since the Bulgarian national revival period, when it competed with the drunken tavern for the attention of the local population.[121] Its use increased in the years following 1923–25, when the movement was forced underground and so had to find front organizations to use as points of mobilization and dissemination of information. In many villages, abstinence organizations working through the local chitalishte were the *only* mass organizations that did educational and other social work for "moral and cultural uplift."[122] As one abstinence leader articulated, "our people were thrown into the war not of their own choosing and returned to their villages with their faith killed and with lower morals."[123] Significantly, the Bulgarian Communist Party grew most rapidly and had the largest base of support among the rural poor.

It is not surprising, then, that urban kafene-krŭchma consumption remained a central issue in abstinence literature even though (or perhaps especially because) the movement was based largely in the Bulgarian village. Youth abstinence societies were particularly popular with a segment of educated rural youth, who appealed to workers and youth from cities to "leave behind the krŭchmas and the cabarets" and instead to gather in reading rooms and work for abstinence.[124] Though rural smoking and drinking also came under fire, the most egregious idleness and engagement with intoxicants were characterized as urban phenomena. Abstinence sources were critical of Sofia as a "many-headed snake" that swallowed the village; this resonated with rural inhabitants who resented the clear imbalance between urban overconsumption and endemic rural poverty.[125] The urban intelligentsia was subject to scathing critiques in youth abstinence literature, charged as "unable to control their passions" and instincts, instead "poisoning themselves."[126] Newly formed left-leaning youth abstinence organizations called on their "parents and educators to crawl out of their krŭchmas and kafenes" and see the light.[127]

The so-called rural intelligentsia—a range of educated semi-elites, including doctors, lawyers and teachers—also came under fire for not setting a good example for the masses.[128] As Tzetko Petkov, an abstinence advocate, lamented,

> The director of an institution [a provincial high school] decided there is no smoking in a public hall. He puts up a sign "No smoking here." One of the leaders of precisely this intelligentsia "a former boss" sits precisely under the sign and smokes right in front of the director every day. There are thousands of such instances among this lower intelligentsia who poison themselves for most of their lives. The real intelligentsia who are relatively small in number in comparison with them are mostly helpless to fight in this environment.[129]

By way of explanation, students and intellectuals were accused of bringing habits from the city to their villages of origin.[130] Students were accused of smoking to be "bohemian," censured for being "proud" of their vices like "drinking and smoking until the wee hours."[131] It was alleged that they then transmitted habits from the West that had filtered through Sofia to the provinces, "infecting" the Bulgarian folk. As one source complained, Bulgarian students studied abroad and returned home as "spiritual invalids" who attempted to imitate "culture" and "civilization."[132] Here as elsewhere it was argued that "in Bulgaria the negative aspects of European civilization are most easily adopted and integrated in the wrong way."[133] Smoking, the author argued, was as much a spiritual poison as a physical one; it harmed not just the body but society as a whole.[134] The city was the explicit conduit of such habits, tied to both Western temptation and capitalist exploitation.

Abstinence was more than just a moralistic impulse among the Bulgarian Left. It became a political imperative after 1923. Until then the communists had actively boycotted abstinence organizations as "bourgeoisie" because they were associated with BANU. While the agrarians were in power from 1919 to 1923 BANU had been a public advocates of abstinence, associating drink and smoke with the evils of the parasitical city and supporting rural referendums to close local taverns.[135] But after the right-wing coup of June 1923 and the failed communist revolt of that September, the search for front organizations brought the Communist Party deep into the abstinence fold.[136] Abstinence associations became front organizations in which the party cooperated with noncommunist elements, including agrarians and Protestants.[137] This cooperation was dictated by the Comintern, the international communist organization in Moscow, in line with the "united front" policy of the 1920s and "popular front" (or second united front) policy of 1935–43.[138] Though endemic tensions continued between the two political movements, both communists and agrarians supported referendums that closed many local krŭchmas.[139] Equally critical was cooperation with Protestants through the organization of larger, neutral abstinence unions.[140] For communist activists, though, abstinence was continually defined as a "revolution in morals... of the soul and the mind, without barricades."[141] Activists pushed abstinence as a "social question," connected to the "exploitation" of the worker and peasant, who gave their "blood and sweat" in exchange for the poisons of the exploitive *krŭchmar* (tavern owner).[142]

As rural populations began to occupy the city in increasing numbers, whether seasonally or permanently, many still felt a deep alienation toward the established and nouveau riche elites of the Bulgarian city. For some of this population the krŭchma may have beckoned, but the urban high life was still out of reach; and for certain party functionaries both were morally repugnant. Leftist writers like Todor Vlaikov commonly included evil krŭchmars and "healthy" abstinent heroes in their work. This in many ways built upon the critical realism school of the 1890s, which highlighted the deleterious effects of the rural krŭchma.[143] These tropes had existed since the nineteenth century, but they grew stronger and resonated with the social concerns of left-leaning intellectuals of the interwar period. At the same time the criticism was more often directed to drinkers, and even avowed and committed abstainers, such as Paun Genov, admitted to smoking, which was patently more acceptable than alcohol.[144]

For many of those, leftist or not, who did choose to abstain from tobacco, abstinence was often less a political statement than a health imperative. This was especially true among aging intellectuals. Brŭzitsov in his gallery of the interwar figures, rarely failed to detail the drinking, smoking, and social patterns of the aging café goers. As Brŭzitsov described him, Stoian Mikhailovski was "not a puritan," but he didn't drink or smoke because he had "smoked a lot as a youth," and his health forced him to quit.[145] There was Iordan Iovkov, who went to the Bŭlgariia every day and smoked incessantly but stopped during his last six years of life because his doctor ordered it.[146] Anton Strashimirov had a "weak heart" so would not go with Brŭzitsov to the krŭchma and instead ate bonbons at home; he reportedly smoked only in public, away from the monitoring eyes of his wife.[147] But while the aging abstained out of necessity, a growing number of younger, mostly left-wing activists abstained out of conviction.

By 1940 Communist Party progress was tracked through membership and work in youth organizations, including abstinence and closely related tourist (mountaineering) organizations.[148] One of the most famous abstinence society activists and poets, the aforementioned Nikola Vaptsarov, played a leading role in both types of organizations.[149] With Aleko Konstantinov's turn-of-the-century tourist movement as inspiration, communist mountaineering movements claimed that "he who loves clean air and the expanse of nature, by no means can be closed up in the smoky and booze-filled cafés or taverns of the cities and villages." Party meetings and even congresses were often held in the mountains, away from the gaze of the state authorities.[150] At least in theory, the communist future in its purist guise was an abstinent one, in which drinking and smoking as capitalist practices (and means for exploitation) would be left behind in favor of a new socialist man with a pure mind and body.

On the grounds of shared notions of abstinence as well as social regeneration there was a certain philosophical synergy between Protestants and communists. Both groups developed similar concerns about the medical, moral, and social effects of alcohol and tobacco use and abuse in Bulgaria. Both targeted drinking and smoking by modern pleasure seekers in the Bulgarian urban kafene or cabaret, which they connected to the ill effects of Western penetration. For both Protestants and communists, modernity was both the problem and the solution, as modern notions of hygiene and discipline supplanted practices of decadent leisure, that could be understood as backward (idle, Eastern) or modern (Western). As an article from a leftist abstinence publication explained,

> The abstinence movement, as a social phenomenon, was the child of modern society. It arose as a reaction against certain social ills: alcoholism, tobacco-smoking, licentiousness, gambling and prostitution, which are inseparably connected to and a product of the modern social-economic structure of society. During the social-economic decline of the current period these social ills have increased markedly, strengthening the processes of demoralization and degeneration.[151]

This resonated with similar claims in Protestant publications from the period, which posited that Western vices and social malaise were central to the problem. Both wings of the abstinence movement believed that modern man should be able to use reason and science to "rein in inimical passions."[152]

More significantly, there was a clear overlap in the gender dimension to both Protestant and communist abstinence messages in terms of the diagnosis and cure. Across the movement activists advocated a deeply gendered moral uplift to counter backward and modern patterns of krŭchma drunkenness and kafene debauchery in the city as well as in the village. Working-class or rural women were seen as the victims of alcoholic and smoking men, who spent sparse family resources on unnecessary intoxicants and were perpetrators of misery and violence against their wives and children.[153] Numerous images and morality tales from abstinence writings depicted working-class men drinking and smoking in neighborhood bars while their wives (and children) literally starved to death at home in cold, unheated flats.[154] This picture is not surprising given that men not only consumed alcohol and tobacco in much greater quantities than women, but did so in public venues where they could be openly judged. According to abstinent observers, women who took care of the household in addition to working in the fields and factory seemed to work much harder than their husbands, who squandered their free time and precious money in the tavern.[155] The social implications of these analyses were clear; women were bearing the brunt of these ruinous habits, and alcohol and tobacco were killing the Bulgarian family, if not the nation.

In connection with this, both Protestants and communists expected women—as "natural abstainers"—to be at the forefront of the movement, enforcing abstinence at home and so playing an important role in the goals of both movements. Although undoubtedly women had long been critical of their husbands' time and money spent in the café and tavern, in this period more and more women began to participate in the rapidly growing abstinence movement for the first time.[156] A number of well-educated and articulate women, like Vera Zlatareva and Ianka Tosheva, lent their names, energy, and intelligence to the cause, contributing regularly to abstinence publications.[157] But even when women were not actively involved in the movement, they comprised the major audience for musical evenings, lectures, and other cultural events organized by abstinence associations. In addition, women were often avid supporters of the referendums to close local krŭchmas that were continuously waged by abstinence organizations, though with only limited success.[158] In spite of these efforts and achievements, abstinence movements continually lamented the lack of participation among women, who accepted the vulgar consumption habits

The caption reads, "And what remains for the wife and children," on the window it reads "krǔchma." \ *Trezvenost* (Ruse) 1921.

of their men.[159] Abstinence leaders continually implored women to become actively involved in organizational work.[160] Indeed, they expected women to do *more* than men and beseeched them to make the men stop their rampant consumption of alcohol and tobacco.[161]

In addition, the fallen woman, smoking, drunk, and often selling herself for sex was a central figure in both radical religious and secular concerns.[162] Fallen women were both the victims of these vices and examples of undisciplined and socially threatening female behavior. More broadly, smoking and drinking women, fallen or not, were a threat not only to traditional mores—now tainted by Western vice—but also to visions of an abstinent future. This reflected deep-seated concerns about the growing visibility of smoking and drinking women in general.[163] It was the modern girl and not just the prostitute who embodied this threat, the moral free fall that would doom the nation. And it was not just men who were alarmed by these implications. As an article by Ianka Tosheva, an educated and vocal advocate of abstinence, amply shows, Bulgarian women had been emancipated in a variety of ways but seemed to be squandering the opportunity.[164] To illustrate, Tosheva tells a story of a young woman from a Bulgarian village who studies medicine at the university in Sofia. Soon after she begins to attend soirées and other such events and falls into "modern company," with whom she begins to "smoke, drink, and flirt." As Tosheva narrates with a clear sense of irony, by the time the girl returns home to the provinces, she has become completely modern. According to Tosheva, however, her understanding of modern is highly misguided and needs to be redirected toward "a true understanding of science and health." If the girl had been a truly modern emancipated woman, she should have returned home with her knowledge of medicine and used it for the common good. As a "good citizen," she would not smoke or drink and would also demand that her future spouse and children abstain. But alas, as Tosheva laments, this was by no means the norm. In fact, only 3 percent of female university students in Bulgaria were members of abstinence associations, which they shunned because of their own "egoism" and the idea that such activities were a "waste of time."[165] In addition to being selfish, most "modern smokers" felt that abstainers were merely "sectarians" (Protestants) who wanted to "limit their freedom."[166] In Tosheva's view, the misguided modern girl could become a modern woman only by being both abstinent and socially conscious. This vision propagated by the Left was not far afield from that of the new Bulgarian woman of the Protestant, feminist, or even right-wing stripe. That is, she was pure, productive, and capable of managing herself and her children in the service of the nation.

But in spite of the clear overlap in message and approach to such issues, this marriage of interests—communist and Protestant—was always an uneasy one. Each embraced abstinence as the path toward a greater good—either communism or God's kingdom.[167] Theoretically, the neutral aspect of the National Bulgarian Abstinence Union constrained the more extreme rhetoric of either group. From the very beginning of the period, evangelical groups were tense and suspicious about the communist "reddening of the movement" and use of it for political ends.[168] Protestants repeatedly and futilely called for political neutrality to be maintained. Communist youth, they complained, would show up at meetings with red banners, attracting the attention of local police, provoking arrests.[169] They also accused nonabstinent communists of infiltrating the movement and using it as a platform for a broader political agenda.[170] Protestant anxieties were heightened by the suspicion of Bulgarian authorities toward these abstinence associations, primarily because of their leftist leanings. Fear of revolutionary ideas and, more concretely, the Soviet threat was a driving force behind right-wing politics in Bulgaria in the interwar period. Protestant activists complained that leftist members only hindered the movement's goal by drawing the attention of the authorities and bringing the "black mark of distrust."[171] In 1928 the movement's organizations and newspapers were temporarily banned because of apparent communist leanings. They were allowed to resurface and even blossom, however, in 1931–34 with the relative tolerance of the political authorities under the umbrella of the newly installed Naroden Blok (People's Block).[172] But by the late 1930s the movement was again under direct fire from Bulgarian authorities, who were concerned with its communist dimensions.[173] Meetings were watched and broken up as "political," and finally in 1938 all abstinence associations and publications were dissolved. By this time various right-wing elements had tried to disrupt and take over abstinence meetings, though many were reportedly drinkers and smokers who brought dancing and debauchery to the meetings.[174] In the early 1940s Brannik (Guardian), a right-wing youth group, paid some lip service to abstinence through the publication *Ruchei* (*Brook*).[175] But generally, the Bulgarian Right, unlike the Right in Germany, was never associated with the impulse of creating a pure and healthy national body through abstinence. Instead, those who saw drinking and smoking men and women as threats to the Bulgarian national future were defined as threats themselves. Consequently, both Protestant and leftist movements were driven underground for the duration of the war. But the abstinence message did not disappear entirely. Though never prevalent, a state-loyal abstinence periodical and youth organization were allowed to exist.

Even more significantly, women's periodicals, as long as they were not overtly leftist, were allowed to propagate a message of abstinence among women. Throughout the interwar period, publications like *Vestink na zhenata* (*Newspaper for Women*)—which published articles from a range of socially engaged women, including feminists and socialists—was very clearly an advocate of abstinence for women. With clearly feminist leanings, the paper pushed women's rights and education and as such carried images of modern Bulgarian women—writers, artists, literati—many of whom were undoubtedly smokers. But pictures of such women never included a smoking cigarette. Instead, frequent articles on abstinence spoke of the moral degradation of Bulgarian society, as well as the duty of Bulgarian women to enforce abstinence at home.[176] As one article on alcoholism pointed out, "[M]en cannot fight this social evil, which poisons and shames, and harms the prestige of all of humanity, without the help of women."[177] The paper was also rife with morality tales on the local krŭchma or the crowed kafene, both filled with smoke that "made your head spin."[178] Smoking women appeared only rarely on the pages of the periodical and only in negative and caricatured images.[179] Instead, the paper's contributors were preoccupied with the "new Bulgarian woman," as a model of "moral purity."[180]

Vestink na zhenata, in fact, depicted Bulgarian women as threatened with falling into the trap of "distorted modernity." Their roles as "reproducers" of the nation, both literally (through childbirth) and figuratively (through child rearing), made their moral stance and consumption of "poisons" a threat to the future of the nation. In conjunction with this, women were assigned the role of moral arbitrators for men and children, not just by Protestants and communists but by more mainstream voices. Even when abstinence newspapers were closed down, *Vestink na zhenata* continued to advocate abstinence. In short, it seems that while abstinence as a general movement was suspect, abstinence among women remained acceptable and desirable. When framed as part of a politically loyal stance, abstinence for women was nonthreatening, and in many respects imperative.

For both Bulgarian women and men, changing patterns of consumption were tightly intertwined with dramatic changes in interwar political participation, patterns of social interaction, and cultural production. With these changes came a range of concerns, in part as a result of the transgression of boundaries that marked this period in particular—between the sober kafene and the drunken krŭchma, between public male and private female sociability, and finally between East and West. As a result, radical models of morality and sobriety, religious (Protestant) and secular (communist), developed and spread as Bulgarians groped for grounding in a rapidly changing landscape of pleasure and propriety. While most of the population was far from responsive to such messages, the passion and insistence of interwar Bulgaria's abstinence movement can hardly be ignored.

Social concerns aside, for Bulgaria's new smokers tobacco was a welcome palliative for pain, a source of pleasure, and even a lively muse. For women, smoking marked their entrance into modern society, while for men it was central to their making of that society. As the smoke-filled café culture that bloomed at the turn of the century expanded in the interwar years, so too did the greatest figures and works in Bulgarian literary and intellectual history. Smoke was both a social lubricant and the muse that inspired a generation of men and women who came of age in this period.

CHAPTER 4

The Tobacco Fortress

Asenovgrad Krepost and the Politics of
Tobacco between the World Wars

On a cool day in April 1922 thousands of people gathered in front of a cluster of tobacco warehouses huddled at the entrance to the town of Stanimaka (renamed Asenovgrad in 1934). Strains of the Plovdiv military orchestra echoed through the valley as a variety of guests including Sofia dignitaries and legions of villagers gathered in the street that morning. After opening remarks by the minister of agriculture, Alexander Obov, the more prominent guests made their way into the salon of one of the warehouses owned by the hosts of the event, the tobacco cooperative Asenovgrad Krepost. There they observed a kind of performance for well-chosen spectators, namely demonstrations of tobacco sorting and packing. It was all part of a ritualistic celebration of the ample achievements of the cooperative located on the tobacco trail, from the dust-choked tobacco factories of nearby Plovdiv to the rugged Rhodope Mountains, where the soil and climate were ideal for tobacco cultivation. Nestled along the northern slopes of the craggy Rhodope peaks, Stanimaka was an ideal location for a tobacco growers' cooperative and processing center that served the town and its surrounding area. Its proximity to Plovdiv assured a constant exchange not just of raw and processed tobacco but also of people, technologies, goods, and ideas, as daily coaches and later buses linked the town with the much larger metropolis of Plovdiv.

On that morning local and visiting dignitaries sampled and admired the local high-quality tobacco and then proceeded down the road along with

23. Асѣновградъ Тютюнева Кооперация Ясѣнова крѣпость

Postcard of Asenovgrad Krepost cooperative buildings with cigarette factory in the center. Author's own collection.

the leaders of Asenovgrad Krepost and a parade of cooperative members. Coming into town, orchestra blaring, the parade crossed an iron bridge, and suddenly the majestic picture of the Stanimaka gorge opened up before them, topped by clifflike peaks and the ruins of the Asenovgrad Krepost (Asenovgrad Fortress). This fortress, the namesake of the tobacco cooperative that organized the day's events, had been the citadel of the medieval Slavic tsar Asen, who ruled from 1189 to 1196. Asen was best known for defying and openly battling the Byzantine Empire. In direct reference to Asen's citadel, the cooperative claimed that it too was a fortress, in which peasant growers of tobacco were protected against the predatory intrigues of speculators, merchants, and other foreign interests. With the ruins of Asen's fortress still in view, the crowd preceded to the north side of town, where they gathered in the yard of the newly built cooperative-owned cigarette factory. Local Orthodox clergy and a student chorus opened the dedication ceremony with prayers and good wishes, followed by speeches. Finally, guests were ushered into the factory, and with a sudden clamor the cutting machines were started, drawing attention to the state-of-the-art equipment recently purchased and shipped from Germany. During the rest of the afternoon, celebrants hobnobbed at the cooperative restaurant, while food, music, drinks, toasts, dances, and a box of cigarettes for every guest made the event on the public square both lively and popular.[1] In a period when only wealthy tobacconists had their own factories, the unprecedented success of Asenovgrad Krepost (AK) brought the cooperative into the public eye domestically and internationally. Its meteoric rise as an economic and social force represented both the possibilities of cooperative agrarian organization and the potential of an interwar boom in tobacco demand to bring security and prosperity to wide segments of the Bulgarian rural population, including refugees from Thrace and Macedonia.

For all its benefits, however, the postwar tobacco bubble also catalyzed the smoldering social and political tensions that made this one of the most turbulent periods in Bulgarian history. The rapid commodification of tobacco, ultimately put Bulgaria on a roller coaster of glut, boom, and crisis. Inevitably AK was unable to provide a true fortress for local peasants or refugees, given the whims of the international market and the tumultuous political landscape.

Peasants in Power

As World War I came to a close, Bulgarians were caught up in the revolutions on the Left that swept much of Europe. The war was particularly devastating for Bulgaria, which lost one in five men—the largest per capita loss in Europe—and was hit hard by shortages, hunger, and discontent by 1918.[2] As elsewhere in Europe, Bulgaria was threatened with a near revolutionary situation, with communist and agrarian parties emerging as moral victors with widespread support, since both had consistently opposed the war. Both parties had been largely decapitated during the war years, their leaders mostly sent to the front or put in prison. Neither party was fully ready to harness the popular protest that threatened to topple the fragile monarchy of Tsar Ferdinand in 1918, as Bulgaria, humiliated and defeated, seemed ready to implode.

With food extremely scarce and expensive at home and men starving on the front, so-called women's revolts shook much of the country, echoing similar revolts across Europe.[3] In Bulgaria, revolts for food had particular vehemence among women tobacco workers of Plovdiv. In May of 1918, a crowd of 250 female workers congregated in front of a tobacco warehouse. Their shouts of "bread" were punctuated by the crash of breaking glass as they began throwing rocks at the windows. The workers inside, a majority of whom were women, streamed out onto the streets and were soon joined by women from other tobacco-processing warehouses and factories. A human stream swelling to two thousand flowed down the streets of Plovdiv with signs reading, "We want bread," "We want our men," and "We want an end to war."[4] In front of the building where wartime food provisioning was coordinated, the women again yelled for bread and threw rocks until they shattered all the windows. But officials from the provisioning office, claiming to have no control over food distribution decisions, directed the crowd to the home of the mayor, Denio Manchev. City police were summoned, but they could not forestall Manchev's panic when his appeals to the women from his balcony failed to calm them. He rashly fired a gun into the crowd, killing a woman and causing the crowd to surge forward in anger. The police were either unwilling or unable to fight off the irate women, who again threw rocks at the windows and finally broke into the mayor's cellar, distributing cheese, soap, chicken, and other stockpiled supplies to the gathered throng.[5] This was just one of many women's food riots that exploded across Bulgaria in 1918, driven by women who were both desperate and empowered by their increasingly important roles in tobacco production and other industries.

World War I was a watershed in European, U.S., and world history because of the dramatic political, social, and geopolitical transformations that accompanied it. All segments of the affected societies were mobilized in a total war that had far-reaching consequences for postwar claims on political rights and social parity. In the history of global tobacco, the war was also a critical turning point. Both during and after the war tobacco production and consumption grew by an unprecedented measure as soldiers provisioned with cigarettes at the front returned as hardened smokers. At the same time, women were mobilized globally into home-front workforces, spurring expectations for political and social rights. Bulgarian working women were disgruntled by the wartime conditions of lower rations and pay.[6] Thousands died of starvation in Bulgarian cities, while children begging for food became a regular feature of late-war city life.[7] In December of 1917 around ten thousand workers, including tobacco workers from across Bulgaria, converged on Sofia, calling for peace and revolution. Antiwar protests were staged across the country, and on the front there were mass desertions.[8] But as worker riots wracked Bulgarian cities, a larger and more menacing wave of peasant protest moved rapidly toward Sofia.

By September of 1918, some fifteen thousand peasant soldiers returning from the front had been swept up in an uprising based in the hamlet of Radomir, 40 kilometers from Sofia. Their main demand was peace, but the rebellion also threatened to topple the Bulgarian monarchy. In response Tsar Ferdinand abdicated in favor of his son Boris III and released Alexander Stamboliski, the leader of the Bulgarian Agrarian National Union (BANU), from prison where he was serving time for his antiwar stance. Having struck a deal with the palace, Stamboliski intervened in Radomir and delivered temporary stability. The palace backing of Stamboliski, who was appointed prime minister, was no doubt provoked by fear of the communist Left that was rapidly coalescing in Bulgaria. BANU, though also radical in many respects, had a larger and more conservative constituency, the peasant majority. With the support of the newly politicized peasant masses, Stamboliski won the 1919 Bulgarian elections by a clear majority, though the Bulgarian Communist Party (BCP) came in second, justifying palace fears of its growing influence. BANU's relationship with the BCP in these years remained uneasy as worker and peasant demands and the approaches of the two parties were often at odds. Stamboliski made a host of enemies in his years in power, not just among communists but also among urban elites, the army, and revanchist refugees from Macedonia. Still, with a peasant mandate, Alexander Stamboliski essentially ruled Bulgaria from 1919 to 1923 as a "peasant republic" or, as many have charged, a peasant dictatorship, albeit under a nominal monarch, the young Tsar Boris.[9]

Among a range of agrarian initiatives, Stamboliski's regime gave an immediate and colossal lift to the agricultural cooperative movement with unprecedented and unqualified governmental support. Yet agricultural cooperatives were by no means new to Bulgaria, and state support was far from a radical departure from past policy. In fact, cooperatives as bases for credit, seeds, tools, and information for peasants had expanded since the 1890s as a result of both grassroots organization under BANU and lines of government-subsidized credit.[10] Cooperative organization took off especially after the 1903 establishment of the Bulgarian Agricultural Bank (BAB) and later the Bulgarian Central Cooperative Bank, whose explicit focus was the funding of cooperative credit and coordination of cooperative formation; there were some 931 cooperatives by 1910.[11] Although controversial, the cooperative idea had enjoyed widespread support from the government and a segment of urban intellectuals since the late nineteenth century.[12] Urban as well as newly educated rural intellectuals were influenced by Russian populism and agricultural cooperative movements abroad, especially Raiffeisen credit cooperatives in Germany. Friedrich Wilhelm Raiffeisen developed the latter model in rural Germany in the 1860s as small-scale banks that catered to the credit needs of agrarian populations. This model had since proven effective in Germany and spread elsewhere on various scales, including the Ottoman Empire. A wide range of interwar Bulgarian thinkers saw cooperatives as an answer to poverty and backwardness connected to the onerous peasant question in the provinces. But they were also an answer to the perceived ravages of capitalist speculation in the rural milieu.[13]

In the prewar years, cooperatives and the agrarian movement had their stronghold in the grain- and wine-growing Bulgarian north, not in the Rhodope Mountains of the south. In the south, fragmented smallholdings, traditional animal husbandry, and the slower commodification of tobacco relative to grain had not lent themselves to cooperative organization. But with the steady rise of tobacco production, tobacco cooperatives had begun to appear in the environs of Haskovo and Dupnitsa by 1909.[14] The rationale for their formation was the same as that for other Bulgarian agrarian cooperatives, to protect the peasantry from predatory creditors and middlemen. In the early years of the industry, Greeks, Armenians, Jews, and other local foreigners had made up the bulk of these merchants. By the time AK was formed, however, Bulgarians were also prominent in the tobacco trade. Hence AK's goals were by no means nationalist or ethnically exclusive, though its leadership was almost exclusively Bulgarian. Indeed, the ranks of Asenovgrad Krepost included non-Bulgarians, primarily local Turkish or Pomak Muslims. Like BANU, it focused on social issues. Massive refugee movements had emptied Bulgaria of large numbers of Turks and Greeks, especially elites, and thus issues related to peasants and refugees generally loomed larger than ethnic tensions.

With an agrarian leader in power, creative answers to Bulgaria's rural plight were critical, and cooperative development became a state priority. In Stanimaka economic transformation since the turn of the century, as well as specific postwar conditions, provided fertile ground for the organization of a large-scale tobacco cooperative.[15] Like Plovdiv, Stanimaka traditionally had an ethnically mixed population—primarily Turks, Greeks, Bulgarians, and Roma—but prominent Turks had emigrated in waves since 1878. Greeks, in contrast, dominated Stanimaka and its primarily grape-based wine and brandy economy until mass migrations were prompted by anti-Greek riots in 1906 and again after the First Balkan War in 1912. As Greeks and Turks moved out, Bulgarian populations immigrated in mass numbers as waves of refugees fled war, random violence, instability, and the ethnic tension that characterized the late-Ottoman and post-Ottoman Balkans. Stanimaka and its surroundings were rapidly Bulgarianized by destitute and dislocated Macedonian and Thracian refugees, who moved into the region armed with tobacco-growing and -processing know-how. Tobacco was ideal for the region, not just because of the climate but because it was labor- but not land-intensive, requiring only small parcels of land. It grew best on the otherwise agriculturally unsuitable sandy plots that dotted the surrounding mountainsides and thrived in the Mediterranean climate of southern Bulgaria. Tobacco, unlike other agricultural export crops, also required a great deal of processing before export, and so refugees and other landless and unemployed Bulgarians could be engaged in this work. Thus the tobacco economy was able to absorb these refugee populations as well as occupy Bulgaria's own rural and urban proletariat, many of them refugees from earlier waves of migration.

As tobacco demand expanded astronomically in the postwar years, it provided an immediate impetus for Asenovgrad Krepost to build its fortress on the foundation of favorable political, economic, and social postwar conditions. Until 1923 the Greco-Turkish War had effectively eliminated Bulgaria's primary competition—Greece and Ottoman Turkey—in the Oriental tobacco market. Within a short period of time tobacco was catapulted to a central place in the Bulgarian national economy as it went from 9 percent of export earnings in 1912 to 79 percent in 1918.[16] Export incentives, along with tobacco consumption tax revenues, were critical to postwar fiscal solvency because Bulgaria faced reparations of 2.25 billion francs, or two times the total national income of 1911.[17] Tobacco revenues, in fact, were tied directly to servicing the debt, and tobacco was Bulgaria's best collateral on the world market, as gold was in short supply.[18] As a result, the Stamboliski regime was intent upon promoting tobacco production in the provinces, and the cooperative structure was the perfect vehicle for mass organization and education of peasant growers. It is not surprising, then, that between 1918 and 1923 the number of tobacco cooperatives in Bulgaria grew from two to forty-one, as kilograms of tobacco produced within cooperatives grew from 137,704 out of a total of 20 million to 6,936,797 out of a total of 54 million.[19] Not only did the amount of tobacco produced nearly double, but the percentage grown within cooperatives also doubled from roughly 6 percent to 12 percent.

During these years Asenovgrad Krepost became a paragon of entrepreneurship and cooperative achievement. By 1923 it had brought together 2,466 members and built numerous tobacco-processing facilities, a cigarette factory, and its own hospital, fire station, restaurant, and two movie theaters. More important, AK, with the support of BANU, beat capitalist middlemen at their own game, conducting direct and highly profitable trade with global partners. Asenovgrad Krepost was very much at the forefront of the tobacco cooperative movement in Bulgaria, a flagship by all accounts.[20] Though the favorable tobacco market provided an enormous opportunity, the AK leadership was far from naive about its inherent vulnerability. This vulnerability stemmed from a "gold rush" for control of the ever-more valuable leaf, which increased the mad scramble among merchant buyers in Bulgaria. The very concept of a fortress assumed an awareness of enemies and the pervasive defenselessness of the tobacco peasant. It also assumed the necessity of building a fortress against exploitation of encroaching middlemen, Bulgarian and foreign, eager to capitalize on the products of local labor. AK was determined to "gather up the ripe fruit of our own labor" emboldened by the "moral and material support" of the Stamboliski regime and the unprecedented credit lines made available by the Bulgarian Agricultural Bank.[21] But as new tobacco firms and cooperatives mushroomed across Bulgaria, bitter struggles over the massive profits of Bulgarian gold seethed under the surface.

From the very beginning the goal was to mitigate such struggles in favor of a kind of utopian tobacco community in which the cooperative protected members from both speculation and risk. Early on, the leadership envisioned a transcendent messianic purpose to their enterprise, which they thought would provide a blueprint for a new future, not just for the tobacco industry but for Bulgaria. With Stefen Ivanov, a former local representative of the BAB at the helm as director, AK rapidly expanded and soon emerged as by far the most enterprising, inventive, and extensive cooperative in Bulgarian history. Support of the regime and the BAB allowed Ivanov and his cohort of BANU supporters to promise consistently good prices—two to four times higher than those offered by merchant buyers—as well as timely and generous advances to tobacco growers.[22] Ivanov used members' land and projected tobacco harvests as collateral to borrow large sums of money from the state-subsidized BAB, which he promptly reinvested in the cooperative enterprise. Using this capital along with enormous tobacco profits in the first several years, Ivanov presided over the building of a cooperative empire that by 1923 included a network of tobacco-drying facilities and processing warehouses, a fleet of cars and trucks, a member restaurant with its own orchestra, a cultural center, and summer and winter movie houses. Asenovgrad Krepost also supplied free medical care to all its members. It had doctors, nurses, and midwives on staff who visited members in the adjacent villages monthly while holding regular hours in a small hospital in Stanimaka. AK cars were frequently used to transport sick peasants into town or even to Plovdiv for medical conditions that needed more intensive care. An AK legal section also offered members free legal advice and services, while experts offered guidance to members on tobacco growing and processing through a cooperative newspaper and field labs. AK also built its own cigarette factory in 1922 to assure control of all stages of tobacco processing and to maximize the profits of cooperative members.[23] Finally, unlike most cooperatives in Bulgaria, AK was also a consumer cooperative, which meant that it purchased and offered members goods at wholesale rates—beans, wheat, and flour as well as gasoline, leather, and textiles.[24] It also gave financial support to members and communities to build houses, tobacco-drying structures, and schools, including a Turkish school built for Turkish members in 1922.[25] As a result of this slew of benefits AK membership grew astronomically in its first few years of existence, from a mere 105 members in 1919 to 2,466 members in 1923![26]

Asenovgrad Krepost leadership sold the cooperative idea to members, not just as an economic association but as a way of life. This was laid out in the cooperative's *Biuletin,* which by 1925 had expanded into a newspaper with the title *Asenovgrad krepost.* Cooperative discipline was a common focus of the *Biuletin* and *Asenovgrad krepost,* which called for regular attendance at meetings, upholding the decisions of governing bodies, the continued cultivation of tobacco, and its delivery to cooperative warehouses. In addition to such demands, AK leadership also implored its members not to "gamble or be drunkards" and to "smoke only cooperative cigarettes."[27] While the leadership viewed drunkenness as a social problem among its members, it generally called for moderation, not prohibition.[28] The cooperative, in fact, sold alcohol at its restaurant and served it at functions such as its annual New Year's party, which rewarded members with food, drink, a lottery, music, and dancing.[29] And unlike abstinence proponents of the period,[30] AK actively encouraged smoking, though only of its own product.[31] With its oft-repeated slogan "Cooperative members, smoke only 'Asenovgrad Krepost' cigarettes!" the cooperative tried to inculcate a sense of corporate loyalty in return for the benefits it provided members.[32] AK leadership apparently did not view the smoking of company cigarettes as conflicting with the notion of healthy and productive, disciplined member bodies, an underlying objective of the AK project.[33]

In addition to member loyalty, AK successes in the early years can be attributed to massive influxes of capital, credits from the BAB, and profits that resulted in direct participation in global trade. Asenovgrad Krepost was one of the first ventures in the immediate postwar period to establish direct trade contacts with Germany, Austria, and many of the new East Central European states. Although Bulgarian trade contacts with Central Europe were developed during World War I, most commerce had been conducted by foreign firms and not local concerns. After the war AK, like other independent Bulgarian merchants, began to engage directly in international trade, further popularizing Bulgarian tobacco on the Central European market.[34] It was unusual—in fact, unheard of—for a Bulgarian agrarian cooperative to send out representatives and conduct direct trade relations with foreign companies and even state monopolies. But after several years of expanding commercial networks, by 1921 AK was loading whole ships of tobacco at the Black Sea port of Burgas before they headed up the Danube for Central Europe. The cooperative opened a trade office in Hamburg and later Vienna, conducting trade not just with Central Europe but also with the United States, the United Kingdom, Holland, China, and India.[35] Through engaging in trade without middlemen, AK was able to foil Bulgarian merchants, its openly and often maligned number-one enemy. The very foundation of the fortress was the organization's ability to forgo domestic and foreign merchants and keep the profits in Stanimaka, in the hands and mouths of the producers. As a 1926 article in *Asenovgrad krepost* triumphantly claimed, "in 2–3 years we have taken from the jaws of the speculator tobacco merchants 236 million leva and given it to the producers."[36] Not surprisingly, most tobacco merchants saw AK and other tobacco cooperatives created in the Stamboliski period as unnatural and impure products of agrarian favoritism and political maneuvering.[37]

On the international stage, in contrast, AK successes brought acclaim in the decade after World War I, as a constant trickle of international guests witnessed this unusually successful cooperative phenomenon.[38] Many of these visitors were from international agrarian, cooperative, or labor organizations, but there was also a wide range of dignitaries including ambassadors, and Western journalists from newspapers like the *New York Times,* the *London Times,* and *Berliner Tageblatt*. From Belgian Nobel prize winner Henri Marie La Fontaine to Albert Toma, head of the International Labor Organization, AK hosted a range of guests, becoming a kind of Potemkin village for the Bulgarian state, during and even after Stamboliski's rule. At least until the late 1920s, Asenovgrad Krepost was a showcase for Bulgarian agrarian economic innovation but also for refugee resettlement.[39] In fact, the first Western loan that Bulgaria received in the postwar period was a "refugee resettlement" loan from the League of Nations.[40] Hence AK became a showcase for the productive use of league funds. Visitors invariably toured the factory and processing warehouses, lunched at the cooperative restaurant, and met with Macedonian and Thracian refugees, who attested to their successful resettlement under the tutelage of Asenovgrad Krepost.[41]

These visits were very much a part of the cooperative's narrative of legitimacy and achievement. They continued even after the fall of Stamboliski and the accompanying lean years from 1923 to 1927, when the cooperative experienced severe economic difficulties. Keeping up its facade of stability, *Asenovgrad krepost* regularly detailed such visits and later printed letters from visitors who marveled over AK successes. AK became a self-proclaimed Jerusalem for the cooperative world,[42] even going on the road to display its concept at international venues such as a trade fair in Rio de Janeiro and an international cooperative exhibition in Ghent, Belgium, in 1923.[43] As the cooperative's *Biuletin* rightly foresaw in a January 1922 issue, "we will soon surprise the world with our drive and our enterprising nature."[44] And the world was surprised by what it encountered in this small tobacco town and its environs tucked into the Rhodope foothills. But in many respects the astonishing and thriving Asenovgrad Krepost of the 1920s was too good to be true, and cracks in the fortress would soon appear.

Fortress under Siege

Asenovgrad Krepost was built on the profits and promise of tobacco in immediate postwar Bulgaria. With Stamboliski in power, AK flourished, creating a community of growers who for the first time were able to reap the benefits of their own labor in unprecedented ways. Though other tobacco cooperatives appeared across southern Bulgarian, no other cooperative was able to build such an elaborate membership or infrastructural base. But AK, like the others, was ill equipped to deal with the ground-shaking political and economic changes that hit Bulgaria beginning in 1923. As tobacco prices entered the roller-coaster years of 1923–34, so too did Bulgarian social and political conflicts intensify. For Asenovgrad Krepost, new enemies emerged outside and within. Battles over tobacco profits spawned economic and political turf wars and undergirded political movements among workers, peasants, and other bases of influence. Between popular unrest, government turmoil, and dramatic fluctuations in the global economy, it would have been a miracle if Asenovgrad Krepost had survived wholly intact.

The events of the summer of 1923 were the first serious blow to AK's political foundations. In June the Stamboliski regime was ousted from power in a violent coup organized by the so-called Naroden Sgovor (People's Accord), an alliance of anti-Stamboliski elements that included urban commercial, industrial, and military factions. In addition to receiving tacit support from the palace, Sgovor's leader, Alexandŭr Tsankov, worked directly (though secretly) with the Internal Macedonian Revolutionary Committee (IMRO), a political organization based in southwest Bulgaria. IMRO followers had become Stamboliski's mortal enemies because of his refusal to support their territorial designs on Macedonian territories held by Greece and Yugoslavia since the Balkan Wars (1912–13). Since 1919, IMRO had been a serious impediment to Stamboliski's foreign policy objectives, which focused on establishing regional stability and cooperation. IMRO openly organized political and paramilitary groups and staged raids, particularly across the border into Yugoslavia. Stamboliski, in an effort to rein in IMRO and its growing power base in Pirin Macedonia (part of Bulgaria since 1913), had signed the fateful 1923 Treaty of Niš, which made a commitment to controlling cross-border terrorism. IMRO willingly cooperated with the Sgovor coup in 1923 and played a direct role in the assassination of Stamboliski. Although thousands of peasants with pitchforks and clubs tried to fend off Stamboliski's pursuers as he fled to the mountains, he was eventually cornered by Bulgarian troops and IMRO operatives. After prolonged torture, IMRO thugs stabbed him sixty times, severed his head (never to be recovered), and cut off the right hand that had signed the Treaty of Niš.[45] As of June 1923, the peasants were no longer in power.

With Stamboliski dead and BANU in disarray, Asenovgrad Krepost faced a series of new challenges beginning in 1923. In the short term, the Sgovor government claimed to support the AK endeavor, and the new prime minister, Alexandŭr Tsankov, even visited the cooperative one month after the change in power.[46] The cooperative movement was by no means buried or even theoretically inimical to the ideology of the forces on the Bulgarian Right. In post-1923 parliamentary discussions, the "unnatural growth" of cooperatives under Stamboliski was hotly criticized but so too was his "most brutal violation of the most basic cooperative principles." Invective against Stamboliski's creation of cooperatives was focused on his "purely political agenda"—garnering support for his regime.[47] Cooperatives per se were not the target of the post-1923 political leadership. Rather, politicians expressed concerns about their rapid and excessive growth due to the overabundant favoritism of Stamboliski. The regime, in fact, saw the urgent need for continued cooperative organization and even a merchant-cooperative rapprochement. But it also saw the necessity of curbing cooperative excess, especially given the huge subsidies granted via BAB credits. It is no surprise, then, that the regime felt compelled to rein in Asenovgrad Krepost and its "bad leadership."[48] Critical state-subsidized loans that came to AK through the BAB were cut off in 1923 as the bank conducted a two-year audit. Supporters of AK in the BAB were abruptly fired, and the bank, according to cooperative spokesmen, fell under the influence of "tobacco capital."[49]

In the middle of this political and financial shake-up there was a severe drop in tobacco prices in 1923, and in the years that followed the price of leaf was extremely volatile. The end of the Greco-Turkish war meant that the market was flooded by Greek and Turkish Oriental tobaccos, creating a glut that came and went in the following years based on harvests and fluctuating demand. In many respects AK weathered the storm of these years better than many, as numerous tobacco cooperatives folded and tobacco merchants went under. Its accumulated capital allowed it to purchase, for example, the tobacco factory of the local Greek owner Karamandi, whose business collapsed in 1924.[50] In addition, the restaurant, medical facilities, movie house, and other services of the cooperative continued until 1927, as did the visits from curious and well-placed foreigners. In the midst of economic instability in the industry, the continued success of AK, as fragile as it was, was enviable.

And at least in part, the survival of the cooperative was a result of the fact that the Sgovor government needed peasant support in the post-1923 years. Sgovor rightly assumed that the Bulgarian Communist Party was a much greater and more immediate threat. The BCP, with the second-strongest electoral showings in Bulgaria, after BANU, since the end of the war, had always been a rival of Stamboliski's party. Although the communists theoretically wanted an alliance of workers and peasants, in practice there were more tensions than harmony between communists and agrarians, who often had conflicting interests. In the interwar period, tobacco workers were more organized and demanding than ever before, in part because of the rising value of tobacco. but also because of their roles as soldiers in the war. Even female workers had contributed to the war effort through continued work in factories, hence satisfying "the needs of smokers on the front."[51] In spite of their sacrifices, factory conditions had actually become worse in the postwar years, while merchants seemed to be living in the lap of luxury.[52] Furthermore, men continued to be displaced by cheap female and child labor, in spite of labor laws that went largely unenforced. Chronic unemployment and underemployment that resulted from the seasonality of processing left working men embittered and radicalized. Strikes broke out in Bulgarian tobacco towns as early as 1919. But then, as in later strikes, the Stamboliski regime called on local authorities to restore order and crush them.[53] This only added to the communist perception that the agrarians harbored bourgeois tendencies, and their cooperation with BANU became increasingly limited to its rather meager left wing.[54] Not surprisingly, BCP activists were unwilling to defend Stamboliski during the 1923 reactionary coup. As a result the party was censured by the Comintern—the international organization based in Moscow that coordinated communist policy—which since 1922 had espoused building a united front against capitalism. For the BCP that meant working with BANU, and as a result of the party's misstep during the coup, the Comintern ordered the Bulgarian communists to organize an uprising against the new regime in the fall of 1923 to prove their loyalty.

Participants in the tobacco economy played a major role in the communist uprising that took place on September 23 of that year. The tobacco proletariat concentrated in Plovdiv and other tobacco depot cities was by this time the largest cohort of workers in Bulgaria with over forty thousand. Tobacco workers were on the front lines of the September uprising, which ended in mass arrests, beatings, and even state-directed assassinations of BCP members.

Plovdiv was literally blockaded as the police descended with rifles and batons, and the prisons were rapidly filled with BCP members. As Stefan Abadzhiev, a key participant in communist organization among tobacco labor described it in his memoirs,

> September, September 1923! A low red dawn. Red glimmers on faces, hands, rifles, clubs. . . . Then white. Deathly white on the white, white, white September nights. In Plovdiv the uprising was paralyzed. Arrests and blockades—a preemptive strike. Even before the red pieces of cloth could fly, tied to poles, before the rifles could thunder. . . . The Prisons were full. The earth slowly soaking with blood.[55]

Anticipating the plot, Tsankov's regime had already declared martial law, and Sofia was largely kept under control. But the struggle was more intense in the tobacco-processing towns of the south like Plovdiv and Stanimaka, where police brutality and round-ups carved a growing narrative of government repression and communist martyrdom.[56]

Stanimaka was an important center in the archipelago of tobacco-based communist labor organizations in this period, most closely tied to tobacco workers in Plovdiv but also to those in Khaskovo, Kirdzhali, Stara Zagora, and other nearby centers. For most of these workers, the abortive movement of 1923 was the culmination of years of bitter strikes waged since the war ended. But in Stanimaka, even more than in larger cities, there was a considerable overlap between the categories of worker and peasant grower. Most workers were either former peasants with families still living in nearby villages or were seasonal workers who still worked the fields during the planting and harvesting seasons. At the same time, the urban proletariat in Asenovgrad, Plovdiv, and elsewhere was attracted to revolutionary circles, whose extreme views often came into conflict with rural interests and agrarian sensibilities. Within Asenovgrad Krepost the organizational dominance of pro-agrarian growers and their advocates created tensions with workers who rightly assumed that most cooperative resources were being spent on infrastructure and benefits for growers and not factory workers. As revealed in worker memoirs and newspapers from these years, Asenovgrad Krepost— like the Stamboliski regime—appeared to be no more responsive to strikes than any other factory owner. Workers' organizations, in fact, perceived AK as just another enterprise where they regularly staged tobacco strikes, even in good times such as 1919 and 1922.[57] As a result, AK sources looked at workers with suspicion, as a continual thorn in the side of the cooperative. Even as early as July 1922, soon after the opening of the new factory, an article in *Biuletin* accused factory workers of acts of sabotage such as putting nails or garbage in the tobacco or the wrong number of cigarettes in cigarette packages.[58] The cooperative leadership was keenly aware that workers had divided loyalties because of their deep associational ties with the international communist movement, as well as with radicalized Macedonian and Thracian émigré associations. While AK considered itself a part of the larger struggle within Bulgaria between labor and capital, it also continually asserted its opposition to Bolshevism and its commitment to democracy.[59] AK leaders cooperated with periodic police searches like the one on March 15, 1926, when a late-night blockade of the city resulted in searches for weapons, "conspiratorial archives," and suspicious literature.[60] In essence AK became a tacit partner against the communist Left, cooperating with post-1923 regimes that offered relatively steady political and fiscal support in exchange. For those regimes AK and other agricultural cooperatives were the lesser of two evils. Nationwide the constituency of 100,000–150,000 tobacco growers was far more trustworthy and necessary than the politically suspect 40,000-strong tobacco proletariat. As a result, the Bulgarian Communist Party became the primary target of the 1923 Law on the Defense of the Government, which accompanied Bulgaria's turn to the right. The BCP was gradually driven underground, especially after its 1925 bombing of the Sveti Nedelia church in central Sofia while Tsar Boris was in attendance. Party members continued to operate abroad and through various front organizations or illegal channels, and communists were routinely put in prison; between 1923 and 1925 some 5,000 communists were killed outright by Tsankov's "white terror."[61]

The 1923 shift right in political power was engineered, at least in part, by Bulgarian tobacco interests. In the words of Georgi Dimitrov, then head of the Comintern and later the BCP, "It was precisely the powerful interests of tobacco capital that framed and organized the Fascist coup of 1923." As he argued in a 1929 article on tobacco labor, the "heroes"—or as he called them, "bloody murderers"—of 1923, like Aleksandŭr Tsankov and Andrei Liapchev, were paid directly by tobacco capitalists who wanted to crush communist interference and run their factories unfettered by communist-backed labor legislation.[62] Although Dimitrov surely overstated his case, Liapchev was known to have been subsidized by Krum Chaprashnikov, one of the most prominent and IMRO-connected tobacco merchants in Bulgaria, who was also a staunch enemy of Stamboliski.[63] Tsankov had also played a role in the tobacco trade before 1923 and was known to be well connected to tobacco interests before and after that year.[64] The more direct tobacco connection to 1923, however—surprisingly unexplored by Dimitrov—was the IMRO one. Since the end of the war, IMRO under Todor Aleksandrov had effectively been building a state within a state in the tobacco-rich Petrich district of

southwestern Bulgaria. Tobacco, in fact, was *the* critical revenue source for
IMRO, which by 1923 had built a local paramilitary of nine thousand men
and an extensive local administration.[65] In light of IMRO's key role in 1923,
the Svogor state was compelled to give even more extensive de facto autonomy to the administration in Petrich, which effectively ruled southwestern
Bulgaria directly until 1934.

IMRO was a kind of mega-tobacco cooperative, or even a tobacco monopoly, which to its great fiscal advantage tightly controlled the buying and selling
of tobacco within the district. There were a number of independent tobacco
cooperatives within the Petrich region in these years, though nothing as elaborate in membership or benefits as Asenovgrad Krepost. At the point of sale,
though, all tobacco growers—or cooperative structures—were expected to pay
a tax of four or five lev a kilogram (tobacco sold for an average of fourteen to
forty-five lev a kilogram). In addition, a "patriotic tax" was levied on all the
more well-off inhabitants of the region, and tobacco merchants appear in IMRO
registers as the largest "donors," contributing as much as three to five hundred
thousand lev a year each to IMRO coffers.[66] IMRO collected this money to
fund local administration, as well as the arming, training, and maintaining of
its paramilitary bands. The ultimate goal of IMRO, and the stated rationale
for the patriotic tax, was the reclaiming of Macedonian territories (also rich
with tobacco) across the border in Greece and Yugoslavia. It was Stamboliski's
obstruction of this greater Macedonian goal through his diplomatic recognition
of the inviolability of borders that made him a mortal enemy of IMRO.

IMRO was less concerned with Stamboliski's agrarian policy, as to a large
degree it was much like their own paternalistic policy toward the peasant
grower. Much of the collected tobacco tax was put into the development of
infrastructure, social security, and hygiene programs for local inhabitants.
As the volatile post-1923 market contributed to a perpetual scramble for
growers to pay the tax, IMRO operatives were concerned about considerable discontent in the villages. Given the threat to stability and their fiscal
base, IMRO was exceedingly flexible with growers, even changing the tax
of four to five lev a kilo to a straight 6 percent tax on the sales price in
1926.[67] The group also tracked and punished "immoral" and "illegal" behaviors of merchants on behalf of peasants who "sought protection from the
Organization."[68] At the same time, IMRO needed supporters among well-off
citizens, and in the years of waning profits cashiers were instructed to use
tact and allow merchants an extra six months to pay off their patriotic taxes.
Still, IMRO maintained a combination of persuasion and intimidation to
keep tobacco revenues coming in. A letter from the Bokhcha cooperative
in Gorna Djumaya, for example, detailed its costs, debts, and the deplorable

financial state of its growers. The cooperative begged for a reprieve on its onerous tax for 1925. In a letter of response, the IMRO central committee expressed sympathy but also noted that all cooperatives in the region were still paying the tax; it stated in capital letters, "IT IS IMPOSSIBLE TO RESCIND THE COLLECTION OF THE TAX—OF 5 LEV PER KILOGRAM OF TOBACCO." Generously, they offered to accept the payments in three or four installments.[69]

In effect, IMRO was run on a tobacco engine, and refusals to fuel that engine were tantamount to treason. The organization seemed to focus its harshest discipline in such matters on its own corrupt members, whom it accused of contributing to the chaos that was taking place in connection with the tobacco tax. One report, for example, complained of 6 million lev in unpaid tobacco taxes from 1923 to 1924 while detailing rampant favoritism and payoffs to IMRO cashiers who turned a blind eye.[70] This state of affairs was especially disturbing to the IMRO central committee, which warned that all the guilty members of the organization would be "punished in the harshest way possible."[71]

The Organization—or the brotherhood, as it was often called—was faced with a range of enemies that it actively observed and punished in the five districts of Petrich. In addition to tax evaders and smugglers, many of these enemies came from rival IMRO splinter groups, which formed after the 1924 assassination of Aleksandrov. Under the new right-wing leader, Ivan Mikhailov, the "Mikhailovists" faction of IMRO maintained power in the Petrich district and protected its turf through wanton terror against rival organizations that claimed to be true heirs to IMRO. The Mikhailovists drove the supporters of the rivals, such as the communist-controlled IMRO-United, out of Petrich, and their members were gunned down on the streets of Sofia, Plovdiv, and elsewhere in the provinces. In its effort to maintain control over the Petrich fiefdom, IMRO sent death squads to cities across Bulgaria, assassinating adversaries and sparking a cycle of retribution that was responsible for some eight hundred murders from 1924 to 1934.[72] IMRO also reached deep into the tobacco warehouses and factories of the Petrich district to root out communism, whether or not it was of the IMRO-United variety. IMRO battled communist influence not only with assassination but also with "material and spiritual support," creating anticommunist youth associations, offering free excursions, and distributing literature on the Macedonian cause.[73] Although such tactics never brought all local activists under Mikhailovist-IMRO control, they did keep strike activity and other communist-directed activism within Petrich to a minimum. At the same time, IMRO maintained elaborate networks of operatives outside Petrich, in Sofia as well as in tobacco-growing and -processing towns like Plovdiv and Stanimaka—anywhere there were large numbers of Macedonian refugees.

Refugees working at Asenovgrad Krepost were connected mainly to IMRO-United, the communist rival of the Petrich-based IMRO. The more radical among them organized in underground communist cells and worked through local émigré organizations, which increasingly became a front for communist activities. Stanimaka's Sveti Georgi neighborhood, otherwise known as Cherveni Kvartal (Red Quarter), became a hotbed of antifascist activism and a stronghold of communist Macedonian (and Thracian) refugees led by such figures as Kostadin Kichukov and Angel Ivanov, who were opposed to the right-wing IMRO of Ivan Mikhailov.[74] As mentioned before, communist-worker tensions with AK leadership had been brewing since the very founding of the cooperative. They became even more acute in the post-1923 years, especially as workers began to implicate AK leadership in cooperation with the new right-wing regime as well as with the Mikhailovist-IMRO.[75] Although a connection between AK and the Petrich-based IMRO seems specious at best, AK leadership did blacklist Communist Party members and truck in strikebreakers from surrounding villages.[76]

IMRO factional turf was decidedly regional, though right- and left-wing IMROs attempted to spread their influence beyond their turf boundaries. Mikhailov's IMRO routinely tracked down and assassinated communist Macedonians (from IMRO-United); its most famous death sentence was against the prominent Bulgarian Communist Party leader Anton Yugov (though the group never succeeded in killing him).[77] The Mikhailovists were the most notorious, but IMRO-United also participated in assassinations, and vengeance shootings were almost daily occurrences on the streets of larger Bulgarian cities, especially between 1924 and 1934. Plovdiv, like Stanimaka, to a large extent became the turf of IMRO-United, as left-leaning refugees from Petrich found jobs in its tobacco-processing depots and factories. Mikhailovist-IMRO often gave IMRO-United tobacco workers "death sentences" as traitors and gunned them down outside tobacco warehouses; the tobacco quarter of Plovdiv became a notorious cite for such drive-by shootings.[78] And while such shootings were relatively rare in Stanimaka itself, other violent incidents occurred. The leftist-IMRO veteran Dimitŭr Nikolov, for example, was "dragged out of his neighborhood" at night and hung outside Stanimaka.[79] Fear for their lives or factory blacklists often drove Macedonian and Thracian communists from Stanimaka to nearby Plovdiv, where they disappeared into communist networks and the anonymity of the city and its tobacco factories.[80]

Like Plovdiv, Stanimika became an important base of operations for the Bulgarian Communist Party. The aforementioned Cherveni Kvartal was IMRO-United turf, and operatives were relatively safe on a daily basis. It was there in private homes that Kosta Kichukov routinely hosted visits from Anton Yugov, Vladimir Poptomov, and other high-ranking Macedonian-Bulgarians, who had always formed a critical core for the wider Bulgarian communist movement.[81] The concentration of tobacco workers and refugees made Stanimaka a hotbed of "revolutionary potential," and the Communist Party demanded that Macedonian communists remain in Asenovgrad Krepost to infiltrate its ranks. In addition, Macedonian (and Thracian) youth and refugee organizations became explicit targets for communist agitation in the late 1920s and early 1930s.[82] Communist operatives routinely attended, disrupted, and even took over refugee association meetings and events.[83] The communist project was further abetted by the 1934 authoritarian coup by the Zveno military league in Sofia, the political configuration that took power that year and dissolved all political parties in Bulgaria. Zveno finally crushed the IMRO stronghold in Petrich and sent the organization into disarray. The coup took place during a mass tobacco workers' strike in Plovdiv and was specifically focused on taming working-class upheaval. But it also took down the rightist branch of IMRO in Petrich, allowing IMRO-United to "fill the Macedonian club" in Stanimaka and establish an uncontested presence.[84] Zveno also targeted IMRO-United, whose nominal leader, Simeon Kabrakirov, was incidentally assassinated in prison in 1934. Still the organization continued to thrive under its de facto leader, Anton Yugov, with financial and organizational support from Moscow.

These political shifts and power struggles could not help but erode the solidarity and political efficacy of AK, particularly in tandem with the economic crises of the period. The loss of Stamboliski as a prime supporter coincided with an increased incidence of open attacks on Asenovgrad Krepost in Bulgarian newspapers, on the floor of parliament, and in public debate. This heightened the siege mentality of the cooperative leadership, and AK publications and documents were preoccupied with enemy attacks as well as internal breaches in discipline. As the cooperative newspaper declared, "[O]ur enemies are waging a ruthless struggle against our successes in tobacco production."[85] The cooperative's main credit source, the Bulgarian Agricultural Bank, conducted a detailed audit from 1924 to 1926 that called into question the financial dealings and expenditures of the cooperative.[86] It revealed huge salaries and "entertainment funds" for the cooperative chief Ivanov and other high-ranking cooperative officials and openly censured irresponsible "expansion" and spending.[87] *Asenovgrad krepost* devoted considerable space on its meager pages to damage control and in particular to countering recurrent attacks on AK leadership. According to the newspaper, numerous sources had accused Ivanov of running the cooperative like a dictator[88] of squirreling away cooperative funds and planning to leave the country.[89] In response to such accusations, *Asenovgrad krepost* challenged its detractors to "leave the noisy capital and come to Stanimaka" to see that we "have not robbed but helped producers"; The four trucks and five cars that AK had purchased, as one article explained, were not Ivanov's but the cooperative's, and his monthly salary was a modest 15,000 lev, not the 150,000 lev that was presumed.[90] As for debt, a 1926 article admitted that AK owed 38 million lev to the bank but also pointed out that with the coming year's tobacco sales, the debt would be more than paid off.[91] In spite of efforts by the cooperative leaders to salvage their reputation, by the mid-1920s members were selling their tobacco to outside merchants rather than the cooperative, many of them leaving AK for good. From the point of view of the leadership such behavior was reprehensible, even traitorous. The AK likened growers who left the cooperative to Judas, particularly as it had given them advances and good prices—at its own fiscal peril—even through times of crisis.[92]

In addition to press attacks and hemorrhaging membership, debt and even individual civil cases brought against the cooperative proved crippling. Finally, in 1927 Ivanov resigned, defeated and discouraged. The new director, Veliu Georgiev was far less ambitious and ultimately more pragmatic but was never able to regain the momentum or sense of mission that had permeated Asenovgrad Krepost in its early years. As a result of a slew of draconian recommendations by the Bulgarian Agricultural Bank, the cooperative leadership, at a meeting of the administration in 1927, announced four hundred pages of changes, including salary cuts and layoffs for workers and employees, the closing of the medical clinic and hospital, and the selling off of various cooperative properties. By 1931 Asenovgrad Krepost had only 657 members and by 1933 only 437.[93] While such numbers seem catastrophically low compared with the 1923 membership of 2,466, the average tobacco cooperative of the time had a mere 135 members. The fall—or perhaps more accurately, the stumble—of Asenovgrad Krepost was in many ways inevitable, a result of the cooperative's (and Bulgaria's) dependence on a single exportable luxury crop. The newly constructed global value of tobacco entangled AK in a complex web of domestic politics, including Macedonian turf wars that were woven deeply into the tobacco world. Remarkably, Asenovgrad Krepost survived the tumultuous period and political rivalries described. It and the cooperative form more generally were given a second life as they came to play an important role in right-wing visions of a Bulgarian national order.

A Corporatist Cooperative

Although a shadow of its former self, Asenovgrad Krepost survived and even thrived in the fascist environment of the 1930s and World War II. Though Bulgaria never had a truly mass fascist movement, that model of governance was exceedingly attractive to a wide range of interwar Bulgarian politicians. Across the region, the failures of free capitalism in the West that had been made especially apparent by the Great Depression were in stark contrast to the order, social mobilization, and economic successes of fascist Italy since 1922 and Germany since 1933. Though not officially or even popularly anti-Semitic, Bulgaria as a revisionist power had a close relationship with Germany, its biggest trading partner in tobacco and other goods.[94] It also was close to Italy, especially after Tsar Boris—with Benito Mussolini in attendance—married the Italian princess Giovanna in 1930. As discussed in earlier chapters, free capitalism had never been widely embraced in Bulgarian economic thought. In this period, then, Italian and German corporatist fascist models of economic organization simply solidified an already deeply embedded desire for protection from unfettered capitalism and sparked the desire for a third way outside capitalism or socialism. Under Stamboliski this had taken the form of a peasant state with a heavy reliance on the cooperative, which proved too radical and alienating for large segments of the urban population. Still, the ousting of Stamboliski was by no means the end of the third way. By all accounts the cooperative remained critical to Bulgaria's image at home and abroad, its calling card for post-1923 regimes.[95] Bulgarian leaders like Alexandŭr Tsankov (1923–26) and his successor Andrei Liapchev (1926–28) supported the cooperative endeavor, though in a more modest form than the AK.[96]

In the post-1923 years a certain measure of government support for cooperatives continued, as the peasant served as a potent symbol and cause for the reactionary Bulgarian right.[97] Partnership with the right allowed AK to function effectively in spite of financial problems. The number of tobacco cooperatives actually grew from 41 in 1923 to 51 in 1924, dropping below the 1923 level to 20 only in 1926. Even this drop cannot be attributed to the post-1923 regime alone, as bad tobacco prices drove many merchants as well as cooperatives out of business. In the years that followed and even through the war years, the average number of tobacco cooperatives hovered around 20, which still was more than in 1921 (when there were only 17).[98] In addition, despite the dropping membership in Asenovgrad Krepost, the number of peasant suppliers who sold their wares to the cooperative was continually on the rise in the 1930s and war years. Although AK membership rose and fell, from 1926 to 1930 there was an average of 1,054 members and 952 suppliers, and from 1936 to 1940 an average of 1,800 growers were selling their tobacco to Asenovgrad Krepost.[99] These numbers reflect the reality that AK, like other cooperatives, continued to thrive after Stamboliski.

In part this was because in many respects tobacco growers—unlike workers and radicalized Macedonians—were the *least* of the political problems encountered by post-1923 Bulgarian regimes. While the social plight of peasants from the tobacco-growing south was certainly a sore spot, as a political force they were generally less threatening than workers and radicalized Macedonian refugees, on the right or left. True, at times communists and IMRO operatives hid among them and sought refuge—especially among relatives. In addition tobacco peasants became more and more organized in growers' unions. Still, these unions espoused government monopoly as opposed to revolution, and they lobbied for better prices, not strikes.[100]

By the 1930s cooperatives openly sought refuge in *more* rather than less government control over the tobacco economy, a sentiment that was shared by many Bulgarian statesmen in Sofia.[101] Certainly a segment of the tobacco merchant lobby with powerful connections in the state apparatus was against cooperative organization. But even many prominent merchants supported the cooperative idea, which they saw as playing an important social and organizational role within the industry. One of the more outspoken of these was the Bulgarian (Sephardic) Jewish merchant and prominent tobacconist Jacques Asseoff.[102] In his 1933 book *Tobacco in the Bulgarian Economy,* Asseoff insightfully details the inner workings of the industry from leaf to cigarette.[103] He presents a lively defense of tobacco cooperative organizations, addressed specifically to his fellow merchant objectors. While critical of "mistakes of certain cooperative leaderships"—possibly a jab at Asenovgrad Krepost—Asseoff also censured certain merchant practices.[104] He expressed concern, for example, about local insecurities created by huge variations in prices offered by merchants; market instability was compounded, he argued, by the common practice of employing "commissioners" who set up shop in local taverns and then made drunken purchases of tobacco regardless of real market prices.[105] Although Asseoff by no means advocated a total suppression of the free market, he believed that cooperatives helped in the regulation and stabilization of prices. He also believed that merchants and cooperatives had a number of shared interests, like keeping tobacco labor costs low and quality good so that market prices and profits could remain high.[106] Although opposed to government monopoly, Asseoff did advocate a greater role for the Bulgarian government in coordinating the tobacco industry. Given the aftermath of the recent economic crisis, as he pointed out, "apostles of economic liberalism" in Bulgaria were "completely dead and buried."[107] Asseoff was quite right in foreseeing a time when tobacco cooperatives and merchants would cooperate under close government control.

But what was particularly insightful and unusual in Asseoff's book on the industry was the larger social if not *national* vision of the role of the cooperative and tobacco more generally within Bulgaria. It was not unusual for works of the period to discuss the critical importance of tobacco for the national economy by tracking its advantages for the grower as well as its revenues for the state in trade and taxes. Asseoff duly covered this ground, but quite unlike other writers, he espoused a model of economic cooperation and government intervention that promised security and benefits for all segments of the industry as well as for the national economy. Starting with his praise for labor legislation, Asseoff by no means advocated squeezing maximum profits out of tobacco workers to the advantage of growers or merchants. Instead, in a period when workers lived and worked in miserable conditions, his firm, Balkantabak, took an active interest in worker welfare, offering free protective clothing and tables and chairs so workers did not have to "sit on the floor cross-legged." Even more unusually, Balkantabak provided a free *pochivna stantsia* (resort or sanitorium) in the mountain town of Samokov where sick workers could convalesce.[108] Finally, Asseoff supported the cooperative endeavor, which he argued "created the preconditions for higher ethics in the tobacco trade."[109] He agreed with the notion that the growth of the cooperative endeavor greatly reduced rampant speculation and criminal methods in dealings with the peasant in the countryside, greatly improving the situation of the local grower. He also believed the cooperative was a force that furthered the "moralization of the tobacco trade," acting as a price stabilizer and hence providing the best organizational structure for the future of the industry. Ultimately, for Asseoff tobacco was Bulgaria's fiscal savior, while the tobacco cooperative was a critical structure for the healthy functioning of the national economy.

Though Asseoff was particularly idealistic for a tobacco merchant, he was by no means alone in his embrace of the cooperative ideal, which long had been embedded in Bulgarian intellectual and economic thought. For many the cooperative seemed to provide a solution not just to the larger issues of the Bulgarian agrarian economy but also to the urban intellectual search for authenticity, for a moral approach to understanding the economy, and for the "Bulgarian spirit" in capitalist relations. By the 1930s the peasant cooperative embodied this spirit in the urban elite imaginary as a repository of national values, with a moral if not messianic role.[110] Although unable to work with Stamboliski or accept the reality of rural "tyranny over the city," urban elites were more than willing to work with the cooperative with its circumscribed boundaries of power in the village. If cooperatives were not an extension of urban power into the village, they were also not an extension of rural power into the city. Instead they were an institution that stabilized and regulated rural–urban relations, albeit dependent on urban credit and governmental regulation. Cooperatives by and large welcomed state intervention against the depredations of *other* urban, rural, or foreign actors of the free capitalist mold. The cooperative became a trope for corporatist rejection of free capitalism and the West as well as the abstract celebration of the Bulgarian peasant and hence the Bulgarian national spirit.

This is not to say that Asenovgrad Krepost or other Bulgarian cooperatives in this period became fascist, as many of their communist detractors later asserted. Nor is it to excuse fascist tendencies in Bulgarian right-wing governments, which were at their worst under direct German influence in the war years. Rather, it is to point out that collectivist and corporatist tendencies were imbedded in Bulgarian economic culture, not just on the left but also on the right; and in interwar Bulgarian society there was not much of a political center.[111] Bulgaria, in fact, was not just following suit with the global Right but also was in tune with left and center interventionist tendencies from Stalinism to FDR's New Deal. For capital-poor and peripheral Bulgaria, the cooperative instinct was part of a larger tendency toward self-preservation that predated this turn elsewhere. Cooperatives were part and parcel of Bulgarian communal capitalism, and unlike those in the West, they were not a corrective to but a replacement for properly "functioning capitalism."[112] As interwar regimes supported the cooperative ideal, they furthered social harmony but also arguably "castrated" capitalism, paving the way for the postwar transition to socialism.[113]

Like the leadership in Nazi Germany, the post-1934 Zveno regime and Tsar Boris's royal dictatorship after 1935 attempted to politically and emotionally co-opt workers into a state-run "patriotic" union. A leading Bulgarian communist from the period, Vasil Kolarov, paints a colorful picture of this endeavor in a pamphlet entitled "How the Fascists 'Buried' the Class Struggle." In 1936 Zveno created the so-called Bulgarian Workers' Union to bring "class harmony" to the strife-ridden industries of Bulgaria, of which the tobacco industry was by far the most contentious. This union, according to Kolarov, was organized and dominated by "fascist henchmen" who attempted to "wean the workers from the Left" through small and temporary concessions. Kolarov pointed out that the union's dues merely imposed an additional tax on already impoverished workers, and its labor leaders were scoundrels who "licked the boots of the fascists" for personal gain. The Workers' Union attempted to take over celebrations such as International Workers'

Day, which during the interwar years was celebrated by the Left-mobilized proletariat with walkouts, parades, and gatherings. In 1936, for example, parades in Sofia and other cities witnessed an "unforgettable picture" of May Day parades that featured priests in "elaborate vestments" blessing the Bulgarian tricolor flag, which replaced the usual purely red communist flags. In addition, military bands marched with high-ranking fascist officials in frock coats and top hats, who accompanied workers along parade routes.[114] The parades apparently did not win over the country's tobacco workers. In June of that year they staged the biggest general strike of the interwar years in Stanimaka (Asenovgrad) as well as Plovdiv, Sofia, Dupnitsa, and elsewhere. AK trucked in peasants to break the strike, and workers lay in front of the trucks so as to not let them through.[115] As Kolarov noted, the class struggle among workers had not been buried, and taming the working class was a losing battle.[116]

The regime had more success in its efforts to work with peasant-growers and the cooperative movement. For one thing it could offer them more, namely political and fiscal stability and a steady market for tobacco through its German and Italian alliances. As rightist regimes in theory embraced and protected the Bulgarian *narod* (people or nation), the cooperative structure remained an important mediating institution for the state-peasant relationship. The post-1927 AK might no longer have been a source of agrarian inspiration, but it did continue to provide credit, tools, and information to its members. In the late 1930s and particularly the war years, Bulgarian Agricultural Bank credits increased, as did the ability of Asenovgrad Krepost and other cooperatives to give advances and attract suppliers. Government intervention, both desired and lobbied for by the Union of Tobacco Cooperatives, became a reality by 1938 when tobacco buying and sales—private or cooperative—began to be closely regulated.[117] Although membership never again reached its 1924 peak, during World War II more than three thousand peasants regularly sold their tobacco to Asenovgrad Krepost.[118] In fact, Bulgarian fascism, with its government regulation of the industry and attendant trade relations with Germany during the war years, was a boon for AK.[119] In practice, it remained a more powerful force than ever in the Rhodope Mountain foothills, a fortress newly fortified by state power.

In many ways the story of Asenovgrad Krepost re-creates the well-known narrative of interwar Bulgaria (and most of interwar Eastern Europe as well). In particular, it follows the plot of postwar devastation that brought misery but also expectations and hope, framed and enacted through radical political experimentation and reform. In Bulgaria the tobacco boom was a major factor in postwar hopes for a better future, as it had the potential to solve a range of social and fiscal problems. Not only did tobacco revenues enable the Bulgarian state to ameliorate postwar fiscal disaster and service the heavy reparations debt, but, more important, they made it possible to absorb the hundreds of thousands of refugees that had flooded the country from Thrace and Macedonia as a result of the Balkan Wars (1912–13), World War I (1914–18), and the population exchange agreements of the postwar years. In the case of Asenovgrad Krepost, tobacco literally financed the dreams of thousands of peasants who pooled their resources, their time, and their hopes into a fortress against exploitation and poverty. To a certain extent these dreams seemed to be realized in the environs of Stanimaka, and the rush of enthusiasm that surrounded Asenovgrad Krepost is still palpable in the documents of the period. By all accounts its achievements were amazing, even if the decisions of its leadership remain controversial.

But ultimately a fortress built on tobacco alone was inherently unstable. Trade in a global commodity inevitably created dependency and vulnerability for Asenovgrad Krepost and Bulgaria more broadly while catalyzing local and national struggles for power. The meteoric rise of tobacco as a commodity after World War I created an even more volatile political and social environment. Tobacco intensified conflict between agrarian and communist, worker and peasant. Nowhere is this more evident than within the walls of the Krepost, where the Left-mobilized working class continually confronted the cooperative leadership, who put growers' interests above theirs. Perhaps even more critically, tobacco funded the creation of an IMRO state within a state in the Petrich district of Pirin Macedonia from which violence and intrigue reached the refugee-populated cities and provinces of Bulgaria. The critical role of Macedonian refugees in interwar Bulgaria has been frequently noted, but rarely are these politics followed from the mountain hamlets to the factories and warehouses of the tobacco world.

Ultimately the political changes that brought right-wing leadership to the fore in 1924 and then in 1934 calmed Bulgarian politics, at least in part, through control of the tobacco trade. IMRO was brought to its knees in 1934 because its critical tobacco revenues were lost. State control was extended by waves of regulatory measures through which cooperative and merchant were brought under government control. By the late 1930s this was coupled with an increasingly stable market in Central Europe, accompanied by solidified political alliances with fascist Europe. While tobacco workers were rattled by the open shift to the right, for most merchants the newly stable market was a boon to business. The turn to the right did not destroy Asenovgrad Krepost or the agrarian cooperative movement in Bulgaria. In fact, fascism ushered in a period of market stability, bolstered by state intervention on the local level in tobacco commerce. In the years after 1934 the cooperative built a partnership of interests against communism and radicalized workers with an interventionist and regulatory state. Business was again booming in the tobacco provinces of the Bulgarian south.

CHAPTER 5

From Leaf to Ash

Jews, Germans, and Bulgarian Gold in the
Second World War

Toward the end of 1940, Jacques Asseoff, a
Jewish tobacco magnate from Bulgaria, got on a ship in Istanbul that was
laden with his company's tobacco purchases. Headed for the port of New
York, the ship had a minor accident at sea but still made it to its destination in April of 1941. Asseoff probably sold his precious cargo—200,000
kilograms of tobacco (worth some $ 256,000)—to the American tobacco
company Liggett and Myers. Since he was Jewish, Asseoff's timing for his
exit from Europe could not have been better. Though Bulgaria was not
at war when he left Istanbul, it had joined the Axis powers by the time he
arrived in New York. But before his departure the writing was already on
the wall. In September of 1940, the Bulgarian parliament had approved the
infamous Law of the Defense of the Nation (LDN), patterned directly on
the Nazi German Nuremburg Laws of 1935. Published in October, the new
law was implemented gradually and sporadically, allowing Asseoff and his
family a window of opportunity to flee the country and settle in New York.
Asseoff's Bulgarian bank accounts were probably frozen in October, but it
took another two years for the Bulgarian authorities to dismantle his tobacco
empire, Balkantabak. And though he ultimately lost the bulk of his Bulgarian
assets, he had already transferred significant funds out of the country. Before
war reached the Balkans, he had managed to depart, accompanied by one last
load of Bulgarian tobacco.

As one of the most successful tobacco merchants in interwar Bulgaria, Asseoff was witness to the growth of a Bulgarian-German commercial partnership. This relationship, in which the tobacco trade was central, ultimately provided one of the foundations for Bulgaria's entry into the war on the Axis side. In the course of the 1930s the development of Bulgarian-German trade relations had profound repercussions for Asseoff and other tobacco merchants. For while Nazi Germany began to swallow up territories in Eastern Europe in 1938–39, its commercial advance across the region came much earlier. German trade with Bulgaria and other countries in Eastern Europe expanded rapidly in the course of the 1930s as a part of Nazi *Grossraumwirtshaft* (greater German economic space). German economic policy promoted a regional economic autarchy that decreased German financial dependence on the West.[1] With the launching of the *Neuer Plan* (New Plan) in 1934, Nazi Germany shifted its trade paths east, increasing its imports of raw materials from Eastern Europe in exchange for exported manufactured goods.[2] The resulting exchange pattern was coupled with increased political influence in the region, heightened by the visible economic and political successes of the fascist model in Italy and Germany.[3] The Neuer Plan targeted all of Eastern Europe, but by 1939 Bulgaria had the largest percentage of trade (67–70%) oriented toward Germany of any state in the region.[4] This did not bode well for Jews like Asseoff. Interwar Bulgarian merchants—Jews and gentiles—had turned to Germany, one of the few willing buyers of their agricultural goods. Yet even before Bulgaria became an Axis state, Jews were gradually shut out of the tobacco trade by Nazi dictate. Bulgarian merchants, in contrast, continued sending Oriental tobacco—Bulgaria's most valuable export in this period—up the Danube to Germany, one of the only options for economic survival as war swept the continent.

Without a doubt Germany needed Bulgarian tobacco to bolster its war efforts. By the 1940s cigarettes for troops had become a wartime necessity. In the annals of tobacco history, World War II, like World War I before it, was a critical turning point in the global consumption of tobacco. Smoking grew to unprecedented levels as Allied and Axis states supplied soldiers on the front and civilians on the home front with cigarette rations. Bored, agitated, hungry, and stressed populations sought a source of comfort in the cigarette. Even in labor and death camps, tobacco was sought after, traded, and smuggled; it was more valuable than currency during the war. German soldiers smoked a path of destruction across Europe; even mass shootings of Jews by Nazi death squads were punctuated by requisite smoke breaks.[5] As in the past, tobacco was not just a palliative, an oasis of comfort and pleasure. It was also, indirectly, a bearer of violence and death. More pointedly, the tobacco trade brought potentially Allied countries like Bulgaria into the Axis fold and played a role in Bulgarian-Jewish policy. That is not to deny Bulgaria's dynastic ties and right-wing political leanings in this period, but rather to say that the tobacco trade made an alliance with the Allies nearly impossible. In addition, Axis states were the only ones who could promise Bulgaria the ultimate war prize, Thrace and Macedonia, then under Greek and Yugoslav control. These tobacco-rich regions became gold mines for the Bulgarian state and the web of tobacco merchants, who provided "New Europe" with its fragrant tobaccos.

The Bulgarian state was compelled to marshal not just its troops, but its tobacco industry as part of its Axis war effort. Tobacco production was intensified at home as well as in Thrace and Macedonia after occupation in 1941. Not only were German and Bulgarian experts and machinery imported into these regions, but cultivation was expanded. More significant, the Bulgarian government took an overtly controlling and regulatory role in the industry, which was officially mobilized for the war effort.[6] But in contrast to the preceding periods, when Turks and Greeks were pushed out of the highest reaches of the industry, Bulgaria's Jews were hardest hit by wartime reshuffling. Not only were successful Jewish tobacco merchants like Asseoff compelled to take their talent and capital out of wartime Bulgaria, but Jewish populations in the tobacco-growing regions became the first targets for deportation by Bulgaria's infamous wartime Commissariat for Jewish Affairs (CJA). In March 1943, commissariat officials in occupied Thrace and Macedonia organized roundups of all Jewish residents under cover of night. Some twelve thousand Jews were herded into massive tobacco warehouses from Drama to Skopje, where they waited amid the tobacco dust and stench for their eventual deportations to Auschwitz and Treblinka. As valuable as Jews might have been in the local tobacco industry, they were apparently more valuable as deportees—emblematic of Bulgarian political loyalty to Germany, their blood the price for Thrace and Macedonia. The commonality of Bulgaro-German interests certainly contributed to partial cooperation in the Nazis' Final Solution (the total annihilation of European Jews) in Bulgarian-occupied territories. But in Bulgaria itself, Bulgarian-Jewish social ties, woven into the highly political, social tapestry of the tobacco industry, played a role in the "saving" of most of Bulgarian Jews.

Asseoff's Leaf

The story of Jacques Asseoff's rise and role in the Bulgarian tobacco industry is not just the subject of dusty documents or passing references in historical manuscripts—though these too have informed the narrative. Asseoff was immortalized in Dimitŭr Dimov's novel *Tiutiun* (*Tobacco*), which remains the most recognized and widely read piece of literature from the communist period.[7] When it was published in 1951, the Bulgarian communist authorities famously denounced the book and pulled it from the shelves. It was reissued after significant revisions in 1961 and made into a popular film, released the following year in an atmosphere of post-Stalinist cultural "thaw." Central to the original controversy over the novel was the fact that the main characters—namely, German, Bulgarian, Armenian, and Jewish tobacco merchants—are bourgeoisie. Although working-class characters also abound, their story and triumphs are mere background to Dimov's vivid if not lurid description of the merchant beau monde of the late interwar and wartime periods. Though Dimov's merchants are depicted as fallen characters who die untimely deaths, their centrality still undercuts the requirement of the socialist realist genre that the main heroes be happy workers.

As for Asseoff, he is the recognized archetype for the character of Koen, arguably the most sympathetic merchant in the book.[8] Although *Tiutiun* is clearly fiction, Bulgarians also widely recognize it as a kind of "documentary novel" because of the author's personal connections to the world of tobacco. Dimov was the stepson of a well-known Bulgarian tobacco merchant, Rusi Genev, who spent the interwar and war years firmly in that world. With the novel in mind, Genev supplied Dimov with hundreds of pages of detailed notes in which Asseoff, among others, was prominently featured. The Genevs, Dimovs, and Asseoffs spent much of their lives in the same town, Dupnitsa, which was a prominent tobacco depot in southwestern Bulgaria. Not far from Sofia, where both families also eventually resided, Dupnitsa was a processing town for tobaccos from adjacent Bulgarian (Pirin), Macedonia, and in the war years it served as a transit point for tobaccos from adjoining occupied Thrace and Macedonia.

Asseoff was born in Dupnitsa in 1896, the son of Rakhamin Moshe Aseo. Aseo was a Sephardic Jewish surname that the family eventually changed to Asseoff to indicate their acculturation to Bulgarian society.[9] Asseoff's father was a rather modest but visible local tobacco merchant who owned the Fernandes tobacco factory until his death in 1926.[10] Local Jews reportedly regarded Rakhamin as an aristocrat of sorts, one of the many prominent Sephardi families who had migrated up the Struma valley from Salonika as traders in the sixteenth century.[11] By the late nineteenth century, tobacco trade and processing occupied a growing place in the Dupnitsa economy. The primarily Turkish population of the town had fled and not returned after the 1877–78 Russo-Turkish war. As a result Jews, as well as newly urbanizing

Bulgarians, filled the roles of tobacco merchants, factory owners, and work-ers. In many respects it was social more than ethnic lines that divided the town, though there was a roughly circumscribed Jewish quarter. After World War I, Dupnitsa became an almost purely tobacco town. Even after the dev-astation of the Great Depression, merchants like Genev and Asseoff used their wits to rebuild an industry and—in the case of Asseoff—their personal fortunes. Dimov, like Asseoff, grew up in Dupntisa amid tobacco affluence but also poverty. As Dimov's wife, Neli Dospevska, later described his child-hood town,

> In the fall the city smelled of drying tobacco. The old grandmas smoked in front of their doors and yelled at the dirty and sunburned kids. Young girls, workers from the tobacco warehouses, went for walks before returning home, hungry for a little fresh clean air. Tobacco workers, tobacco merchants, tobacco experts—tobacco was every-where. In the field, still green, in the dark dusty warehouses, in the minds and conversations of people, fragrant, poisonous, it damaged the body and corrupted the mind. It brought power, but also ruin; once a happy fate, another time a bitter end.[12]

In her memoirs Dospevska implies that such impressions surrounded the young Dimov, shaping his leftist sympathies, which became politically expe-dient after the war. Not surprisingly, his disdain for merchants and respect for the working class permeate his novel, along with the aromas of the old tobacco world. Dupnitsa is clearly the model for the provincial tobacco depot town that is one of the central settings for the novel. As the book details, the interwar period was a particularly bumpy one for the tobacco industry, with surges in supply and activity punctuated by huge falls in prices and ruin for growers, workers, and traders alike.[13]

Jacques Asseoff was particularly adept at navigating these ups and downs with his company Balkantabak, which he and his brother Uriel founded in 1926. Balkantabak slowly grew in scale in spite of the devastating effects of the Great Depression from 1929 to 1933. In large part, the Balkantabak advantage was a German one, as Asseoff was well positioned to ride the wave of the success of Reemstma—a highly successful German tobacco company—into the late 1920s and much of the 1930s. The rise of Reem-stma has been described as "one of most stunning success stories in the his-tory of German business," generally attributed to the entrepreneurial skills of both Phillip Reemstma and his associate, David Schnur, a Jewish refugee from Bolshevik Russia. Reemstma rose from a small concern with one ciga-rette factory to a business that dominated 20 percent of the German market by the end of the 1920s and 70 percent by 1939.[14] Though the company was owned by Phillip Reemstma, its rise to prominence in the 1930s is often credited to the entrepreneurial skills of Schnur, who among other things was deeply involved in the importation of raw tobacco from Bulgaria. According to Rusi Genev's notes on the industry—later used as a basis for Dimov's novel—Schnur first came to Bulgaria in 1926 to establish a local import-export office. There he met Jacques Asseoff, with whom he shared social-democratic political leanings as well as business acumen. Asseoff became Schnur's local supplier, and over the next decade he provided between 1 and 12 million kilograms of tobacco a year to Reemstma, earning a 5 percent commission on the sales.[15] This arrangement was highly profitable but also, in the eyes of certain Bulgarian tobacco merchants, somewhat monopolistic. Certainly Asseoff could not help but arouse envy and resentment in some of his colleagues, including Genev, who watched his fortune grow and his business concerns branch out to movie theaters and even a Buick car dealership in Sofia.[16] In spite of the Depression, both Asseoff and Schnur managed to build huge personal fortunes and successful companies on the basis of German-Bulgarian tobacco trade and domestic cigarette operations.[17] Riding the wave of Reemstma, Balkantabak soon became the largest export firm in Bulgaria with branches in Sofia, Dupnitsa, Plovdiv, Kiustendil, and Haskovo.

Accordingly, Asseoff became one of the richest men in Bulgaria, and with money came influence and a web of social ties. In the course of his business dealings, he inspired envy as well as respect and gratitude. He developed a highly elaborate web of political and commercial contacts, gaining considerable clout through his philanthropic and organizational activities. Far from monopolizing the tobacco trade, Asseoff was known to work through a number of local merchants, helping many to get into the business, including the later prominent Bulgarian merchant Kiril Bozhkov and the well-known Armenian merchant Takvor Takvorian.[18] Asseoff also developed social and political ties to such high-ranking Bulgarian politicians as Alexandŭr Tsankov, who had also worked in the tobacco trade at one time. Asseoff worked for Tsankov's nationalist Zveno (Link) movement in Dupnitsa, which had a clearly articulated Bulgarian nationalist program, and both Asseoff and Tsankov, along with numerous other Bulgarian political and economic elites, belonged to the Masons.[19] Asseoff's collectivist (if not corporatist) strategies would have resonated with Bulgarian economic thinkers—on both the Right and the Left—who had long been alarmed by the ravages of the free market in Bulgaria.[20] While opposed to a government monopoly, Asseoff supported Bulgarian government coordination of the tobacco industry, agricultural tobacco cooperatives, and labor legislation.

This presaged not only wartime state control, support of cooperatives, and labor policy but also to a certain extent the postwar order.[21] Perhaps Dimov presented his Koen/Asseoff character with relative respect—in spite of his right-wing contacts—because Asseoff was well known not only for his business acumen but also for his socially progressive ideas.[22]

With the triumph of Hitler and the National Socialist Party in Germany as of 1933, however, Asseoff's networks of support, at home and abroad, became increasingly fragile. On the German side, Reemstma was waging a quiet miniwar with the Nazi Party. Even before the Nazis rose to power, the Nazi Sturmabteilung (SA), or storm troopers, had launched an attack in the party press on *Reemstma*'s "Jewish" Cigarettes—given Schnur's role in the company. SA campaigns against Reemstma from 1931 to 1932 were driven in part by the fact that the SA was manufacturing its own cigarettes, the so called Storm Cigarettes, as a way of funding its activities. As Reemstma was its biggest competitor, the SA dispatched rabble-rousers to break the windows of the company's distributors. Holding its ground, Reemstma threatened to pull company advertising from Nazi Party publications, a significant source of revenue at the time. Only a meeting between Phillip Reemstma and Hitler himself brought a temporary truce and an end to SA attacks.[23] Around the same time, Reemstma also met with the top Nazi official Hermann Göring, committing huge sums of money to the Berlin opera and a total of 7.276 million Reichmarks to the "Adolph Hitler fund."[24] Reemstma's "blood money" did not imply a political connection to the Nazi Party. If anything, it was the price of business as usual, and the company continued to operate with high-placed Jewish employees and suppliers, including Schnur and Asseoff. By 1936, however, Nazi pressure compelled Reemstma to shuffle David Schnur off to France, and within a year he had permanently emigrated to the United States. Schnur's role in the direct importation of Bulgarian tobaccos was subsequently filled by Kurt Wenkel, who, according to Rusi Genev, was "not a Hitlerist" but simply a German businessman.[25] Political leanings aside, Wenkel had the correct *racial* profile. Asseoff, however, did not.

In the short term, the Schnurr-Asseoff partnership had continued from 1933 to 1936 as the Nazi Party consolidated power at home and spread its political reach into Bulgaria. After the passing of the German Nuremburg laws in 1935, Nazi officials began to aggressively push Jews out of German commercial activities, at home and abroad. Reemstma pushed Schnur out in 1936, and Asseoff was soon to follow. By 1937 the German consulate in Bulgaria reported home to Berlin that Asseoff was a "Bulgarian merchant of Jewish extraction" who was personally responsible for some

65 percent of all German purchases of tobacco from Bulgaria, some 10 million kilograms in 1935 alone. Several reports that focused solely on the activities of Asseoff defamed the "Spanish Jew," who, they claimed, was the richest and most influential Jew in Bulgaria, worth an estimated 150 million lev.[26] In no uncertain terms, the consulate recommended that "[f]or economic reasons it is critically important to transfer the purchasing and exporting of tobaccos out of Bulgaria from Jewish into Aryan hands, Bulgarian or German. In this way we will force the recognition of the validity of the main tenets of National Socialism on the Jewish question in the realm of foreign representatives of German companies."[27] Note here that Bulgarians are referred to as "Aryans," though according to Nazi ideology Bulgarians, as Slavs, were not Aryan in the racial sense. This was clearly an ideological compromise that was politically expedient given the German need for Slavic cooperation in Bulgaria.[28] The post-1941 Aryanization of industry meant that the economy would be transferred into mostly Bulgarian hands. As the Germans sought to Aryanize Bulgarian-German tobacco, Asseoff was their primary concern. They were worried that in addition to being Jewish, he was involved in anti-Nazi activities. In 1937 the German consulate discovered an anti-Nazi brochure featuring commentaries from sixty Bulgarian public figures, including the well-known nationalist and longtime associate of Asseoff, Alexandŭr Tsankov. In essence it countered Nazi and Bulgarian anti-Semitic propaganda while touting Bulgarian Jews as loyal patriots. The German consulate was especially irked by the pamphlet's attacks on New Germany and tried to confiscate as many of the publications as possible, though a second edition was quickly released. Both pamphlets were funded by Asseoff, whom the consulate accused of "using our money," that is, profits from the tobacco trade. Asseoff's pamphlet advocated "finding new markets" to avoid Bulgaria's potentially "fateful" dependence on "a few big governments."[29] Also troubling for the Germans was the fact that Asseoff controlled the major film houses in Sofia and the provinces. His chain of movie theaters had begun in 1933 to shift away from purchasing and distributing German films to focusing on American and French. Reports back to Berlin commented on the disturbing fact that five years after the Nazis had seized power almost all the profits of Reemstma were still "pouring into Jewish hands." To make matters worse, this "German money," was "being used expressly against the political and cultural interests of New Germany."[30]

Since at least 1936, the Nazi Party had been corresponding directly with the Bulgarian Ministry of Foreign Affairs, requesting cooperation in the ousting of Jews from commercial positions that involved trade with Germany. In the case of Jacques Asseoff and Balkantabak, influential Bulgarian merchants and politicians were openly hostile to German demands. They not only rejected the principles of Germany's race war, but they were openly concerned about becoming a "colony" of Germany. Articles in trade publications like *Sofiiski tŭrgovski vestnik* (*Sofia Trade Journal*) insisted that Bulgarian Jews, who kept and invested their capital at home, were preferable to German merchants, who took their profits out of Bulgaria.[31] With public opinion in mind, Bulgaria officially played no part in Germany's efforts to Aryanize trade until officially entering the war in 1941. In the meantime, Reemstma, apparently under Nazi influence, dropped Asseoff's contract in 1937. The lack of German business meant that Asseoff quickly reoriented his business toward tobacco trade with the United States, France, and the United Kingdom. The UK in particular continued to pursue trade relations with Bulgaria with a decidedly diplomatic objective, aggressively seeking ways to expand its role in Bulgaria's Oriental tobacco trade market as a way to counter German influence in the region.[32] This was something that German tobacco trade journals watched closely and with concern.[33] As time would tell, British efforts were too little too late, as Germany remained Bulgaria's predominant trade partner. In the short term, though, trade with the West allowed Asseoff a continued source of revenue while he slowly began moving capital out of the country in preparation for his eventual departure.

Bulgarian Gold

As Asseoff and other Jewish merchants were cut out of the Bulgarian-German tobacco trade, Bulgarian merchants like Stoian and Alexandŭr Chaprashikov, Todor Radev, Kiril Bozhkov, and Takvor Takvorian stepped in. According to Rusi Genev, some of them were exceedingly duplicitous, accepting commercial favors from their friend and colleague Asseoff while whispering anti-Semitic platitudes in a servile manner to the Germans behind his back.[34] New firms mushroomed during this period, many of them staffed by Bulgarian political and military figures, anxious to take advantage of the golden opportunity in the rapidly expanding German tobacco market.[35] As the beginning of the war definitively cut off overseas trade routes, Bulgaria became the primary supplier of Oriental tobaccos to the German cigarette industry and to occupied or quisling New Europe. Virtually every war-time issue of the German SA newspaper, *Die SA,* included full-page ads for tobacco featuring pastoral scenes in the Bulgarian countryside, emblematic of relative peace and escape.[36] For the German and Austrian tobacco merchants and experts who spent much of the war in Bulgaria, it was by no means a hardship post. In Dimov's *Tiutiun,* Reemstma's Kurt Wenkel is immortalized as the character Von Gauer, with his Austrian counterpart Likhtenfeld depicted in the novel as Lerkhtenfeld. For Von Gauer and Lerkhtenfeld, Bulgaria is a playground where they spend as much time womanizing, drinking, hunting and frequenting Bulgarian cabarets as attending to business.[37] While Lerkhtenfeld indulges in orgies in the provinces, Von Gauer has an affair with the glamorous but tragic Bulgarian antiheroine Irina, a fallen woman. In Dimov's novel, German and Bulgarian merchants live a life of luxury amid wartime deprivation, in sharp contrast to the appalling condition of tobacco workers. For Germans, Bulgaria perhaps represented a kind of escape, where the horrors of war and Nazi Party discipline were fairly distant. Unlike at home, Nazi officers could enjoy evenings of jazz in the smoky nightclubs of Sofia without political fallout.[38]

Smoking was still allowed in Germany, but it was widely stigmatized by the Nazi leadership. With the purity of the German body at stake, the Nazi Party conducted the "world's most powerful antismoking campaign" in this period.[39] Hitler in fact attributed his success and rise to power to his own breaking of the habit.[40] A legion of pro-Nazi doctors and scientists carried out groundbreaking research that for the first time conclusively linked tobacco to cancer. Nazi theorists associated tobacco and the disease with cultural degeneracy and, predictably, with "Jewish capitalism."[41] They also traced its potential ill effects for German men as soldiers and women as reproducers. An avalanche of measures restricted smoking in public places, eliminated cigarette rations for women, and raised taxes on tobacco products. A deluge of antismoking "scientific" literature and congresses was supplemented by quit-smoking programs and even the introduction of special stop-smoking gums. But in spite of these efforts, the rise in smoking rates in Germany continued unabated, rising from 512 cigarettes per capita in 1935 to 1,022 in 1940![42] No matter how loudly the Nazi voices railed against smoking, Reemstma continued to do business as usual, and business was booming. Phillip Reemstma rejected the call of Bernhard Kohler, head of the Nazi Party's Economic Policy Commission, to start slowly converting cigarette factories to munitions. The request was linked to policy goals of both ramping up war production and reducing smoking among Germans. Reemstma, in a ten-page letter of protest, defended tobacco as a substance and pointed to the larger foreign policy significance of maintaining the tobacco-importing relationship with Bulgaria.[43] Ultimately Reemstma's arguments won out, and tobacco continued to secure German dominance in Bulgarian trade. At the same time, the Nazi desire to create a nonsmoking *Übermensch* (Superman) was subordinated to the war effort, which required the funds that tobacco trade and taxes—as well as Reemstma donations—brought into Nazi coffers. As in Bulgaria, tobacco taxes and trade were important sources of revenue for the Nazi war effort, an estimated one-twelfth of German national income in 1941.[44] In addition, forcing Germans to quit smoking, especially men—who presumably needed the comfort of smoking at the front—was simply a political impossibility.[45] Still, only a few top Nazis, like Hermann Göring, smoked publicly, and smoking was ardently discouraged among Nazi Party members; the notorious SS were even banned from smoking on duty. Quite ahead of their time, the Nazis banned all public smoking by 1943.

This was quite the opposite of the state of affairs in Bulgaria. The Bulgarian Ministry of Trade, in fact, was concerned with the Nazis' attempts to limit smoking, which would lessen their demand for tobacco imports. The ministry assumed these attempts were primarily for financial reasons, though it noted that the propaganda pointed to social and political rationales. With some alarm, it noted that "these measures of the German government are of interest to us…because they will inescapably affect our importation of raw tobacco into Germany." At the same time the ministry was reassured by the fact that German smoking had increased by 10 percent in 1939.[46] In Bulgaria itself, only isolated antismoking articles appeared in the Bulgarian press, all with open references to Nazi literature and congresses on the subject.[47] But generally the antismoking lobby, which had grown in strength between the world wars, was actively suppressed in Bulgaria during the war years. Abstinence associations and newspapers were closed down and censured, their members watched by wartime authorities. The reason for this was not, as might be assumed, the efforts of the tobacco industry lobby but rather the politically suspect nature of these associations in the wartime political climate. For without exception, the abstinence movement in this period was peopled by Bulgarian Protestants under direct American missionary tutelage or by left-leaning communists with clear Soviet connections. Moreover, as in Germany and around the world, smoking was sinking more deeply into daily practice as soldiers, workers, and the general populace got regular cigarette rations. Across Europe tobacco was becoming more and more golden.

This gold played an important role in bringing Bulgaria finally and fatefully into war on the Axis side in 1941. Admittedly Bulgaria had dynastic as well as cultural and commercial links to Germany in the late 1930s, along with a shared bitterness about the outcome of World War I. Still, entering war on the German side was hardly a foregone conclusion, and Bulgarian statesmen under the royal dictatorship of Tsar Boris (since 1935) struggled to stay neutral for as long as possible.[48] But the conclusive onset of war in Europe in 1939 made neutrality increasingly difficult. Attempts to avoid engagement were typified by the tsar's famous quote from the period, "My army is pro-German, my wife is Italian, my people are pro-Russian, I alone am Bulgarian."[49] Ultimately Germany offered the best possibility for satisfying Bulgarian revanchist desires. Bulgaria's appetite was whetted with the preemptive gift of southern Dobrudja, transferred from Romania under German pressure on September 7, 1940. More important, only Germany was able to promise Bulgaria the territories of Thrace and Macedonia. Bulgarians, and especially its large populations of former refugees from these regions, had deep emotional ties to them. But it was also extremely important that these regions produced tobacco of a quality and quantity that exceeded those of tobacco grown in Bulgaria proper. If tobacco was gold, Thrace and Macedonia were definitely gold mines. After signing the Tripartite Pact on March 1, 1941, Bulgaria followed German troops into Yugoslavia and parts of Greek Macedonia and western Thrace. By April, only Salonika—the prime port city in the region with some fifty thousand Jews, the largest concentration in the region—and its environs remained in German hands. As bitter a pill as the loss of Salonika was to swallow, Bulgarians were still euphoric when their troops marched into the rest of Thrace and Macedonia. This territory included the Aegean port city of Kavala, more of an active tobacco depot than Salonika and a respectable consolation prize. But before taking over these areas, the regime also offered a major political concession to Nazi Germany.

A mere four days after the transfer of Dobrudja but still almost a month before signing the Axis pact, the Bulgarian government published its official proposal for the infamous LDN. The law was drafted by Alexandŭr Belev, who came to play a key role in anti-Semitic legislation and actions in wartime Bulgaria. Belev was a member of the small but vocal association called Ratnik (Warrior), one of a very few anti-Semitic organizations in Bulgaria in this period. Ratnik had been established in 1936 to prepare the ground in Bulgaria for Hitler's "new order."[50] Until 1940, these organizations were kept in close check by Tsar Boris and were even considered political opponents of the parties that cooperated closely with his regime. In 1940, however, a clear shift was indicated with Boris's appointment of Bogdan Filov, a known Germanophile, as prime minister and Petŭr Gabrovski, a Ratnik member, as minister of the interior. Belev, a lawyer and close associate of Gabrovski, was dispatched to Berlin in the same year to study the Nuremburg laws and draft a version suitable for Bulgaria.[51] The Bulgarian law was almost identical to its German counterpart in its call for the disenfranchisement of Jews and its limitation of Jewish professional life in Bulgaria through occupational restrictions and *numerus clausus* ("closed number," or educational or occupational limits for Jews). The most glaring difference, and one that was amended in 1942, was that Jews were defined by religion in the LDN, not by blood or race. This and other exceptions made the Bulgarian law considerably more flexible, though it was still an unmitigated disaster for Bulgaria's Jewish community.[52] To a large degree, the announcement of the law was tantamount to a declaration of Bulgaria's political loyalty to Germany. This loyalty, however, was tempered by vocal opposition from the outset.

The Law of the Defense of the Nation was hotly debated in the Bulgarian parliament, which received a flurry of telegrams, letters, and delegations in the months after it was proposed. These protests are still the pride of Bulgarian historians and citizens and have been collected and published in numerous books on the subject.[53] A wide range of Bulgarian and Jewish social actors sent in letters, from occupational associations to the Holy Synod of the Orthodox Church, from famous persons to the tobacco workers of Plovdiv. The latter wrote, "We energetically protest against the Law of the Defense of the Nation, which brings alarm to and tries to take away the last dry morsel from the mouths of our Jewish colleagues. These patriotic Jewish tobacco workers, who work shoulder to shoulder with us in this sector of the national economy, deserve a more humane treatment and guarantees of the same."[54] Here the left-leaning tobacco workers relied on arguments that stressed Jewish patriotism as well as their contribution to the national economy. These types of arguments spanned the political spectrum, though they were used most frequently by the Bulgarian Left. The Communist Party, which had been illegal since 1925, was able to show its public face during the short-lived German-Soviet alliance of 1939–41, precisely the period when the LDN was introduced. Communist delegates in the Bulgarian parliament launched attacks on the "real robbers" of national wealth, namely, the Bulgarian bourgeois and the Germans. According to the communists, the German-allied, Bulgarian bourgeoisie harbored purely "economic motives"—that is, the confiscation of Jewish properties—and were using the law to divert attention from their exploitation of the masses.[55] In hindsight, there was more than a grain of truth in these astute observations. As Gabrovski openly suggested, the law "opened up economic horizons" for Bulgarians.[56]

The promise of profit seemed to have attracted very few supporters of anti-Semitic legislation in the short term, but opportunism eventually reared its ugly head. While most workers' and petty trade associations openly protested the LDN, the Union of Tobacco Merchants was one of the few organizations to actually express support.[57] The union in its enthusiasm even called for the immediate replacement of Jewish traders with Bulgarians ones, a striking reversal from earlier resistance to German colonial domination. This enthusiasm extended beyond the tobacco industry, as expressed in a communiqué of Bulgarian industrialists: "The time has finally arrived for the Bulgarian economy, that huge, vital current which nourished the people and the state, to be exclusively in Bulgarian hands."[58] But while many were openly supportive of the anti-Semitic law, many tobacco merchants later secretly offered moral support to Jewish friends and colleagues.[59] Major Jewish traders like Asseoff had already been pushed out of export trade with Germany. Consequently the LDN affected mostly smaller-scale Jewish merchants. In fact, the resultant new economic opportunities for Bulgarians were exceedingly sparse, not enough to create widespread support for the LDN at this juncture. Furthermore, the bulk of the population simply did not see Jews as a threat to Bulgarian society, and anti-Semitism met with almost no popular response in Bulgaria.[60] For one thing, Jews made up a relatively small portion of the population, less than 1 percent, and they were fairly well acculturated into Bulgarian society. In addition, other ethnic groups—namely, Turks (and in a different way Roma), were far more likely to be perceived as a contemporary threat in the Bulgarian national imagination. One parliamentarian argued against the law on just these grounds: "In Bulgaria there are half a million Turks who represent a bigger danger for the nation than the Jewish minority."[61] The perception of a Turkish threat, however, was not connected to their role in tobacco industry.

While support for the LDN was not universal, a vocal anti-Semitic minority played an important role in pushing it through parliament. The fascist Ratniks were clearly influenced directly by German (and global) anti-Semitic formulations, and once in positions of power they played their role as agents of Germany with direct lines of communication to Berlin.[62] These and other proponents of the law argued that Jews controlled the most profitable branches of industry in Bulgaria and so had significant political control. As one parliamentarian, Demi Kostov, argued, Jews controlled 80 percent of the railroads and 50 percent of the tobacco industry. Kostov highlighted Asseoff's role in "earning hundreds of millions of lev" at the expense of the "blood, sweat, and suffering... of the unhappy Bulgarian peasant." Asseoff had used this money, he charged, to buy off supporters on the Right and Left and to exert considerable political control. Going further, he implicated Asseoff and many of his "entourage" in the "franco-masonic" conspiracy that wanted to control Bulgaria and the world.[63] The most prominent in this presumed conspiracy, he charged, was the right-wing parliamentarian Aleksandŭr Tsankov, whose protest of the LDN seemed to confirm his ties to Asseoff and the Masons. As Kostov railed, "Your place is in Palestine,

Mr. Professor. I will send you there with the automobile of Jacques Asseoff. You Jewish agent of Jacques Asseoff!"[64] Tsankov's resistance to the LDN was almost certainly the result of the law's targeting of Masons and other international organizations to which he belonged, though ties to Asseoff may have also played a role.

It was the Left, however, who most vociferously challenged the LDN. One communist delegate, Dimo Kazasov, in a letter of protest from November 1940 argued that in addition to "awakening the darkest instincts" in Bulgarians, the liquidation of Jewish properties would deliver a severe "blow to the Bulgarian economy."[65] In his testimony after the war, he noted that his suspicions had been correct as Jewish firms that were taken over and sold off had "fallen to waste." Ultimately Kazasov, like many others in the context of the postwar "people's court" trials, blamed German pressure for the ultimate adoption and implementation of the LDN. At the same time, however, they noted the role of "crude careerism" and Bulgarian envy of "certain rich Jews."[66] Asseoff certainly fell into the latter category, as his domestic assets came up for grabs after the passing of the LDN.

Yet as the parliamentary debates on the LDN raged, Asseoff was on his way to New York, a fact that was openly noted in the debates. This detail was used by an open opponent of the law to point out the problem of capital flight:

LIUBEN DIUGMEDZHIEV: But who helped Jacques Asseoff get his millions out of Bulgaria?

IVAN GŬRKOV: Bulgarians who were bought off.

LIUBEN DIUGMEDZHIEV: Find them and punish them. But you will do nothing. . . . Look into it and find out who is responsible for allowing the millions of Jacques Asseoff and Angel Kuiumdzhiiski [another prominent Jewish tobacco merchant] to be taken out of Bulgaria. But that is not the real question. Bulgarian millionaires are waxing their palms for the chance to drop their million-dollar fishing poles into these murky waters and hook some Jewish capital. I ask you: how many Jews even have such capital? Our existing laws are fine to regulate them. But the others, the majority of Jews live in poverty.

CHAIRMAN NIKOLA LOGOFETOV: Finish, Mr. Diugmedzhiev.

LIUBEN DIUGMEDZHIEV: I am finishing. Have you been to Iuchbunar [Sofia's Jewish quarter], along Pozitano Street? Do you know the miserable situation in which these people live, which in no ways inhibits the Bulgarian economy, hardly allowing for a loaf of black bread to be brought to the family? If you have the desire to limit the

participation of Jews in our economic life, so we won't be totally
controlled by them, I ask who are guilty among these poor Jews,
who represent 95 percent of the Jewish masses; why do you pursue
them? I maintain that even if the question is one of speculative capitalists, there are also Bulgarian capitalists-speculators.

IVAN GŬRKOV: Their turn will also come.[67]

Gŭrkov's words were an odd foreshadowing of the postwar communist
transformation. But as far as Diugmedzhiev was concerned, the Bulgarian
bourgeoisie was to blame for the capital flight of rich Jews like Asseoff
(and Kuiumdzhiiski). More pointedly, he implied that only a few Bulgarian
capitalist-speculators would benefit from the LDN, noting the utter poverty
in which most of the Jewish community lived. As for Asseoff, Diugmedzhiev
was scarcely concerned with his role in the Bulgarian economy, past or present. Instead, his focus was on Bulgarian millionaires who wanted to "hook
Jewish capital" or accept payoffs. Though Asseoff did get out of Bulgaria
with significant assets, he lost many more that were left behind in Bulgaria
and appropriated after the LDN was passed in January of 1941. Asseoff's
Balkantabak with its millions of lev in assets was dismantled in the years that
followed. But the documents that detail the dismantling of the firm and its
transfer to a Bulgarian owner, a certain Asen Ivanov Pobornikov, were not
processed until December of 1942. This attests to the very drawn-out nature
of Bulgaria's actual implementation of the law.

Incessant complaints about Bulgarian laxity, in fact, had prompted the
dispatch of a new German consul—Adolph Bekerle, a high-ranking SA offi-
cer in the Nazi Party—in July of 1941 to put more direct pressure on the
Bulgarians to enforce their anti-Jewish legislation. Over the next eighteen
months a series of laws and decrees called for enforcement of the LDN as well
as additional measures, including the redefinition of Jewishness as a racial
rather than religious category. In addition, Bulgarian authorities imposed a
special 20 percent tax on all Jewish possessions, while a wide range of real
estate and industrial properties were confiscated. Preliminary provisions were
also made to mark Jewish businesses and homes with signs and clothing
with a yellow star. In practice, however, the enforcement of many of these
measures—in particular the wearing of the yellow star—was quite difficult.
By October of 1942 only 20 percent of Bulgarian Jews had been provided
with stars, the smallest number by far in Eastern Europe.[68]

On the other hand, financial appropriations and property confiscation
were pursued with gusto.[69] By a decree of August 1942 the Commissariat of Jewish Affairs (CJA) was created under the leadership of Alexandŭr

Belev, the aforementioned lawyer (and openly anti–Semitic Ratnik) who had drafted the LDN. Belev presided over a legion of some seventy-six clerks—most of them lawyers and accountants—who were charged with the massive freezing and appropriation of Jewish property and the coordination of other anti-Jewish measures.[70] Given the draconian and inhumane range of activities that were included in CJA affairs, including mass deportations of Jews from Thrace and Macedonia, it is unsettling that the job was directed mainly by a bunch of legal and financial professionals. In the postwar trials for crimes connected to CJA activities, most of the employees claimed they were involved only on the "technical" end of things and had taken the jobs primarily for the money. And there was a lot of money to be made by CJA employees, who took massive bribes and fees to help Jews elude oppressive legislation. The payola would only increase in the course of the war years, as Jewish fortunes and homes were dismantled and desperate Jewish families offered bribes for exit visas to Palestine. As elsewhere in Eastern Europe, the distribution of Jewish properties, even petty goods, was a way in which the CJA could implicate common Bulgarians in its insidious policies, while buying support on the local level. While the participation of local Bulgarians in such a process requires further research, it is certain that Belev and many of his associates inside and outside the CJA made vast fortunes on the appropriation of Jewish property. Much of the estimated billions of lev taken from Jewish individuals and organizations was used to directly pay CJA salaries and fund their activities on the ground. Jewish money was used to further persecute Jews.[71]

As Diugmedzhiev pointed out in the parliamentary debates, however, 95 percent of Jews were destitute. As such they offered little booty for what one Jewish witness in the postwar trials, Isak Frantsez, called the "organized official robberies" by the CJA.[72] Asseoff's Balkantabak, on the other hand was the largest tobacco concern in Bulgaria. At the time of liquidation, the firm's assets were worth some 65 million lev, including 16 million in cash, 7 million in tobacco, and the rest in various movable and immovable properties.[73] Eighty-three percent of these assets were in Jacques Asseoff's name, with another 16.3 percent in the names of his brothers (Iakob, Haim, and Uriel) and the rest in the name of Asen Pobornikov, an apparent Bulgarian "partner" of sorts and now the "buyer" of the property. By the time of the liquidation by the CJA employee Boian Zlatarov, the firm was reportedly inactive, a result of the firing of almost all Jewish employees in October of 1942. Although Pobornikov was presumably going to buy the firm in installments, it is quite clear that the money never made it into the hands of the Asseoffs, who were already in the United States and purportedly owed millions of lev in taxes and fees to the Bulgarian state—most conspicuously, the 20 percent Jewish property tax. Asseoff also supposedly owed a certain bank the "security money" that guaranteed the load of tobacco that had accompanied him to America in late 1940. In short, given the gargantuan list of taxes and fees, on paper Asseoff did not own any of the assets that were appropriated by the CJA.[74]

As the CJA began to conclude its work on confiscation and the enforcement of other Jewish measures in old Bulgaria and the newly occupied territories, more ominous measures loomed. In January of 1943, the SS captain Theodore Dannecker came to Bulgaria as a special representative of Adolph Eichmann to begin negotiations with Belev about the deportation of Bulgarian Jews to occupied Poland. A year earlier Nazi officials had announced the Final Solution at the famous Wannsee Conference outside of Berlin. By the winter of 1943 Bulgaria was expected to comply with this larger Nazi objective.

From Dust to Ash

Bulgaria's occupation of western Thrace and most of Macedonia in the spring of 1941 was followed by a wave of national euphoria at home. Tsar Boris was hailed as the "Tsar Obedinitel" (Tsar Unifier) as preparations were made to integrate these "liberated" territories into their presumed rightful homeland. Technically, however, the territories remained zones of German occupation and appeared as administratively separate from Bulgaria on German maps. Although this fact annoyed Bulgarian officials, it didn't stop them from administering these territories as if the annexation were permanent, and Bulgarian citizens certainly saw it that way. In the region itself, a portion of the "Bulgarian" (or Macedonian-Slavic) populations initially welcomed the occupying forces with open arms, but many were quickly disillusioned by the dominance of Sofia over local affairs. For the Jews, the occupation was understandably unwelcome, as the German troops who led it sacked their shops and businesses, ruining Jews economically within a matter of days.[75] In addition, the Law for the Defense of the Nation was immediately announced and gradually implemented on the local level. Certainly Jews who ended up under adjacent Albanian-Italian territories fared better (and many Jews fled there), but direct German occupation in Salonika and environs was also a potentially worse fate.[76]

While Jews were being rapidly pushed out of trade and industry in the cities and towns of Thrace and Macedonia, rural areas were being Bulgarianized through a variety of means. Beginning in 1941, the regime offered land, free passage, and free medical care to people of "Bulgarian descent" willing to settle in the occupied zones.[77] In general, the occupation brought intense state campaigns against foreign presences broadly defined, including communists after Germany went to war against the Soviet Union in April 1941. And while repression increased in Bulgaria proper, in certain respects the occupied territories were more of a security concern as the regime's hold on these regions was more tenuous.[78] In large part, the imperative to keep order in the occupied territories was linked to their critical economic importance. With the occupation of Thrace and Macedonia, Bulgarian production of tobacco, or Bulgarian gold, doubled overnight, and Bulgaria virtually obtained a natural monopoly over Oriental tobaccos.[79]

Germans were directly involved in the appropriation and reshaping of the industry for wartime needs, even appointing a temporary Commissar for Tobacco in 1941. A certain Bilovitski, who assumed this post, had lavish apartments across the region and even took over Asseoff's former villa outside Sofia.[80] Probably a Slav of some Habsburg stripe, he was a former employee of the Austrian Tobacco Régie (state monopoly) and also the son-in-law of the German finance minister. Bilovitski, along with Wenkel, rode out the war with his relatively safe and profitable post in Bulgaria. The wartime tobacco sector was undoubtedly lucrative for a small coterie of German and Bulgarian merchants precisely because private enterprise was put under tight government control. This meant, that only government-approved merchants could make tobacco purchases for prices set by Germany.[81] For those on the approved list, profits were astronomical as peasant growers were paid sums that were artificially low, especially given the hyperinflation that made basic supplies so hard to procure.[82]

A host of measures brought about the rapid Bulgarianization of the industry in the course of wartime confiscations. In the former Yugoslavia, Germany declared all tobacco-processing facilities "war booty," since before the war they had been under the umbrella of a state monopoly. Subsequently, tobacco concerns were put under the private control of state-approved Bulgarian experts and merchants, which effectively put Bulgarians into key positions in the industry.[83] In contrast to the former Yugoslav lands, the formerly Greek territories of eastern Macedonia and western Thrace were in private hands before the war, a situation that required more careful negotiation with prewar interests. Though many Greek traders fled immediately after occupation, Bulgarians continued to work with local Greek merchants, factory owners, and workers. Their labor and local knowledge were simply too important to lose, especially since Jews were being pushed out by the LDN and other legislation. Macedonian and Thracian Jews, with Salonika as their traditional mother-city, were deeply imbedded in the industry at all phases, even more than in Bulgaria itself, as exporters, clerks, factory owners, and workers.[84] These networks began to slowly unravel as Jews were pushed out of the upper and middle echelons of the industry after 1941. And certainly the loss of their labor and coordination added to the challenge of putting the industry into overdrive to meet the overwhelming demand, what one Bulgarian author called the "tobacco hunger" of New Europe.[85] But the elimination of Jews also facilitated Bulgarian-German domination of the industry.

Not surprisingly, tobacco entrepreneurs and experts from Bulgaria and Germany descended on the region, expanding cultivation, requisitioning tobacco warehouses and factories, and opening new ones.[86] A tobacco institute was set up in the town of Drama for the development and diffusion of technologies for growing, cultivating, and processing.[87] Labor was relatively scarce in the region and in factories, like the cigarette factory Pobeda (Victory) in Kavala, the director incessantly complained about the need for more trained personnel from Bulgaria. Since the tobacco industry was considered an industry mobilized for war, men were often sent to work in its factories in lieu of military service. The bulk of tobacco, some 80 percent annually, was exported to Germany and other Axis states. But as required by law, the remaining 20 percent was kept for domestic consumption, to supply (tax-free) cigarettes for the Bulgarian and German troops stationed in Bulgaria or adjacent regions, as well as rations for domestic civilians.[88] Cigarettes were also regularly offered as gifts to visiting German officers, officials, and consuls. Tobacco seemed to undergird or, more aptly, lubricate the workings and daily politics of war. More important, supplying smokes kept many people relatively satisfied with their lot, whether they were on the top or bottom of the social ladder.

Keeping the peace domestically, in and outside the industry, was certainly a critical goal of Bulgarian statesmen in this period. Though working conditions remained deplorable during the war, there were concerted efforts on the part of the state-directed industry to improve conditions and keep workers relatively satisfied. Worker unrest was curbed by wage hikes and other measures, like the opening of factory cafeterias, a special ration of ten cigarettes a day, and wages to cover seasonal unemployment.[89] This along with modest hikes in tobacco prices meant the end of most urban strikes and rural protest until the fall of 1944.[90] But the proverbial stick was undoubtedly more of a determining factor than the carrot. Significantly, the tobacco proletariat and peasant growers, though often in conflict, had comprised one of the most organized and mobilized segments of workers and peasants in interwar Bulgaria.[91] After a mass strike of thirty thousand tobacco workers in the spring of 1940, the government passed the draconian law of "citizen mobilization." From this point on all strikes or labor organization would be punishable by a prison sentence. This meant the dissolution of most work- ers' and growers' associations (though not growers' cooperatives) and the eventual internment of labor leaders in camps.[92] As a result, strikes and other political activity tended to die down during the war, and resistance move- ments within old Bulgaria were exceedingly weak. Still, communist tobacco workers played a major role in the existing organized resistance; an estimated 80 percent of all partisans and political prisoners during the war were tobacco laborers.[93]

In spite of the relative social calm, state fears were heightened by the first act of terrorist sabotage to be carried out in wartime Bulgaria, com- mitted in October of 1941 by Jewish activist, Leon Tadzher.[94] Later, in February of 1943, Bulgarian General Lukov—leader of the right-wing officers association the Legionaries—was killed by a Jewish partisan, Vio- leta Iakova. This incident in particular was used to spark an anti-Semitic campaign in the press.[95] The perception of Jews as a potential source of resistance had special significance in the occupied territories. Jewish intellectuals and activists had been long involved in labor unions and associations, particularly among tobacco workers in Thrace and Mace- donia. In fact, tobacco workers—Jewish or non-Jewish—in this region exceeded those in Bulgaria before the war, in both numbers and scale of labor organization.[96] The authorities certainly viewed Jews as a potential hotbed of resistance, and the fact that they had been pushed out of the tobacco industry did little to alleviate such fears, given the fact that they had been left idle and bitter. While this was also the situation in Bulgaria proper, Thrace and Macedonia had the added threat of relative proxim- ity to the largest and most-organized communist resistance movements in Europe, centered in occupied Greece and Yugoslavia. The majority of Jews were by no means communists, but a visible minority did join the movement, notably out of proportion to their percentage of the total population.[97]

All of this became significant when German pressure for Jewish deporta- tion come to bear in the spring of 1943. Since the Wannsee Conference in 1942, the Germans had been putting pressure on Bulgaria to move forward toward finding a solution to the Jewish question on Bulgarian soil. Belev's Jewish Commissariat actively planned such measures for the near future, though other Bulgarian authorities continually cited their need for Jewish labor as an overriding obstacle. With the arrival of Dannecker in January of 1943, a series of negotiations resulted in the only written "contract" in the history of the Holocaust. The famous agreement signed by Dannecker and Belev on February 22, 1943, promised that Bulgaria would "provide" twenty thousand Jews to the Germans for labor in the "new territories" of eastern Poland. Specifically, these Jews would consist of the approximately twelve thousand Jews of Thrace and Macedonia and another eight thousand hand-selected "undesirable" Jews—rich, influential, or politically suspect— from old Bulgaria.[98] The Bulgarian government approved the agreement on March 2, 1943, and the first *Aktsia* (Action) took place on March 4 in the formerly Greek territories of western Thrace and eastern Macedonia (or, in Bulgarian, Belomorie).

At four o-clock on the subzero morning of March 4, 1943, towns were blockaded across Belomorie. Soldiers and local police, coordinated by representatives from the CJA in Sofia, went to cities and towns with Jewish populations—Drama, Kavala, Ksanti, Seres, Giumiurdzhina, Dedgedatch— and knocked on doors, banking on the element of surprise.[99] Families were given thirty minutes to vacate their homes and each family member was allowed to take personal possessions weighing no more than 40 kilograms.[100] They were told they were being moved to old Bulgaria for use in labor brigades, but it is unclear how many Jews actually believed this. They were taken on foot, by horse cart, or by truck to local collection points, or camps. Almost without exception these were tobacco warehouses, which were the largest buildings in these tobacco depot towns. Because March was considered off season for tobacco processing, they would have been mostly empty, with the last year's harvest sold off and that year's yet to come in.

The Jews of Belomorie were held in these camps for several days and then transported by open truck or cattle car to collection points within southwest Bulgaria—Kuistendil, Dupnitsa, Gorna Djumaya, and Radomir. Coincidentally these were all tobacco towns, and again tobacco warehouses were used as temporary holding camps. Here internees were held for two weeks amid the ubiquitous, suffocating tobacco dust, sleeping on concrete floors and on the convenient bunklike wooden tobacco-drying platforms.[101] In Gorna Djumaya the warehouse of Anton Rainov housed 2,980 Jews, with one toilet for every 300–500 people.[102] In Kuistendil Jews were interned in the Fernandes factory, once owned by the Asseoff family.[103] In Dupnitsa, 1,460 Jews were packed into the four-story cartel tobacco warehouse, which had two toilets and one water tap. The conditions were miserable, and local Jews were prevented from providing supplies to internees. Ivan Popov, the commissariat official in charge of setting up a temporary camp in Radomir, was assigned an older, abandoned tobacco warehouse to house the internees. In his postwar trial he testified that the windows were broken out and he could "not imagine children staying there." He claimed to have had the windows replaced to protect against the subzero temperatures and to have had the building cleaned and supplies purchased for the internees before they came.[104] Popov was undoubtedly trying to portray himself in the best possible light before his accusers. Still, according to Jewish testimonies, Bulgarian behavior toward the deportees ranged from cruel to more accommodating. In many cases Bulgarians actively intervened to help Jews. In one instance a gentile tobacco merchant from Dupnitsa, Boris Dimitŭr Ushev, who lived next door to a tobacco warehouse camp, intervened on behalf of a nine-year-old orphaned Jewish girl, for whom he found a home with a Jewish family in Plovdiv.[105] But because the deportations were conducted quickly, in a surprise fashion, and mostly outside Bulgaria proper, no immediate actions were taken to stop them.

At the same time, commissariat officials were preparing orders for the arrest and deportations of the eight thousand undesirable Bulgarian Jews covered in the Belev-Dannecker agreement. Significantly, however, there was no effort to individually identify and extract 8,000 undesirables from across Bulgaria. Instead, specific towns were chosen for total clearance, most often the very collection points where Jews from Thrace and Macedonia were still being interred, like Dupnitsa and Kiustendil. The plan might have been to simply coordinate these deportations with the others, using the same tobacco warehouse collection points, the same train lines, the same police. But it was probably no accident that other randomly selected towns, like Plovdiv and Pleven, were also major centers for tobacco production, collection, and export. They were also all conveniently located along railroad lines that led to Danubian port cities. It was to one of these ports, namely Lom, that Thracian Jews were sent by train after their two-week internment in the tobacco depots of the Bulgarian southwest. On March 19 the Jews of Belomorie were loaded onto four barges in Lom and sent up the Danube to Vienna and then on to Auschwitz. Ironically, they followed the path of tobacco export; they arrived in Auschwitz and Treblinka reeking of tobacco.

Within old Bulgaria, and internationally, the deportations provoked a flurry of protests, letters, telegrams, and delegations. As with the Law of the Defense of Nation, a broad range of actors witnessed or found out about deportations, and concrete actions followed. The Orthodox Church, Bulgarian professional organizations, domestic Jewish associations, and most important, some highly placed Bulgarian politicians began to actively seek intervention on the highest levels. Although public mobilization was too late for the Jews of Belomorie and the rest of Macedonia, the deportations of undesirable Jews from old Bulgaria were literally stopped in their tracks on March 10. In some cases, as in Plovdiv, Jews had been already arrested and rounded up on the evening of March 9, only to be let go the next morning when official orders canceling the deportations finally made their way to Plovdiv. The field of public protest was broad, but the main center of political action was Kiustendil, where witnesses to the transports reported the situation to their representative in parliament, Dimitŭr Peshev. Peshev drew up a massive petition signed by forty-three members of parliament, including an impressive array of government figures like Aleksandŭr Tsankov. He also actively confronted Gabrovski and other high-ranking government officials until the deportation orders were finally canceled. But others had also witnessed and protested against the transports of Jews through Bulgaria, most notably the Sofia Metropolitan, Stefan. Stefan, who saw the Jewish internees while passing through Dupnitsa on his way to the Rila monastery, wrote a personal letter of protest to Tsar Boris, implying that the tsar would "go to hell" if he allowed Bulgaria's Jews to be deported.[106] A variety of factors were at play, but the efforts of Peshev, Stefan, and many others had the important and permanent result of stopping the deportation of Jews from old Bulgaria.

But international factors were also significant. Jacques Asseoff, from his new residence in New York, personally played an important role. Numerous sources point to the importance of the Bulgarian-American Committee that he founded in the fall of 1942. Tirelessly working to get moral and diplomatic support from every possible corner, Asseoff worked with Jews across the Americas, especially Latin American Sephardic organizations, as well as with Jews in Palestine and the World Jewish Congress.[107] He wrote letters and met with Swiss diplomats while launching radio campaigns in the West informing people of the deportations that had been carried out and were being planned in Bulgaria.[108] At the same time he coordinated broadcasts four times daily to Bulgaria from New York, London, Cairo, and Bari during the critical month of March 1943, imploring Bulgarians to save the Jews. One such broadcast consisted of the following:

> In today's fateful times, of major historical significance, the vital interests of Bulgaria are close to our hearts here in America. That is why we are appealing to all Bulgarians who love their homeland to do everything in their power to impede the horrible fate of the Bulgarian people. Don't forget that you will be responsible for all collaboration with the Germans. Be rid of the horrific Jewish laws, for which there is no forgiveness or redemption. Get rid of the inhuman regime.... Don't forget that Mr. Roosevelt, president of the United States of America,

proclaimed unequivocally that the behavior of enemy countries toward
their Jewish minorities will be taken into account when the fate of
these states is decided. No excuses will be taken into account as justi-
fication for ill treatment of Jews.[109]

Here Asseoff appealed to Bulgarians as patriots as well as to their basic sense of
humanity. But he also warned of a day of reckoning, trying to inspire fear of
punishment in addition to other more positive human impulses. Such fears certainly haunted some members of the Bulgarian elite as an Axis victory became
ever more unlikely by 1943. But at the same time the participants and narratives
of protest against deportations in 1943 were quite similar to the cast of characters and script from the 1941 LDN debates. This continuity suggests the sincer-
ity and bravery involved in the Bulgarian remonstrations against deportations.

At the same time it must be kept in mind that only "Bulgarian citizens"
were saved by the halt of the deportation orders on March 9–10. Unfortunately, the Jews of Thrace and Macedonia had never been extended Bulgarian
citizenship. As the Jews of Thrace were on their way to Auschwitz, the Jews
of Macedonia also faced quick and effective deportation measures beginning
on March 11. In towns across the region, blockades were again set up and the
same process was carried out against Jews who had lived in the region since
the sixteenth century. In Skopje the Jewish quarter was sealed, and 3,943
Jews were arrested and marched off to the Monopole tobacco warehouse,
the former property of the Yugoslav tobacco monopoly.[110] Under the cover
of night 3,342 Jews were brought from Bitola and put into the same compound.[111] This came to be known as the "tobacco camp," where inmates had
to live and breathe as the "the galling stench of tobacco permeated the skin,
the hair, the bones."[112] According to the testimony of one survivor, Avram
Tadzher, at one point a child looked out the window "for a moment to forget
the unbearable tobacco dust in the warehouse" and was shot.[113]

After two weeks of internment, on March 24–29, 7,144 Macedonian
Jews were taken straight to Treblinka in three cargo-train transports without
passing through old Bulgaria and without riding on ships up the Danube
as had the Thracian Jews.[114] The choice of this route was undoubtedly a
strategic decision, a way to avoid alarm or the rallying of more opposition
from Bulgarians who continued to fight for the Jews in old Bulgaria. But
few voices of protest were raised for Macedonian Jews, who were outside
of the legal institutional parameters of Bulgaria proper. Silence about the
fate of these Jews—many of whom had assimilated into interwar Greek and
Serbian culture—was the price paid for saving the Bulgarian Jews of the old
kingdom, a negotiation that was still in progress.

Within Bulgaria itself the fight was far from over in the spring of 1943. Bulgarian and Jewish opposition to deportations continued, and the respite was generally seen as temporary. In fact, Belev continued to ply the Germans with promises of an eventual solution, and on March 21 he issued an order for the Jews of Sofia and other Bulgarian cities to be deported to towns in the Bulgarian countryside.[115] In spite of protests, Sofia's Jews were expelled, and most lived in miserable conditions in provincial towns for the rest of the war with virtually no source of livelihood. The presumed ringleaders of the protests, however, like other politically active Jews, were arrested, and twenty-four new labor camps were set up for two thousand inmates. One was in Samovit (near the Danube), and the other, the notorious Tabakova Chesma (Tobacco Fountain) was near Pleven.[116] These internal camps were in addition to concentration camps that had already been set up in 1941 for "politically suspect" Bulgarian citizens regardless of ethnicity.[117]

Jews who ended up in camps suffered far more than those in internal exile. With sparse rations, forced labor, and a generally more regulated existence, they were also separated from their families. Among other everyday inconveniences, they were not allowed to smoke cigarettes in camps or during transport.[118] This may seem a trivial matter under the circumstances, but for many being deprived of this familiar and addictive comfort was exceedingly difficult. Khaim Eshkenazi, an eyewitness to conditions in the camps, claimed in his postwar testimony that food packages were allowed in labor camps in Bulgaria, but cigarettes were not. In particular, he described the apparent agony of an old man who claimed that he could live without food but cried out all day, "Cigarettes! Cigarettes!" Cigarettes, as Eshkenazi pointed out, were the old man's last comfort, now gone.[119] It is no wonder that they were reportedly being sold in camps by profiteering Bulgarians for one hundred to two hundred lev![120] While some Bulgarians later claimed to have supplied Jews in the camps with cigarettes as a humanitarian gesture, for others it was a ready source of profit. Cigarettes came to play the role of currency in and outside camps across Europe, a phenomenon that would continue in economically devastated postwar Europe.[121]

As World War II took the lives of Macedonian and Thracian Jews, it also destroyed the social world of old Bulgaria's Jews. Sofia's Jews lost their homes, and influential Jews from across Bulgaria were stripped of commercial and personal assets and in a sense their future in Bulgaria. Thus World War II furthered not only the Bulgarianization of the tobacco industry[122] but also the unraveling of the complex ethnic tapestry of the eastern Balkans by pulling out the Jewish thread. Still, in exile or in camps, Bulgaria's Jews were able to wait out and, most important, *survive* the rest of the war.

The Dust Settles

It is unclear whether Bulgarian Jews would have survived if Axis fortunes had not turned so dramatically in the months that followed. Belev and other Bulgarian officials had implied to the Germans that the deportations to the provinces were a temporary measure and that a Final Solution was forthcoming. Belev personally was incensed that the deportations had been halted and he went forward, drafting detailed plans for their resumption. Although Tsar Boris's stand on the deportations is much less clear, many sources claim that he was the final voice in halting them. Bulgarians were stricken with grief when he mysteriously died after a visit with Hitler and other high-ranking Nazis in August of 1943. Later some posited that his stand on the Jews was the reason for his untimely death.

But Boris's death also coincided with a turn in the tides of the war; as the Axis lost ground, there was renewed hope for Bulgarian Jews. By the summer of 1943 the Germans were losing ground on the eastern front, following the fateful loss in Stalingrad in February. By August Italy had fallen to the Allies, and Germany was scrambling to cover formerly Italian occupied territories in the Balkans. Meanwhile Balkan resistance movements, especially in Yugoslavia and Greece but also in Albania and Macedonia, rapidly expanded into the power vacuum. With shake-ups in the Bulgarian government, Belev was pushed out of the Commissariat for Jewish Affairs, and under his replacement, Khristo Stomaniakov, conditions for Jews got gradually better. In the meantime, the Allies intensified negotiations with Bulgaria, and the regime slowly distanced itself from Germany.[123] From November 1943 through the spring of 1944, Allied air strikes intermittently shook Sofia and other Bulgarian cities. Thousands were killed, and many more fled to the provinces, where fear and hunger were suddenly not just a Jewish problem. At the same time, communist resistance in Bulgaria was finally gaining traction, and the regime was suddenly under attack. Communists, and particularly their partisan military *cheti* (armed bands), were by far the most active and violent opponents of the regime. Whereas there were only 180 active partisans in 1943, by the end of the summer of 1944 there were 10,000.[124] Political opposition was also coalescing—albeit somewhat uncomfortably—around the Fatherland Front, a broad coalition of oppositional groups formed in 1942 under communist leadership. In short, the Bulgarian regime was in an untenable situation: the Red Army was on its way, partisans were on the attack, and members of the government were quietly joining the Fatherland Front. Negotiations with the Allies—who were providing supplies to the partisans—continued, though Bulgaria's unwillingness to sign away Thrace and Macedonia was a serious sticking point in the conclusion of a separate peace.

Meanwhile there were dramatic changes in the government and in Jewish policy. In February of 1944, the new prime minister, Ivan Bagrianov, met with prominent Jewish leaders and assured them that the regime had a new outlook on the anti-Jewish question. By the end of August the Law of the Defense of the Nation, though curiously kept on the books, was fundamentally altered. The LDN was still applied to foreign organizations but no longer to Jews as a people. Other anti-Jewish legislation was repealed or altered, and basic rights of Jews were restored, including the freedom to travel, live, and work where they pleased. Yellow stars and other markings were abolished, as were special taxes. In addition, the Commissariat for Jewish Affairs was transformed into a Jewish-run institution, whose explicit focus was to ensure the promised restoration of confiscated properties. By this time Germany was carrying out complete evacuations of its embassy as well as pulling troops out of Bulgaria and the region.

The war was lost for Bulgaria, and last-minute changes in government and declarations of neutrality could not change that fact. Nor could they stop a Soviet invasion on September seventh. With the Red Army moving quickly through Bulgaria, political changes were inevitable. The communist-led Fatherland Front coalition took power in Sofia on September ninth· in what would later be dubbed a "people's revolution." September ninth followed a week of intense protests from many sectors of Bulgarian society, including tobacco workers, who for the first time since 1940 took to the streets calling for peace and the end of fascist rule. In Dimov's *Tiutiun,* written in the immediate postwar years, the spontaneous strikes of tobacco workers in September of 1944 were the denouement of the story. Indeed, tobacco workers were a traditional stronghold of communist influence, and partisan units had quickly formed in tobacco-growing regions.[125]

As the military and political tides in the war turned, the tobacco world was immediately inundated with change. Trains and barges of tobacco headed to Germany were abruptly halted, and now transports of Bulgarian tobacco were directed to Moscow or slated for consumption by occupying Soviet troops. One of the first acts of the Fatherland Front was the proclamation of a state tobacco monopoly and an almost doubling of tobacco prices, a boon to Bulgaria's peasant growers.[126] Furthermore, tobacco workers and growers, along with labor and cooperative organizers, claimed positions of responsibility in the new regime because of their presumed political reliability. This was in stark contrast to the situation of tobacco merchants and financiers, who became prime targets of postwar justice.

Dimov famously countered accusations about his undue focus on bourgeois merchants in *Tiutiun* by pointing out, "Before describing the bloody birth of a new world, he needed to describe the ruin of the old."[127] And the birth of the communist new world in Bulgaria was certainly bloody. Political change was immediately accompanied by political vengeance, as the guilty were identified and tried in the famous people's courts that were in session before the end of 1944. The three regents, the members of every wartime cabinet, most of the deputies of parliament, court advisers, and bureaucrats were brought to trial. Most of these trials were quickly resolved. Top officials were executed, while others were given life in prison or extended sentences. On the local level, people's courts mushroomed, and political scores were settled. In fact, it is estimated that in Bulgaria three thousand people were executed within a year, a higher percentage of the population than in any Axis state, in spite of the relatively few war crimes committed.[128] A whole set of these trials that were categorized and numbered as "process 9" indicted Bulgarians involved in the Ministry of Trade or in direct trade relations with Germany. Twenty-two tobacco merchants were indicted for their trade activities with Reemstma, which was seen as "bringing harm to the Bulgarian people."[129] But not all tobacco merchants met untimely ends.

In the famous memoirs of Stefane Groueff, *My Odyssey,* he bears witness to the lives of émigrés who managed to get out of Bulgaria before the dramatic political turn. His intimate circle of elite Bulgarian émigrés included the remnants of tobacco families in exile, those who had managed to escape. He spent ample time in those years with the remaining Chaprashikovs and the Takvorians, who lived in exile in Geneva and Paris. Through his connection to Takvor Takvorian, the Armenian merchant who had managed to escaped prosecution, Stefane was hooked up briefly with a job as a "tobacco taster," for which he eventually conceded he "was not gifted."[130] Although the young Stefane was "adopted" by the Takvorians and other rich émigrés, his family had to face a new reality in Bulgaria. His father, Pavel Groueff, a former palace adviser, was found guilty of treason. And as his fate was being decided in Sofia, Stefane placed his hopes for his father's survival on "all the Jewish friends he had helped." Indeed, his family had been part of the elite cosmopolitan world of Sofia, into which Bulgarian Jews were tightly woven. Many Bulgarians were reported to have turned to Jewish friends during these years of transition, with the assumption that all Jews would be somehow favored by the regime.[131] True, virtually no Jews were in a position to be dubbed collaborators or war profiteers, as most of them had been financially ruined or remained in exile. But certainly if Asseoff or any other prosperous Jew had returned to Bulgaria in this period, he would have met his financial (if not mortal) end, not as a Jew but as a bourgeois exploiter of the people.

Still, Bulgaria was a relatively secure, even welcoming, environment for Jews amid the immediate postwar chaos. In Bulgaria there were no pogroms or waves of anti-Semitic violence, as in Poland, Slovakia, and Hungary.[132] In addition, Bulgaria was remarkably the first state in postwar Europe to hold trials that specifically focused on wartime crimes against Jews, beginning on March 7, 1945. Elsewhere in the Soviet-occupied zone of Eastern Europe people's courts were aggressively prosecuting collaborators and war criminals of various stripes, but separate trials that highlighted crimes against Jews were still unheard of. Even the Nuremburg trials, which did not start until November of 1945, were focused on war crimes more broadly—particularly against Allied citizens—and not specifically on crimes against Jews.[133] Trials with a focus on crimes against Jews occurred only sporadically in Eastern Europe—in Hungary in 1946, in Poland in 1949, and in the Soviet Union in the 1960s.[134] In Bulgaria, in process 7 of the people's court, fifty-three defendants were brought to trials, mostly employees of the Commissariat for Jewish Affairs and a few other notorious public anti-Semites.

In the course of the trials, crimes against Jews were examined, discussed, and prosecuted in a language that was astoundingly free of communist rhetoric or politics—from either the prosecutors, the defendants, or the witnesses. The language was more evocative of opposition to anti-Jewish measures taken before and *during* the war than of a postwar turn to communist ideology. And certainly the intelligent and pointed lines of questioning by the mostly Jewish prosecutors provided excellent documentation of the details of the crimes. More important, the trials located blame and established motive. Ultimately they were a cathartic moment in Bulgarian-Jewish history because they recognized not only individual Bulgarian crimes against Jews but also the "innocence" of Bulgarians as a whole. One of the very few Bulgarian individuals whom witnesses demonized in the trials was Alexandŭr Belev. According to them, he was an "enthusiastic" anti-Semite if not a German agent, who took joy in the deportations and was "depressed" when such measures were thwarted by the palace. In contrast, commissariat officials claimed that they had little choice but to follow orders on their technical jobs.[135] Oddly enough, most of these employees also thought that Belev was secretly Jewish—because of his Italian grandfather's surname, Milanezi (which sounded plausibly Sephardic).[136] While Belev's actual background is still unknown, his underlings seemed to see no contradiction between his Jewishness and his Nazi inclinations. In a sense, the guilt of Belev and a few other notable Bulgarians was critical in establishing the benevolence of the rest of the Bulgarian population. And indeed, most testimonies—Bulgarian and Jewish alike—revealed that Bulgarians as a whole were opposed to anti-Semitic measures.[137]

According to trial testimonies, only a minute number of extreme anti-Semites believed the elimination of Jews would solve the "social question" or provide an economic boon to Bulgaria. One of these was Nikolai Rashkov, who was not in the commissariat but was a known anti-Semite who had translated the *Protocols of the Elders of Zion* into Bulgarian. At his trial Rashkov explained that even though there were only fifty to a hundred prominent Jewish merchants, he still felt that the anti-Jewish measures were justified in terms of solving Bulgaria's social question.[138] He and other anti-Semitic intellectuals like Aleksandŭr Pudrev were brought to trial not on the basis of their active participation in anti-Jewish crimes but because of their influence on the development of anti-Semitic thought (an unheard-of indictment in the Nuremburg trials). On the stand, Purdev explained that he was not "against Jews in general" but was against only "very rich Jews." In particular, he noted that Jacques Asseoff "holds in his hands all of the influential journalists, movie theaters, and politicians."[139] His use of the present tense when Asseoff was long gone from Bulgaria spoke to Asseoff's lasting impression as representative of Jewish wealth and power in Bulgaria. But voices raised against Asseoff or Jews in general were in the minority. Most defendants admitted that they did not believe anti-Jewish measures would help the Bulgarian economy as a whole.[140]

Still, commissariat staff who personally profited from Jewish persecution were heavily condemned in the highly public trial settings. Prosecutors came down hard on most witnesses when they claimed that they had helped Jewish friends through securing documents or leaking crucial information. In one case, defendant Asen Paitashev tried to cull favor with the prosecutor (and audience) by pointing out that he had procured cigarettes for Jews, even as he participated in their transport and detainment in Dupnitsa. This admission inspired "mirth" from the audience. While Paitashev may have seen offering cigarettes as a humanitarian act, the fact remained that these internees were on their way to their death, a death facilitated by Paitashev himself.[141] Undoubtedly there were many who did help Jews find sustenance and comfort and even escape. But such excuses did not hold water when the prosecution was able to present detailed figures on fees taken, revealing a widespread system of bribes for procuring visas to Palestine or allowing families to stay together when relocating from Sofia to provincial towns.[142] In no uncertain terms, prosecutors made clear the guilt of such technocrats, in spite of their purported lack of anti-Semitism or knowledge.[143] When Iaroslav Kalitsin, a high-ranking commissariat official, claimed that he didn't know Germany was going to liquidate the Jews, the public literally burst into laughter, while his prosecutors balked that all of Bulgaria and "the whole world knew what it meant to be deported to Poland!"[144] Kalitsin countered that "[t]here is not a Bulgarian who would agree to work in an institution if they knew that the institution would send 12,000 people to their death." The prosecution came back at him with the indictment, "But you sent them to their death and the deaths of 12,000 men, women and children are on your conscience!" At this point the crowd shouted "BRAVO!" clapped, and then shouted "Shame! Death!" as the Jewish prosecutor, M. Rakhaminov, finally pronounced, "Mr. Kalitsin, you have committed a crime not just against Jews, not just against the Bulgarian nation, but against humanity."[145]

All in all, however, the sentences for crimes against Jews were quite mild. Of 53 defendants, 40 were found guilty, but only two individuals were sentenced to death, both in absentia (and assumed dead).[146] One of them, Alexandŭr Belev, had mysteriously disappeared, though he was rumored to have been killed (by a Jew) and left in a ditch somewhere in the provinces.[147] The other, Kliment Dalkalŭchev, had already been tried in a local tribunal, where he was interrogated and executed in the Metokha tobacco warehouse, used as a makeshift court.[148] In other areas of criminal prosecution, there were not only more defendants but harsher punishments. In the realm of economic crimes, for example, there were 89 indictments, 22 of them tobacco merchants, 6 of whom were killed via vigilante justice before reaching the court. Of the 160 Bulgarian wartime parliamentarians, 126 were tried; 67 were sentenced to death and 23 to life in prison, while the rest received shorter sentences.[149] Ironically, Dimitŭr Peshev, the representative from Dupnitsa who had played a primary role in stopping deportations, was also tried and sentenced to fifteen years as a Nazi collaborator in spite of his "good Jewish lawyer."[150]

Given these trial outcomes, it seems that in postwar Bulgaria selling tobacco to Germany (as in the cases of process 9, explored further in chapter 7), was as great a crime as robbing and disenfranchising Jews and sending them to their death. In a sense the confiscation of properties from bourgeois Jews had furthered the nationalization process, which now shifted its focus to Bulgarians. The politics of nationalization were also simplified by the fact that all Bulgarians involved in the upper echelons of the wartime tobacco trade—as in other sectors of the economy—could easily be labeled fascist. This would not have been the case for Jews if they had survived the war in Bulgaria with their fortunes intact. More pointedly, Asseoff's Balkantabak was already in state hands, soon to become part of the state monopoly, Bulgartabak. In the formulations of the new communist government, Bulgarian gold was now in the hands of the people; Bulgarianization was complete.

Tobacco permeated the complex Bulgarian-Jewish-German relationship that unfolded directly before and especially under the extreme conditions of World War II. The Bulgarian-German commercial knot that grew out of the interwar trade in tobacco was tied with a Jewish thread, the Schnur-Asseoff-Reemstma link. But by the late 1930s and certainly during the war itself, German-Jewish and Bulgarian-Jewish ties unraveled. Jews like Jacques Asseoff were restricted and then expelled from the tobacco industry and ultimately lost all grounding in Bulgarian economic life. For many Bulgarians this was a bitter pill to swallow, an example of German imperialism tainting Bulgarian traditions of tolerance. Others, though, cooperated and personally profited, and the short-term rewards for Bulgaria were tremendous. One of the biggest rewards was the occupation of Thrace and Macedonia, which gave Bulgaria a virtual monopoly on Oriental tobacco and made it the biggest producer of tobacco in Europe.

But for Bulgaria, selling itself to the Germans in exchange for access to tobacco-rich Thrace and Macedonia meant further compromises that were not always readily accepted by the population. The continued persecution of Jews and their ultimate deportation from Thrace and Macedonia was one of these compromises. Dragged from their homes and pushed into the dust and stench of tobacco warehouses, Jews were traded, much like tobacco, for Bulgarian political favor and profit. But many Bulgarians also protested against and successfully stopped these deportations, in part as a result of Jewish social ties. Still, the fact that Jews were ultimately eliminated from the high and middle reaches of the industry, as Turks and Greeks had been in the past, seemed to mark the final chapter in the Bulgarianization of the industry.

On the other hand, it might be seen as its prelude, since with the coming of the Fatherland Front and the nationalization of the industry *all* private interests were pushed out of their exploitative role in the tobacco industry. Hence the end of Asseoff's era would soon become the end of the capitalist era. In many ways, it was not 1941 but 1944–47 that was the final step in the total Bulgarianization not just of the tobacco industry but, in part, of Bulgaria itself. For during the first few years of communist rule, a mass exodus of Jews responded to the pull of a new life in the new state of Israel. Leaving behind the violence and uncertainty of the transition to communism, 90 percent of Jews had emigrated from Bulgaria to Palestine by 1948.[151] For better or worse, a new Bulgarian world was in the making.

CHAPTER 6

Smoke-Filled Rooms

Places to Light Up in Communist Bulgaria

In August 1964 an article called "A Day of Rest" appeared in *Turist,* the Bulgarian communist journal dedicated primarily to hiking and mountaineering but also leisure and holiday travel. It was accompanied by a photo-essay that walks the reader through a carefully crafted parable of leisure in which the industrious, healthy Ivan Markov is juxtaposed to the slovenly and lazy Dimitŭr Ivanov. Both are enjoying their day of rest in diametrically opposed fashions, Ivan in a properly socialist, productive fashion and Dimitŭr in an idle and ultimately counterproductive way. On this precious Sunday off, Ivan Markov travels to an unspecified mountain in an unnamed mode of transportation, with his compliant and happy wife, Vania, and their content son, Asko. They hike, breathe the crisp air, and return home happy and refreshed. They sleep well and get up the following morning invigorated and ready for another day of work. To illustrate, the series of six photos ends with an image of Vania smiling at her job as a switchboard operator. Dimitŭr Ivanov, in contrast, first appears in a photograph in which the clock reads 10:00 a.m. and he is still in bed, leaning on one elbow reading the paper with a bulbous puff of cigarette smoke obscuring his mouth. As the text accusingly elaborates, "His eyes are closing. Why this laziness? From the stale air and the cigarette smoke that is perpetually on his lips!" Meanwhile, Dimitŭr's wife, Dora, sullenly cleans the floor on hands and knees, while their son, Vanio, is ignored. Dimitŭr is then shown settling down to *rakia* (brandy), cards, and cigarettes with a friend, a state of affairs that appears to last for the rest of the day. Dimitŭr is shown the next morning at work, straining to lift some kind of barrel. As the article relates, he and his wife reportedly felt "as if they had worked a double shift." Presumably lacking exercise or fresh air, they were unready to face the week of labor and by extension the task of "building socialism."[1]

If the message of the two pictorial storyboards and their simple texts was not clear enough, the words that follow spelled it out: "Tourism more and more has entered into the life of the nation. Workers and especially manual laborers should spend their rest time in nature, like the Markov family and not like the Ivanov family!" Here, as historically, the word "tourism" refers primarily to hiking, which had become an institutionalized practice since the days of Aleko Konstantinov's founding of Bulgaria's first tourist society in 1880s. It was in the interest of the communist regime to promote tourism as something that was healthy and refreshing, complementary to worker productivity. While the regime continued to stress healthy tourism in periodicals like *Turist,* Bulgarian tourism was changing form as the period progressed. Ultimately Bulgaria, like other socialist states, showed remarkable flexibility, responding to the shifting demands of its population and even catering to the Dimitŭrs of its citizenry, who probably far outnumbered the Ivans.

By the 1960s, recently urbanized, educated, and professionalized Bulgarians were being encouraged to become tourists in the sense not only of avid hikers but also of visitors to leisure venues that were being consciously expanded by the state. The meaning of the word "tourism" was slowly evolving to include a vastly expanding web of *pochivni stantsi* (rest stations), hotels, resorts, and even restaurants and cafés in Bulgarian cities, mountain ski and spa areas, and especially the Black Sea coast. These sites catered not only to Bulgarian workers and cultural or political elites but also to foreigners who began to pour into the country to visit Bulgaria's "Red Riviera" (the Black Sea coast).[2] Post-Stalinist Bulgaria, like other countries in the Eastern Bloc, sought to soften the blow of admittedly egregious Stalinist mistakes and turn from heavy to light industry and services for its disgruntled population.[3] Not only was there popular demand for such sites of rest, but the very rationale of the regime required that tourism in all its forms was available to the people and not merely to the elite, as in the prewar years. Indeed, increased tourism and other leisure consumption opportunities were couched in party theory as signs of "advanced socialism" and the approach of "ripe" communism. This was the final stage in history, the utopian promise of a "bright future" as understood in the Marxist-Leninist thought espoused by Bloc leadership. In the short term, the socialist "good life" was a sure sign of this impending transition.

In practice this meant that the Dimitŭrs and Ivans of Bulgaria found cafés and bars perched in mountain resorts. Hiking was no longer the only option for spending one's free time. At the Black Sea coast, luxury hotels, restaurants, and bars spilled right onto the golden sands that were lined with gleaming new resorts. In Sofia and other Bulgarian cities venues for leisure consumption also sprouted, providing a refuge from work and monotony in the city, while satisfying the modern demands of newly educated socialist citizens. More pragmatically, tourism (along with tobacco export) became one of the Bulgarian state's major sources of foreign currency, necessary to economic viability and the very building of socialism. But the provision of places of leisure—or places to smoke and drink—might also have been an attempt to corral leisure into a collective environment; here consumption took place under the gaze of the self-regulating crowd, if not the eyes and ears of the socialist state.[4] While *Turist* was able to record, as if by hidden camera, Dimitŭr's smoking in bed, the concentration of Bulgaria's other Dimitŭrs in public leisure venues brought smoking (and drinking) starkly into the public eye. Hence as the communist period progressed, Bulgarians were taking part in leisure consumption on an unprecedented scale, but not always in acceptable *socialist* ways. As a result state actors continually attempted to orchestrate productive and rational forms of socialist leisure and consumption, even as the state continued to build resort hotels, restaurants, and bars with gusto. Late-communist efforts in Bulgaria to control or direct leisure consumption, were, perhaps surprisingly, far more rigorous than they had been during the Stalinist period.[5]

Official attitudes toward smoking in particular were rife with contradiction, revealing the deep inconsistencies and problems of socialist leisure theory and practice. Part of the problem was the legacy of practical and philosophical divisions between smokers and antismokers within the interwar communist movement. More pointedly, there was the problem of tobacco production, so deeply embedded in interwar, wartime, and now postwar Bulgarian agriculture and industry. Not only were tobacco sales critical to the Bulgarian economy, but a large percentage of Bulgarians were involved in the tobacco and tourist economy, making it exceedingly difficult to censure the consumption of these goods and services—the products of their own labor. But in spite of such issues, by the 1960s and 1970s the Bulgarian Communist Party (BCP) began to sponsor rather vigorous abstinence efforts—leveled against both drinking and smoking; in official publications both were defined as examples of "irrational" leisure consumption.[6] As in the case of Dimitŭr, the cigarette became emblematic of both benign idleness and waste and more deliberate and threatening social deviance, linked to an imagined Western influence.

Yet ironically, out of the smoke-filled rooms of the communist leadership, plans were hatched for the production of ever-more luxurious and tantalizing Bulgarian cigarettes that were actively marketed and sold in Bulgaria's new places of leisure activity. The appearance of flashy new Bulgarian brands with luxurious hard packs and shiny cellophane was lauded by the tobacco industry as emblematic of Bulgarian socialist progress and the state's ability to provide leisure and luxury to the laboring masses. But when Bulgarians actually smoked these state-produced cigarettes in state-provided leisure venues, state-sponsored abstinence advocates became alarmed. This alarm was particularly intense because of the rapidly expanding numbers of women and youth among the irrational consumers of tobacco, so starkly smoking in the public eye.[7] While Dimitŭr, was central to the problem in 1964, increasingly it was Vania and Vanio (his wife and child) who turned to the cigarette and in so doing seemed to pose a greater threat to the future of socialism and the nation.

Smoking and Stalinism

In the early years of communist consolidation of power in Bulgaria, deep divisions within the party on the questions of abstinence—in relation to smoking and drinking—were apparent. A segment of Bulgarian communists, particularly in rural areas, had been deeply involved in the interwar abstinence movement. Many communist intellectuals and party leaders, however, moved in the café (and tavern) circuit in Bulgaria's larger cities and in some cases smaller towns. Numerous party leaders were hardened and passionate smokers who were less apt to put messages of abstinence at the forefront of party programs, and in the immediate postwar years it was a low priority. Though many local communists were tied to abstinence initiatives, many of the returning "Muscovites" (that is, communists who had spent the war in the USSR) were hardly sold on the abstinence message, which had largely run its course in the Soviet Union in the 1920s.[8]

It was true that the Comintern—the Communist International dominated by the Soviets from 1919 to 1943—had approved the use of abstinence associations in interwar Bulgaria as front organizations for party work. In Soviet society smoking and drinking were not only socially acceptable, but embraced as part of deserved socialist leisure. Stalin himself was an avid smoker, and he and Georgi Dimitrov—Bulgaria's first communist leader and head of the Comintern from 1934 to 43—were said to have enjoyed many a pipe together at Stalin's dacha. Both smoked publicly, and there was no overt stigma attached to the practice in the early postwar years.[9] On the contrary, the regime faced a pervasive ethos of smoking, not just among the intelligentsia but also among workers, partisans, soldiers, and the emancipated women that they actively courted. Furthermore, the party could hardly expect Bulgarians to go cold turkey while it initiated extensive political and economic programs, using not only force but also compromise and patience.

In the immediate postwar years some abstinence-related measures were taken. But they were concentrated in the 1945–48 period, that is, *before* political power was consolidated. They appear, in fact, to have been something of a compromise with a large segment of so-called home-communists (those who had spent the war years in Bulgaria) whose organizational stronghold had been in interwar abstinence associations. Why else other than political compromise, would the party have pushed forward abstinence legislation and associations when political chaos, severe shortages of basic goods, and other problems loomed so large? Such measures resonated with Bulgarian communists from rural locales but also with certain abstinent socialists, other leftist parties, Muslims, Christians (especially evangelicals), and many women. Hence, after taking power in September 1944, Bulgaria's communist-led coalition, the Fatherland Front, approved the organization of a national conference for the abstinence movement. In March of 1945, committed Bulgarian abstainers saw their dream of an open and state-supported movement finally come to fruition, and a large number of abstinence societies mushroomed across Bulgaria, their representatives making the pilgrimage to Sofia amid general euphoria. Petko Tsonev was named director of the newly established "politically neutral" Bulgarian National Abstinence Union, which immediately began to organize associations in every village. As in the interwar period, the village rather than the city was the immediate focus of organizational efforts, and a range of leftist activists organized youth associations, lectures, plays, films, and exhibitions. In 1945 newspapers with national circulation were launched, such as *Trezva borba* (the *Abstinence Struggle*) and *Vŭzdŭrzhatelche* (*Little Abstainer*). At the same time, the more politically suspect abstinence societies, primarily those run by evangelical Christians, were liquidated or taken over by loyal party members or left-leaning fellow travelers.[10] In spite of the apparent enthusiasm among the committed abstainers, state resources for this effort were sparse in this brief "glory period."[11]

For those most involved, the krŭchma seemed to best represent the immoral vestiges of the past, emblematic of the backwardness and malaise in Bulgarian rural life. As one communist reporter and abstinence activist had observed in his interwar reportage, "Krŭchmas are overflowing with the smell of sour alcohol fumes and tobacco smoke. The peasants drink spoiled wine and smoke low-quality tobacco. They read newspapers. They spit on politics, life, themselves."[12] The Fatherland Front confiscated many krŭchmars (tavern owner) properties along with those of the tobacco merchants.[13] In addition, the last act and crowning achievement of the abstinence lobby was the so-called law on krŭchmas that the Bulgarian communist-dominated parliament enacted in June 1947. The law placed limitations on the number of krŭchmas in Bulgarian towns or villages. Towns with under thirty thousand people were limited to one krŭchma per eight hundred people. In settlements bigger than thirty thousand the ratio was one bar for every thousand people. The law also prohibited krŭchmas from existing within two hundred meters of mines, schools, factories, military bases, chitalishtas (reading rooms), and military clubs.[14] In some more enthusiastic villages referendums on the interwar model were held, and in many cases more than the required number or even all krŭchmas were closed.[15]

Although such measures apparently bore some fruit, by 1949 all abstinence efforts were shelved, subordinated to other state priorities. Although the law for krŭchmas stayed on the books, it is unclear how aggressively it was enforced in the early decades of communism. In many cases krŭchmas were simply nationalized and then renamed *pivnitsa* (beer hall or cantina) and then business proceeded as usual. After 1948, abstinence associations were not only a low priority, but they were actually disbanded and their newspapers canceled, though their activities were theoretically put under the umbrella of the chitalishta. In the words of Khristo Stoianov, a committed *trezvenik* (abstainer) and organizer from the period, abstinence was "put on the back burner."[16] During the post-1956 "thaw" in Bulgaria, when policy decisions from the Stalinist period were openly censured, Stoianov and other prewar abstinence veterans were publicly critical of this lull in state support for the movement. According to Pavel Petkov, another prominent abstinence activist, by the late 1940s abstinence was "out of fashion," a state of affairs that lasted for some seventeen years. Indeed, there was a gap in the abstinence literature from 1949 to 1958, and only in the mid-1960s and particularly 1970s did this literature return in force.

This makes sense in a period when the new regime was struggling to establish a base of support among broad masses of the population; perhaps it was more prudent to alienate the abstinence lobby than to estrange smokers and drinkers—many of whom made up the symbolically and ideologically important leftist intelligentsia. In the interwar period, these communists were known regulars of the smoke-filled cafes of Sofia—most notably Sredets and Bu˘lgariia—where they had been watched by police from the "agent's corner" in the interwar period.[17] For this intelligentsia, interwar café culture as they knew it no longer existed.[18] For one thing, many buildings, like the one that housed the kafene Tsar Osvoboditel, had been bombed out of existence by American shelling. Other establishments were quickly nationalized in the postwar period. In addition, many of the communist and other left-leaning intellectuals who frequented such cafés were now behind desks with portfolios and major responsibilities, without time to hang out writing poetry in the cafés of the capital or provincials towns. While smoking itself was socially acceptable, the kafene ethos of holding court and spending endless hours slacking in public view was decidedly frowned upon. Still, certain kafenes survived. The Sredets, for example, although renamed Zad Teatra (Behind the Theater), weathered the communist storm. And clearly, there was never a period in which *all* of the party was behind ascetic notions of communist morality. On the contrary, for many communist intellectuals smoking had always been their muse and for a large percentage of average citizens it had increasingly become an indispensable (and addictive) part of their way of life.

As mentioned, Georgi Dimitrov, Bulgaria's first communist leader in the postwar period, was an avowed, passionate smoker. With all his prestige within the communist movement, Dimitrov appeared quite publicly with a pipe in hand. A pipe, no less! A decidedly bourgeois form of paraphernalia in comparison with the more working-class cigarette. Still, while not averse to flaunting his habit, Dimitrov did openly demand "healthy pleasures" for communist youth. At a meeting of the communist youth group the Septembrists in 1947, he was said to have announced:

> Do not get carried away by superficial, temporary, and often times harmful pleasures! I am a smoker and a passionate one. This happened in the last few years, as until 1927 I did not smoke. Septembrists should not smoke! For them there should be a law against it! In everything else, imitate me, but not in smoking—No!…You should choose healthy pleasures, which increase your physical and moral strength and not those which harm your health and break your will.[19]

Needless to say, Dimitrov's "do as I say, not as I do" approach never bore fruit. A law against smoking never materialized. Nor did the regime, in spite of its seemingly vast control over Bulgarian society, impose any restriction on sales or consumption in the postwar period.[20] For while smoking was (at least theoretically) connected to vestiges of the bourgeois past and excess, it was also part and parcel of working-class culture, masculinity, women's emancipation and, by extension, socialist modernity. In the short term, political consolidation, economic control and development, industrialization, and collectivization of agriculture were more immediate and pressing tasks than denying ordinary citizens a routine smoke break.

Places to Smoke

To a large extent lighting up was a more and more central part of life under Bulgarian socialism. The numbers of smokers steadily climbed in the postwar period regardless of political shifts. After the death of Stalin in 1953, the Soviet Union initiated a wide range of policy changes that affected consumption, leisure, and, by extension, smoking. While the "new course" began as early as 1953, reform was more dramatic after Nikita Khrushchev consolidated power and denounced Stalin in his famous secret speech of 1956. Vŭlko Chervenkov, who had replaced Georgi Dimitrov after his death in 1949, was quietly shuffled aside in 1956 in favor of Todor Zhivkov. Following the Eastern Bloc line, Zhivkov, introduced a cultural thaw, albeit brief, along with calls for greater attention to the satisfaction of consumer needs.[21] But in post-Stalinist Bulgaria, as in the Soviet Union under Khrushchev, a quickening of revolutionary ardor was also expected as "past mistakes" were corrected. Khrushchev announced that the Bloc was on the fast track to "ripe communism," which was to be achieved by 1980. For him this paradoxically meant both an overtaking of the West in standard of living and a rather austere and rational approach to consumption.[22] This created a set of practical and theoretical contradictions that played out in a variety of ways within in the Bloc. In Bulgaria, in general, there was a relaxation of state control but also a theoretical hastening of revolution, most immediately evident in the Chinese-inspired, though less ambitious, 1958–80 "cultural revolution," and "great leap forward."

Changes in communist-state attitudes towards leisure and consumption were a critical part of the changes in this period.[23] Between 1956 and 1960, the Soviet Union put into effect a shortened workweek, from roughly forty-eight down to forty-one hours, with Saturdays off.[24] Bulgaria, like many other states in the Bloc, followed suit and made more free time a new part of socialist reality that accompanied the widely noted post-Stalinist boom in leisure and consumption.[25] But the presumed socialist achievement of increased free time—as sparse as free time may have been in the reality of socialist life— also became the subject of Bulgarian communist (and general Bloc) angst. The modernizing effects of the first decade of communism brought new consumers to the fore, with expectations for a better life. De-Stalinization only heightened such expectations and, for many, the reality of more free time created a market for leisure and consumption that the party had to address.[26]

But even as the state responded to this market, it also tried to direct and educate consumers. Under Zhivkov state agencies actively encouraged the mass expansion of the tourist movement as a presumed healthy and productive form of leisure.[27] In 1957 the Bulgarian Tourist Union was established, and in the years that followed, tourist organizations expanded across the country with the fiscal and moral support of the regime. Under the umbrella of Balkantourist, established in 1948, new specialized associations emerged— for example, Orbita, which coordinated youth travel, and Pirintourist, which administered chains of primitive chalets for hikers in the various Bulgarian mountain ranges.[28] Local and national chapters of these organizations proliferated beginning in the late 1950s and 1960s, with the Union of Bulgarian Tourists growing from 41,256 members in 1957 to 800,000 in 1965.[29] The periodical *Turist* began publication in 1956, promoting a tourism that was still generally associated with healthy and mostly outdoor pursuits. As the opening anecdote from this chapter illustrates, as late as 1964 (and arguably throughout the period) the proverbial Ivan was clearly idealized over the smoking, lazy Dimitŭr. In spite of real changes in tourist opportunities and infrastructure, the bulk of articles in *Turist* featured pastoral images of nature as well as tips or stories on outdoor adventure.

Perhaps not surprising, the focus of *Turist* was on healthy, active tourism, or hiking. It built on the historical development of the concept of tourism in Bulgaria, which was closely linked to partaking in the beauties of the natural environment. This focus not only accommodated the larger communist project of promoting clean living but also tapped into the growing use of national sentiment to encourage political engagement—or in this case proper leisure behavior. *Turist,* for example, openly co-opted Bulgaria's two most famous nineteenth-century literary figures, Aleko Konstantinov and Ivan Vazov, as "founding fathers" of Bulgarian tourism. The journal lauded Konstantinov, the well-known author and world traveler who founded Bulgaria's first tourist association in the 1890s, for first making tourism a "mass phenomenon."[30] Though Vazov was not a hiker or tourism organizer, he too was known for his travels in the provinces of Bulgaria, described in loving detail in his well-known travelogues.[31] Of course, *Turist* presented an exceedingly selective reading of Konstantinov and Vazov that obscured the fact that they were both heavy smokers. Smoking permeated their touristic—and literary—personas,—as was typical of people with their education and stature in the nineteenth century. They were certainly not celebrated for their vices. But neither was smoking entirely vilified in the early 1960s.

Instead, by then the contradictory approaches of communist leaders in relation to smoking had begun to intensify. In line with the global smoking

phenomenon, smoking rates among all segments of the Bulgarian population soared. The forces of socialist modernization seemed to inevitably lead
to smoking, especially in a country that was the eighth-largest producer
of tobacco in the world and number one in terms of cigarette exports by
1966.[32] Cigarettes were cheap and available, and their packaging and branding were increasingly seductive. The rise in tobacco consumption was closely
linked to the strategies of Bulgartabak (the Bulgarian state tobacco monopoly)
in terms of both quantity and quality of cigarette production for Bulgaria
and the Bloc. By the 1960s the party recognized that a new modern type
of consumption had emerged with a growing demand for quality items.[33]
With this in mind, the tobacco industry announced its intent to provide a
premium product. The industry trade journal, *Bŭlgarski tiutiun (Bulgarian
Tobacco)*, discussed in lavish terms the specific attributes of Bulgarian Oriental tobaccos—"excellent flavor, exquisite aroma, and good burning properties," which provided a "complete taste sensation and satisfaction when
[the cigarettes were] smoked."[34] Articles also bragged about the increased
use of "luxurious packaging materials" like metallic cartons, cellophane, and
zip-fasteners, which "gave the smoker comfort and aesthetic pleasure" and
"associated the cigarettes with their renowned luxury."[35] In a country where
there was little to no branding of other products, cigarettes came in a wide
variety of ever-proliferating brands—many of which had foreign names like
Victory and Opal. The use of such words heightened the association of the
cigarettes with the West and hence with premium products.[36] Significantly,
the tobacco industry went above and beyond to "satisfy the socialist consumer" and purposely sold and marketed (yes, marketed) its goods abroad
and at home, at Bulgarian leisure venues that proliferated in the 1960s and
1970s.[37] Cigarettes were sold not only in lively kiosk displays on the streets
of Sofia and other cities but also in cafés and bars and at Black Sea resorts,
where pretty girls were hired to work in sleek kiosks that were open twice as
long as equivalent city stalls. They were sold not just in kiosks for Bulgarian
lev but also—and more profitably—for hard currency in Bulgarian hotels
and *Corecom* (hard currency stores) that abounded in coastal resort cities.
Not surprisingly, this provision both responded to and provoked an orgy of
demand and consumption at home and across the Bloc.

This carnival of consumption could hardly be blamed on the presence
of foreigners at Bulgaria's new tourist venues. The fact that a large percentage of foreign tourists were from other socialist states certainly made such a
state of affairs more palatable. But the fact of the matter is that Bulgaria's new
leisure venues and consumption opportunities were also, if not especially, for
its own citizens, and not just the party elite. Although the latter certainly had

the best access to such abundance, gardens of leisure blossomed everywhere and for everyone—from new eating and drinking establishments in urban centers to resorts that were built all over the country. From the Black Sea coast to the mountains, from hot-springs spa locations to cultural monuments, cabins, hotels, restaurants, cafés, and bars mushroomed in the 1960s and 1970s to provide Bulgarian citizens with state-provided vacation venues.

Smoking was an essential part of these new leisure opportunities. In fact, Bulgartabak's branding and (albeit limited) advertising specifically crafted cigarettes as part of a tableau of holiday-oriented leisure consumption. Brand names such as Varna (a city on Bulgaria's Black Sea coast) and Stewardess evoked travel and tourist locales, while advertisements showed seductive images of airplanes, glasses of wine, candles, and cards that made an acceptable and desirable connection between cigarettes and leisure.[38] This connection was especially overt for Bulgaria's tobacco workers, who were endlessly praised in *Bŭlgarski tiutiun*. The journal was filled with articles and photographs showcasing resort hotels that were built solely for Bulgaria's tobacco workers in some of the most desirable Black Sea locations. One 1963 article guides the reader through the rooms of one such hotel, the recently built Palace Among the Dunes at Sunny Beach with twenty-three rooms and seventy beds: "Of course on every table you will see various things according to the tastes of those staying in the room—books, fishing gear, needlework, cigarettes, toys, radios, letters, etc. . . . Is this not your house, workers with the golden hands, through which passes the gold of our homeland—tobacco!" Given their substantial contribution to the Bulgarian economy, tobacco workers were presented as naturally deserving of their time in the sun, lounging on the beach, fishing, playing cards, and of course smoking. But it was not just tobacco workers who deserved these amenities.

By the early 1960s *Turist* began to change its tune on the acceptable and desirable parameters of Bulgarian leisure. The magazine began to feature photo spreads of hotels, restaurants, and sunbathers subtly slipped into its pages alongside the familiar treed mountainsides and highland lakes. Meanwhile party sources boasted a 27 percent per annum growth in available tourist services by the mid-1960s, with an entirely different kind of tourism in mind. Voices for the official tourist industry tracked the meteoric rise in available seats at restaurants, cafés, and bars and beds at hotels as "socialist achievements."[39] Even mountain tourism, as these sources readily pointed out, had begun to develop a new material base, which meant more hotels, restaurants, and cafés in mountain resort areas.[40] Balkantourist coordinated an ever-more impressive range of such venues from the Black Sea coast to the mountains as well as in Bulgarian cities. Urban tourism was given considerable attention,

Опитайте
цигари
BAPHA

Cigarette advertisement for Varna brand from back of *Bŭlgarski tiutiun*, 1969. It reads "Try Varna Cigarettes."

and events like the biannual Plovdiv trade fair became jumping-off points to further develop the tourist industry in Bulgaria as a whole.[41]

Balkantourist, as well as a variety of other state agencies, inadvertently provided the infrastructure for a vastly expanded web of social drinking and smoking venues to entertain the pleasure-seeking hoards. In part the expansion of Bulgarian tourism was a critical economic imperative.

ROPOTAMO, THE SECOND BLEND
VARIETY WHICH FULLY SATISFIES
SMOKERS USED TO THIS TYPE OF
CIGARETTES.

Cigarette advertisement for Roptamo cigarettes, a Bulgarian blend presented at the Plovdiv International Tobacco Symposium in 1965. *The First Tobacco Symposium, Plovdiv Bulgaria* (Plovdiv: Conference Publication, 1965).

Bulgaria did not have many commodities that were marketable to those inside (and especially outside) the Bloc, beyond its sunny climate and golden sands. Tourism was a set of services with accompanying goods that could be sold to foreigners, for both soft (Bloc) and hard (Western) currencies. This was a critical factor in the rapid development of tourist facilities in the post–1956 period. Tourism—along with the cigarette industry—was the most important engine driving the Bulgarian economy which in the 1960s and 1970s enjoyed the highest rate of growth per capita in the Bloc.[42] In a sense, tourism (and cigarettes) funded the increased ability of the Bulgarian state to provide a range of other goods and services to its urbanized and modernized populations. Tourist sites and cigarettes could also be readily provided to Bulgarians as rewards for exemplary work or party service, or more generally (and less luxuriously) to the population at large—even when other kinds of goods were scarce.

Bulgaria—much like nonaligned socialist Yugoslavia—turned to the development of tourism on a grand scale for foreign as well as domestic visitors. As proof of the efficacy of industry developments, it charted with pride the rising number of foreign visitors, as 1 million in 1965 rose to 3 million in 1972.[43] While this was far fewer tourists than in Yugoslavia, which already had 2.6 million tourists in 1965 and 8.4 million in 1985, it was still impressive, given Bulgaria's size and resources.[44] Whereas in Yugoslavia the majority of foreign tourists were from the West, in Bulgaria, as late as 1989, 80 percent of all tourists were from the former Bloc. For these visitors Bulgaria was infinitely more affordable and accessible.[45] The country became an important provider of beach vacations to social-ist citizens, with an expanding network of hotels, resorts, tourist com-plexes, campsites, roads, and restaurants. Bulgaria's development of its Black Sea coast became a critical part of its niche in Comecon (the Council for Mutual Economic Assistance, which coordinated economic activities among Eastern Bloc states). Its southern climes and sandy beaches were in high demand among Soviets as well as citizens of other communist Bloc partners. The People's Republic of Bulgaria increasingly became a safe escape for a captive audience, that is, locals and Bloc citizens who could have their day in the sun in an ideologically sound setting.[46] Beginning in the 1960s, increasing numbers of Bloc visitors poured in, on trains, deluxe buses, planes, and Black Sea ships.[47] Though these sites were firmly behind the Iron Curtain, the presence of Westerners, who also vacationed there in significant numbers, provided an atmosphere of an international party and certainly heightened the appeal.

During the 1960s the Black Sea coast became a place of East-West encoun-ter amid the Bulgarian sands, sun, and resort pleasures. The regime, in fact, actively worked to promote Bulgaria as a tourist site to Americans and West-ern Europeans, even working through diplomatic channels. To a large extent this was a common experience in post-Stalinist Eastern Europe—including Yugoslavia and the Bloc—where commercial and political interests made communist states market their countries to these consumers.[48] As the French journalist Edouard Calic noted, by the 1960s Bulgarian beaches had become gold mines with a "long string of resorts with their hotels, casinos, villas, and rest homes" along a newly built panoramic highway, some 700 kilometers long.[49] In this period, the Bulgarian state produced pamphlets, books, and periodicals in English and other Western languages that sold Bulgaria as a tourist vacation destination, not just because of the Black Sea but also because of its verdant mountain ranges, its mineral baths, and its unique history and architectural monuments. Western visitors were lured with images of the "velvety sands" of the Black Sea coast, as well as the many amenities in its large-scale resort complexes.[50] Calic likened Golden Sands, one of the newest beach resorts near Varna, to Cannes or Le Touquet in France, noting its "proximity to linden forests, its countless restaurants with dance floors, its 1000 colorful bungalows, its terraces, its pensions, its neon-lit highway."[51] The glitz and glamour of what he called the Red Riviera was coupled with camel rides, "folk taverns," folk orchestras, and dance performances, along with excursions to ancient Byzantine and Ottoman cultural monuments. And of course, there was the unforgettable pirate ship restaurant-bar, permanently lodged on the sands of the Sunny Beach resort, where one could drink and smoke the night away, served by young Bulgarians dressed in pirate attire.[52] Both the foreign thirst for the exotic and the domestic desire for fantasy were quenched in a region where natural beauty met modern comfort, glamour, and entertainment. The communist state expended considerable efforts to satisfy these assorted appetites.

And at least some Westerners began to take notice. By the mid- to late 1960s, travel pieces began to appear in the *New York Times* and other Western publications that touted Bulgaria as both beautiful and inexpensive. Far from complaining about bad service or low-quality goods, the writers were enamored by Bulgaria's layered history, its "magnificent beaches," and even its range of accommodations and restaurants.[53] Those who came were a mix of the more adventurous, leftists or working-class members on a budget, willing to suffer some discomfort and uncertainty for a taste of the East, a Cold War adrenaline rush, or just a cheap beach vacation. By 1969 some fifteen thousand Americans had been lured to what the *New York Times* called the "sophisticated seaside" of Bulgaria, where visitors were impressed by "folk restaurants" and other unusual venues like a resort bar with stools that "hung from the ceiling like swings."[54] With only gentle jabs at the "institution-like" white hotels, articles in the *Times* also marveled at the tolerance for nudism—purportedly initiated by East Germans—as well as the general atmosphere of "free East-West mixing," calling Bulgaria a veritable "coexistence bazaar."[55] Of course, as one British traveler noted, the Bulgarians on holidays were relegated to a "sort of barracks accommodation that the tourist authority would not dream of offering to foreigners," but he also pointed out that for them resorts like Golden Sands were still "marvelous, a dream country." At the same time, he described how "[f]raternizing breaks out when you go for a camel ride, a motorboat trip, a meal in one of the folk restaurants which have seized, sterilized and served up palatable dollops of old Bulgarian ways, from fire-walking to dancing bears."[56] Of course, certain forms of segregation because of socioeconomics or fear were certainly present. Westerners were unquestionably restricted in their travel, while secret police and informers observed Bulgarians in their interactions with Westerners.[57] But the Black Sea coast also became a site of interaction for citizens of East and West to listen, gawk, and even interact—with the requisite social lubricants, namely, Bulgarian drinks and cigarettes. By the early 1970s there were as many West German as East Germans tourists and the coast became a known meeting ground for German families divided by the wall.[58] As Calic explained, "If the inhabitants of East and West Berlin wish to meet, all they have to do is come to these parts. The same sea, the same sand, the same food for the tourists who have come from abroad."[59] The Black Sea Coast, Calic opined, had "not become socialist, but sociable."[60]

But this transnational sociability was by no means a diversion from socialism; rather, its origins and goals were deeply imbedded in socialist rationale and objectives. Foreigners were welcomed to Bulgaria both to see for themselves socialist progress on display at the Plovdiv fair or in a coastal resort and to actively contribute to it by spending their money on Bulgarian goods and services. Modern tourist facilities were built in these locales with global standards in mind, to impress foreigners (as well as locals) as part of Bulgaria's active role in East-West competition.[61] In terms of the regime's objectives, providing such escapes to foreigners had obvious financial benefits, while for its own citizens it was both cheaper and politically safer than sending them abroad. The development of tourist venues not only provided a replacement for travel abroad but also brought Bulgaria's socialist citizenry into the public eye, where its leisure practices could be watched and critiqued. Even if Bulgarians could not be like Ivan, new places to smoke and drink might guarantee that they would not be like Dimitŭr, who smoked in bed and drank at the kitchen table. New leisure venues could theoretically take such unproductive and polluting activities out of the home and also the workplace, containing them in a leisure environment that was at least theoretically under direct or indirect state supervision. Here officials could watch and comment on citizens' understanding of socialism and modernity as expressed through patterns of leisure and consumption.

Cigarettes, of course—along with alcohol and food—were an important part of the Bulgarian offerings at the coast and other tourist or urban leisure sites. Bulgaria's agricultural abundance in its processed and unprocessed forms—cigarettes, alcoholic drinks, and food products—were ideal supporting industries to supply the visiting multitudes and vacationing locals. Bulgarian cigarettes were abundantly displayed and available for sale in kiosks and Corecom (hard currency) shops that abounded in coastal resort cities, and the connection between tourism and smoking (as between tourism and drinking) became natural and unshakable in this period. Of course, drinking and smoking had long been associated with leisure and sociability. But under communism, the scale of public drinking and smoking was unprecedented, as was their spread to women and youth. Of course, the expansion of smoking in the postwar period was global—among women, youth, working classes, and rural populations. On both sides of the Iron Curtain, under capitalism and socialism, tobacco triumphed, and in both worlds its meteoric rise was the cause of increased public scrutiny.

Please Don't Smoke

In direct competition with the goals and efforts of Bulgartabak and Balkantourist, a state-sponsored abstinence movement reemerged in force in the 1960s and 1970s. In January of 1966—the year Bulgaria became the number one exporter of cigarettes in the world—the BCP called a national convention on the theme of abstinence. Party organizers appointed a permanently active national committee and launched the organization of abstinence youth clubs and regional and municipal committees with a new range of local initiatives and measures. Many of the old abstinence veterans were called upon to organize everything from plays, brochures, evening events, exhibitions, and contests to lectures on abstinence.[62] Such efforts gained momentum in the 1970s and 1980s as a whole antismoking literature blossomed, including revived periodicals like the newspaper *Trezvenost* (*Abstinence*). While health issues were central to this literature, behavioral and moral questions with clear political implications were equally fundamental. Smoking as a fashionable and luxurious pursuit came under direct fire by abstinence publications as a remnant of capitalism and hence indicative of a failure to evolve in a sound and socialist manner. Smoking was quite clearly equated with the Bulgarian capitalist past and a malignant present in the West. But tobacco consumption was also viewed as an unavoidable social phenomenon explained by urbanization, the scientific technological revolution, and other changes in postwar Bulgarian life.[63] Bulgarian analysts recognized that smoking was a direct result of modernization but also problematic understandings of modernity.

At issue was not just the nature of *modernity* but the closely related question about the nature of socialism and more critically the presumed rapidly approaching communist future. Was there a place for smoking, drinking, and other intoxicants in this imminent utopia? If so, how should these practices be tolerated or regulated in the socialist present? The biggest problem was that Bulgaria's economic base was firmly rooted in the profits of tourism and tobacco. To tone down smoking or leisure offerings would be economic suicide for a regime that already faced an array of economic problems. Yet the reality of Bulgarian smoking, especially as it spread to ever-wider segments of the population and was increasingly visible to the public and party, was rather alarming for actors in other state sectors. The smoking habit, far from withering away, was deepening its hold on women, working classes, and youth. As cities grew, as women left the home, as ever-larger segments of the population, including youth, enjoyed more leisure time, smoking seemed to fill a void, to provide a needed escape or source of pleasure, here as elsewhere in the modern world.

Attuned to a growing critique of smoking in the West, the communist East also began to wage its own miniwar against smoking by the 1970s. Ultimately, Western campaigns were far more successful in curtailing the habit and putting the industry on the defensive. The combination of new scientific studies, grassroots campaigns, and legal battles against the industry created an environment in which the public demonization of smoking slowly but surely put down deep-seated roots. In contrast with far fewer resources and public will, campaigns in Bulgaria as elsewhere in the Bloc were state-directed in a period when the communist state or at least its core ideology was losing its luster. Unable to fund their own research about the medical or social harms of tobacco, Bulgarian abstinence sources generally, and perhaps ironically, were compelled to cite American or Western European studies (with an occasional Russian study). Working at cross-purposes to other agencies within the communist authoritarian state—namely, the tobacco, alcohol, and tourist industries—the hands of the abstinence movement were tied to a large degree. No large-scale campaigns or lawsuits against the industry were possible, though the abstinence press did contain more than occasional jabs. One antismoking source, for example, after enumerating the various medical and social problems associated with smoking, noted, "I have no doubt that the increase in production and advertisement of produced or imported cigarettes is a meaningful factor which psychologically stimulates smoking."[64] Other sources directly connected

Bulgarian consumption of cigarettes with trade interests, which presented a "difficult problem for the battle with smoking."[65] According to yet another source, in spite of its proven harm to "the socialist way of life," smoking was continually on the rise in socialist Bulgaria because of "planning and material interests."[66] But such subtle digs at the industry were not enough to provide an impetus for major change.[67] Without widespread popular support, the antismoking message often fell on deaf ears, and demand for cigarettes was steadily on the rise, even as it leveled off and eventually dropped in the West.

And supply, of course, readily kept up with demand as the industry provided increasingly attractive, luxurious, and addictive offerings.[68] One would think that a command economy structure would have provided the perfect context for the elimination of smoking simply by decreasing or even eliminating supply. But such an approach was out of the question given the already shaky legitimacy of the Bulgarian communist and other Bloc regimes—a legitimacy that was very closely connected with their ability to supply not only necessities but the luxuries seen as essential to modern life. Still, the state continued to support a fairly extensive network of abstinence organizations, periodicals, and operatives throughout the country, allowing their soft jabs at other state agencies that worked counter to their abstinence program. Clearly there was something in the program that spoke to the deep-seated anxieties about the unintended consequences and social costs of modernity that seemed to run counter to the core tenets of socialist ideas.

At issue was the fear that certain kinds of consumption had political undertones. The question was, were certain consumer desires among socialist citizens indicative of a hunger for the West? While the cigarette itself, unlike the miniskirt or rock music, was not overtly Western in origin, its specific forms (that is, brands) could be. Abstinence sources began to look at smoking as potentially associated not with healthy and deserved workers' leisure but rather with weakness, conformity, snobbery, and the evils of the West. Critics routinely described smokers as flaunting their "luxurious imported cigarettes or packs of tobacco."[69] Even outside abstinence circles, socialist analysts of domestic consumption were appalled that consumers were willing to pay higher prices for foreign cigarettes and other luxurious goods. Notably, *imported* cigarettes were seen as part and parcel of the onerous lure of luxury and "prestige consumption":

With the continuing increase in wages and expansion of the *nomen-klatura* [bureaucratic elites] there is an increased demand for jewelry, artwork and goods, which demonstrate a high standard of living and social prestige, goods connected with snobbism of certain groups of society. In connection with that it is interesting that there is a change in the consumption of alcoholic beverages and tobacco products. With a rise in income, certain groups of the population, especially from the intelligentsia have an increased demand and consumption of concentrated alcoholic beverages and above all "imported" and "luxurious" alcoholic concentrates and cigarettes.[70]

The fact that "imported" and "luxurious" are in quotes is telling. Most of the so-called imported cigarettes in the Eastern Bloc in this period were actually produced in local factories but with American labeling and markedly higher prices.[71] Both were offered to the public in 1976. Ironically, in the same year the State Council of Bulgaria issued an antismoking decree with the aim of "curbing and gradually doing away with this Western imperialist evil."[72] As hypocritical as it was, there was some sense that the evils of smoking could, at least to some degree, be contained in foreign packages. This stance was, of course, quite appealing to the Bulgarian tobacco industry, which openly claimed that its own cigarettes were the lesser of the evils. While the industry continually rejected claims until the 1980s that all tobacco was cancer-causing, it did admit that "American type" tobaccos were. *Bulgarian* tobaccos, in contrast, had enough "anticarcinogens" to counter any possible cancer risk.[73] Nevertheless, Bulgartabak continued to incorporate American-type tobaccos (some grown on Bulgarian soil) into its cigarettes to an unprecedented degree.

Most critics, however, did not limit their critique to Western brands or types of tobacco but rather saw smoking more broadly as linked to "incorrect"—and by implication Western—forms and notions of modernity. Smoking, as one antismoking activist asserted, was indicative of a "wrongly understood feeling of modernity," specifically one that was not on a sound socialist footing: "Over time we ourselves will laugh at the absurdity and senselessness of many of today's fashionable pursuits. We will laugh, that is, if we are able to save ourselves from these excesses which the West has brought us. Imitation in its most harmful form can only make us ludicrous and ugly. Imitation can liquidate us as a nation and we will be lost."[74] Smoking, he went on to argue, far from being a sound pursuit for socialist workers was an imitative and Western practice, connected specifically to the "contradictions of capitalism" that threatened not only to derail socialist progress but to liquidate the distinctiveness of the Bulgarian nation itself. Echoing these ideas, sources even outside the narrow circle of abstinence advocates began to connect smoking with the newly articulated concept of "irrational consumption." Economic analysts were appalled by the growing phenomenon of consumer *veshtomania* (thing-o-mania), when people limited "expenditures on food or the fulfillment of other more appropriate necessities in order to buy luxurious and new models of clothing, furniture, and luxurious, imported drinks and cigarettes."[75]

Smoking was also connected to the problem of the irrational use of free time, one shared by Bulgarian youth and adults.[76] As one pamphlet on the topic claimed, "He who smokes tobacco, for example one pack a day, loses a minimum of 10 minutes per cigarette because it is smoked as a ritual—slowly, ceremoniously, as they say for 'kef' [from the Turco-Arabic *keyf* for pleasure or bliss]. And so unnoticeably for the smoking of one or two packs of cigarettes in a day, hours disappear from one's valuable free time."[77] Significantly, not only work but free time was squandered by smoking and drinking, which "deflected one's thoughts" to pleasure and bliss.[78] The notion of partaking in kef clearly evoked a sense of prolonged and shiftless laziness of a decidedly backward and Oriental character. The Ottomans were even blamed in some antismoking literature for having introduced tobacco to Bulgaria.[79] Hence the danger came from the backward East as well as the decadent West.

The solution to the apparent problem of free time was closely connected to abstinence efforts in this period. In terms of time, smoking was seen as more insidious, more harmful to worker productivity, than drinking because alcohol was generally confined to after-hour consumption. Smoking, in contrast, was practiced from morning to night, at home, at work, and at play. Historically, this was the beauty of the compact and mobile cigarette; it was perfect for the modern world where one could play at work and work at play. But in Bulgaria, such a symbiosis became synonymous with slacking, which was indeed a problem in most socialist countries. The ubiquitous legions of administrators and bureaucrats who smoked the day away while their customers waited seemed to be a problem mired in smoke and ash. In truth, since under communism these people had almost total job security and little incentive, smoking was just a symptom and not a cause of the disease. But for antismoking theorists of the communist era, smoking itself was the problem.

Numerous publications of the antismoking genre were particularly concerned about the amount of time wasted on smoking in the workplace. They had elaborate schemes of calculating time lost—above and beyond projected sick days. Anxieties over work time were behind a directed movement to limit places where smoking was permitted, as in the 1976 decree that limited smoking within the workplace. Still, numerous sources complained about the laxity with which such laws were actually enforced.[80] Even when special smoking areas were provided, this seemed to actually compound the problem of time lost. As one antismoking theorist argued, "If one smoker smokes twenty cigarettes a day, and spends 10–12 minutes per cigarette, plus 14–16 minutes in getting to and from his smoking area he will lose some 140–160 minutes a day!"[81] Though in no way realistic, the ideal was to separate smoking entirely from the time and place of work and—if indeed it could not be eliminated—to locate it firmly in free time and more pointedly in leisure places.

According to abstinence voices, even smoking in the home was problematic, in part because it was outside the gaze and regulatory purview of the state. As in the case of Dimitŭr, *Turist* clearly disproved of his smoking at home, lazily in bed. One antismoking tract openly attacked smoking in the home environment: "Smokers also often destroy the demands and principles of socialist aesthetics and ethics. It isn't difficult to see how many of them unceremoniously damage their appearance, how they ruin their teeth with smoking, how they make everything reek with tobacco, how they dirty the air, they destroy moral principles and how their smoke pollutes the environment of nonsmokers and defiles household objects."[82] Here, concerns about socialist morals and ethics also involved aesthetics but most of all pollution— the impurity (dirt and smell) of the body and household environment. By the 1970s an increasing awareness, mostly from openly cited Western sources, of the dangers of secondhand smoke abounded. As one abstinence tract argued, "Under no circumstances should a person from a socialist society pollute the air because of their personal pleasure and ruin the health of those around them."[83] And later, "Of course it is not fair…that the smoker lights up for 80–100 minutes of their day while others around them are in the clouds of smoke they have created."[84] Among these others were of course women and children, whose importance for the future of socialism and the nation brought concerns about smoking in the home environment to a feverish pitch. Worries about the effects of smoking on women and children in public venues also were on the rise.

Considering that socialist thinkers and abstinence activists wanted smoking out of the workplace and home, Bulgartabak's focus on leisure marketing and sales was not entirely contradictory. Perhaps providing workers with leisure venues could purify the workplace of slacker tendencies? Workers would have the incentive—and vacation packages indeed were part of factory incentives—to work hard and play hard after hours. Leisure separated from work would be refreshing and regenerative and make workers happier and more productive on the job. Perhaps even some smoking and restful café and bar sociability could be part of this deserved break from the daily grind. In practice, however, smoking in the workplace persisted and even intensified in the decades of late communism. At the same time, tourism and urban socialist leisure practices began to seem shockingly debauched to many observers. The reality of chain-smoking men, women, and youth, along with rampant alcohol consumption during leisure hours in public venues, drew harsh criticism from party circles even as the party directly enabled such practices.

The role of the state agencies in creating the problem was not lost on the abstinence press. Though themselves state-sponsored, abstinence publications were surprisingly frank and critical about how competing state interests had intensified the problem. One source, for example, questioned the "tendency here in Bulgaria for the increase in production of cigarettes" given the various medical and social problems associated with smoking.[85] More strikingly, state-provided restaurants, bars, pivnitsas, and *kafene-sladkarnitsas* (coffee and pastry shops) were incessantly critiqued in the abstinence press.

Their ubiquitous nature, particularly in sites of leisure, in and of itself was seen as an affront to the abstinence movement and the closely associated tourist movement. A 1964 cartoon from *Turist,* for example, depicts a rather puzzled hiker on a mountain top, surrounded by taverns, bars, and restaurants.[86] A quite similar image from the abstinence newspaper *Trezvenost,* with the caption "a romantic night in the mountains," shows four buildings, labeled "restaurant, hotel, bar, and mekhana," obstructing the pristine view.[87] From the point of view of *Trezvenost,* such temptations were an unwanted distraction not just from the landscape but from proper and productive communist leisure pursuits. This critique was not just about the sullying of the pristine mountain environment. The Black Sea coast came under an even more scathing attack. In a cartoon from 1975, a rather innocent-looking young girl stands on a sandy beach with her suitcase in hand, surrounded by a bar, pivnitsa, and café, while a man lies dead drunk in front of her on the sand.[88] The clear message is that beach resorts, with their pervasive culture of leisure consumption, were a debauched and corrupting environment for all Bulgarians but especially for youth.

Youth were the clear focus of the antismoking and antidrinking message. Perhaps more than any other segment of Bulgarian society, youth were continually depicted in abstinence caricatures and exposés. For example, a 1964 "criminal photo story" in *Turist* depicted a group of hip young Bulgarians smoking and drinking in a mountain cabin on Mount Vitosha, within an easy driving distance from Sofia. A picture of the aftermath of their debauchery was equated with a crime scene—complete with sheets muddied by the boots of one of the Sofia "hooligans." Cigarette butts and bottles defile

Exo-o-o-o!

Карикатура от С т. Г р о з д е в

A hiker on a mountaintop in a sea of consumption venues. *Turist*, February 1974, 32.

the pretty little cabin nestled on the pristine mountainside, now tainted by the urban visitors.[89] Far from leaving behind urban blight in favor of nature's delights, Sofia youth allegedly holed up and partied in the state-provided cabin meant to facilitate communion with nature and healthy, productive tourism. Similarly, in a fictionalized feuilleton in *Turist*, two young men from Sofia visit wintery Mount Vitosha to stay at the Shtastlivets Hotel.[90] The young men brazenly park themselves in the hotel restaurant, where they drink Czech beer and smoke, viewing the natural scene around them indirectly through a large picture window. One of the pair, Ivan, retires to his room to sleep, and they plan on "meeting in the café and bar later." On his way out of the restaurant Ivan looks at the snowy trees through the "glass and cigarette smoke," commenting, "I don't understand what it is that people think is so exciting and romantic in the winter. . . . There is only boredom as in the city."[91] The young men have a rather idle approach to winter tourism—idly enjoying nature through the smoky glass. Their excessive sleep, intoxication, and boredom are equated with "laziness and licentiousness."[92] The communist predicament was how to provide the population with free time and provide the good life without encouraging such debauchery and waste.

"Ivan" and friend smoking in a café in the Shtastlivets Hotel on Mount Vitosha. *Turist*, November 1974, 30.

As state-provided leisure venues multiplied, official sources expressed hopes that such establishments could somehow be schools of modernity, indicative of the "refined taste and high culture" of their visitors.[93] In fact, many of the new venues were built with the express purpose of countering "irrational consumption" among youth as well as adults.[94] Such establishments were meant to provide a place to "satisfy the growing demands of both youth and adults, to appease the need to express social prestige and at the same time exclude the use of alcohol and tobacco products." Yet as one source on the problems of youth describes,

> They [discotheques] were created for the more effective use of free time for youth. But do they fulfill these functions? In my opinion, categorically "no." Especially where they are under the control of Balkantourist. . . . Discotheques have turned into places where young people spend a lot of money and learn how to smoke and drink imported alcoholic drinks. And if there is something that they learned from the propaganda on sobriety [and antismoking], then it is lost and forgotten in the atmosphere of these luxurious, smoke-filled venues.[95]

The fact that these establishments, whose express purpose was supposedly abstinence from tobacco and alcohol, were not smoke- and drink-free is telling. The notion of clean leisure ran counter to the goals and needs of Balkantourist and Bulgartabak to stay solvent and fulfill their plans for domestic sales. Abstinence sources were particularly caustic in their attack on the role these public establishments took in the shaping of misguided Bulgarian youth. In one particularly telling image from *Trezvenost* with the caption "worldview," a young boy limply holds a toy car while despondently looking out his apartment window. The view consists of signs reading "bar," "pivnitsa," and "tsigari"(cigarettes). In another image a young man gazes at the entrance to a "youth club," which is locked, a movie theater that says "no tickets," and finally a pivnitsa with a sign saying "dobre doshli" (welcome). Youth were not to blame for the world of pleasure and temptation that had been created by Bulgarian adults.

By way of remedy, abstinence organizers became involved in local efforts to close bars and taverns and replace them with sladkarnitsas or other alcohol-free (and ideally smoke-free) venues for youth to spend free time. In 1972 in Ruse the local abstinence organization transformed a krŭchma-pivnitsa, where presumably older male "drunks and loafers" hung out, into an alcohol-free kafene-sladkarnitsa, where kids, moms and, in short, all clients would be served. A sign on the wall now read "Please don't smoke."[96] Such transformations were the result of a general call for the closing of krŭchmas-pivnitsas or their transformation into food or sweets venues without alcohol and smoking. A great of number of such changes were reportedly made, but it is unclear whether they were substantive or merely semantic. Critique of apparent abuse of the new spate of transformations came out in numerous lampoons of the process in the pages of *Trezvenost*. In one image from 1975, for example, an elderly couple looks on and claps during the closing of a pivnitsta. In the next frame, however, to their utter dismay a new sign is hoisted above the storefront that reads "bar."[97] In another image, a red-nosed old man coming out of a pivnitsa yells out at a smoking young man who is walking down the street, "Young man, don't waste your life in a pivnitsa, your place is in a bar!" In both of these images, "bar" is written in the Latin script, an allusion to the presumed Western influence of the newly named establishments.[98] In other words, whether replacing or rivaling old forms of leisure, new forms were equally, if not more, insidious.

The fact that children smoked in these places of public sociability was an increasingly prevalent concern, especially given their flaunting of the practice in front of adults in an apparent show of disrespect for their elders. In one case, *Trezvenost* describes having placed a hidden camera in a park in Sofia, where the reporters found an appalling scene of as many as fifty to a hundred kids smoking in the park right across from their high school. Immediately upon exiting the school, the offenders brazenly asked passersby for a light and crossed the boulevard with cigarettes in their mouths. Most disturbingly, according to the journalistic observers, "the Students of the capital smoke en masse and in front of everyone, in school, on the street, in the park, and in establishments. They smoke without shame and without any desire to hide it."[99] In addition, the menacing "need to be fashionable" was constantly cited as a contributing factor to the dangerous rise in youth smoking.[100] Again, incorrect notions of what was rightfully modern were highlighted, as was the more problematic notion of fashion (*moda*) as a destructive Western phenomenon, a blot on the aesthetic face of socialism.[101]

Bulgarian youth, of course, were not impervious to the contradictions in such messages, given the fact that their parents and teachers, doctors, and other public figures smoked.[102] Even antismoking sources decried such facts and laid considerable blame on these authority figures, who set a bad example for proper socialist behavior. The following testimonial from a Bulgarian eighth grader in the health journal *Zdrave* illustrates the way that antismoking messages were often deployed and received. In a rather humorous vein, this probably fictional student tells the story of how his teacher, comrade Patlazhanov, was reading a lecture to the class on the evils of smoking:

> When he gave the example of how one drop of nicotine could kill a horse . . . everyone turned to Pesho Konia the leader of the smokers in the class and giggled [his surname was based on the word for horse]. Because the teacher thought the students were laughing at him he called them hooligans and low-life. He ran out of the room and slammed the door, but the students opened it again to see that he did not even wait until he had gone into the teachers' lounge to light a cigarette with trembling hands in the hallway. The students were not so impatient. They lit up in the bathroom.

The students were caught and taken to the principal, and the author's father later scolded him at home. While yelling, however, the stressed-out father "filled a whole ashtray with butts." Finally, the father sent the boy to buy him a pack of Sluntse (a Bulgarian brand of cigarettes), fortuitously leaving him enough change to buy himself some Arda (a cheaper brand). As the narrator sarcastically pointed out, "Shouldn't I follow my father's example?"[103] Although probably fictionalized, this story was most certainly describing a common scenario from Bulgarian life in the communist period. In spite of state control under socialism, mixed messages abounded. The regime promoted and provided leisure and luxury while berating it. Parents and teachers spouted slogans while ignoring them. The nearer it came to achieving ripe communism, the more the government felt the need not only to appease the population with the good life it had promised them but also to make sure that that life would *reflect* an idealized notion of communism.

In *Trezvenost* images of parents smoking in front of, over, and onto children abounded. Their "crime" was especially egregious, for even if they were to eventually die out as a generation, their habits would not die with them. The future, then, relied not just on youth but on parents and particularly on young women, who were most directly responsible for literally and figuratively reproducing the nation in the proper socialist mold. The prominence of smoking boys and young men in many of the images described make it clear that they had a major if not predominant presence among Bulgaria's public smokers. But women, especially young women, were also viewed with alarm as part of a new army of smokers.

Since the beginning of the period, women had been drawn into the service of the state not only as producers but consumers. The female worker and consumer citizen was critical, in fact, to the regime's larger goal of material modernization.[104] Within the expanding Bulgarian city and, to a lesser extent, within the village, women played important roles in the visible discarding of rural backwardness in favor of a modern material life. They were targeted as productive consumers who would bring the artifacts of modernity into their homes and wear them on their bodies.[105] Via smoking women would consume modernity throughout the 1960s, and Bulgartabak targeted women in ads that featured images of smoking women promising that its cigarettes could "satisfy even the most capricious smoker."[106] A specific brand for "women's tastes," Femina, was developed, and smoking was deemed acceptable, almost required, for the emancipated and modern women that the regime courted and sought to shape. Bulgartabak's branding and (albeit limited) advertising invited, and expected, women to take part in the public leisure consumption.

But an increasing awareness of the link between smoking and women's emancipation presented a theoretical dilemma for state officials by the late 1970s and 1980s, when the number of women smokers skyrocketed. On the one hand, citing the American suffragettes as an example, numerous sources admitted that smoking was historically linked to emancipation and "progressive change" for women.[107] On the other hand, health officials and economists alike from the Bulgarian communist elite were concerned by the phenomenon that "equality with men drives women to smoke." Ironically, they extolled the virtues of the village tradition—otherwise maligned as backward—for providing a shelter from the evils of smoking for Bulgaria's rural women.[108] And while Bulgarian communists had always gone to great lengths to promote and cultivate the image and economic reality of the modern woman, they also began to disparage newly urbanized and emancipated women who smoked to "appear modern."[109] Never mind the fact that images of women smoking were prevalent in film, novels, and tobacco ads from the 1950s and 1960s. By the late socialist period, these luxury-seeking, smoking creatures of ripe socialism presented the regime with a critical challenge. In fact, precisely as the number of women smokers increased, anxieties were heightened about the social costs of smoking and the implications for a Bulgarian communist future. Smoking women, in a sense, posed a concerted threat to the Bulgarian nation itself because of issues related to reproduction and child rearing.

The antismoking writings of the late 1970s and 1980s incessantly expressed alarm about the particular problem of women smokers. Although a smaller percentage of women than men actually smoked in this period, the number of women smokers rose at a rate alarmingly faster than that for men. In a period when Bulgarian birth rates were lower than ever, the connection between smoking and women's reproductive capacity was a particular concern. In a 1976 collection of "conversations" among health professionals, connections between emancipation, smoking, reproduction, and femininity are explicit:

> The cigarette has become one of the required markers of the emancipation of women, of their independence. In essence this ill-conceived independence is costly in terms of the unshakable dependence of the woman smoker on the cigarette with severe consequences for her health. For women the poisonous tobacco substances have negative effects on their ovaries. Their activities are disturbed, and as a result the appearance of the woman is changed—she takes on a manlike appearance. The tender color of her face takes on an earthy hue, the woman either grows thinner or abnormally fatter. The regularity of her menstrual cycle is disturbed. Her voice becomes hoarse and with a base tone.[110]

In succumbing to the vice of tobacco, women allegedly endangered the reproductive health of the nation. Not only did they have an erratic cycle, but smoking purportedly "negatively affects her sexual desire."[111] The image of the smoking woman was unflattering, manly. Smoking, it was argued, was customarily "connected with the image of a man." And as one source openly complained, "cigarette smoke coming out of the lips or nose of a woman is something uncommon that appears to us as something vulgar and unnatural."[112] In the lexicon of the antismoking literature, smoking obscured and sullied the very essence of woman.

The smoking woman was not only a "manly" and "unnatural" sight, she was also perilously de-sexed. The antismoking literature decried the damage done to the unborn when women smoked during pregnancy. It also claimed that these women had more planned and spontaneous abortions, and if they did manage to conceive, lactation was depressed and their milk was "lacking in vitamin C."[113] Even more problematic, it argued, was that smoking, especially women's, had a significant impact on men's sexual function:

> It is proven that smoking negatively affects the sexual abilities of men and sexual desire of women. Nicotine depresses sexual function. As a result there is a sexual weakness in men and sexual frigidity in women, although not in all smokers, in a significant percentage. The smell of smoke from the lips of women diminishes the attraction for men and acts as an inhibitor to the sexual act....Many men said that they reacted negatively even to the smell of smoke on the clothes of female smokers.[114]

Admittedly, smoking men's sexual weakness and "abnormal sperm" were evidently part of the reproductive predicament. But the literature attached more importance to the sight and smell of smoking women as a supposed sexual turnoff.[115] As another source argued, "Men in our surveys said that a smoking cigarette in a woman's mouth lessens or eliminates their sexual attraction. Even if we accept that tobacco has no ill effect on the female organism, then isn't this last fact enough of an argument against smoking among women?"[116] It is unclear here whether the primary concern was over the negative effects on reproduction in general or, more narrowly, men's sex lives.

At the same time, and in contradiction to such arguments, women who crossed conventional gender boundaries into the traditionally male space of the tavern or bar were often depicted as oversexed, a latter-day image of the interwar fallen woman. In *Trezvenost* image after image of Bulgarian women smoking in bars and cafés or on park benches depicts them as buxom and leggy, scantily clad, and alluringly posed.[117] The ample cleavage and apparent Western miniskirts clearly marks them as deviant, given the rather puritanical norms of dress for the time. What's worse, there is a recurring theme of bad mothering: in one unflattering image a sexily dressed woman is shown with her baby peering out of his carriage as she blows smoke in his face. The caption reads, "The first lesson."[118] But perhaps equally damning, most smoking women were depicted without children, as in an image of a sexy and seemingly drunk woman with a cigarette in her mouth, who leans against a smoking man with glazed eyes. The caption reads, "Full equality."[119] The implication is clear. Smoking women had gravely misunderstood the meaning of equality and modernity and were shirking their duties as reproducers and caregivers of the nation's children.

But in spite of the seriousness of such charges, critiques of leisure consumption were generally light-hearted, comic lampoons that probably evoked a chuckle rather than mass fear of incarceration. By 1982 approximately 50 percent of Bulgarian men and women smoked; of these, a large percentage smoked an average of twenty or more cigarettes a day—more than one a waking hour.[120] Eliminating smoking from socialist society by this period was far from feasible given that half the population smoked and a fourth worked in the tobacco industry.[121] The more the regime railed against smoking, the more Bulgarians smoked, with ever-higher percentages of their income devoted to the purchase of tobacco.[122] In a period of increasing deficits of bare necessities like certain food items and toilet paper, the declining legitimacy of the socialist regime made serious attempts to require the population to give up cigarettes simply unrealistic. Although many goods were in short supply, the regime continued to supply cheap and even luxurious cigarettes to the Bulgarian population and the Bloc. Its legitimacy and very survival depended on it. Certainly there seem to have been a number of committed voices calling for abstinence, but they were working with severely limited resources against rather onerous odds. Not only was the population at large unresponsive to the message, but the state itself had an extreme conflict of interest. Economic as well as political imperatives assured that tourism and smoking would flourish in this period among men, women and Bulgaria's youth. It is quite clear that a certain degree of irrational consumption was not only tacitly accepted but also required for the building of socialism. As tourism and cigarette sales were connected to state economic imperatives, they also continued to be critical to the appeasement of the growing needs of an increasingly modern population.

By the end of the communist period, Bulgaria was a country of smokers. Bulgaria, the former Bloc nations, and China had, and generally still have, the highest rates of smoking in the world. This is revealing, given that in the Eastern Bloc advertising was meager if not nonexistent in comparison with the robust multimillion-dollar campaigns in the West. Even without advertising, smoking expanded at the same rate (or faster) than the West. This fact was used by Western companies in their own defense to decouple the presumed link between the expansion of smoking and advertisement. And perhaps they were right. Maybe it was not the advertisements paid for by the

American tobacco industry that created smokers after all. The production of a desirable and inherently addictive product on both sides of the Iron Curtain clearly played a role, but smoking also seemed to have a momentum all its own.

This momentum was severely curtailed in the West, beginning in the 1970s and 1980s, by a series of legal actions and campaigns waged by individuals, class-action groups, a grassroots antismoking lobby, and eventually an interventionist state. Under communism, however, in spite of a range of state concerns and state-sponsored campaigns, smoke permeated Bulgarian life as never before. For unlike in the West, there was no grassroots movement or legal mechanism to question or rein in the industry. And there was no desire to stop on the part of the Bulgarian population. On the contrary, smoking was a luxury and a freedom that was offered on a grand scale in a period when both were in short supply. In the final analysis, antismoking was an unwelcome message. Perhaps it was the messenger that was the real problem.

CHAPTER 7

Smokes for Big Brother

Bulgartabak and Tobacco under Communism

In the summer of 1973 Dimitŭr Iadkov, the director of the Bulgarian state tobacco monopoly, Bulgartabak, was in the New York City headquarters of Philip Morris at the end of his tour of tobacco facilities in the American South. After a whirlwind tour of the sights and smells of American tobacco, Iadkov had the pleasure of coffee, smokes, and a chat with Hugh Cullman, then CEO of Philip Morris. It was in Cullman's office that Iadkov was apprised of the real reason that the Bulgarian tobacco delegation had been wined and dined across the South:

A few things were clarified in the office of Philip Morris during our last meeting in New York. . . . I looked at the map behind the president's desk and BULGARTABAK was written across it from East Germany, over the Czechs, to the huge area of the USSR all the way to Vladivostok. . . . I told him I felt like I was in the Pentagon and he said—"You are not mistaken, Mr. Iadkov, this is the 'pentagon' of Philip Morris. We look at the world this way." The president stood and pointed at the map. "You see the spheres of interest. Look here is BAT's [British American Tobacco's] market, here is Reynolds [R. J. Reynolds], this is Reemtsma [a German firm]. And these are the markets of Philip Morris. I would say that we are almost everywhere with the exception of this huge territory that is held by Bulgartabak. I have to admit,

Mr. Iadkov, that I really envy you. I always dream of those markets. I say this with sincere envy, because for our company the market rules.[1]

In the course of his American tour, Iadkov had been exposed to a great deal, from new tobacco harvesting and processing technologies to new ways of conducting business and finally to the capitalist notion of markets, as opposed to simple provisioning of goods. All of this would have a profound influence on the future of Bulgarian tobacco. At the same time, Iadkov began to fully appreciate the benefits of the Bulgarian position within the Bloc's integrative economic institution, Comecon. For within the context of Comecon specialization, Bulgaria provided cigarettes for the Bloc, which became a kind of captive market for Bulgartabak. The jewel in the crown of this market, of course, was the Soviet Union; by 1972 the USSR was the biggest importer of cigarettes in the world, and Bulgaria was its main supplier. Armed with this market and considerable resources to respond to its demands, the leadership of Bulgartabak eventually propelled the tobacco concern to a place of prestige in the jet-setting, international circles of global tobacco.

This image of a communist, state-run industry might be hard to reconcile with common assumptions about the system as a colossal economic failure, with subsidized agriculture and industry that was unproductive and not market-oriented. However, such assumptions are closely tied to the shortages and economic crises of the late communist period and Western triumphalist views of the system's collapse. Certainly many socialist enterprises were eventual failures, especially by the later decades of the period when the result of heavy industrial development was a gargantuan rust belt from the Urals to the Oder River. This makes it all the more astounding that Bulgartabak was such an unmitigated success, especially in the late communist period. For the first time in Bulgarian history, one centralized enterprise—under the state—controlled tobacco production from seed to cigarette. Ever attuned to Soviet and Bloc tastes, Bulgaria became the biggest exporter of cigarettes in the world between 1966 and 1988 (or in some years second only to the United States), exporting roughly 80 percent of overall production.[2] About 90 percent of Bulgartabak's exported cigarettes went to its closest trading partner and political ally, the Soviet Union.[3]

As Iadkov—in the position of director from 1971 to 1991—points out in his voluminous memoirs, "tobacco and politics were always connected."[4] As Nazi troops withdrew and the Red Army moved into Bulgarian territory in the fall of 1944, tobacco shipments were detained and redirected. At home the social landscape of tobacco production was gradually and thoroughly transformed as pro-Nazi tobacco merchants were brought to trial, and trade, along with Bulgaria itself, came under the full control of the Bulgarian Communist Party. After the state tobacco monopoly was formed in 1947, it stood at the helm of a total reordering of the industry. Not only did it replace personnel with more politically reliable individuals, but it created a more socially equitable system in which a larger percentage of tobacco profits was made available to local producers and workers, through direct payment as well as social services. Although communism introduced a period of well-documented political repression, for the average tobacco peasant and worker it was also a boon. Indeed, both groups were embraced and wooed by the new regime as the revolutionary core of the new socialist society it sought to build.

Without a doubt, tobacco revenues played an important role in the larger modernization projects that accompanied Bulgaria's socialist transformation, one that had far-reaching implications not just for workers—many of whom were women—but also for Bulgaria's Muslim minority populations. As Bulgarian populations rapidly urbanized, Muslims—Turks and Pomaks (Bulgarian speaking-Muslims)[5]—generally remained rural, a large number of them in the tobacco-rich Rhodope and Pirin Mountains. The tobacco industry became increasingly dependent on Muslim growers, which encouraged a certain degree of integration of these populations into Bulgarian socialist society. On the other hand, the organization of the tobacco economy enabled a measure of social separation for Muslims, as it allowed (and even required) that they remain in their mountain hamlets, where they could retain distinct cultural attributes. Even as Muslim difference became anathema to the communist state, their potential emigration posed larger problems for Bulgaria's tobacco economy and hence the economy as a whole. In complex ways, then, tobacco was intimately involved in the "Muslim question," a perennial issue in Bulgarian communist politics.

Without question Bulgarian tobacco, or Bulgarian gold, played a critical role in domestic as well as international political dynamics. The Iron Curtain, to a large degree, protected Bulgarian Bloc markets from Western penetration, which along with local initiatives brought Bulgartabak into a position of global leadership in cigarette exports. At the same time, by the 1960s and 1970s, détente gave Bulgarian tobacco the means to reach outside the Bloc for technology, resources, and business models. Soviet demand, in fact, necessitated the Bulgarian adoption of Western technologies—and the employment of almost a quarter of the population—to fill ever-growing yearly quotas. Only in 1989, the year of the collapse of communism, was Bulgaria for the first time unable to fulfill these quotas. The collapse of the communist system was closely tied to the intricacies of the tobacco economy with its deep dependency on its own periphery.

Tobacco Loyalties

As World War II came to a close, Bulgarian tobacco interests were in serious need of reordering. After all, during the war 80 percent of its tobacco had gone to Bulgaria's closest ally, Nazi Germany.[6] Not only were German soldiers stationed in Bulgaria and the nearby Balkan provinces provisioned with Bulgarian cigarettes, but the bulk of Bulgarian raw tobacco and cigarette shipments went to the Third Reich, other Axis states, and the quisling governments of Hitler's New Europe. After Red Army occupation, Bulgaria's newly established communist-dominated regime abruptly redirected shipments of tobacco as it began to provision Soviet soldiers and direct massive shipments of raw tobacco and cigarettes to Moscow. As the so-called Fatherland Front took over, directives were sent to every tobacco enterprise and factory, requiring inventories and itemized promises of supplies for the population, the Bulgarian troops (now supporting Allied war efforts), and Soviet troops. In 1944 alone some two thousand tons of tobacco were requisitioned for the Soviet troops, deemed necessary (like food and alcohol) for their basic comfort.[7]

In many ways the new Soviet trade partner filled the immediate void in demand for raw Bulgarian tobacco left by the collapsing German state and cigarette industry. In early 1945, the USSR bought twenty-four thousand tons of tobacco that would otherwise have languished in Bulgarian warehouses in the midst of political and administrative chaos. Apparently a good deal of tobacco that was exported to the Soviet Union was never paid for; perhaps it was considered part of the war restitution connected to Soviet looting of properties in occupied German and other formerly Axis territories across Eastern Europe. While tobacco peasants and workers were rewarded and wooed as heroes in the struggle against fascism, tobacconists were put on trial and the Fatherland Front began the mass confiscation of tobacco industry properties.[8]

People's courts, though present across the region of Red Army occupation, were particularly harsh in Bulgaria.[9] A whole set of these trials (process 9) focused on Bulgarians engaged in economic crimes with alleged political consequences, namely, direct trade with Germany. Sixteen tobacco merchants were brought to trial as servants of Reemstma and hence Nazi Germany. In the indictment prosecutors charged the Reich with "enslaving Bulgaria" on the "colonial principle,"[10] in order to secure an economic base for its war machine. Although other industries and merchants were also implicated, Bulgarian tobacco, the court charged, was a central facet of this Germany policy, as it made up 75 percent of all export in the period and was worth some 14 billion lev in 1943 alone. Bulgarian merchants, prosecutors alleged, had enabled the German economic penetration of Bulgaria and hence the plundering of Bulgarian gold and, more pointedly, the tobacco peasant and worker. Bulgarian (as well as Macedonian and Thracian) tobacco, as laid out in the indictment, was sold to Germany at prearranged and ruinous prices and then consumed in Germany or re-exported for a premium to German trade partners in occupied and Nazi-allied New Europe. This "sucked the last lifeblood out of the Bulgarian economy" and funded German expansion. While a host of state actors were at fault for the "clearing agreement" of October 1940 that enabled this trade, economic actors were also "traitors," as "buying tobacco for Germany was not just an economic but a political act."[11] A core group of twenty-two merchants who supplied Reemstma was brought to trial for economic sabotage and treason.[12] Of these, only sixteen actually made it to trial, as the other six were killed in various pretrial acts— "death sentences" of an unofficial order.

Stefan Chaprashikov was one of these merchants from a prominent tobacco merchant family who lost his life as social hostilities exploded in vigilante justice that is as yet not well documented. His brother Aleksandŭr, however, who denied any commercial connection to his brother, was given the fairly light sentence of one year in prison and a hefty fine. In fact, fourteen of the sixteen merchants got similar sentences. In the end, as one prosecutor noted, the accused had delivered 75 percent of "our tobacco" into German hands in acts that were antinational and traitorous but ultimately not treasonous. For "already in 1905, 81.3% of Bulgarian tobaccos went to Germany and Austria, and by 1935, 75% of all tobacco went to Germany." The court therefore concluded that these merchants had not created but simply enabled an "already existing situation."[13] Many of those who received commuted sentences, such as Dimitŭr Bozhkov (the nephew of Stephan and Aleksandŭr Chaprashikov), used their past relationship to Jewish merchants (such as Jacques Asseoff) and interwar Jewish firms to establish credibility with the court.[14] But perhaps even more common were references to purported good works in relation to tobacco peasants, workers, and partisans. In addition, the accused and their defense witnesses stressed the merchants progressive or apolitical nature, their open conflicts with Reemstma, and/or the alacrity with which they had sought trade deals with the Soviet Union in 1940–41 (while it was still a Nazi ally). As one merchant exclaimed in his own defense, "Even the Soviets worked with the Germans."[15] But while sentences were relatively light, these merchants also lost their livelihoods, most of their property, and certainly their future within the Bulgarian socialist state, as they were stigmatized and demonized as part of the exploitative bourgeoisie. Only those who went abroad were able to continue their business, and many of the tobacco families of Bulgaria had the resources and connections to make it out in time.[16]

Meanwhile, the Iron Curtain slowly dropped. As Bulgarian communists consolidated power at home with the aid of the occupying Red Army, American influences, including tobacco interests, were penetrating Europe. Cheap—and higher-nicotine—American cigarettes flooded the Western European market in Marshall Plan aid packages, becoming a kind of valued local currency in this tumultuous period of reconstruction and also trickling into parts of the Bloc.[17] In fact, the United States, along with several Western European countries, was a participant in the Plovdiv trade fair of 1947. Relative flexibility in trade relations meant that in these immediate postwar years, Bulgarian tobacco began to quickly regroup. In addition to making an export deal with the Soviet Union in 1948 for eighty thousand tons, Bulgaria sold some fifteen thousand tons to France and other Western European states.[18] But while Bulgaria was dabbling in relations with other European states, it also became increasingly clear that the Soviet colossus was critical to its economic future. When Foreign Minister Vasil Kolarov opened the 1947 Plovdiv trade fair, he pinned Bulgaria's future on the now national and rational control of its resources under the tutelage of the Soviet Union, which was poised to save the country from a past of "waste and abuse."[19] In the Bulgarian communist mind, the Soviets were defined as neither foreign nor exploitative but rather the great white hope of Bulgarian political and economic cooperation.

The tobacco trade was central to this highly politicized and rapidly tightening cooperation. In the now-famous show trials that swept Eastern Europe beginning in the late 1940s, involvement in trade with the West was linked to accusations of espionage for many of those accused and executed. In the trials of 1948, Traicho Kostov, the former president of the Economic-Financial Committee of the Council of Ministers, was the central figure. Kostov was accused not only of treason, Titoism, Trotskyism, and Anglo-American espionage but also of committing acts aimed at the "disorganization of the national economy" and the supply system of the country. His presumably anti-Soviet criminal activities included attempts to sell tobacco to France and the supposed withholding of information on tobacco prices from the Soviet Union.[20] Ironically, Kostov—unlike the tobacco merchants tried some four years earlier—was a faithful and loyal communist who had been an active partisan during the war. But, as elsewhere in the Bloc, the ax was meant to fall on the most loyal so that everyone, no matter what his station, would have something to fear. Kostov's loyalty to Moscow had come into question when he openly criticized the Soviet practice of buying Bulgarian tobaccos at low prices and then re-exporting them on the world market.[21] As a result, he, unlike most of the merchants mentioned above, was given the death sentence and executed in 1949 for a completely bogus spate of crimes. Along with Kostov, ten other prominent communists were tried, receiving a range of sentences from life imprisonment to twelve to fifteen years, all harsher sentences than tobacco merchants received in the people's courts trials. Angel Timov, the head of the newly spawned Bulgarian state tobacco monopoly, was both a witness to the trade-related crimes of his peers and a victim of the purge trials that accompanied the Kostov case. He was imprisoned in 1949 and not released and "rehabilitated"—meaning proclaimed innocent—until 1956, when he again become director of Bulgartabak.[22] Bulgarian gold was deeply imbedded in the process of establishing political loyalties, but it was not only trade that became steeped in politics.

Tobacco workers had been among the first to take to the streets to protest the Bulgarian regime in its last days before the Soviet occupation. They and a segment of peasant growers were strong supporters of the new regime and were handsomely rewarded for their loyalties with social mobility. One of the first acts of the Fatherland Front was to double tobacco prices, a godsend to tobacco-growing peasants.[23] In addition, on April 26, 1947, the Bulgarian parliament voted for the establishment of a state-run tobacco monopoly, a move that was strongly supported by workers and growers, who had been agitating for a monopoly for decades. Ivan Pitekov—who later became a key translator and functionary in the industry—described this in his memoir from the postcommunist period as a "a long cherished dream of hundreds of thousands of tobacco laborers—from the field and stuffy factories."[24] The monopoly, many workers and growers had believed, was the best way for the fickle tobacco trader and factory owner to be reined in by state regulation that would protect growers and workers. As Iadkov, ever the convinced communist, later reported, finally "the people became the masters of one of our greatest riches"—tobacco.[25]

Pitekov, a keen observer of Bulgartabak, observed that the communist state was determined to make the tobacco sector into a fiscal cash cow for Bulgaria. Tobacco revenues would not be directed toward the amassing of personal fortunes, as they had been in the past, and at least initially increased production would be achieved through incentives. Even before the first five-year plan was launched in 1949, the Fatherland Front government put into place a new system of stimulus for growers, providing a certain amount of rations for every decare (.25 acre) planted—74kg of flour, 20kg of fodder, 1kg of soap, 1 liter of margarine, 2 meters of cloth, 1 pair of shoes, etc.[26] In a time of severe postwar shortage these extra rations, as well as high prices, were ample enticement, and tobacco production increased rapidly. Meanwhile the Bulgarian tobacco monopoly closed many factories and smaller workshops and worked to streamline the system of production by consolidating every phase.

Loyalties of the tobacco-growing populations of the Bulgarian south were also a critical issue. Many of these regions were ethnically mixed, with Bulgarian, Turkish and/or Pomak populations. This heightened party anxieties, as neighboring Turkey was a NATO member as of 1950. In these years, party surveillance revealed that only Turkish and Pomak tobacco *workers,* and not the population at large, supported the Communist Party and the Fatherland Front. Muslim opposition to the Fatherland Front regime came more from Muslim peasants, out of the fear that their land would be taken.[27] As a way of relieving this fear, distribution of land to Muslim peasants became a critical part of party work in Muslim districts; from 1944 to 1947 some eighty thousand Muslim families were given about 1,500,000 decares, an average of about 50 per family.[28] But Muslim loyalties continued to be highly suspect, and the Ministry of War did not hesitate to advance various proposals to cleanse the vulnerable Bulgaro-Turkish border from the "tried and true reserve of Turkey and Imperialism, which is located on our territory."[29] As a consequence, in 1948–49 the state resettled about a thousand Pomak families away from southern border regions to the interior.[30] As local party officials all over Bulgaria reported, there was apparently a growing desire among Turks and Pomaks to emigrate, further heightening suspicions about Muslim loyalty.[31] And while initially only selective emigration (from border areas) had been encouraged, eventually emigration emerged as a viable political alternative for resolving both perceived security problems and domestic policy dilemmas.

Since 1947, the Communist Party had aggressively moved toward rationalizing small-scale, "backward" agriculture through the creation of cooperative (or, in Soviet parlance, collective) farms.[32] By the end of 1948 the BCP initiated a mass push for "voluntary" collectivization, holding thousands of meetings on the local level, but by 1949 only 11.3 percent of all arable land had been collectivized.[33] The peasants openly resisted collectivization, which drove many rural Bulgarians into the larger cities and regional capitals. The Muslim population, though it also was generally opposed to collectivized agriculture, chose to remain in primarily rural areas throughout the period, increasing its social and cultural isolation from the Bulgarian mainstream.[34] Both BCP suspicions of Muslim loyalties and problems with incorporating Muslim populations into rural transformation projects were mainly responsible for the large-scale expulsion of some 140,000 Turks from Bulgaria in 1950–51.[35] The focus of the expulsion was the Turkish populations of the agriculturally rich plain of Dobrudja in the Bulgarian northeast, with the intent of furthering the collectivization of that region.[36]

Yet large numbers of Turks in the country's southerly regions were also part of the mass migration. As early as 1949 local reports noted that emigration of Turks and Pomaks in the Rhodopes was under way, with severe consequences for the local tobacco fields, which "lay abandoned." The tendency of local Muslims preparing for emigration to neglect their traditional activities in the tobacco economy was seen as none other than "sabotage."[37] In response, state officials announced to the local population in the Rhodopes that emigration was banned until "after the tobacco harvest."[38] Ultimately party officials hoped to resettle these areas with "Bulgarian populations, who understand how to cultivate tobacco."[39] For Bulgarians, however, these regions, and especially the more remote mountain hamlets where tobacco was grown, were hardly a draw. Instead, opportunities were sought in cities and provincial towns, in and outside the burgeoning tobacco industry. As the period progressed, urbanization brought about a situation in which, for the first time in Bulgarian history, the face of the tobacco grower was predominantly Muslim. Arguably, this heightened economic interdependencies in the provincial and national economies. But it also meant that the tobacco question and the Muslim question became tightly connected. This would have far-reaching implications in the later decades of the period. But in the meantime, with at least some of the more reactionary Muslims gone from Bulgaria after the 1950–51 exodus, the process of integrating the rest of them into Bulgarian socialist society began in earnest; The tobacco industry was a part of this process.

Tobacco Tastes

It was a long and bumpy road from the tobacco towns of the south to Sofia, where Bulgarian smoking rapidly increased and Bulgartabak operations were based. In the postwar years Bulgartabak was increasingly forced to fulfill centrally dictated plans for production, as tobacco consumption grew to astronomical proportions in Bulgaria and across the Bloc. East or west, the postwar years were the smoking era par excellence as women and youth, along with men, took up the habit in unprecedented numbers. The return of soldiers who had been provisioned at the front and newly mobilized women became the foundation for a new world of smokers. Furthermore, coming on the heels of postwar shortages, an economic boom on both sides of the

Iron Curtain translated into the growth of ever-larger urban, professional, and relatively well-off working-class consumers. As a 1954 article in the *New Yorker* noted, for the first time there were ashtrays placed around the table at the UN Security Council in "recognition that the common man's right to a good cigarette transcends ideological differences."[40]

In the early years, Bulgarian tobacco was far from the top priority in terms of investment, overshadowed by basic heavy industry and infrastructure. By the mid-1950s, however, in line with the consumer turn in the Bloc, Bulgartabak was streamlined and production numbers expanded. As the world's tobacco concerns watched in envy, Bulgaria's export numbers rose astronomically, particularly after the 1960 Soviet-Sino spilt.[41] This meant that China no longer functioned as a key supplier of tobacco to the Soviet Union, and exports of tobacco and cigarettes from Bulgaria to the USSR increased from seven hundred tons in 1955 to five thousand by 1960.[42]

Rising Soviet as well as Bulgarian and Bloc demand for cigarettes drove explosive growth in tobacco production and export in Bulgaria in the course of the next few decades. Ever-rising expectations of production in Bulgaria's annual and five-year plans drove Bulgartabak directors to seek out any means to fulfill and overfulfill quotas. When this was achieved, tobacco production, and especially the manufacture of cigarettes, was charted with pride by the tobacco industry as a clear marker of socialist achievement.[43] As Comecon began to demand that Bulgaria specialize in cigarette production for the Bloc, cigarettes became what Iadkov called the "locomotive of the Bulgarian economy."[44] Bulgarian gold essentially became the currency with which the state obtained machinery and other means of industrialization from other the Bloc countries. Meanwhile, the slow opening of the Iron Curtain to trade with the West in the 1960s offered new possibilities for Bulgartabak to exploit the experience and technologies of the West while still holding on to its coveted Soviet market.

By the mid-1960s in spite of right-wing opposition in the United States, the Lyndon B. Johnson administration was actively encouraging American firms to establish trade with the Eastern Bloc.[45] The tobacco industry immediately began stepping up its efforts to penetrate Bloc markets in any way possible. In 1964, Justus Heymans, representative of Philip Morris International, went on a fact-finding mission to Moscow. Although provided with a tour of the Dukat cigarette factory, which Heymans reported was "not up to date," the American was generally given a rather cold shoulder in the Soviet capital. This is not altogether surprising considering that, along with cigarette samples and the Philip Morris annual report, Heymans brought a particularly unwelcome message. "American blend" cigarettes, he reported to the Soviet representative, were increasingly in demand across the globe and hence the wave of the future for cigarette aesthetics. Since 1913 with the famous "Coming of the Camel" campaign, American cigarette production had been dominated by the American blend, composed primarily of Virginia and Burley broad-leafed tobaccos with a smaller amount of the narrow-leafed Oriental types.[46] The Soviets, however, were not buying what Bulgarians in the cigarette industry later referred to as "trade tricks of the capitalists."[47] In fact, the Soviet response was rather categorically contrary, namely "that their taste was mainly Oriental."[48] By this the Russian trade representative meant the types of cigarettes that were produced in Bulgaria, still made almost from exclusively Oriental tobaccos. At this juncture it became clear to Heymans that, in terms of cigarette aesthetics, there was an Iron Curtain of taste that divided East from West. This divide, however, was soon to be breached.

Usually grown in mountain regions in a particular climate, Oriental tobaccos had a much stronger natural flavor than broad-leafed tobaccos but were significantly lower in nicotine. The American broad-leafed varieties (like Virginia and Burley) had a lighter flavor and desirable burning properties and were also were easier to "aromatize" and "saucify"—to infuse with aromas and flavors that were pleasing to a wide variety of palates. Their higher nicotine content gave a quicker "high" to smokers and they were more chemically addictive. In limited amounts, Virginia tobacco had been grown in Bulgaria since 1937, and Burley would be introduced in 1967, but high-quality Oriental tobaccos dominated, and in the early 1960s purely Oriental cigarettes were the main types available to smokers in Bulgaria, the USSR, and elsewhere in the Bloc. This type of tobacco was in no way inferior to Western types. In fact, it had historically been deemed superior and was still highly coveted by the West—which acquired it mainly from Greece and Turkey—to use in its famous blends. But as Western packaging and advertising underwent significant development in the early postwar period, many Bloc inhabitants, imagining a superior West, also harbored the illusion that Western cigarettes, like other goods, were of a higher quality. Certainly Bulgarian and other Bloc cigarette papers, packaging, and wrappers were of a lower quality, and filters were still scarcely available. But in spite of such deficiencies, Oriental cigarettes were still king in the East as late as the 1960s. Whether this was a result of taste, cost, or availability is unknown. But change was in the air and, to a certain degree, predated American industry contact.

By the late 1950s Bulgartabak had begun to respond dynamically to perceived changes in consumer taste through aesthetic adjustments in packaging, branding, blending, and flavor variety. Its efforts to exponentially increase quantity and experiment with quality and flavor variety took place firmly within the context of Bloc technologies and tastes. As early as 1961 a Bulgarian publication entitled *Tobacco and Cigarettes* presented a wide variety of cigarette brands that "achieve the full satisfaction of desires of the most demanding smokers in the country and abroad." As the text continued, "Bulgarian cigarettes were greeted extraordinarily well by consumers [*konsumatori*] in the USSR, Czechoslovakia, the GDR, etc."[49] In lavish detail thirty-seven different Bulgartabak brands were featured, all with distinct names, labels, and flavor profiles. The names of the various Bulgarian assortments were derived from "Bulgarian history and nature" (Shipka, Vitosha, Dunav), tobacco regions and types (Rhodope, Dzebel) and were based on Bulgaria's "friendship with other socialist countries" (Laika, Baikal). But Bulgartabak also found no apparent contradiction in the simultaneous description of brands with more Western (English) names printed in Latin script (Derby, Sport, Travel, and Virginia). Significantly, the distinguishing features of each brand—strength, flavor, in some cases filters, and even size and shape—were described in direct reference to the Bloc consumers who preferred them. For example, the Soviets liked Vega and Rodopi; the Czechs, Marica; the East Germans, Yaka; and so on, not because of the names but because of the specific flavor profiles that seemed somehow suited to their national characters.[50] In a period when branding was sparse in Bulgaria, Bulgartabak openly discussed the "importance of branding" for cigarette manufacturing. As an article in *Bŭlgarski tiutiun* pointed out, "It is easier for a passionate smoker to change a number of other things, like food, clothes, etc. than cigarettes for which he has an established taste."[51] Courting a range of consumers, foreign and domestic, through taste and branding became critical to Bulgartabak's success.

Admittedly, to produce a number of these brands Bulgartabak dabbled in a range of techniques, some of which were associated with interwar and postwar American industry practices, including artificial (or natural) aromatization and blending of Oriental with non-Oriental tobaccos. But in 1961 these methods were still overshadowed by elaborate blending of Oriental varieties, a practice that had been common in the local tobacco industry since the nineteenth century. In fact, so-called American blends were not so different from purely Oriental blends. They were only a variation on the time-honored tradition of blending among tobacconists. They were a special recipe that mixed American varieties with Oriental ones, though infusion of natural and artificial flavoring was certainly an American novelty. In 1961 Virginia was still the only Bulgarian cigarette brand produced that used (locally grown) American varieties of tobacco, with a smaller percentage of Oriental tobacco. But Bulgaria was growing more and more American varieties of tobacco in this period and introducing Bulgarian blends that utilized them.

This process accelerated after Bulgartabak increased its direct contacts with the American tobacco industry. After receiving the cold shoulder in Moscow in 1964, Philip Morris began to pursue market penetration at the source of the Oriental tobaccos that the Soviets claimed to prefer. It began by canvassing various officials in Bulgaria, including the American ambassador and embassy staff in Sofia, directors and vice directors of Bulgartabak and Corecom (the hard-currency store chain), and other export officials, with samples of cigarettes.[52] As trade meetings and correspondence slowly began to increase, scientific and technological exchanges were also beginning to occur in the tobacco world across Cold War boundaries. Encouraged by the Soviets to tap into Western technologies, Bulgaria was particularly proactive. In September of 1965 it hosted its first ever tobacco symposium in Plovdiv, one of the primary sites of cigarette production. In attendance were not only representatives from the Soviet Union and across the Bloc but also those from the United States, a number of Western European countries, Turkey, Greece, Yugoslavia, Egypt, and Israel.[53] In the same year, Bulgaria also joined the international tobacco organization, Coresta, and by the 1970s would play a leading role, even hosting the first Coresta conference behind the Iron Curtain in Varna in 1978. As Iadkov later reported, among global tobacconists there was a certain camaraderie of the traditional "guild type," though certainly Cold War tensions still seethed under the surface of their relationships. Such meetings were sites of technology transfer, trade relations, and also aesthetic influence.

The timing of American industry's focus on the Eastern Bloc was undoubtedly more than just a response to de-Stalinization and détente. In 1964 an American study came out that definitively linked smoking to cancer. Though previous studies, including those done in Nazi Germany, had also come to this conclusion, this one had a breakthrough quality, leading to the first surgeon general's warnings on cigarette packaging and ads in the United States. As American smoking growth rates leveled off, smoking was still on the rise worldwide. Philip Morris, like other U.S. tobacco concerns, was well aware that U.S. smoking rates had slowed to 5.6 percent by 1966 while in the Eastern Bloc smoking was up 7.5 percent.[54] By 1966 initial agreements allowed for the very limited sales of American cigarettes at hard-currency stores and foreigner-oriented hotels in Bulgaria, as elsewhere in the Bloc. After a trip to Bulgaria in 1967, the Philip Morris director of research and development, Helmut Wakeham, reported to headquarters that Marlboro and now its com-

Delegates in the main conference hall at the Plovdiv International Tobacco Symposium in 1965. *The First Tobacco Symposium, Plovdiv Bulgaria* (Plovdiv: Conference Publication, 1965).

petition Kent (a product of British American Tobacco) were available in all major hotels for hard currency or in some cases local currency. "There seems to be a market here," he reported, "among the better classes everywhere" for American-type cigarettes.[55] But though only a certain segment of the local population was getting its hands on the rare and desirable forbidden fruit of Western cigarettes, greater efforts to spread American cigarette aesthetics had begun. At the Plovdiv symposium of 1965, for example, virtually all the papers presented were on boring technical subjects such as "Resistance of Tobacco to Thrips," a paper by Dr. Ternovsky of the USSR.[56] The sole American presenter, Fred Triest, who might have been expected to share information about advances in tobacco growing or processing, instead gave a paper entitled "The Function of Tobacco Flavor." It offered a detailed description of the complex chemical process of creating a consistent and pleasing flavorful cigarette using a blend of tobaccos and aromatic additives—everything from vanilla, licorice, and cocoa to rose, jasmine, and wood resins. In positively seductive terms, Triest described how the "taste and aroma of tobacco" was heightened by synthetic mixtures that could achieve "honey and fruit notes," "jasmine top notes," "spicy effects," and "flowery sweetness."[57] The Bloc tobacconists could not help but be seduced by the aesthetic possibilities of

Delegates look at new tobacco-drying technologies at the Plovdiv International Tobacco Symposium in 1965. *The First Tobacco Symposium, Plovdiv Bulgaria* (Plovdiv: Conference Publication, 1965).

American blend technologies, which along with filter technologies began to slowly penetrate tobacco production practices.

By 1965 Bulgartabak and its trading partners from across the Bloc were demanding filters, the American-type king size cigarette (85mm), and American blends.[58] While the Soviets increasingly gave the Bulgarians a green light for industry development and cigarette specialization within Comecon, Bulgartabak looked to the West for trade relations that would enable the transfer of technology and information. Western technology, in fact, was critical to the mechanization and modernization of tobacco processing and cigarette production, simply to meet the growing production quotas, which were so impossibly high that they were frequently not met. But Bulgartabak also explicitly began to recognize that the know-how to make American blends was needed both for increasing internal demand and "so we can enter THEIR [capitalist] markets with the appropriate cigarettes."[59] And Bulgartabak was well on its way to doing just that. At the 1965 Plovdiv symposium, in fact, it amply impressed delegates with its already impressive array of tobacco technologies and its lavish program filled with flashy advertisements of fashionable models smoking "new Bulgarian blends." Some of these, like the brand Luna, explicitly featured Virginia tobaccos with aromatic enhancements, boasting a "new type of Bulgarian scented cigarette, combining the mild pleasant flavor of Oriental tobacco with the peculiar flavor and strength of Virginia tobacco." Another brand, Ropotamo, was lauded as the "second blend which fully satisfies smokers used to this type of cigarette."[60] By 1965 Bulgartabak was moving in an American-blend direction as nicotine-rich Virginia tobaccos made their way into Bulgarian blends. In the decades that followed, local cultivation of Virginia and Burley broad-leafed tobaccos would dramatically increase under the direct tutelage of American specialists.

Negotiations between Bulgaria and Philip Morris began as early as 1966 but would last for almost a decade. In spite of Bulgaria's need for American technology, suspicions abounded. From early on, Philip Morris was ready to move ahead with a full-blown joint venture based in Bulgaria in which it would own a 51 percent *controlling* share. This proposal was deemed "unacceptable" by Bulgartabak managers, who were rightly fearful that "this is their effort to control the socialist market."[61] In addition, in a meeting of Bulgartabak discussing these negotiations, higher-ups expressed well-grounded fears that American-blend cigarettes would supplant Oriental cigarettes on the socialist market. Some questioned the notion that Bulgaria should increase production of American-style cigarettes, which could ultimately be harmful to the market for *Oriental* cigarettes in the Bloc. One tobacco official claimed that in Bulgaria the market for American-type cigarettes was "limited to only Sofia youth," but there was a wider recognition of "the luxury and fashionable nature of American cigarettes" in a global context, which included Bloc consumers.[62] In spite of fears about American intentions, the Bulgarian need for knowledge about fashionable American blends

KOM. ONE OF THE THREE NEW BULGARIAN BLENDS WITH FILTER, SCENTED, KING-SIZE AND IN MOLLINS PACKING.

Cigarette advertisement for Kom cigarettes, a Bulgarian blend presented at the Plovdiv International Tobacco Symposium in 1965. *The First Tobacco Symposium, Plovdiv Bulgaria* (Plovdiv: Conference Publication, 1965).

and especially technology and hard currency was clear. As one Bulgartabak official noted with obvious pragmatism, "If we become partners with the devil, so be it. The form is not important, but the outcome." In light of this attitude, the Bulgartabak relationship with Philip Morris began to go beyond mere words to take the form of "technical help and the exchange of specialists," culminating in an eventual licensing agreement signed in 1975.[63] In the same year a similar agreement was signed with R.J. Reynolds, and within a year Marlboro (Philip Morris) and Winston (R.J. Reynolds) cigarettes were being produced in Bulgarian factories with machines imported by the two companies. Bulgarian specialists were trained to use and maintain the machines while in exchange Bulgartabak paid a royalty on cigarette sales and provided Bulgarian Oriental tobacco to these companies. In this way American companies slowly penetrated the Iron Curtain with their branding as Marlboro, Winston, and also Kent (BAT) became desirable status symbols. In reality, of course, most of these cigarettes were actually produced in the region (unbeknownst to their buyers).

Still, in the midst of contact and exchange with the West, there was an attendant revolution in cigarette aesthetics. Bulgarian studies conducted primarily at the Tobacco Institute in Plovdiv concluded that even Bulgarian smokers seemed to prefer the flavor and "smokability" of blends.[64] As a result, considerable resources were put into attempts to reorient the industry toward "modern aesthetics."[65] The institute conducted taste tests and experimented with aromatization and sauces to emulate American blends and also create "Bulgarian compositions"—hybridized blends with higher contents of Oriental tobacco.[66] In 1966 it signed a licensing agreement with Eastman Kodak for filters and the machinery to produce and attach them to cigarettes.[67] The production of filters was on the rise, as was the use of soft over hard packs and outer cellophane wrappers. Some cigarette technology was procured within the Bloc. For example, the Czech company Škoda had ongoing agreements with Bulgartabak to provide cigarette machines in exchange for cigarettes.[68] But in order to obtain the other needed state-of-the-art technologies, Bulgaria was increasingly exporting raw tobacco to Western markets—particularly West Germany, France, and Japan. The USSR, however, was still getting 75 percent of all Bulgarian raw tobacco exports and 90 percent of cigarette exports (the other 10 percent stayed within the Bloc). But the nature of these exports was changing. By 1975, 82 percent of Bulgarian cigarettes had filters (as opposed to 20% in 1967), 62 percent were king size (only 11% in 1967), and 30 percent were American-blend types (a mere 8% in 1967), but most of them had Bulgarian names, packing, and materials. These changes, as Bulgartabak documents readily show, resulted from market research in Bulgaria and across the Bloc.

In the 1970s and 1980s, in particular, Bulgartabak quite aggressively canvassed its Eastern European market, showering the Bloc with samples and eliciting opinions. Cigarette displays and free samples were constant features at Cold War trade fairs at home (Plovdiv) and around the Bloc (Leipzig,

Riga, Kharkov, Poznan, Moscow, Warsaw, Berlin, and Bratislava).[69] In addition, more orchestrated events, such as taste tests and "promotional weeks," punctuated the period starting in the mid-1960s primarily in the Bloc but also in potential emerging markets like Afghanistan (1976).[70] Though tests revealed a wide range of tastes, American blends began to score higher on test results, especially in the ostensibly more Western-oriented Bloc states of Poland, Czechoslovakia, and Hungary but also among a more select population in the Soviet Union and Bulgaria.

This aesthetic turn, of course, may in part be explained by the fact that the newly produced American blends were by nature higher in nicotine and tar. To be fair, the increased use of filters had some ameliorative effect, but regardless, the switch to American blends meant a switch to a more addictive and carcinogen-laden cigarette. At a time when a revolution in production had brought about a rapid turn to "lights" and other lower-tar and nicotine varieties in the United States, Americans were exporting—or as some would complain, "dumping"—higher-tar cigarettes on world markets. In the Eastern Bloc dumping was severely limited, but technology transfer favored recipes that were of the American classic high-tar and nicotine varieties. Bulgartabak must have been aware of the implications of this change. It had been studying nicotine content and tar in tobaccos themselves in this period and produced numerous widely read (in the West as well) studies on the low-nicotine properties of Oriental tobaccos. In fact, Bulgartabak sources claimed that whereas Western tobaccos were highly carcinogen-laden, Bulgarian tobacco actually contained anticarcinogens![71] Such claims continued in the Bulgarian tobacco industry literature until about the mid-1970s and then were mysteriously silenced. But amid increasingly proactive antismoking campaigns in Bulgaria and the Eastern Bloc as whole, the industry quietly continued to produce and improve quality at a breakneck pace, even as various health officials and politicians began to make attempts to squelch the smoking habit—which had now reached epidemic proportions.[72]

This flurry of activity within the industry required a more willing and able workforce to fulfill ever-expanding quotas. After 1965, economic reform articulated through the so-called New Economic Mechanism required that individual local tobacco enterprises be more productive and fiscally solvent. This drove local collective farms, processing plants, and cigarette factories to spur on growers and workers to produce with a range of incentives from greater pay for higher productivity to sumptuous free vacations. In addition, tobacco revenues were poured into a vast network of free social services, pensions, and the development of housing and local infrastructure in the remote and undeveloped districts of the Rhodope Mountains. As Ivan Pitekov of

Bulgartabak later described the situation, "[Tobacco] profits made their way into tobacco villages," where one could see the gradual appearance of "massive two-story structures [houses], asphalt streets, stone squares, new schools and other buildings for social services."[73] While such services and infrastructure might have seemed substandard to Western observers, local populations saw a huge improvement in standard of living as well as opportunities for education and social advancement.

Tobacco cultivators and workers were showered with these services but also publicly lauded for their revolutionary past and their inordinate contributions to building socialism. In *Bŭlgarski tiutiun,* for example, every issue was a veritable orgy of praise for the workers with their "golden hands" fulfilling and overfulfilling production quotas for tobacco. In a column called the "golden page," there were in-depth biographies and work profiles of workers from various regions. The standard narrative in such stories was the transition that workers or growers had experienced from the "miserable" days before to the "glorious" days after 1944. Workers were openly fetishized with hyperbole and poetic language. As one article claimed, it was not tobacco but tobacco workers that were the true "gold of Bulgaria."[74] As in the past, the overwhelming majority of tobacco producers—in both field and factory—were women. This was reflected in the veritable deluge of biographies, profiles, and articles in *Bŭlgarski tiutiun* on women growers, pickers, factory workers, and specialists. Women in the factory were called the *maistorki na tsigari* (masters of cigarettes), their work described in loving detail—"leaf by leaf the gentle hands of women sort it."[75] In one article entitled "These Golden Hands" the life and work of a woman named Velika was explored, beginning with an adoring description of her hands, "Look at them—nimble, roughened by labor—pure gold. They can tell you many things."[76] And another article asserted, "[T]oday tobacco is the gold of Bulgaria, and women are its creators."[77] In fact, women's significance was so great that in one map of tobacco-growing regions featured in *Bŭlgarski tiutiun* in 1979, each region was marked by a woman in traditional Bulgarian dress. This is somewhat ironic considering that many of these areas were heavily populated by Muslims (Bulgarian- or Turkish-speaking) who mostly did not identify culturally with Bulgarians.

The achievements of Muslim workers and growers, especially women, were quite prominently glorified on the pages of *Bŭlgarski tiutiun.* Here their stories were told through formulaic descriptions of the dark days of capitalism followed by a happy ending resulting from the changes wrought by the communist regime.[78] Their exemplary labor was always a central theme. For example, there was Zatie Khodzhova, who reported that she had worked in tobacco in the precommunist period, hating it since childhood. As she recalled, "Work, work, you didn't know when it was day, night, the work-week or holidays," and there was little to no compensation for your toil. Now (in 1962) she was a "shock-worker," highly productive and so rewarded with various honors in a cigarette factory in Shumen. As Khodzhova exclaimed "the people's government takes care of me like a nurturing mother"; she had a nicely furnished house and received 1,100 lev a month, and her son was studying to be an engineer in Sofia. Her "love for work," as *Bŭlgarski tiutiun* explained, had gained her a new life under a new regime that appreciated and rewarded her.[79] The journal was peppered with frequent pictures of robust, smiling women in the tobacco fields, Muslim and Bulgarian, exuding health, happiness, and a bright future.

Providing Muslims with homes, education, infrastructure, agricul-tural technologies, and places within the tobacco or party hierarchy was linked to efforts to integrate this population into a homogeneous and loyal labor force. These attempts were all the more imperative given the rapid out-migration of Bulgarians from the rural Rhodope Mountain districts in the late 1960s and 1970s. This left a potential labor shortage that only the remaining Muslims with their continually high birthrates could fill. Only Muslims were willing to live and stay in these areas, which in part protected them from the very integration that the socialist state so wanted to promote. In fact, even as the state moved to fully collectivize Bulgarian agriculture by the late 1950s in the name of both economic and social integration, it was always unable to fully, properly collectivize the predom-inantly Muslim mountain districts where most tobacco was grown. These districts, if collectivized at all, fell under the rubric of the so-called family accord, a compromise that allowed for essentially small-scale family plots that drew seed, technology, and equipment from a village-based coopera-tive farm.[80] While the tobacco economy created connections and interde-pendencies between Muslims and the socialist state, it also enabled cultural isolation and insularity, which became a political thorn in the side of the regime.

Throughout the period, Bulgarian Communist Party campaigns to elimi-nate the backward influence of Islam and all its cultural accoutrements were rife. From 1965 to 1975, the Pomak population was targeted by party officials in a so-called rebirth process, which first encouraged and then demanded the changing of Pomaks' Turco-Arabic names to Bulgarian names.[81] In other realms of culture as well, including clothing choice, the Bulgarian-speaking Pomak population was encouraged to proclaim and embrace their true Bul-garian nature and shirk any cultural remnants that connected them culturally to Islam or to the local Turkish populations. Women's dress and the so-called veil or Pomak head scarf, as well as *shalvari* baggy Turkish pants), were an issue of special concern among both Pomak and Turkish women in this period. And along with door-to-door consultation and meetings, the party also organized competitions to encourage the shirking of "Turco-Islamic" clothing, such as fashion shows of, in one case, work clothes "especially for tobacco production."[82] But while various organs of the party attempted to intervene in dress choices of Muslim women, the tobacco industry seemed to maintain a comparative sensitivity on such issues. Certainly most Muslim women were shown in the pages of *Bŭlgarski tiutiun* with Bulgarian-style scarves or even bare-headed. But also, and quite unusually, a picture of Pomak cooperative women from 1975 showed them in more traditional head scarves tied conspicuously under the chin.[83] Of course, such an image was unusual even for *Bŭlgarski tiutiun,* and by 1979 the map of tobacco regions depicting Bulgarian women in folk dress was a harbinger of the future. But overall, Bulgartabak seemed to stay out of the intense minority politics that plagued the central regime, though to a large degree these politics were played out in the tobacco fields and factories. With or without Bulgartabak complicity, tobacco became inseparably linked to the question of the Muslim presence in Bulgaria. And this question sharpened in the later decades of the period, the golden years of *Bulgartabak.*

Tobacco Markets

In 1972 Dimitŭr Iadkov, at age forty-two, was promoted from his position as head of regional tobacco production in Blagoevgrad to the head of Bulgartabak. The industry was in a moment of temporary crisis. In spite of technological improvements, the ever-increasing demands of the plan were still beyond the organization's resources, and Iadkov was ordered by his superiors to "fulfill the plan at any cost...especially shipments to the USSR."[84] During his second week on the job, Iadkov got a call from the Soviet trade representative concerning the belated delivery of one thousand tons of cigarettes. Aware of the importance of the Bulgaro-Soviet political relationship, Iadkov promised that the delivery would be Bulgartabak's "highest priority."[85] With a flurry of meetings, pep talks across the country, and added initiatives for production, he somehow managed to actually overfulfill the plan for 1972 and make all needed deliveries for that year, a feat for which he received an award in Moscow in 1973; it would be his first of many. Between 1972 and 1991, Iadkov became world-renowned for his business prowess. In his four hundred- plus-page memoir published in 2003, *Bulgartabak: Spomeni*

(*Bulgartabak: Memories*) he relates in colorful detail the story of his "tobacco years" and the "Bulgarian phenomenon in the tobacco world." He narrates the story of the monopoly's "heady rise" in a period when he had "free rein in accessing the experience, technology, and technical know-how of the American tobacco companies."[86] In his years as director, Iadkov traveled the globe searching for technology, developing trade relations, collecting various awards and honors, and becoming the toast and envy of Western tobacconists.

Soon after assuming the directorship in 1972, Iadkov realized that—ironically—the only way to fulfill the unrealistic production plans that were supposed to be indicative of socialist achievement was through cooperation and massive technology transfer from the West. But unlike many of his predecessors, Iadkov seemed to have few if any reservations about this kind of cooperation. Fortuitously, President Nixon had initiated a more aggressive policy of trade and contact with the Eastern Bloc beginning in 1972. In fact, before Iadkov had time to initiate expansion of trade with the West, the West came knocking. In October of 1973 Bulgartabak got a call from the Macedonian branch of Yugoslav-Macedonian tobacco monopoly. Apparently representatives from R.J. Reynolds and its close American partner, Sokotab (specializing in purchasing raw Oriental tobaccos for American firms) were in Skopje and had requested a trip to Bulgaria to establish trade relations. Bulgatabak representatives were quite excited by the prospect, and as one official joked, "If Mohammed can't come to the mountain, the mountain will have to come to Mohammed." The next day the Bulgarians met the Macedonians and their American guests at the Bulgaro-Macedonian border, where Jack Wonder, the representative of R.J. Reynolds, and five others were driven across in two luxury cars. Ushered to Dupnitsa, they visited a tobacco field and factory and then engaged in what Iadkov describes as the "special ritual of bringing out the tobacco." As he later remarks, "No other commodity has such a specific and emotional ritual for sales."[87] Over coffee they looked at samples, and as Iadkov proudly reports, Wonder "got tears in his eyes" when he put his nose in a ball of Dzhebel Basma (a local Oriental variety). "Stroking the leaf with his hand he [Wonder] said 'oh my old friend, after 30 years apart we have lived to see each other again.'" As it turns out, Wonder had been a pre-World War II representative of R.J. Reynolds in Kavala (then part of Greek Macedonia) and had been a buyer of Bulgarian tobaccos for the company's blends.[88] In a sense, with the arrival of Wonder and his delegation, the Iron Curtain was irreversibly opened.

Soon enough, Iadkov himself would "go to the mountain," namely, the United States. His first brush with Western technology, however, was not in the United States but Japan. A trip there in early 1973 was eye-opening for

Iadkov, who saw for himself that, in spite of official Bulgartabak pronounce-ments, Bulgarian industry was significantly behind the West in terms of pro-cessing and cigarette production technologies. Having witnessed this, he was shocked by the reactions of a Soviet delegation from Glavtabak that visited Bulgaria in February of 1973 and marveled that the country had "moved significantly further ahead in industrial processing, in science and especially in cigarette production." Iadkov assumed this comment was just insincere flattery until he visited the Dukat and Iava factories in Moscow that June. There he was positively astounded by the low level of Soviet technology, the seeming lack of cleanliness and order, and the fact that much work was still done by hand. He was honest, he claimed, with the director of the Soviet tobacco industry, Glavtabak, who glumly agreed, noting that upgrades were not expected any time soon. This, he explained, was because Soviet priorities were strategic, and he added, "It is accepted that Bulgaria specializes within Comecon in this direction."[89] For Iadkov it was clear that he bore the burden of bringing Bloc tobacco technologies up to world standards.

On the invitation of Jack Wonder and R.J. Reynolds, later that year Iadkov and his Bulgarian tobacco colleagues did a grand tour of American tobacco. Starting with the obligatory meeting with political figures in Wash-ington, D.C., Iadkov was then flown on an R.J. Reynolds jet to Winston-Salem, where he met the company president, William Hobbs. He was very impressed by the R.J. Reynolds operation. This was, he wistfully recounted, by far the most mechanized and modern facility that he had ever visited. Toward the end of his trip, he met with Hugh Cullman of Philip Morris in New York. As recounted above, Cullman enlightened him regarding issues of the market and American interest in Bulgartabak and the Soviet market.[90] Iadkov and his people were positively energized by their experience in the United States and reported back to the authorities at home that "the study and introduction of American experience into all the stages of our tobacco production will allow us to move ahead, to build a modern, productive and competitive tobacco economy."[91] This visit laid the groundwork for the licensing agreement signed with R.J. Reynolds in 1973 and the release in early 1974 of Bulgarian-produced Winstons on the Bloc market. By August of 1975, an agreement was finally made with Philip Morris, and Marlboros were also rolling off production lines. In exchange for Bulgarian tobaccos and licensing royalties, the American companies provided machines and training for the increased cultivation of Burley and Virginia tobaccos, as well as the sorting, curing, and fermenting of tobacco and the production and packaging of cigarettes.[92] Not only did the Bulgarians obtain machines, but they also purchased the license for machines that they were trained to build themselves for export within the Bloc and in the developing world.[93] In spite of the very real and perhaps well-founded "superstitions" against foreign capitalism among many communist functionaries, Iadkov moved forward his agenda of rapid technology transfer and modernization. He of course remained in close contact with the Soviets on these matters and on his next visit to Moscow in 1974 was given another green light for working with the Americans as long as the Bulgarians stayed within the parameters of Comecon and, above all, met their obligations for deliveries to the Soviet Union.[94]

By 1976 Bulgartabak's hard-currency profits had increased by 158 percent, from $252 million to $400 million.[95] Bulgaria was on the cover of *Tobacco International* in 1977, and Iadkov was awarded a trophy for industry achievement at the Coresta meeting in Rio in the same year. In the years that followed, Iadkov proved himself to be a master of maneuvering within the tobacco world. Under his leadership Bulgaria began a whole new phase of export and production practices that reached to the far ends of the globe. Iadkov began to reorient the work of Bulgartabak away from simply fulfilling the plan—which was not a problem anymore with the new technologies in place. Now the focus was above all on quality, which in this period meant the explicit emulation of the American blend model of cigarettes. This was part of Iadkov's larger vision of Bulgarian exports outside the Bloc, not just raw tobaccos but ideally cigarettes, which would bring larger profits.

Bulgaria first spread its cigarette export wings beyond the Bloc after the revolution in Iran in 1979. In that year, under Ayatollah Khomeini, Iran broke off relations with the United States, which had been its major supplier of cigarettes (namely, R.J. Reynolds's Winston) up to that time. Iran, in fact, was the largest importer of cigarettes in the capitalist world and now that it was alienated from that world, Bulgaria was an ideal trading partner.[96] Bulgaria was already exporting tobacco to Iraq, and now the Iran-Iraq war, which broke out in 1980, created an increased demand on both sides. During trade negotiations, the Iranians informed the Bulgarians that they were used to American-type blends like Winston. By then this was an easy recipe for the Bulgarians to follow, and before long they had produced cigarettes closely akin to Winston but in elegant red packages with Islamic symbols on them; the cigarettes were named Azadi—the Persian word for freedom. Later the packs were redesigned in the requested, "more appropriate" green.[97] Within a few years the Bulgarians would also be asked to change the name to Tir (a character from Persian mythology) so that "freedom" would not be crumpled up and stepped on when packaging was discarded.[98] Responsive to such demands, the Bulgarians became the biggest supplier of cigarettes to Iran for the next decade, and the hard-currency profits were astronomical. As Bulgaria began to export cigarettes to other states, mostly in the Near and Middle East, it also became a major *importer* of tobacco for processing in its factories. In general, it still exported raw Oriental tobacco, but with the new focus on blends it also required broad-leafed tobaccos from outside the country.

As Iadkov grew more ambitious in extending the reach of the industry Bulgarian central planners were slowly demanding curtailed investment within the industry. In the 1981–85 five year plan, for example, they projected no growth—for the first time ever—in tobacco production and exports, with a view to "developing other industries" like chemicals and machine making. The move was justified in light of antismoking campaigns in Bulgaria and elsewhere and a foreseen leveling off in demand. Iadkov was stunned by the assertion that "tobacco had no future." Enterprising as he was, he decided to ignore the plan and move forward in the most aggressive trade and development plan that Bulgartabak had pursued to date. Because of the New Economic Mechanism inaugurated in 1979, enterprises were allowed a certain amount of initiative in planning and production—as long as quotas were met. Iadkov took this and ran with it, all around the world. Like American corporations in this period, Bulgartabak begin to look to the developing world for markets. Having conducted a prognosis on the growth of smoking rates from 1980 to 1981, Bulgarian industry studies concluded that in the West smoking was up only 1.3 percent, in the Bloc 2.3–2.5 percent, but in the Near East and Africa it was up 3-5 percent. As Iadkov put it, given these numbers, there was "no reason for pessimism."[99]

He continued to travel the world with delegations, seeking new contacts and customers in the Near East and developing world. Political instability and decolonization—which had battered Western economic interests in Africa, southeast Asia, the Middle East, and Latin America—were a boon for Bulgartabak. The Iranian contract alone was enough to warrant a new factory in Blagoevgrad, the administrative center of the tobacco-rich region of Bulgarian (Pirin) Macedonia. Iadkov met with the Bulgarian leader, Todor Zhivkov, personally to ask for permission to build the factory. And although Zhivkov readily agreed, in reference to antismoking campaigns he also rather sarcastically retorted, "But won't they say we are supporting smoking?"[100] With new technologies pouring in, Iadkov began to travel the world exporting tobacco technologies and cigarettes in exchange for the needed raw tobacco to meet the huge and growing demand. Among other places, Iraq, Tunisia, Morocco, Afghanistan, Vietnam, Cambodia, Zimbabwe, Somalia, the

Philippines, Nicaragua, and Cuba became involved in trade with Bulgaria, many of them as suppliers of raw broad-leafed tobaccos in exchange for technology, training, or cigarettes.[101] Iadkov, who continued his contacts in the West, now was wined and dined in the developing world. In Nicaragua, for example, Iadkov was shown around the tobacco estate of the former dictator, Anastasio Samoza, where he noted the irony in the fact that they signed an official protocol "under the roof of Samoza's secret lover, connected with a secret tunnel to his residence."[102] Iadkov and his retinue of Bulgartabak men went on safari in Zimbabwe and lounged on Cuban beaches at the Tropicana Hotel—a resort for Soviet cosmonauts. Bulgaria became a kind of proxy for Soviet influence abroad, also exporting weapons and foodstuffs to many of these new trading partners as part of the project of "spreading global communism."[103] Bulgartabak became in essence a neocolonialist multinational corporation, quickly and successfully reversing its own role as importer of technology and exporter of raw tobacco. Now it imported raw tobacco and hard currency and exported machines and cigarettes, fanning out globally while holding on to its Bloc partners.

In spite of these successes, the 1980s were not without challenges. After the Chernobyl nuclear disaster in neighboring Ukraine, many of Bulgaria's partners were reluctant to buy tobacco or "radioactive cigarettes." Bulgartabak was relieved, of course, when first Philip Morris, then Poland and the USSR resumed orders.[104] Comecon remained Bulgaria's most loyal market, but even there, temporary dips in orders from everyone including the USSR required Bulgartabak to be proactive in terms of keeping its traditional markets.[105] It developed new brands—many of them American blends—with higher-quality packaging, cellophane wrappers, and other desirable features It battled not only the real and potential penetration of Western brands but also antismoking tendencies. In marketing strategies for the Bloc, Bulgartabak sought "effective forms and methods of advertisement of our cigarettes in socialist countries with the goal of popularizing these products in spite of the existing bans in advertisements of tobacco products."[106] But significantly, according to Bulgartabak marketing strategists, the Soviet Union, along with Romania and Mongolia—but unlike East Germany, Czechoslovakia, Hungary, and Poland—still preferred Oriental cigarettes as late as 1985.[107] Perhaps Western aesthetic hegemony could get only so far behind the Iron Curtain. On the other hand, Bulgaria could still sell Oriental cigarettes for significantly lower prices—so perhaps economic, not aesthetic, choices were being made by Bloc consumers.

Still, in spite of imports of raw tobacco, the dependency of Bulgartabak on its Bulgaria-based workforce was tremendous. Consequently the issue of compact Muslim enclaves across the Bulgarian south was increasingly seen as an economic as well as a security issue. As the birthrates of urbanized Bulgarians fell precipitously in the late decades of the communist period, the Muslim population maintained high birthrates and also proved generally resistant—publicly and privately—to state integration efforts. Maintaining a visible and hence potentially disloyal presence was a seeming affront to Bulgarian communist efforts to provide economic resources and the promise of a modern life under socialism. Paradoxically, Muslim emigration was an even greater potential threat. An agreement with Turkey in 1969, spurred by post-Stalinist détente, allowed for the emigration of eighty to ninety thousand Turks with family members across the border over a ten-year period. News of the agreement prompted huge numbers of Turks to file for emigration in the years that followed, in some districts as much as 70–80 percent of the population.[108] This only heightened anxieties about the political disloyalty of Bulgarian Muslims, and party work in the decades that followed was filled with propaganda against emigration.[109]

One of the most prominent fears about the repercussion of the mass emigration of Turks—was the economic destruction that such an exodus would leave in its wake. Apprehensions about the place of Turks on Bulgarian soil grew, especially after the Turkish invasion of Cyprus in 1974 and the international spread of Islamic fundamentalism. But as one party report from 1980 confided,

> For our country a massive emigration of Bulgarian Turks would create serious economic difficulties, it might even destroy certain sectors of our economy. What would happen to tobacco production in the Kirdzhali region, with construction, to a certain degree with agriculture and industry, without a few hundred thousand workers, working as you can see in the most difficult sectors, some of which Bulgarians avoid.[110]

With emigration a looming threat in the tobacco sector and beyond, the Communist Party turned to another, rather extreme solution to the Turkish problem. Beginning in 1984–85, the Bulgarian regime initiated the now famous "rebirth process," which compelled the Turks of Bulgaria to be "reborn" as Bulgarians. Although they were technically allowed to remain Muslim, they were forced to embrace a Bulgarian national identity, most symbolically through changing their Turco-Arabic names to Slavic-Bulgarian ones. After the initial assimilation drive, significant resistance and difficulties in enforcement made it clear, however, that Todor Zhivkov's famous statement of 1985 "There are no Turks in Bulgaria," was far from the truth.[111]

By 1989 protests had gained momentum across Bulgaria, both those related to the Turkish question and those in response to the crumbling communist regimes across Eastern Europe. On the Turkish question, mass protests and hunger strikes in the spring of 1989 were the probable impetus for Todor Zhivkov's opening of the border with Turkey that May. Having abandoned his goal of total integration, Zhivkov made his famous announcement on Bulgarian national television that all Bulgarian-Muslims who still believed themselves to be Turks should leave Bulgaria immediately. In response some three hundred thousand Turks headed for the border with Turkey, leaving fields of tobacco fallow or, later, unharvested for that season.[112] Immediately there were reports of massive absenteeism in Turkish districts as populations were in a frenzied preparation for a mass exodus. Many officials in border regions, such as Kirdzhali and Khaskovo, requested that the borders be closed as tobacco export orders needed to be filled. If such measures were not taken, one report warned, "the tobacco will fall into ruin," and plans would be underfulfilled by some 50 percent.[113] In some areas, Turks were accused of "organized inactivity, tantamount to sabotage," and officials recommended that "passports should not be issued until the tobacco was harvested."[114] In the throes of the exodus, which lasted from late May until August 21, Zhivkov confided Bulgarian woes to the Russian leader, Mikhail Gorbachev. The country's two biggest problems, he disclosed, were first of all, the economy and second, the Muslim question; the two, it seems, were tightly connected, and the Soviet Union was not impervious to the fallout.[115]

In spite of Iadkov's desperate measures to save the situation, for the first time ever Bulgaria could not make promised deliveries to many of its cigarette and raw tobacco export trade partners. Iadkov was extremely distraught by this turn of events, recalling his own promise to himself from 1973 that "As long as I am in the Union [Comecon] I will not fail to supply the Soviet market."[116] He even went to Moscow himself to personally apologize for the situation. On his return he reported back home that when he saw the lines for cigarettes in Moscow, he felt that he was personally responsible. As communism collapsed across the Bloc in the months that followed, Iadkov watched with horror as American and other Western cigarettes inundated the markets of the East, and Western tobacco companies became major investors and buyers of former state-owned tobacco enterprises, many of which were closed down. Iadkov's empire, like communist Bulgaria and soon the Soviet Union, eventually collapsed.

In the course of the Cold War, Bulgartabak used the complex political landscape of domestic and Bloc loyalties, tastes, and markets to its own advantage.

It was able to flourish as Soviet demands for cigarettes drove industry mechanization and modernization. In the course of the period, Bulgaria was able to work with and borrow technology and cigarette aesthetics from the West, using these technologies to maintain Eastern Bloc markets and take over former markets abroad, like Iran. It was also able to appropriate and replicate American and Soviet neoimperialist techniques of global trade in the Middle East and the developing world. But while this seemed like a win-win situation for Bulgartabak, ultimately America's indirect penetration of the Eastern Bloc market was a long-term success. Western brands—Marlboro, Winston, and Kent—became known and desired behind the Iron Curtain, if for no other reason than their Western cachet and air of luxury. More important, Western cigarette aesthetics that favored American blends and hence predominantly broad-leafed tobacco varieties (Virginia and Burley) had a permanent impact on the status and demand for Oriental tobaccos. As in other arenas of the Cold War, the West had won.

As communism collapsed, so too did the Bulgartabak empire. While the industry had cultivated a largely loyal and hard-working labor force, state assimilation projects also alienated the Muslim segment of the tobacco economy. By the late 1980s the fallout from the 1984–85 rebirth process and the subsequent 1989 expulsion brought the collapse of the tobacco industry and subsequently the Bulgarian economy. Tobacco and ethnic politics were an important component in bringing down communism in Bulgaria. The collapse of communism, in turn, brought down the tobacco industry.

Conclusion

As the world gradually pushes tobacco smokers out into the cold, in Bulgaria they are still welcome inside. Smoking is still central to leisure culture; the gleaming new postcommunist café, cocktail bar, pizzeria, and even McDonald's are still smoker-friendly. As of 2005, a law limiting smoking in public buildings did go into effect, though its enforcement has been sporadic. Having visited Bulgaria every year from 2005 to 2010, I do remember watching as the female staff members at the national archive moved their smoke breaks from the reading room to the hallway and eventually to the women's bathroom. There they camped out, leaving behind their smoke and ash. A quick visit to the small stall-like bathroom meant that the smell of smoke would linger in your clothes and hair as if you had been out clubbing. A 2010 bill to prohibit all smoking in restaurants, bars, and other leisure establishments failed to pass through the Bulgarian parliament. Smokers are digging in deep in order to maintain what one Bulgarian friend told me is their way of life.

For many, smoking is still a beloved activity. The 2009 memoir of Ivan Pitekov, a longtime interpreter for Bulgartabak, is nothing short of a treatise on the joys of tobacco. His essays, lumped under the provocative title *S aromat na tiutiun* (*With the Aroma of Tobacco*), celebrate the smells and the aura of the industry and the leaf in titillating detail. Pitekov's writings are also full of open disdain for the opponents of the smoking habit:

> What does this plant represent in and of itself? This is an agricultural genus that is teeming with poisons and bitter substances and has an unpleasant smell and taste! This is what nonsmokers say. But offer a smoker (or even better a female smoker) a box of aromatized cigarettes and a bag of potatoes. He (or she) will pass over with contempt the blessing of the potato and will open the box and slowly light up. And a miracle will inevitably occur. Their mood will get better, their pulse will increase, their outlook will become kind and gracious. It is no accident that wise people say that one can't live on bread alone. Bread and potatoes are food for the body, and tobacco is food for the soul.[1]

Like so many Bulgarians today, Pitekov embraces smoking with abandon from a personal and a philosophical standpoint. Though the country has an increasing number of nonsmokers and even antismokers, the smokers, it seems, still have the upper hand.

It remains to be seen whether new definitions of "Western" and "modern"—which seem to require snuffing out the global cigarette—will resonate in postcommunist Bulgaria. Although it has been under the umbrella of the European Union since 2008, conformity to norms of severely restricting public smoking is controversial at best. While Bulgaria fought long and hard to get into the EU, it is also among the most forthright Euro-skeptics in the union. It fights to maintain independent policies in as many areas as possible. Given the country's history of ambivalence toward the West, it is not surprising that many see antismoking as a Western import. For others, antismoking messages may be too reminiscent of abstinence propaganda from the communist period. Yet for all their efforts to curtail smoking, the communist authorities never actually banned it. Thus there is a certain irony in the fact that smoking restrictions and proposed bans have been introduced by postcommunist governments. Many smokers surely see this heightened interference in leisure activity and curtailment of freedoms as onerous. Whatever the reason, Bulgaria's antismoking lobby is weak, and antismoking bans will meet with opposition for many years to come. For many, such bans openly threaten Bulgarian autonomy and entrenched modes of leisure. It might also be argued that the introduction of Western fast food, automobile culture, and other by-products of the transition to capitalism is as harmful to public health as smoking.

Postcommunist Bulgaria—like the rest of the Eastern Bloc and China—continues to maintain some of the highest smoking rates in the world. As I have argued in this book, smoking accompanied and even drove Bulgaria's political and cultural coming of age since the nineteenth century. Bulgarian modernity was infused with smoke as ever-larger segments of the population entered a new world of public sociability, cultural production, and political interaction. Smoking had a chemical and social effect that hastened Bulgarian initiation into the modern world, for better or worse. Part of this initiation was a growing awareness of the poisonous effects of tobacco on the body. This, as well as anxieties about the transgression of social boundaries by female and child smokers, drove modest antismoking impulses throughout Bulgarian history. Still, the lure of the cigarette would ultimately win out. Indeed, the rapid rise in smoking, for whatever reason, was a natural if not necessary accompaniment to postwar modernity. The concentrated modernization drive under communism brought the Eastern Bloc into the big league as global smokers. After the fall of communism in 1989–91, Western tobacco companies penetrated the region, brandishing their slick and sexy advertisements and dumping their more addictive cigarettes. After 1989 the explosion of Western products was accompanied by sleek new cocktail bars and other, more enticing smoke-filled establishments. Smoking rates continued to climb after the fall of communism, contrary to trends in the West.[2]

The question remains, why has the antismoking message failed to become deeply rooted in Bulgarian soil? The answer to this question is undoubtedly different than it would be, say, for the French or other cultures that have hung on to smoking as it fades out elsewhere. In Bulgaria, antismoking was always connected to foreign and/or radical outside influences, Protestant and communist. These groups found pockets of unmitigated support, but by and large their abstinence programs were never willingly embraced by the bulk of the smoking population.

The credibility of the messenger was surely an issue in the widespread rejection of the message. In part, the state's credibility was eroded by the fact that it also owned and operated Bulgaria's tobacco monopoly, which distributed increasingly luxurious brands of cheap cigarettes. Thus the state's antismoking message must have seemed insincere, empty propaganda to be ignored, and it is not surprising that even after the fall of communism, public support for an antismoking message would still ring hollow. The small antismoking lobby that has emerged is subject to public accusations of foreign ties and funding.[3] If nonsmoking is now the hallmark of global modernity, Bulgaria has been left behind.

One outcome of the complicated changes of 1989 is indisputable; for the Bulgarian tobacco industry the fall of communism was an unmitigated disaster. As mentioned in the last chapter, a crisis in the tobacco industry may even have precipitated the fall. But this crisis occurred not because Bulgartabak was unsuccessful or insolvent. Rather, the expulsion of Turks created a severe shortage of labor in the tobacco provinces, which spelled disaster for the industry in the short term. After 1989 the problems increased exponentially. Foreign brands of cigarettes began to inundate the Bulgarian market. Highly seductive cigarette advertising—which is closely regulated in most of the West—had relatively free rein in Bulgaria. Bulgartabak markets collapsed overnight as former Bloc partners faced a severe economic crisis. Old barter arrangements were thrown out as the Comecon collapsed and Bloc countries looked for new trading partners. The domestic market also went into a tailspin as hyperinflation meant that real incomes were cut in half. Although a Bulgarian new rich emerged and slowly expanded, average household consumption declined severely after 1989, as did vacation time.[4] Even as late as 2003, the Bulgarian GDP was still not up to its 1989 level, and the average Bulgarian family was spending 60.5 percent of its income on food, a dramatic rise from pre-1989 levels.[5]

Bulgartabak also became a controversial political and economic sore spot in post-1989 Bulgaria. Soon after the transition to capitalism it was fragmented into twenty-two subsidiaries, which were still tied to centrally fixed prices. It was racked with scandal during various attempts to privatize in the years that followed. Every such attempt failed when the Bulgarian media revealed associated scandals—payoffs, bribes, and corruption—that brought the process to a halt. The sell-off of Bulgarian gold to a foreign company, even when it had lost some of its luster, was an emotionally charged issue for many Bulgarians. Was this tantamount to handing over the profits, once again, to foreign exploiters? Bulgartabak employees protested privatization, fearing the worst for the future of their livelihoods. There were a lot of reasons for this, including a history in which a private tobacco industry had benefited only a select few. Given that history, Bulgartabak under communism truly represented a golden age for its numerous employees. The situation following the collapse of the industry in 1989 seems to have confirmed that perception.

Soon after the fall of communism, scores of individuals and communities that used to be supported by Bulgartabak revenues were in a dire situation. The tobacco-growing south, in particular, had lost many of the managerial and technical jobs associated with the industry after decollectivization and industry reorganization. Dropping prices and the decrease in demand for Oriental tobacco meant a loss of jobs in tobacco-growing regions. Today the market for Oriental tobaccos is very small even within Bulgaria as domestic demand has shifted to the more addictive American blends. Though these types of tobacco are also grown in Bulgaria in a more limited way, the bottoming out of the Oriental market has translated into 25–90 percent unemployment in Muslim districts of the Bulgarian south as opposed to the national average of 16 percent. Some of these populations have found other means of survival, like gathering herbs and mushrooms, but most live in dire poverty. This has contributed to the political tensions between Muslims minorities and other Bulgarian citizens as their tobacco interdependencies have disappeared.

Since the late nineteenth century the commodification of tobacco has brought prosperity but also social disparity and violence to the region. In Thrace and Macedonia, right across the Bulgarian border, this violence had deep social roots. Its causes cannot be reduced to the commodification of tobacco, but this certainly played a role in the ethnic, social, and political struggle for Macedonia. As refugees poured into Bulgaria, particularly after World War I, they brought both tobacco skills and political violence to politics and social life. They also helped fuel Bulgarian desires to reacquire Macedonia and Thrace. This along with its interwar tobacco commerce with Germany brought Bulgaria firmly into the Axis camp. Ultimately this meant the wartime occupation of Thrace and Macedonia but also the purging of Jews from Bulgaria's tobacco world. Whereas at home Bulgarian-Jewish merchants lost their businesses and properties, in Thrace and Macedonia they also lost their lives. World War II was one of the last steps in the Bulgarianization of the industry, at least of its upper echelons. Turks and Greeks had slowly migrated out of Bulgaria since 1878 and lost their stronghold in the domestic tobacco trade. The nationalization of the industry under the umbrella of Bulgartabak in 1947 was the denouement of this process.

Despite all the problems with communism as a system, it was actually a boon to the development and functioning of a world-class tobacco industry in Bulgaria. For those entrepreneurial individuals and families who lost their fortunes along the way—Turkish, Greek, Armenian, and Bulgarian—this nationalization was a personal tragedy. But as never before, the industry benefited the state as a whole by bringing in massive revenues, furthering the unprecedented development of infrastructure, education, and state services. In addition, Bulgaria's tobacco-growing peasant farmers and factory workers now had the highest wages, the best working conditions, and the most developed webs of social services in their history. They enjoyed free medical care, pensions, and paid vacations. In the undeveloped regions where they lived, resources were available for new homes, schools, and roads. The gradual urbanization of Bulgarians, though, meant that many of the tobacco-growing regions of the south were populated primarily by Muslim minorities. These populations both benefited from the industry and were critical players in it, which furthered Bulgarian-Muslim interdependencies.

All this came tumbling down after 1989, not just because of the introduction of capitalism in Bulgaria but because of the collapse of the entire Comecon market. In the postcommunist period the global marketplace reduced Bulgarian tobacco to a mere shadow of its former self, a heap of ash in the dustbin of history. Bulgartabak, which had once exported the largest number of cigarettes in the world, is now reduced to a domestic supplier, albeit with a healthy market share. But it is no longer the fiscal cash cow it once was, and Bulgaria has a small and faltering economy that is exceedingly vulnerable to the current economic crisis. The state has held onto Bulgartabak for the time being, but privatization talks continue. Perhaps Bulgarian gold will one day be in the hands of foreigners. In the meantime, Bulgarians will continue to smoke it in their cocktail bars, sidewalk cafés, and archive bathrooms. Ivan Pitekov, however, after his extensive defense of smoking, admitted that he eventually had to quit. Apparently he got winded after climbing a flight of stairs and so realized that he could no longer indulge in his favorite source of pleasure.

NOTES

Introduction

1. There are numerous global histories of tobacco. One of the classics is Jordan Goodman, *Tobacco in History: The Cultures of Dependence* (London: Routledge, 1993). For more recent studies see Iain Gately, *Tobacco: A Cultural History of How an Exotic Plant Seduced Civilization* (New York: Grove Press, 2003).

2. One of the best studies of tobacco in twentieth-century America is Allan Brandt, *The Cigarette Century: The Rise, Fall and Deadly Persistence of the Product That Defined America* (New York: Basic Books, 2007). See also Howard Cox, *The Global Cigarette: Origins and Evolution of British American Tobacco* (Oxford: Oxford University Press, 2000), and Marcy Norton, *Sacred Gifts, Profane Pleasures: A History of Tobacco and Chocolate in the Atlantic World* (Ithaca: Cornell University Press, 2008).

3. For a few in-depth studies of tobacco in non-American locales see Relli Shechter, *Smoking, Culture and Economy in the Middle East: The Egyptian Tobacco Market 1850–2000* (New York: I.B. Tauris, 2006); Matthew Romaniello and Tricia Starks, *Tobacco in Russian History and Culture: From the Seventeenth Century to the Present* (New York: Routledge, 2009); and James Grehan, "Smoking and 'Early Modern' Sociability: The Great Tobacco Debate in the Ottoman Middle East, Seventeenth to Eighteenth Centuries," *American Historical Review* 111 (2006): 1352–76.

4. Dimitŭr Iadkov, *Bulgartabak: Spomeni* (Sofia: Izdateslvo "Sibia" 34, 2003), 102.

5. *Bŭlgarski Tiutiun,* no. 4 (1975): 46.

6. I am clearly indebted here to the influential work of Arjun Appadurai. See his "Introduction: Commodities and the Politics of Value," in *The Social Life of Things: Commodities in Cultural Perspective,* ed. Arjun Appadurai (Cambridge: Cambridge University Press, 1986), 3–4.

7. Several works have dealt with the history of tobacco in the context of other intoxicants or drugs. See, for example, Wolfgang Schivelbusch, *Tastes of Paradise: A Social History of Spices, Stimulants, and Intoxicants* (New York: Vintage Books, 1992); David Courtright, *Forces of Habit: Drugs and the Making of the Modern World* (Cambridge, MA: Harvard University Press); and Richard Davenport-Hines, *The Pursuit of Oblivion: A Global History of Narcotics* (New York, W.W. Norton, 2002).

8. On the social construction of value for commodities see Appadurdai, "Introduction," 3–4.

9. James Grehan argues that British traders were most likely responsible for the plant's import. See Grehan, "Smoking and 'Early Modern' Sociability," 18. Suraiya Faroqhi, however, suggests that the plant more likely crossed into Ottoman territory via Italian or Habsburg trade. See Suraiya Faroqhi, *Subjects of the Sultan: Culture and Daily Life in the Ottoman Empire* (London: I.B. Tauris, 2005), 217.

10. See Grehan, "Smoking and 'Early Modern' Sociability," 12–22, and Shechter, *Smoking, Culture and Economy,* 17.

11. Ottoman tobacco was grown mainly in the eastern Balkans—Macedonia, Thrace, and the Aegean Coast region—but also the Black Sea coast of Anatolia and northern Syria. Grehan, "Smoking," 13.

12. Schivelbusch, *Tastes of Paradise,* 9–10.

13. Maria Todorova, *Imagining the Balkans* (Oxford: Oxford University Press, 1997), 13.

14. An Ottoman Armenian, Pasqua Rosee, was purported to have set up the first coffeehouse in London in 1652. Alan Weinberg and Bonnie Bealer, *The World of Caffeine: The Science and Culture of the World's Most Popular Drug* (New York: Routledge, 2002), 154.

15. Brian Cowan, *The Social Life of Coffee: The Emergence of the British Coffeehouse* (New Haven: Yale University Press, 2005). On the evolution of the nineteenth-century French café see Scott Haine, *The World of the Paris Café: Sociability among the French Working Classes* (Baltimore: Johns Hopkins University Press, 1996).

16. For more on Ottoman consumption see the groundbreaking volume, Donald Quataert, ed., *Consumption Studies and the History of the Ottoman Empire, 1550–1922* (Albany: State University of New York Press, 2000).

17. Debates about the meaning and usefulness of "modernity" as an analytical category have raised more questions than they have answered. See, for example, Anthony Giddens, "The Nature of Modernity," in *The Giddens Reader,* ed. Phillip Cassel and Anthony Giddens (Palo Alto: Stanford University Press, 1993), 284–316; see also Fredrick Cooper, *Colonialism in Question: Theory, Knowledge, History* (Berkeley: University of California Press, 2005), 113–52.

18. *Bŭlgarski Tiutiun,* no. 7 (1977): 4.

19. See for example, *Bŭlgarski Tiutiun,* no. 2 (1966): 1.

20. For this line of thinking on East-West interaction see the influential work of Alexei Yurchak, *Everything Was Forever, Until It Was No More* (Princeton, NJ: Princeton University Press, 2006), 158–206.

21. See, for example, Sander Gilman and Xhou Zun, eds., *Smoke* (London: Reaktion Books LTD, 2004); Ilene Barth, *The Smoking Life* (Columbus, MS: Genesis Press, 1997).

22. The questions of which came first, the early modern consumer revolution or the Industrial Revolution, is a matter of intense historical debate. See, for example, Don Slater, *Consumer Culture and Modernity, Polity* (Cambridge: Polity Press, 1999), 16–23.

23. On the history of consumption see, for example, Woodruff Smith, *Consumption and the Making of Respectability, 1600–1800* (New York: Routledge, 2002); and Peter Sterns, *Consumerism in World History: The Global Transformation of Desire* (New York: Routledge, 2006); and Quataert, *Consumption Studies.*

24. See especially Gilman and Zun, *Smoke,* and Schivelbusch, *Tastes of Paradise.*

25. See for example, Georg Kraev, ed., *Kafeneto Kato Diskurs* (Sofia: Nov Bŭlgarski Universitet, 2005); and Raia Zaimova, ed., *Kafene Evropa* (Sofia: Izdatelstvo Damian Iakov, 2007). For notions specifically raised here see Lilia Kirova, "Razmisli za neprekhodeniia char na Balkanskite kafeneta," in Zaimova, *Kafene Evropa,* 27–28.

26. Schivelbush, for example, credits the coffeehouse for fueling Western commercial and material success. Schivelbusch, *Tastes of Paradise,* 15–24. For newer work on the Ottoman coffeehouse, see Cengiz Kirli, "The Struggle over Space: Coffeehouses of Ottoman Istanbul, 1780—1845" (PhD diss., State University of New York, Binghamton, 2001); Cengiz Kirli, "Coffeehouses: Public Opinion in the Nineteenth Century Ottoman Empire," in *Public Islam and the Common Good,* ed. Armando Salvatore and Dale F. Eickelman (Boston: Brill Academic Publishers, 2004), 75–98; and Selma Özkoçak, "Coffee Houses: Rethinking the Public and Private in Early Modern Istanbul," *Journal of Urban History* 33, no. 6 (September 2007): 965–86.

27. For the best discussion of consumption after Stalin in Eastern Europe see David Crowley and Susan Reid, eds., *Style and Socialism: Modernity and Material Culture in Postwar Eastern Europe* (Oxford: Berg Publishers, 2000); David Crowley and Susan E. Reid, eds., *Pleasures in Socialism: Leisure and Luxury in the Bloc* (Evanston, IL: Northwestern University Press, 2010); and Paulina Bren and Mary Neuburger, eds. *Communism Unwrapped: Consumption in Cold War Eastern Europe* (New York: Oxford University Press, 2012).

1. Coffeehouse Babble

1. Ivan Vazov, *Under the Yoke* (New York: Twayne Publishers, 1971), 163. (Quotation in epigraph on page 110.) It is unclear whether Vazov was familiar with Balzac's famous novel *The Peasants,* in which he called the café the "parliament of the people," but it is entirely likely that he would have been exposed to the work of the French writer.

2. Here I use the term "Bulgarian" as shorthand for Slavic-speaking Christians, but with the assumption that much of this population had a rather fluid national consciousness until well into the twentieth century.

3. I use the term "awakening" not in the traditional primordial sense of awakening preexisting national identities but rather in the modernist sense of the imagining or constructing of national identities by national elites. For the concise discussion of the modernist-primordial debate see Anthony D. Smith, *The Ethnic Origins of Nations* (Oxford: Blackwell, 1986), 6–18.

4. Recent Bulgarian historiography has begun to draw a direct connection between the kafene and Bulgarian urbanization, cultural revival, and political emancipation. With the recognition that the Ottoman kafene had long functioned as a type of public sphere, new scholarship has begun to trace how Bulgarians entered and eventually carved out an autonomous place within this public field of discussion. See, for example, Georg Kraev, ed., *Kafeneto kato diskurs* (Sofia: Nov Bŭlgarski Universitet, 2005).

5. I am by no means questioning the notion of Europeanization as a whole, which I employ in my own work; see *The Orient Within: Muslim Minorities and the Negotiation of Nationhood in Modern Bulgaria* (Ithaca: Cornell University Press, 2004). Rather, I am questioning the existence of "Europe" as an autonomous and essential whole, somehow independent and unaffected by the "Orient." A similar approach can be found in the works on nineteenth-century Bulgaria by Rumen Daskalov and Raina Gavrilova. See, for example, Rumen Daskalov, *Mezhdy iztoka i zapada: Bŭlgarski kulturni dilemi* (Sofia: Izdatelstvo Prosveta, 1994); Rumen Daskalov, "Images

of Europe: A Glance from the Periphery" (Working Paper SPS No. 94/8, European University Institute, Florence, 1996); Raina Gavrilova, *Bulgarian Urban Culture in the Eighteenth and Nineteenth Centuries* (London: Associated University Press, 1999), and Raina Gavrilova, *Kolelota na zhivota: Vsekidnevieto na Bŭlgarskiia vŭzrozhdenski grad* (Sofia: Universitetsko izdatelstvo Sv. Kliment Okhridski, 1999).

6. See James Grehan, "Smoking and 'Early Modern' Sociability: The Great Tobacco Debate in the Ottoman Middle East, Seventeenth to Eighteenth Centuries," *American Historical Review* 111 (2006):12–22, and Relli Shechter, *Smoking, Culture and Economy in the Middle East: The Egyptian Tobacco Market 1850–2000* (New York: I.B. Tauris, 2006), 17. Numerous sources discuss this cultural transference. See, for example, Danilo Reato, *The Coffee-house: Venetian Coffee-houses from 18th to 20th century* (Venice: Arsenale, 1991), 13; and Markman Ellis, *The Coffee-House: A Cultural History* (London: Weidenfeld and Nicholson, 2004), 75.

7. Many historians of tobacco, for example, have noted that the Crimean War, which brought large armies of Western Europeans onto Ottoman and (what would become) Bulgarian soil, contributed to the rapid spread of the cigarette and the niche market for Oriental tobaccos grown in the region. Shechter, *Smoking, Culture and Economy*, 75.

8. Several works have tried to make sense of this huge body of Western travel writings on the Balkans and the role they played in the process of defining, and culturally colonizing the region as either part of or in contrast to the Orient. See, for example, Maria Todorova, *Imagining the Balkans* (Oxford: Oxford University Press, 1997); John Allcock and Antonia Young, eds. *Black Lambs and Grey Falcons: Women Traveling in the Balkans* (New York: Berghahn Books, 2000); and Bozhidar Jezernik, *Wild Europe: The Balkans in the Gaze of Western Travelers* (London: Saqi Books, 2004).

9. Todorova argues that "Balkanism" is distinct from "Orientalism" in that the Balkans are seen as a European hybrid as opposed to pure "other." For an elaboration on this and other debates on these issues see Todorova, *Imagining the Balkans;* Neuburger, *The Orient Within;* Milica Bakić-Hayden, "Nesting Orientalisms: The Case of Former Yugoslavia," *Slavic Review* 54 (1995): 917–31; and John Allcock, "Constructing the Balkans," in Allcock and Young, *Black Lambs and Grey Falcons,* 170–91.

10. While it is tempting to try to make sense of the discourse on the region as Orientalist or Balkanist, the inconsistencies in these writings make such a venture at best flawed. Still one has to note that Orientalist themes do seem to pervade these writings.

11. "Turk" is in quotes here because though the appellation was widely used by foreign observers, it was still rarely used by Ottoman-Turks themselves, who were among the last in the empire to undergo a national awakening.

12. Fanny Blunt, *My Reminiscences* (London: Murray, 1918), 91, 228.

13. Such pictures would have been taken by both Westerners and locals to sell for foreign consumption. See, for example, Engin Özendes, *Photography in the Ottoman Empire, 1839–1919* (Istanbul: Haset Kitabevi, 1987), 74, 80, 81, 83, 125, 130. See also Charles Newton, *Images of the Ottoman Empire* (London: Victoria and Albert Publications, 2007), 54, 60–61, 63.

14. For images of women see Özendes, *Photography in the Ottoman Empire,* 84, 120, 124, and Newton, *Images of the Ottoman Empire,* 119, 121, 124. Such imagery of women has been looked at elsewhere as indicative of the "penetration" of the colonial

gaze. See Malek Alloula, *The Colonial Harem* (Minneapolis: University of Minnesota Press), 4–5.

15. Jezernik, *Wild Europe,* 152–53.

16. Jezernik argues that, the Habsburg administration, after occupying Bosnia-Hercegovina in 1878, "took great pains to keep people from lazing about in coffee-houses." Ibid., 152–53.

17. Ibid., 165.

18. Earlier accounts of Ottoman leisure, such as the famous letters of Lady Montagu, reflect more fascination than judgment in relation to the smoking men and harem women of the empire. See Mary Wortley Montagu, *Turkish Embassy Letters* (Athens: University of Georgia Press, 1993).

19. As cited in Gavrilova, *Kolelota na zhivota,* 307.

20. The Ottoman Empire, including the Ottoman Balkans, had been an important destination on the British "grand tour" since the eighteenth century. By the nineteenth century, the region, and in particular the Bulgarian lands adjacent to Istanbul, became a major destination for Americans and British citizens of various stripes—adventurers, diplomats, traders, and Protestant missionaries. See, for example, Stanislas St. Clair and Charles Brophy, *Residence in Bulgaria: or, Notes on the Resources and Administration of Turkey: The Condition and Character, Manners, Customs, and Language of the Christian and Musselman Populations, with Reference to the Eastern Question* (London: J. Murray, 1869), 116.

21. Ibid., 408.

22. Brophy was quite shocked that Bulgarian hosts, who gave him shelter in a remote village, offered him wine in the morning before travel instead of coffee, as offered by Muslim hosts. Ibid., 22.

23. As Todorova points out, such imagery was guided by class bias and echoed British writings about their own lower classes of the period. Todorova, *Imagining the Balkans,* 102.

24. I take this term from Joseph Grabill's insightful study *Protestant Diplomacy and the Near East: Missionary Influence on American Policy, 1810–1927* (Minneapolis: University of Minnesota Press, 1971), 5.

25. As van Ilchev and Plamen Mitev argue, American missionaries lived in more direct and intimate contact with Bulgarians than did any other foreigners during the nineteenth century. Ilchev and Mitev, eds., *Bŭlgaro-Amerikanski kulturni i politicheski vrŭzki prez XIX–pŭrvata polovina na XX v.* (Sofia: Universitetsko izdatelstvo Sv. Kliment Okhridski, 2004), 12. See also James Clarke, *Bible Societies, American Missionaries, and the National Revival of Bulgaria* (New York: Arno Press, 1971).

26. The American Board is short for the American Board of Commissioners for Foreign Missionaries, which was established in 1810 and was the primary conduit for missionaries from the United States in the nineteenth century. By 1899, the American Board in Bulgaria alone had established four missionary stations, fifty outstations, with twenty-four missionaries, seventy-seven Bulgarian employees, and sixteen churches with 1,998 members. James F. Clarke, *Sketch of the European Turkey Mission of the American Board* (Boston: American Board of Commissioners for Foreign Missionaries, Congregational House, 1901), 10.

27. As George Washburn, the college's second but longest-reigning president articulated in his memoirs, the goals of Robert College were to inculcate "moral

strength" in young men from the region. Washburn, *Fifty Years in Constantinople and Recollections of Robert College* (New York: Houghton Mifflin, 1909), 298.

28. Ibid., 95. A women's college was also set up in Istanbul that attracted numerous Bulgarian women. It was run by American missionary women and funded by, among other people, the Rockefeller family.

29. This was how Istanbul was described by Mary Patrick Mills, who was based in Istanbul from 1875 and was president of the American College for Girls from 1889 to 1923. See her memoir, *Under Five Sultans* (London: Century Co., 1929), 170.

30. Cyrus Hamlin, *My Life and Times* (Boston: Congregational Sunday School and Publishing Society, 1893), 230.

31. Ibid., 159.

32. Washburn, *Fifty Years,* 70, 298.

33. *Zornitsa* was a weekly paper published in Istanbul that was said to be circulated in more than three hundred towns in the Bulgarian provinces. By 1882 the circulation was about four thousand. Though the population was largely illiterate, this paper, like others, was regularly read aloud in Balkan kafenes, and it was mentioned in Vazov's *Under the Yoke,* 51–52, which attests to its fame. See also William Webster, *Puritans in the Balkans: The American Board Mission in Bulgaria, 1878–1918, A Study in Purpose and Procedure* (Sofia: Studia Historico-Philologica Serdicensia, 1938), 22, 82.

34. Hamlin, *My Life and Times,* 436.

35. Washburn, *Fifty Years,* 70.

36. Blunt, *My Reminiscences,* 27, 231.

37. St. Clair and Brophy, *Residence in Bulgaria,* 2.

38. Khristo Danov, *Za teb mili rode* (Plovdiv: Izdatelstvo Khristo G. Danov, 1978), 113.

39. St. Clair and Brophy, *Residence in Bulgaria,* 234.

40. Ibid., 227. It is noteworthy that the French café was always a site of consumption for alcohol and coffee, as well as tobacco. But it is also worth mentioning that the coffeehouse (and its goes without saying also the tavern) was not beyond reproach in England or elsewhere in the West. Perceptions of early modern British coffeehouses, for example, ranged from "serene and sober" to "chaotic and conflict-ridden," depending on the perspective of the observer. See Brian Cowan, *The Social Life of Coffee: The Emergence of the British Coffeehouse* (New Haven: Yale University Press, 2005), 225. The French café had even more complex social connotations, since it was associated with alcohol as well as coffee and was more politicized because of its connection to revolution, sedition, and the political potential of the masses. See, for example, W. Scott Haine, *The World of the Paris Café: Sociability among the French Working Classes, 1789–1914* (Baltimore: Johns Hopkins University Press, 1996).

41. St. Clair and Brophy, *Residence in Bulgaria,* 230.

42. This transition took place, Wolfgang Schivelbusch argues, when such substances became commonplace in Protestant Europe, while hot chocolate and beer (even for breakfast) were then still the beverages of choice for the elite and commoners, respectively, in Catholic Europe. Schivelbusch, *Tastes of Paradise: A Social History of Spices, Stimulants, and Intoxicants* (New York: Vintage Books, 1992), 110. On the public sphere see Jürgen Habermas, *The Structural Transformation of the Public Sphere: An Inquiry into a Category of Bourgeois Society* (Boston: MIT Press, 1992). Though his notion of a public sphere as distinct from the private one has received considerable criticism, his work is still influential in explaining the rise of modern political

structures in the "West" His emphasis on the division between public and private has been hotly challenged even in the European context. See, for example, Nancy Fraser, "Rethinking the Public Sphere: A Contribution to the Critique of Actually Existing Democracy," in *Habermas and the Public Sphere,* ed. Craig Calhoun (Cambridge, MA: MIT Press, 1992), 109–42.

43. See, for example, William Rowe, "The Public Sphere in Modern China," *Modern China* 16 (1990): 309–29, and Srirupa Roy, "Seeing a State: National Commemorations and the Public Sphere in India and Turkey," *Comparative Studies in Society and History* 48 (2006): 200–232.

44. See, for example, Cengiz Kirli, "The Struggle over Space: Coffeehouses of Ottoman Istanbul, 1780—1845" (PhD diss., State University of New York, Binghamton, 2001); Cengiz Kirli, "Coffeehouses: Public Opinion in the Nineteenth Century Ottoman Empire," in *Public Islam and the Common Good,* ed. Armando Salvatore and Dale F. Eickelman (Boston: Brill Academic Publishers, 2004); Selma Özkoçak, "Coffee Houses: Rethinking the Public and Private in Early Modern Istanbul," *Journal of Urban History* 33 (2007): 965–86.

45. Grehan, "Smoking," 18. While Grehan does not invoke the notion of the public sphere directly, he does frequently speak of smoking and "public spaces," and his fundamental assumptions support the notion of the development of an Ottoman early modern public sphere.

46. Grehan, "Smoking," 31–32, and Kirli, "Struggle over Space," 31–32.

47. See Özkoçak, "Coffee Houses," 975.

48. Grehan, "Smoking," 37, 31–32.

49. Since the seventeenth century, concerns about the transgression of social boundaries had driven anxieties about the coffeehouse environment. Ibid., 21–22.

50. Ibid., 41.

51. Tobacco (and coffeehouses) had also been prohibited by Selim II (1566–74), Murat III (1574–95), and by Murad IV (1623–40), who was said to have "personally patrolled streets to punish those who smoke" and opened or frequented coffeehouses. He had the latter thrown into the Bosphorus "sewn in leather bags." Kirli, "Struggle over Space," 49–51.

52. Ibid., 2.

53. Ibid., 140.

54. Ibid., 156, 11.

55. It is also unclear whether in Balkan Orthodox Christian or Jewish writings there were polemics against tobacco consumption as it entered Ottoman society. In Russia, the clergy preached against tobacco in sermons dating from the early modern period, but no work has been done on this period and tobacco consumption in Bulgaria. On Russia see Nikos Chrissidis, "Sex, Drink, and Drugs: Tobacco in Early Modern Russia," in *Tobacco in Russian History and Culture,* ed. Matthew Romaniello and Tricia Starks (New York: Routledge, 2009).

56. Jezernik, *Wild Europe,* 148.

57. In fact, those who became Janissaries dominated the coffeehouse guild in Istanbul by the nineteenth century. Grehan, Smoking," 120.

58. As Raina Gavrilova argues, it was not rare for Bulgarian women to smoke, and even Bulgarian nuns were known to "smoke the chibouk and drink rakia." Gavrilova, *Koleloto na zhivota,* 308.

59. Grehan, "Smoking," 9–10. See, for example, the writings of diplomat William Miller from the 1890s. William Miller, *Travels and Politics in the Near East* (New York: Arno Press, 1971), 418.

60. D. C. Bloomer, *The Life and Writings of Amelia Bloomer* (New York: Schocken Books, 1975).

61. Mills, *Under Five Sultans,* 239.

62. There has been some work done on the social world of elite Ottoman women. See, for example, Suraiya Faroqhi, *Subjects of the Sultan: Culture and Daily Life in the Ottoman Empire* (London: I.B. Taurus, 2005), 101–23.

63. Blunt, *My Reminiscences,* 99, 27.

64. Georgi Traichev, *Grad Prilep: Istoriko-geografsko i stopansko pregled* (Sofia: Pechatnitsa "fotinov," 1925), 137. Baba Nedelia was also known for taking Bulgarian women on frequent outings into the countryside and so perhaps overstepping her bounds as a teacher in the eyes of local men.

65. For a more thorough exploration of gender and smoking see chapter 3.

66. Viktoria Tileva, *Bŭlgarsko pechatarsko druzhestvo 'promishlenie' v Tsarigrad: 1870–85* (Sofia: Narodna biblioteka Kiril i Metodi, 1985).

67. Kirli, "Struggle over Space," 112.

68. Although Hattox assumes that Muslim ownership meant Muslim clientele, Kirli asserts that at least during the nineteenth century there was not necessarily a correlation. "Struggle over Space," 137, 179.

69. A number of scholars have severely challenged traditional notions of the static and segregated "Islamic" city. See, for example, Edhem Eldem, Daniel Goffman, and Bruce Masters, *The Ottoman City between East and West: Aleppo, Izmir, and Istanbul* (New York: Cambridge University Press, 1999), and Gavrilova, *Bulgarian Urban Culture,* 78 and 92.

70. See, for example, Malte Fuhrman, "Cosmopolitan Imperialists and the Ottomans Port Cities: Conflicting Logics in the Urban Social Fabric," *Du cosmopolitisme en méditerrannée* 67 (2007): 1–50.

71. Kirli, "Struggle over Space," 114. Of course, many of those designated "foreign" could have been locals who took foreign citizenship in order to enjoy certain trade privileges.

72. Hüseyin Mevsim, "Balkapan han" as Social and Private Place of Bulgarians in Istanbul in the Nineteenth Century," *Balkanistic Forum* 1–2 (2006): 61.

73. See chapter 2 for more on this.

74. Naiden Nachov, *Sbornik na Bŭlgarskata akademiia na naukite, kniga XIX* (Sofia: Pechatnitsa P. Glushkov, 1925), 180.

75. Ibid., 178.

76. Ibid., 53.

77. The well-known tract of Paisii Khilendarski, *Slavianobŭlgarska Istoriia,* which appeared in 1762, first articulated the need for Bulgarians to reclaim their past, their homeland, and their language from the foreign Greek presence. Khilendarski, *Slavianobŭlgarska Istoriia* (Sofia: Bŭlgarski pisatel, 1963).

78. Nachov, *Sbornik,* 53.

79. Khristo Brŭzitsov, *Niakoga v Tsarigrad* (Varna: Dŭrzhavno izdatelstvo, 1966). Some of the most prominent figures in the pantheon of the Bulgarian nationalist revival were Istanbul men of letters like Petko Slaveikov, and most Bulgarian nine-

teenth-century figures spent some time in the city along the way. This connection is indicated in names like Stefan Stambolov and Alexander Stamboliski, which are linked to the capital (Stambul in the Slavic languages).

80. Brŭzitsov, *Niakoga v Tsarigrad,* 39.

81. Brŭzitsov, *Niakoga v Tsarigrad,* 40. Karagöz—an Ottoman everyman—ridiculed exaggerated social and ethnic types from Ottoman society, providing a source of bawdy and carnivalesque entertainment that drew multiethnic Ottoman crowds of men, women, and children. Kirli also elaborates on the well-known Karagöz (meaning black eye in Turkish) phenomenon as a popular mode of social critique, in which there was an intense social mixing based on religion, gender, or age. Kirli, "Struggle over Space," 156.

82. Brŭzitsov, *Niakoga v Tsarigrad,* 36.

83. Biser Toshev, "Kafeneta. Galeriia ot tipove i nravi Bŭlgarski v Tursko vreme," in Kraev, *Kafeneto kato diskurs* (Sofia: Nov Bŭlgarski universitet, 2005), 27.

84. See for example, Ivanka Iankovo and Mincho Semov, *Bŭlgarskite gradove prez vŭzrazhdaneto: Istorichesko, sotsiologichesko i politichesko izsledvane, chast pŭrva* (Sofia: Universitetsko izdatelstvo Sveti Kliment Okhridski, 2004), 388.

85. Ibid., 388.

86. Ibid., 27–28. Bulgarian-dominated *krŭchmar* (tavern owner) guilds formed or grew to prominence where they already existed by the mid-nineteenth century, and many krŭchmars developed into powerful merchants in their own right. Iankovo and Semov, *Bŭlgarskite gradove,* 387.

87. Since Roman times, Plovdiv has been called the city of three hills (Trimontium); though it has had other names too, the city of three hills (although there are indeed more hills in Plovdiv) has remained a nickname. Matei Mateev, *Stara arkhitektura v Plovdiv* (Sofia: Izdatelstvo septemvri, 1976), 3.

88. This apparent "collaboration" of elite Bulgarians with the Greek and Turkish ruling classes to a large degree compromised their status in the Bulgarian historical record. According to Konstantin Dufev, for example, "Their [rich Bulgarians'] familiarity with the privileged castes ensured them a place in the hills of Plovdiv, where along with the rich Turks and Greeks they were set up in luxurious houses, which they had built." Many members of this group, however, were later exonerated by their participation in the national revival or liberation movement. See Dufev, *Tam gore na trikhŭlmieto: Kniga za rodoliubitsi* (Plovdiv: Telerpres, 1993), 15. For the debates on, and more recent rehabilitation of, çorbacıs, see Mikhail Grŭncharov, *Chorbadzhiistvoto i Bŭlgarskoto obshtestvo prez vŭzrazhdaneto* (Sofia: Universitetsko izdatelstvo Sveti Kliment Okhridski,1999), 105.

89. See the memoir of Andonov for an exploration of the complicated loyalties of the Christians of old Plovdiv. Ivan Andonov, *Iz Spomenite mi ot Tursko vreme: Suedinenieto, chast 1 i chast 2* (Sofia: Akademichno izdatelstvo Marin Drinov, 1995).

90. Gavrilova, *Bulgarian Urban Culture,* 149, 82–83.

91. Milko Bichev, *Bŭlgarski Barok: Prinos kŭm problemite na Bŭlgarskoto izkustvo prez epokhata na vŭzrazhdaneto* (Sofia: Nauka i izkustvo, 1954), 12.

92. Gavrilova, *Kolelota na zhivota,* 308.

93. Gavrilova points out that for the first time coffee and tea were prepared and consumed at home rather than in the coffeehouse. See *Bulgarian Urban Culture,* 150.

94. Mateev, *Stara arkhitektura,* 4.

95. Jordan Goodman, *Tobacco in History and Culture: An Encyclopedia* (New York: Thomas Gale, 2005), 144. According to Shechter, Egyptians had developed cigarettes for use in the Ottoman army in the 1830s and were influential in popularizing smoking among European soldiers during the Crimean War. *Smoking, Culture and Economy,* 30–31.

96. See, for example, the criticism of Bulgarians who "imitated" European dress in Petko Slaveĭkov, *Sŭchinenie* (Sofia: Bŭlgarski pisatel, 1989), 7:201.

97. Khristo Peev, *Plovdivskata kŭshta prez epokhata na vuzrazhdaneto* (Sofia: Tekhnika, 1960), 450.

98. Gavrilova, *Bulgarian Urban Culture,* 145.

99. The economy was based on sheep husbandry and wool processing, especially wool fabric and braid used for Ottoman military uniforms. The tobacco-growing regions of Bulgaria were primarily south of the Balkan range, but certainly tobacco was one product that was circulated by the merchants.

100. See Gavrilova, *Kolelota na zhivota,* 308.

101. In another Vazov novella, *Chichovtsi: Galeriia ot tipove i nravi Bŭlgarski v Tursko vreme,* he uses the kafene to represent diverse social types in this period.

102. Vazov, *Under the Yoke,* 48.

103. According to Gavrilova, as a rule shepherds smoked pipes, the çorbacı smoked (and routinely displayed in their homes) long, decorated chibouks, and the young intelligentsia smoked cigarettes. *Kolelota na zhivota,* 308. This is consistent with the tobacco paraphernalia that Vazov assigns to his archetypical characters in *Under the Yoke* and *Uncles.*

104. Vazov, *Under the Yoke,* 164.

105. Ibid., 164.

106. Kristo Stoianov, *Dvizheniie za trezvenost v razgradski okrŭg* (Razgrad: Okrŭzhen komitet za trezvenost, 1983), 6. Stoianov also claims that the Bulgarian revival figures Georgi Rakovski and Todor Kableshkov were abstinent.

107. Mercia MacDermott, *Apostle of Freedom: A Portrait of Vasil Levsky against a Background of Nineteenth Century Bulgaria* (South Brunswick, NJ: A.S. Barnes, 1969), 258.

108. A communist proponent of abstinence even claims that Levski organized the first abstinence organization in Karlovo in 1869, though I have found no evidence to substantiate this claim. See Pavel Petkov, *Borbata za trezvenost vŭv vrachanski okrŭg, 1920–1980* (Sofia: Izdatelstvo na otechestveniia front, 1982).

109. As cited in Mac Dermott, *Apostle of Freedom,* 269.

110. As cited in ibid., 108.

111. Gavrilova, *Kolelota na zhivota,* 45–46, and Petur Karaivanov, *Vasil Levski po spomeni na Vasil Karaivanov* (Sofia: Izdatelstvo na otechestveniia front, 1987), 138. See also Nikola Alvadzhiev, *Plovdivska khronika* (Plovdiv: Izdatelstvo na Khristo G. Danov, 1971), 336.

112. Washburn, *Fifty Years,* 109.

113. See, for example, Petŭr Tashev, *Sofiia; arkhitekturno gradoustroistveno razvitie: Etapi, postizheniia i problemi* (Sofia: Tekhnika, 1972), and Khristo Ganchev, Grigor Doinchev, and Ivana Stoianova, *Bŭlgariia 1900: Evropeĭskata vliianiia v Bŭlgarskoto gradoustroĭstvo, arkitektura, parkove, i gradini 1878–1918* (Sofia: Izkustvo i arkitektura, 2002).

114. For example, see Mark Mazower, *Salonica City of Ghosts: Christians, Muslims, and Jews 1430–1950* (New York: Vintage, 2006). On Budapest see Robert Nemes, *The Once and Future Budapest* (Dekalb: Northern Illinois University Press, 2005).

115. Alvadzhiev, *Plovdivska Khronika,* 100.

116. Ibid., 93.

117. Ibid., 112.

118. Ibid., 217.

119. Ibid., 240.

120. Ibid., 182.

121. Ibid., 49.

122. Neli Zhelova, "Kafenetata na stariia Shumen," in Kraev, *Kafeneto kato diskurs,* 45, 47, and 52.

123. Alvadzhiev, *Plovdivska khronika,* 200–201.

124. Ibid., 185.

125. Ibid., 184.

126. Ibid., 226.

127. Ibid., 112.

128. A *vakf* is an endowed property whose proceeds generally go to fund religious (in this case Muslim) intuitions or other services of public benefit.

129. Alvadzhiev, *Plovdivska Khronika,* 37.

130. Ibid., 183–84.

131. Sofia was chosen as the capital, historians seem to have concluded, in part because Plovdiv was outside the principality until 1885 but also because of its centrality in relation to the coveted territories of Macedonia that had slipped through Bulgarian fingers as a result of the "catastrophic" Treaty of Berlin.

132. Ganchev, Doinchev, and Stoianova, *Bŭlgariia 1900,* 34.

133. Much has been written about the razing of large sections of Paris in the 1850s and 1860s as part of Georges-Eugène Haussmann's grand scheme for remaking the city in a "modern" image. For a recent synthesis and interesting take on the phenomenon see David Harvey, *Paris: Capital of Modernity* (New York: Routledge, 2005).

134. Boriana Sergeeva, "Kafeto—Luks, koito vseki mozhe da si pozvoli," in Kraev, *Kafeneto kato diskurs,* 96.

135. For more on Sofia in this period and after see chapter 4.

136. Petŭr Neikov, *Spomeni* (Sofia: Izdatelstvo na otechestveniia front, 1990), 81.

137. Raina Gavrilova "Kafeneto: Vreme i miasto," in Kraev, *Kafeneto kato diskurs,* 94–95.

138. Aleko Konstantinov, *Razkazi i feiletoni* (Sofia: Knigoizdatelstvo fakel, 1937), 57.

139. Ibid., 53.

140. Konstantinov had traveled extensively in Central and Western Europe and even to Chicago in 1893 for the World's Fair. For an excellent recent translation of this work into English by Robert Sturm see Aleko Konstantinov, *To Chicago and Back* (Sofia: National Museum of Bulgaria, 2004). For a discussion of this work see Mary Neuburger, "To Chicago and Back: Aleko Konstantinov, Rose Oil, and the Smell of Modernity," *Slavic Review* 65 (2006): 427–45.

141. Konstantinov, *Razkazi i feiletoni,* 49.

142. Ibid., 43.

143. Ibid., 47.

144. Danov, *Za teb mili rode,* 113.

145. Ibid., 111, 116.

146. James F. Clarke, *Temperance Work in Bulgaria: Its Successes* (Samokov, Bulg.: Evangelical School Press, 1909, 3).

147. Webster, *Puritans in the Balkans,* 88.

148. See, for example, James Clarke, *Bulgaria and Salonica in Macedonia* (American Board of Commissioners for Foreign Missionaries, 1885), 5, and Webster, *Puritans in the Balkans,* 22–23.

149. Stoianov, *Dvizheniie za trezvenost,* 6.

150. Edward Haskell, *American Influence in Bulgaria* (New York: American Board of Commissioners for Foreign Missionaries, 1913), 7.

151. Ibid., 7.

2. No Smoke without Fire

1. For an in-depth look at this exhibition as part of a cluster of articles about this phenomenon in Eastern Europe, see Mary Neuburger, "Fair Encounters: Bulgaria and the 'West' at International Exhibitions from Plovdiv (1892) to Chicago (1893) to St. Louis (1904)," *Slavic Review* 69 (3): 547–70, Fall 2010.

2. Several books have chapters or sections that deal with Eastern European fairs. See, for example, Cathleen Giustino, *Tearing Down Prague's Jewish Town: Ghetto Clearance and the Legacy of Middle-Class Ethnic Politics around 1900* (Boulder, CO: East European Monographs, 2003), 65–69; Alice Freifeld, *Nationalism and the Crowd in Liberal Hungary, 1848–1914* (Baltimore: Woodrow Wilson Center Press, 2000), 230–54; Patrice Dabrowski, *Commemorations and the Making of Modern Poland* (Bloomington: Indiana University Press, 2004); and Maureen Healy, *Vienna and the Fall of the Habsburg Empire: Total War and Everyday Life in World War I* (Cambridge: Cambridge University Press, 2004), 87–122. See also Mary Neuburger, "To Chicago and Back: Aleko Konstantinov, Rose Oil, and the Smell of Modernity," *Slavic Review* 65 (2006): 427–45.

3. *Nasheto pŭrvo izlozhenie,* 8 August 1892, 6.

4. Ibid., 24 October 1892, 7.

5. Ibid., 8 July 1892, 3.

6. On emigration of Muslims see Justin McCarthy, *Death and Exile: The Ethnic Cleansing of Ottoman Muslims, 1821–1922* (Princeton, NJ: Darwin Press, 1996).

7. Michael Palairet argues that the loss of these urban markets was more harmful to local manufacturing than was the influx of European goods. Palairet, *The Balkan Economies c. 1800–1914: Evolution without Development* (Cambridge: Cambridge University Press, 2003), 175–78.

8. See for example ibid., 186–97, and Rumen Daskalov, *Bŭlgarskoto obshtestvo: Dŭrzhava, politika, ikonomika, 1878–1939* (Sofia: IK Gutenberg, 2005), 307–11.

9. Although Palairet, John Lampe, and others argue that the penetration of the West was relatively insignificant during this period, it is clear that the *perceived* impact was still significant. See Palairet, *Balkan Economies,* and Lampe, "Imperial Borderlands or Capitalist Periphery? Redefining Balkan Backwardness, 1520–1914," in *The Origins of Backwardness in Eastern Europe: Economics and Politics from the Middle Ages until*

the Early Twentieth Century, ed. Daniel Chirot (Berkeley: University of California Press: 1989), 200–202.

10. *Nasheto pŭrvo izlozhenie,* 8 February 1892, 3.

11. Plovdiv Okrŭzhen Dŭrzhaven Arkhiv (hereafter PODA), F-455, O-1, E-29, L-66.

12. Stambolov was also quoted as saying that the fair had been staged in response to his fear that Bulgarians would "become slaves to them [the West]." *Nasheto pŭrvo izlozhenie,* 8 February 1892, 6.

13. Indeed, Bulgarian Marxist historians, with little affection, credit Stambolov with bringing full-blown capitalism to Bulgaria. For an excellent survey of the Stambolov period see Duncan Perry, *Stefan Stambolov and the Emergence of Modern Bulgaria, 1870–1895* (Chapel Hill, NC: Duke University Press, 1993).

14. Richard Crampton, *Bulgaria* (Oxford: Oxford University Press, 2008), 303.

15. It has been documented that in Lom and the surrounding district only Turks grew tobacco. Bulgarians opened cutting shops in the city, however, right before liberation. See Ivanka Iankova and Mincho Semov, eds. *Bŭlgarskite gradove prez vŭzrazhdane: Istorichesko, sotsiologichesko, i politichesko izsledvane* (Sofia: Universitetsko izdatelstvo Sv. Kliment Okhridski, 2004), 387.

16. Although this phenomenon has been widely noted, the most famous elaboration of it is the seminal article of Traian Stoianovich, "The Conquering Balkan Orthodox Merchant," *Journal of Economic History* 20 (1960): 234–313.

17. Since the seventeenth century Greeks had been shipping tobacco along with most other products from Salonika and other port cities to Istanbul, the Italian lands, and elsewhere. See John Lampe and Marvin Jackson, *Balkan Economic History, 1550–1950: From Imperial Borderlands to Developing Nations* (Bloomington: Indiana University Press, 1982), 40. See also Gelina Harlaftis, *A History of Greek-Owned Shipping: The Making of an International Tramp Fleet, 1830 to the Present Day* (New York: Routledge, 1996), 3–142.

18. Snezhka Panova, *Bŭlgarskite tŭrgovtsi prez XVII vek: Izsledvane* (Sofia: Nauka i izkustvo, 1980), 79–80.

19. Palairet, *Balkan Economies,* 46.

20. The relative benefit of export to Ottoman, or specifically Balkan, development is a matter of considerable controversy among economic historians. Neo-Marxist historians have persuasively characterized the penetration of the global economy into the Ottoman Balkans as detrimental to the Ottoman Empire, transformed into an exploited "semi-periphery" of Europe. In contrast, classical economic theorists tend to blame the Ottoman "command economy" and a relative *lack* of European contact prior to World War I for the backwardness that plagued the region. See Lampe, "Imperial Borderlands," 200–202.

21. Lampe and Jackson, *Balkan Economic History,* 138–39.

22. V. N. Duravenski, *Dunavskata problema* (Sofia: Izdatelstvo na Bŭlgarskata rabotnicheskata partia, 1947), 12.

23. According to Dakov, there were 64 Austrian ships cruising the lower Danube by 1873 and 190 by 1897. See Vasil Dakov, *Reka Dunav i neinoto stopansko znachenie za Bŭlgariia* (Sofia: Nauka i izkustvo, 1964), 63.

24. According to Kemal Karpat, from about 1850 until 1914 European imports greatly exceeded exports. Karpat, *Studies on Ottoman Social and Political History* (London: Brill, 2002), 31.

25. Şevket Pamuk, "The Ottoman Empire in the 'Great Depression' of 1873–1896," *Journal of Economic History* 44 (1984): 112.

26. See, for example, Donald Quataert, "Ottoman Manufacturing in the Nineteenth Century," in *Manufacturing in the Ottoman Empire and Turkey, 1500–1950,* ed. Donald Quataert (Albany: State University of New York Press, 1994), 87–122.

27. See, for example, Şevket Pamuk and Jeffrey G. Williamson, *The Mediterranean Response to Globalization before 1950* (New York: Routledge, 2000), 111.

28. By an agreement in 1881, the Bulgarian annual tribute was paid directly to the Ottoman Public Debt Commission established in that year. See Stanford Shaw and Ezel Shaw, *The History of the Ottoman Empire and Turkey,* vol. 2, *Reform, Revolution, and Republic* (Cambridge: Cambridge University Press, 1977), 223–24.

29. Iordan Iordanov, *Istoriia na Bŭlgarskata tŭrgoviia do osvobozhdenieto: Kratŭk ocherk* (Sofia: Pechatnitsa S.M. Staikov, 1938), 150.

30. Even before 1878, there is significant evidence of the expansion of tobacco cultivation, along with cutting and sorting workshops, in a range of cities that came under the purview of the Bulgarian principality. See, for example, Iankova and Semov, *Bŭlgarskite gradove,* 87, 710, 521.

31. By the mid-nineteenth century, there were fifty different trades practiced in Plovdiv with some four hundred workshops. The merchants of Plovdiv were engaged in trade with Central and Western Europe, Anatolia, Egypt and even Calcutta, where there was an active colony of Plovdiv-based merchants. Elena Uzunska, "Plovdiv v navecheriia na osoboditelna voina," in *Plovdiv, 1878–1968: 90 Godini ot osvobozhdeniie na grada i Plovdivskiia krai,* ed. Ivan Undzhiev (Plovdiv: Izdatelstvo Khristo G. Danov, 1968), 61.

32. By 1873, 1 million *oka* (1.3 million kilograms) of tobacco were being produced and processed annually. Iankova and Semov, *Bŭlgarskite gradove,* 521.

33. Milko Bichev, *Architecture in Bulgaria: From Ancient Times to the Late Nineteenth Century* (Sofia: Foreign Language Press, 1961), 42.

34. *Bŭlgarski tiutiun,* no. 2 (1991): 35.

35. PODA, F-455, O-1, E-29, L-122.

36. After the fair was over, in fact, Stavrides gave the pavilion to Madras, who reconstructed it in his residential courtyard. PODA, F-455, O-1, E-29, L-116.

37. Though prerolled cigarettes became increasingly popular both locally and globally in the second half of the nineteenth century, they were still generally an expensive niche product in most markets. In Bulgaria it was still more common to buy and sell tobacco in packets for self-rolled cigarettes and pipes, including narghile. Nikola Alvadzhiev, *Plovdivska khronika* (Plovdiv: Izdatelstvo Khristo G. Danov, 1971).

38. *Bŭlgarski Tiutiun,* no. 2 (1991): 35.

39. For names of Bulgarian tobacconists see Iankova and Semov, *Bŭlgarskite gradove,* 87, 538, 564, 434, 710, 997.

40. Ibid., 282.

41. Ibid., 148–51.

42. Ibid., 287.

43. See Georgi Vangelov, *Tiutiunopabotnitsi: Spomeni iz borbite na tiutiunopabotnitsite* (Sofia: Profizdat, 1955), 58.

44. See, for example, Georgi Nachovich, *Tiutiuneva industriia v Bŭlgarskoto kniazhestvo* (Sofia: Pechatnitsa na Bŭlgarski glas, 1883), 5.

45. A. Jochmus, "Notes on a Journey into the Balkan, or Mount Haemus, in 1847," *Journal of the Royal Geographic Society of London* 24 (1854): 41; Iankova and Semov, *Bŭlgarskite gradove,* 834.

46. On the Jews of Salonika and their role in tobacco trade see Mazower, *Salonica, City of Ghosts: Christians, Muslims, and Jews, 1430–1950* (New York: Vintage, 2007).

47. Vasil Kutsoglu, *Spomeni i razmisli* (Sofia: Izdatesltvo na otechestveniia front, 1989), 9.

48. Ibid., 10.

49. Karl Müller, *Proizvodstvo, obrabotvane i tŭrgovie c tiutiunĭa v Evropeska Turtsia, a sega nova Bŭlgariia* (Sofia: Dŭrzhavna pechatnitsa, 1916), 18, 44.

50. His sons later changed their surname back to Kutsev, presumably after Smolian was incorporated into Bulgaria in 1912. On the culture and politics of names in the region see Mary Neuburger, *The Orient Within: Muslim Minorities and the Negotiation of Nationhood in Modern Bulgaria* (Ithaca: Cornell University Press, 2004), 142–68.

51. Nachovich also advocated the "bringing of farmers"—clearly Bulgarian ones—from Macedonia and Thrace to plant tobacco in the Bulgarian lands. Nachovich, *Tiuiuneva industriia,* 10.

52. Ibid., 4.

53. American Tobacco Company, *"Sold American!" The First Fifty Years, 1904–1954* (New York: American Tobacco Company,1954), 33.

54. Pamuk and Williamson, *Mediterranean Response,* 122.

55. Cotton was reduced from 5 million to 1.2 in the same period. Tsvetana Todorova, ed., *Bŭlgariia v pŭrvata svetovna voina: Germanski diplomatichecki dokumenti* (Sofia: Glavno upravlaniie na arkhivite pri ministerkiia sŭvet, 2005), 324.

56. On the widely divergent ethnographic maps produced during this period see Henry Wilkinson, *Maps and Politics: A Review of the Ethnographic Cartography of Macedonia* (Liverpool: Liverpool University Press, 1951). On the amphibious nature of identity in Macedonia, particularly as regards Bulgarians, Greeks, and Vlachs, see Keith Brown, *The Past in Question: Modern Macedonia and the Uncertainties of Nation* (Princeton: Princeton University Press, 2003); and Anastasia Karakasidou, *Fields of Wheat, Hills of Blood: Passages to Nationhood in Greek Macedonia, 1870–1990* (Chicago: University of Chicago Press, 1997).

57. Tara Zahra has made a powerful case for the role of "national indifference" in driving the vehemence of nationalist movements in Bohemia and Moravia in this same period. See Tara Zahra, *Kidnapped Souls: National Indifference and the Battle for Children in the Bohemian Lands, 1900–1948* (Ithaca: Cornell University Press, 2008).

58. John Foster Fraser, *Pictures from the Balkans* (London: Cassell and Co., 1912), 169–70.

59. Ibid., 170.

60. See also Fredrick Moore, *The Balkan Trail* (New York: Macmillan, 1906), 172.

61. H. N. Brailsford, for example, associates the blatant disregard for the tobacco monopoly in Albania as indicative of "Albanian defiance" of Ottoman authority. See H. N. Brailsford, *Macedonia: Its Races and Their Future* (London: Methuen, 1906), 262.

62. On Skopje or (Üsküb) see Luigi Villari, ed. *The Balkan Question: The Present Condition of the Balkans and of European Responsibilities by Various Writers* (London: John and Murray, 1905), 170.

63. Egypt was one of the Ottoman provinces with the highest demand for Balkan tobaccos, both for internal consumption and for re-export as manufactured "Egyptian cigarettes."

64. Villari, ed. *The Balkan Question,* 169–70.

65. Ibid., 170.

66. Ibid.

67. George Abbot, *Tale of a Tour in Macedonia* (London: Edward Arnold, 1903), 280.

68. As early as 1895 and continuing through to the Balkan Wars (1912–13), Austria and Germany (combined in the statistics) were the number one exporters of Ottoman tobacco by a large margin. See Müller, *Proizvodstvo,* 107.

69. By 1914, 20 percent of all Ottoman exports went to the United States. See Joseph Grabill, *Protestant Diplomacy and the Near East: Missionary Influence on American Policy, 1810–1927* (Minneapolis: University of Minnesota Press, 1971), 36. See also Müller, *Proizvodstvo,* 109.

70. Müller, *Proizvodstvo,* 73.

71. Direktsiia na Statistika, *Vŭnshnata tŭrgoviia na Bŭlgariia prez godinite 1897– 1903* (Sofia: Pechatnitsa na P.M. Buzaitov, 1905), 292. *Papirosi* (cigarettes) were exported in small numbers, mainly to the Austro-Hungarian Empire but also to other countries. For example, 91 kilograms went to Germany in 1900.

72. On the Egyptian tobacco industry and the use of Balkan tobaccos see Relli Shechter, *Smoking, Culture and Economy in the Middle East: The Egyptian Tobacco Market 1850–2000* (New York: I.B. Tauris, 2006), 33–4.

73. Egypt, which was not listed as a separate entity in Bulgarian export statistics until 1902, moved easily into second place in that year, importing about 220,000 kilograms in 1902 and 1903. Direktsiia na Statistika, *Vŭnshnata tŭrgoviia,* 292.

74. Crampton, *Bulgaria,* 157.

75. Koitcho Velchev, *Tobacco in Bulgaria* (Sofia: Marco Beltchev and Sons), 1950), 3.

76. Ibid., 163.

77. John Keiger, ed. *British Documents on Foreign Affairs: Reports and Papers from the Foreign Office Confidential Print: Part 1, Series F, V15* (London: Great Britain Foreign Office, 1952), 86–87.

78. Theodora Dragostinova, *Between Two Motherlands: Nationality and Emigration among the Greeks of Bulgaria* (Ithaca: Cornell University Press, 2011). Dragostinova offers an excellent review of the vast literature on this issue.

79. See, for example, Duncan Perry, *The Politics of Terror: The Macedonian Revolutionary Movements, 1893–1903* (Durham, NC: Duke University Press, 1988).

80. On Geogri Chaprashikov see Iankova and Semov, *Bŭlgarskite gradove,* 148.

81. See, for example, Basil Gounaris, ed., *The Events of 1903 in Macedonia as Presented in European Diplomatic Correspondence* (Thessaloniki: Museum of the Macedonian Struggle, 1993), 73.

82. See, for example, ibid., 79, and Voin Bozhinov, and Dimitŭr Kosev eds., *Macedonia: Documents and Material* (Sofia: Bulgarian Academy of Sciences, 1978), 506.

83. Bozhinov and Kosev, *Macedonia,* 515.

84. Perry, *The Politics of Terror,* 25.

85. Ibid., 139–40.

86. There are no available figures on Muslim noncombatant deaths. Ibid., 140.

87. Ibid., 100.

88. Brailsford, *Macedonia*, 17.

89. Hristo Andonov-Poljanski, *Documents on the Struggle of the Macedonian People for Independence and a Nation-State* (Skopje: Kultura, 1985), 52.

90. From a letter written by Gote Delchev and Gyorche Petrov, in Bozhinov and Kosev, *Macedonia*, 448.

91. See William Eleroy Curtis, *The Turk and His Lost Provinces: Greece, Bulgaria, Servia, Bosnia* (Chicago: Fleming and H. Revell Co., 1903), 228.

92. For a recent narrative of these bombings see Mazower, *Salonica*, 268. It seems unlikely that it is a coincidence that IMRO staged the famous Ilinden Uprising precisely in the "American year."

93. Keith Brown, *The Past in Question*, 63.

94. P. L. Martin Wills, *A Captive of the Bulgarian Brigands: Englishman's Terrible Experiences in Macedonia* (London: EDE, Allom, and Townsend, 1906), 11–13.

95. Ibid., 21.

96. D. Vlakhov, *Rezhima na tiutiuna v nova i stara Bŭlgariia* (Burgas: Pechatnitsa N. V. Velchev, 1914), 12.

97. Andonov-Poljanski, *Documents*, 537.

98. Mete Tunçay and Erik Jan Zürcher, *Socialism and Nationalism in the Ottoman Empire, 1876–1923* (London: Palgrave Macmillan, 1994), 41–58.

99. Andonov-Poljanski, *Documents*, 548.

100. Since 1878, the Bulgarian administration had impeded the return of Muslim refugees by granting their lands to Slavic refugees from Macedonia and Thrace. Georgi Todorov, "Deinostta na vremenoto Rusko upravlenie v Bŭlgariia po urezhdane na agrarniia i bezhanskiia vŭpros prez 1877–1879 g," *Istoricheski pregled* 6 (1955): 36.

101. See Crampton, *Bulgaria*, 434. For a thorough discussion of these events and the Greek minority in Bulgarian history see also Dragostinova, *Between Two Motherlands*.

102. See, for example, Dragostinova, *Between Two Motherlands*, 39–41.

103. Stefan Abadzhiev, *Spomeni ot izminatiia put* (Sofia: Profizdat, 1982), 9.

104. See Vangelov, *Tiutiunopabotnitsi*, 10. See also Abadzhiev, *Spomeni*, 8.

105. Abadzhiev, *Spomeni*, 9.

106. Vangelov, *Tiutiunopabotnitsi*, 34–35.

107. Iankova and Semov, *Bŭlgarskite gradove*, 834.

108. On strikes and the labor movement in Ottoman Macedonia in this period see Tunçay and Zürcher, *Socialism and Nationalism*.

109. Nikola Gospodinov, *Zhiznen pŭt: Publististika, dokumenti, spomeni* (Sofia: Profizdat, 1977), 7.

110. For a discussion of Blagoev's contacts with the Internal Macedonian Revolutionary Organization see Mercia McDermott, *For Freedom and Perfection: The Life of Yane Sandansky* (London: Journeyman Press, 1988), 48.

111. Ibid., 7.

112. *Tiutiunopabotnik zashtitnik,* 13 November 1910. In 1910, of new members in the union, 345 were reportedly "Bulgarian," while only 47 were "other."

113. See, for example, ibid., 15 January 1909, 4.

114. Ibid., 15 March 1908, 3.

115. Ibid., 1 May 1910, 2.

116. Ibid., 21 May 1910, 2–3.

117. Dragostinova, *Between Two Motherlands,* 40–41.

118. One way worker solidarity was eroded was through the use of so-called *bashii* (singular, *bashiia,* from the Turkish word for head), or spies. They were paid extra and allowed perks—such as samples of tobacco or cigarettes—in exchange for reporting on discontent or organizing among workers. This practice was widely reported on in the workers' press. See, for example, the discussion of Stavrides's use of bashii in *Rabotnicheska borba,* 25 January 1904, 1.

119. Gila Hadar, "Jewish Tobacco Workers in Salonika: Gender and Family in the Context of Social and Ethnic Strife," in *Women in the Ottoman Balkans,* ed. Amila Buturovic and Irvin Cemil Schick (London: I.B. Tauris, 2007), 128.

120. Tunçay and Zürcher, *Socialism and Nationalism,* 94.

121. Ibid., 64–65.

122. *Rabotnicheska borba,* 25 January 25 1904, 1.

123. Vangelov, *Tiutiunopabotnitsi,* 14.

124. *Tiutiunopabotnik zashtitnik,* 30 October 1909, as cited in Gospodinov, *Zhiznen pŭt,* 40.

125. Todor Belchov, "Iz borbite na tiutiunopabotnitsite v grad Plovdiv (1891–1920g.)," *Godishnik na museite v Plovdivski okrŭg* 2 (1956): 17.

126. *Tiutiunopabotnik zashtitnik,* 6 July 1910, 2.

127. *Rabotnicheska borba,* 25 January 1904, 2.

128. Ibid., 1.

129. Ibid.

130. For an exploration of similar dynamics in the tobacco labor movement in Ottoman Salonika see Hadar, "Jewish Tobacco Workers," 127–52.

131. *Tiutiunopabotnik zashtitnik,* 15 March 1908, 3.

132. *Tiutiunopabotnik zashtitnik,* 21 May, 1910, 4.

133. Ibid., 1 April 1908, 2.

134. Ibid., 13 November 1910, 2. For example, of the new members in the union in 1910, 222 were women and only 160 were men.

135. Ibid., 21 July 1910, 2.

136. There are many chronicles of these years that were published during the postwar period. See, for example, Belchov, "Iz borbite na tiutiunorabotnitsite," 11–37, and Vangelov, *Tiutiunopabotnitsi.*

137. See, for example, Allan Brandt, *The Cigarette Century: The Rise, Fall, and Deadly Persistence of the Product That Defined America* (New York: Basic Books, 2007), 51–54.

138. Richard Hall, *The Balkan Wars 1912–3: Prelude to World War One* (New York: Routledge, 2000), 24.

139. For a more detailed discussion of this process see Neuburger, *The Orient Within,* 91–97, 113–14, 176.

140. See, for example, George Kennan, ed., *The Other Balkan Wars: A 1913 Carnegie Endowment Inquiry in Retrospect* (Washington, DC: Carnegie Endowment for International Peace, Brookings Institution Publications, 1993).

141. Ibid., 11.

142. Maria Todorova, *Imagining the Balkans* (New York: Oxford University Press, 1997), 4–6.

143. For more discussion of this see Brown, *The Past in Question,* 59.

144. Keiger, *British Documents,* 26.

145. B. Destani, ed., *Ethnic Minorities in the Balkan States,* vol. 2, *1888–1914* (London: Archive Editions Limited, 2003), 355.

146. Theodoros Zaimes, *The Crimes of Bulgaria in Macedonia: An Authentic Document, Based on Facts and Records* (Washington, DC: 1914).

147. On the Doxato, Serres, and Kavala massacres see Kennan, *The Other Balkan Wars,* 79–81. On tobacco and development in Ksanti (in Greek Xanthi) see Destani, *Ethnic Minorities,* 354.

148. This is according to an Austrian consular dispatch as cited in Zaimes, *The Crimes of Bulgaria,* 18.

149. Destani, *Ethnic Minorities,* 358.

150. Ibid.

151. Leon Trotsky, *The Balkan Wars: 1912–3* (New York: Monad Press, 1980), 362.

152. Bulgarians have widely used the term "national catastrophe" to characterize the outcomes of the Second Balkan War and World War I.

153. D. Vlakhov, *Rezhima na tiutiuna,* 131.

154. Belchov, "Iz borbite na tiutiunopabotnitsite," 14.

155. Todorova, *Bŭlgariia v pŭrvata svetovna voina,* 124.

156. In a case reported from Serres, a *cavass* (porter) of a Mr. Arrington of the American Tobacco Company was arrested under Bulgarian occupation as a suspected "Greek guerrilla." Arrington found the man in jail, where he had been wounded but not killed during a massacre of Greek prisoners. See Kennan, ed., *The Other Balkan Wars,* 85.

157. Although American Tobacco temporarily lost access to "Turkish" leaf, World War I was a boon to the cartel, which began to supply Allied Western Europe, as well as the Allied military with American leaf. The Allies were also cut off from Ottoman leaf for much of the war. See *New York Times,* 15 July 1918, 10.

158. Todorova, *Bŭlgariia v pŭrvata svetovna voina,* 51.

159. Ibid., 10. See also Alfred Bekhar, *Tiutiun v Bŭlgariia* (Sofia: 1927).

160. Todorova, *Bŭlgariia v pŭrvata svetovna voina,* 389. See also Belchov, "Iz borbite na tiutiunopabotnitsite," 15.

161. Todorova, *Bŭlgariia v pŭrvata svetovna voina,* 389.

162. Belchov, "Iz borbite na tiutiunopabotnitsite," 15.

163. Todorova, Ibid, 619.

164. Ibid., 125, 171, 203.

165. Ibid., 178.

166. Ibid., 116.

167. Vangelov, *Tiutiunopabotnitsi,* 24.

168. Belchov, "Iz borbite na tiutiunopabotnitsite," 33.

169. For more on this late war period see Crampton, *Bulgaria,* 211–14.

170. Belchov, "Iz borbite na tiutiunopabotnitsite," 34. While Belchov puts the numbers in the hundreds, Vangelov argues for thousands of participants. Vangelov, *Tiutiunopabotnitsi,* 99–100.

171. On women rioting for food in Vienna see Healy, *Vienna and The Fall of the Habsburg Empire,* 32–33.

172. Crampton, *Bulgaria,* 215.

3. From the Orient Express to the Sofia Café

1. See Raina Kostentseva, *Moiat roden grad Sofiia v kraia na XIX–nachalo na XX vek i sled tova* (Sofia: Riva, 2008), 80–81.

2. Scholars have long explored how patterns of consumption are both embedded in and foster social change, including momentous shifts in gender roles. On gender and consumption see Victoria de Grazia and Ellen Furlough, eds., *The Sex of Things: Gender and Consumption in Historical Perspective* (Berkeley: University of California Press, 1996). For analyses of the global modern girl in relation to consumption see Alys Eve Weinbaum et al., *The Modern Girl Around the World: Consumption, Modernity, Globalization* (Durham, NC: Duke University Press, 2008).

3. David Courtright, *Forces of Habit: Drugs and the Making of the Modern World* (Cambridge, MA: Harvard University Press, 2001), 9.

4. Irina Gigova, "Writers of the Nation: Intellectual Identity in Bulgaria, 1939–1953" (PhD diss., University of Illinois at Urbana–Champaign, 2005), 29.

5. *Trezvenost* (Sofia), October–November, 1921, 1.

6. See Rumen Daskalov, *Bŭlgarsko obshtestvo,* vol. 2, *Naselenie, obshtestvo, kultura* (Sofia: IK Gutenberg, 2005), 152–56.

7. See Petur Mirchev, *Kipezhŭt: Kniga za Sofiia, 1878–1884* (Sofia: Otechestven front, 1971), 36–40.

8. Dimo Kazasov, *Vidiano i prezhiviano. 1891–1944* (Sofia: Otechestven front, 1969), 114.

9. *Trezvenost* (Sofia), 22 May 1922, 7. This was compared with 246 taverns per person in Germany, 350 per person in the United States, 430 in Japan, and 927 in Russia.

10. *Trezvenost* (Sofia), 22 May 1922, 7.

11. Kostentseva, *Moiat roden grad Sofiia,* 230.

12. Ibid., 13–14. See also Mirchev, *Kipezhŭt,* 94.

13. See also Mirchev, *Kipezhŭt,* 44.

14. Kostentseva, *Moiat roden grad Sofiia,* 229.

15. Ibid., 172–73; Mirchev, *Kipezhŭt,* 36–37.

16. Naiden Sheimanov, "Preobrazhenie na Bŭlgariia," in *Zasto sme takiva: V tŭrsene na Bŭlgarskata idenitichnost,* ed. Rumen Daskalov and Ivan Elenkov (Sofia: Izdatelstvo prosveta, 1994), 267.

17. Ibid., 267.

18. Daskalov, *Bŭlgarsko obshtestvo,* 2:164–65.

19. Ibid.,153–58.

20. Kostentseva, *Moiat roden grad Sofiia,* 172.

21. Ibid., 223.

22. Ibid., 80.

23. Mirchev, 39–44.

24. *Trezvenost* (Sofia), 1922, 11.

25. In the United States the problem was so bad that the temperance movement kicked into high gear and made alcohol (though not tobacco), illegal on January 16, 1919. This day became celebrated as "abstinence day" among all abstinence groups

in Bulgaria, and the United States was always at the forefront of global abstinence efforts, whether religious or secular, even after prohibition was abolished in 1933. At the same time, the Bolsheviks made alcohol illegal in the newly formed Soviet Union, providing a model of attempted total abstinence on the Left to complement that on the Right. On temperance in the Soviet Union, see Laura Phillips, *Bolsheviks and the Bottle: Drink and Worker Culture in St. Petersburg, 1900–1929* (DeKalb, IL: Northern Illinois University Press, 2000); see also Kate Transchel, *Under the Influence: Working-Class Drinking, Temperance, and Cultural Revolution in Russia, 1895–1932* (Pittsburgh: University of Pittsburgh Press, 2006).

26. Khristo Brŭzitsov, *Niakoga v Sofiia: Spomeni 1913–1944* (Sofia: Bŭlgarski pisatel, 1970), 67–68.

27. See also Kazasov, *Vidiano i prezhiviano.* 332.

28. Brŭzitsov, *Niakoga v Sofia,* 14.

29. Rumiana Pashaliiska, "Santimentalna razkhodi iz literaturnite kŭtcheta na Sofiiska khudozhestvena bokhema," in *Kafene Evropa,* ed. Raia Zaimova (Sofia: Izdatelstvo Damian Iakov, 2007), 150.

30. Kazasov, *Vidiano i prezhiviano,* 114.

31. Ivan Radoslavov, Lilia Radoslavova Popova, and Ivan Sestrimski, *Spomeni, dnevnitsi, pisma* (Sofia: Bŭlgarski pisatel, 1983), 69.

32. Konstantin Gulubov, *Spomeni veseli i neveseli za Bŭlgarski pisateli* (Sofia: Bŭlgarski pisatel, 1959), 81.

33. Pashaliiska, "Santimentalna razkhodi," 150–51.

34. Kostentseva, *Moiat roden grad Sofiia,* 124–55, 231.

35. She knew, for example, that Stoian Mikhailovski, the famous Leftist poet, was a regular at the Okhrid café. Kostentseva, *Moiat roden grad Sofiia,* 168.

36. See chapter 1 for a discussion of this memorable ethnographic memoir of Plovdiv. Nikola Alvadzhiev, *Plovdivska khronika* (Plovdiv: Izdatelstvo na Khristo G. Danov, 1971).

37. Brŭzitsov, *Niakoga v Sofiia,* 39. This was in reference to an Orthodox Christian ritual in which a flame was carried from Jerusalem to Sofia during Easter holy days.

38. Ibid., 40. For descriptions of social life in Iuchbunar see also Tsola Dragoicheva, *Poveliia na dŭlga: Shtŭrmŭt, v2* (Sofia: Profizdat, 1975), 160.

39. Brŭzitsov, *Niakoga v Sofiia,* 55. On the mekhana as an institution see Malamar Borisov Spasov, "Balkanski mekhani-zmi," in Zaimova, *Kafene Evropa,* 110–16.

40. Brŭzitsov, *Niakoga v Sofiia,* 60.

41. On Pelin see Gulubov, *Spomeni veseli i neveseli,* 161, 174. On Konstatinov, see discussion of his feuilleton "Strast" in chapter 1. For the text of the feuilleton see Aleko Konstantinov, *Razkazi i Feiletoni* (Sofia: Knigoizdatesltvo Fakel, 1937), 57.

42. Petŭr Neikov, *Tekhnite obrazi: Spomeni* (Sofia: Bŭlgarski pisatel, 1956), 95.

43. For the place of Vazov and generational shifts within Bulgarian intellectual life see Boian Penev, "Uvod v Bŭlgarskata literature sled osvobozhdenieto," in Daskalov and Elenkov, *Zasto sme takiva?,* 158.

44. Petŭr Mirchev, *Sofiia tŭzhna i vesela: Spomeni na edno Sofiianche* (Sofia: Otechestvo, 1978), 217–18.

45. Kazasov, *Vidiano i prezhiviano,* 161.

46. Pashaliiska, "Santimentalna razkhodka," 140.

47. Blaga Dimitrova and Iordan Vasilev, eds., *Mladostta na Bagriana i neinite sput-nitsi* (Plovdiv: Izdatelstvo na Khristo G. Danov, 1976), 162, 175.

48. Konstantin Konstatinov, *Pŭtuvane kŭm vŭrkhovete: Portreti, spomeni, eseta* (Varna: Knigoizdatelstvo Georgi Bakalov, 1976), 111–12.

49. Kazasov, *Vidiano i prezhiviano,* 161.

50. Lora Shumkova, "Mechtaniia za kafene sredets," in *Kafeneto kato diskurs,* ed. Georg Kraev (Sofia: Nov Bŭlgarski Universitet, 2005), 68.

51. Pashaliiska, "Santimentalna razkhodi," 155.

52. Rosen Takhov, *Golemite Bŭlgarski senzatsii* (Sofia: Izdatelstvo iztok-zapad, 2005), 230–33.

53. I put "Bulgarians" in quotes here because the ethnic identification of Cyril and Methodius is disputed; they are claimed as Bulgarian, Macedonian, and Greek, Because they lived in the ninth century, when such identities were in a premodern state of flux.

54. Takhov, *Golemite Bŭlgarski senzatsii,* 232.

55. Ibid.

56. The current world record, of eight hundred cigarettes in less than six minutes, was set by Stefan Sigmond of (neighboring) Transylvania, but Sigmond used a special device to smoke all eight hundred simultaneously, which is in no way comparable.

57. See, for example, Milena Georgieva, "Kafeneto kato atelie, ili na bohemstvo kato nachin na zhivot v Bŭlgarskoto izkustvo prez pŭrvata polovina na XX vek," in Zaimova, *Kafene Evropa,* 201.

58. For a description of Zlatorog's internal dynamics and kafene life see Georgi Tsanev, *Sreshta s minaloto: Spomeni* (Sofia: Bŭlgarski pisatel, 1977), 183–229.

59. See Plamen Doinov, "Kafene, meniu, literatura: Tekst i literaturen protocol v Evropeĭski i Bŭlgarksi kafeneta," in Zaimova, *Kafene Evropa,* 166.

60. Katiia Kuzmova-Zografa, "Ot imaniarski legendi do mornata utopia 'Viensko kafene,'" in Zaimova, *Kafene Evropa,* 161.

61. Georgi Georgiev, *Sofiia i Sofiiantsi, 1878–1944* (Sofia: Nauka i izkustvo, 1983), 124–25.

62. Pashaliiska, "Santimentalna razkhodka," 152.

63. Gigova, "Writers of the Nation," 29.

64. Brŭzitsov, *Niakoga v Sofiia,* 170.

65. Gulubov, *Spomeni veseli i neveseli,* 161, 174.

66. Brŭzitsov, *Niakoga v Sofiia,* 170–71.

67. Georgiev, *Sofiia i Sofiiantsi,* 124–25.

68. Konstatinov, *Pŭtuvane kŭm vŭrkhovete,* 115.

69. Ibid., 115–16.

70. Takhov, *Golemite Bŭlgarski senzatsii,* 233.

71. Brŭzitsov, *Niakoga v Sofiia,* 69; Konstatinov, *Pŭtuvane kŭm vŭrkhovete,* 144.

72. Konstatinov, *Pŭtuvane kŭm vŭrkhovete,* 115.

73. For a biography of Dora Gabe see Ivan Sarandev, *Dora Gabe* (Sofia: Izdatelstvo Nauka i izkustvo, 1986).

74. According to Manning, both Gabe and Bagriana were better writers than their male contemporaries. Clarence Manning, *The History of Modern Bulgarian Literature* (New York: Bookman Associates, 1960), 239.

75. Strashimirov, *Zheni i mŭzhe v zhivota i v literaturata* (Sofia: S.M. Staikov, 1930), 69.

76. Konstatinov, *Pŭtuvane kŭm vŭrkhovete,* 115.

77. For the image and a list of all the figures in the painting see Aleksandŭr Dobrinov and Adelina Fileva, *Alexander Dobrinov, 1898–1958* (Sofia: Sofia Municipal Art Gallery, 1998).

78. Konstatinov, *Pŭtuvane kŭm vŭrkhovete,* 144.

79. Pashaliiska, "Santimentalna razkhodka," 152.

80. Konstatinov, *Pŭtuvane kŭm vŭrkhovete,*113.

81. Kazasov, *Vidiano i prezhiviano,* 111–14, 127.

82. Dimitrova and Vasilev, *Mladostta na Bagriana,* 162; Khristo Nedialkov, *Bŭlgarski kulturni deitsi za trezvenostta* (Sofia: Meditsina i fizkultura, 1977), 50–52.

83. Kazasov, *Vidiano i prezhiviano,* 332.

84. As described by British writer Henrietta Leslie, the Bulgarian PEN Club held a salon in the home of Anna Kamenova, who incidentally was described as a smoker. According to Leslie, married women of means had more time for writing than men, who also had to hold employment as civil servants. Henrietta Leslie,*Where East Is West: Life in Bulgaria* (Boston: Houghton Mifflin, 1933), 47, 60.

85. Irina Gigova, "The Feminisation of Bulgarian Literature and the Club of Bulgarian Women Writers," *Aspasia* 2 (2008): 109.

86. Kazasov, *Vidiano i prezhiviano,* 290.

87. Outside Sofia, where there were fewer of such places, women were more restricted.

88. Brŭzitsov, *Niakoga v Sofiia,* 60.

89. Kostentseva, *Moiat roden grad Sofiia,* 38.

90. Ibid., 229–30.

91. Tsola Dragoicheva,*Poveliia na dŭlga,* vol. 2, *Shturmŭt* (Sofia: Profizdat, 1975),75.

92. In one case she did meet with operatives in a luxury café in Ruse, but her discomfort was palpable in the text. Dragoicheva, *Poveliia na dŭlga,* vol. 1, *Spomeni i razmisli,* 129.

93. Ibid.,160.

94. Ibid., 160–66.

95. Ibid., 153.

96. Petkov, *Borbata za trezvenost vŭv Vrachanski okrŭg, 1920–1980* (Sofia: Izdatelstvo na otechestveniia front, 1982), 52–53.

97. Nedialkov, *Bŭlgarski kulturni deitsi,* 14–22.

98. Dragoicheva, *Poveliia na dŭlga,* 2:110–11.

99. See Elena Bogdanova, *Vela Blagoeva: Biografichen ocherk* (Izdatelstvo na BKP, 1969).

100. Dona Bogatinova, *Trudno i slavno minalo* (Sofia: Partizdat, 1973), 72.

101. Dragoevicha, *Poveliia na dŭlga,* 2:333–34.

102. Ibid., 1:153.

103. Paun Genov, *S Fakela na trezvenostta: Momenti ot borbata protiv pianstvoto i tiutiunopusheneto pres 1300-godishnata istoriia na Bŭlgariia* (Sofia: Natsionalen komitet za trezvenost, meditsina i fizkultura, 1980), 43.

104. Dragoicheva, *Poveliia na dŭlga,* 2:160.

105. As described, for example, in ibid., 1:186.

106. See for example, Ivan Nachev, "Politicheski aspekti na vŭzrozhdenskoto kafene," in *Kafeneto kato diskurs,* ed. Georg Kraev (Sofia: Nov Bŭlgarski Universitet, 2005), 41–42.

107. See for example, *Bŭlgarski tiutiun,* 1 November 1936, 1.

108. Khristo Kulichev, *Zaslugi na Protestantite za Bŭlgarskiia narod* (Sofia: Universitetsko izdatelstvo Sveti Kliment Okhridski, 2008), 273.

109. Ibid., 267.

110. Khristo Marinov, "Ivan Pavlov," in *Iubileen nauchen sbornik, 1922–37,* ed. Krum Akhchiiski and Ianka Tosheva (Sofia: Studentska vŭzdŭrzhatelno druzhestvo, 1937), 34–35.

111. Khristo Dimchev, "Pŭrvi iskri," in Akhchiiski and Tosheva, *Iubileen nauchen sbornik, 1922–37,* 10.

112. Petkov, *Borbata za trezvenost,* 21.

113. *Trezvenost* (Ruse), April 1922, 7.

114. As Kostentseva noted in relation to this period, "[T]here was something revolutionary in the work of the Protestants that attracted many people." Kostentseva, *Moiat roden grad Sofiia,* 181.

115. Ibid., 180.

116. See, for example, Phillips, *Bolsheviks and the Bottle,* and Tricia Starks, "Papirosy, Smoking, and the Anti-Cigarette Movement," in *Tobacco in Russian History and Culture from the Seventeeth Century to the Present,* ed. Matthew Romaniello and Tricia Starks (New York: Routledge, 2009), 132–47.

117. See Jukka Gronow, *Caviar with Champagne: Common Luxury and the Ideals of the Good Life in Stalin's Russia* (Oxford: Berg, 2003); and Julie Hessler, *A Social History of Soviet Trade: Trade Policy, Retail Practices, and Consumption, 1917–1953* (Princeton: Princeton University Press, 2004).

118. Shumkova, "Mechtaniia za kafene sredets," 68.

119. In Bulgarian villages, where religious and social strictures remained firmly in place, the village kafene and krŭchma remained an exclusively male space until after World War II. See Dobrinka Parusehva, "Politicheska kultura na kafeneta," in Zaimova, *Kafene Evropa,* 85.

120. In Vaptsarov's hometown of Bansko, for example, the local chapter of the "narrow socialist" (later Bulgarian Communist) party was formed at a local krŭchma. Boika Vaptsarova, *Nikola Vaptsarov: Letopis za zhivota i tvorchestvoto mu* (Sofia: BAN, 1978), 22.

121. See Stefan Karakostov, "*Chitalishte i vŭzdŭrzhatelno dvizhenie,* in Akhchiiski and Tosheva, *Iubileen nauchen sbornik, 1922–37,* 55–56.

122. Petkov, *Borbata za trezvenost,* 43.

123. Stefan Cholakof, "U.N.V.S.—Shkola na podvig i samozhertva," in Akhchiiski and Tosheva, *Iubileen nauchen sbornik, 1922–37,* 18.

124. Tsentralen Dŭrzhaven Arkhiv (hereafter TsDA), F-1027k, O-1, E-38, L-34.

125. *Trezvenost* (Ruse), 6, April 1923, 96–97.

126. Tzetko Petkov, "Vŭzdŭrzhane i intelligentsia," in Akhchiiski and Tosheva, *Iubileen nauchen sbornik, 1922–37,* 252.

127. *Trezvenost* (Ruse), year 5, book 7–8. 1922. See also TsDA, F-1027k, O-1, E-8, L-46.

128. TsDA, F-1027k, O-1, E-22, L-9–10.

129. Petkov, "Vŭzdŭrzhane i intelligentsia," 252.

130. TsDA, F-1027k, O-1, E-16, L-67.

131. Liuben Abadzhiev, *Psikhologiata na nachunaishtia pushach* (Sofia: Pechatnitsa khudozhnik, 1933), 43, 48.

132. Ibid., 52–53.

133. Trezvenost (Ruse), April 1922, 4–5.

134. Abadzhiev, *Psikhologiata na nachunaishtia pushach,* 37.

135. Paun Genov, *S Fakela na trezvenostta: Momenti ot borbata protiv pianstvoto i tiutiunopushteneto pres 1300-godishnata istoriia na Bŭlgariia* (Sofiia: Natsionalen komitet za trezvenost, meditsina i fizkultura, 1980), 54. These initiatives were supported by the Bulgarian Communist Party in 1919. Petkov, *Borbata za trezvenost,* 49.

136. Petkov, *Borbata za trezvenost,* 9.

137. Ibid.

138. Ibid., 15–16.

139. Ibid., 272.

140. Kristo Stoianov, *Dvizheniete na trezvenost v Razgradski okrŭg* (Razgrad: Okrŭzhen komitet za trezvenost, 1983), 6–7.

141. *Trezvenost* (Ruse), year 6, 1922, 1.

142. Petkov, *Borbata za trezvenost,* 8. See also *Trezvenost* (Ruse), year 5, book 5, 1922.

143. Authors such as Pencho Slaveikov and Peiu Iavorov were part of this school. Nedialkov, *Bŭlgarski kulturni deitsi,* 39.

144. Genov, *S Fakela na trezvenostta,* 38–39.

145. Brŭzitsov, *Niakoga v Sofiia,* 67.

146. Ibid., 190.

147. Ibid., 190.

148. Nedialkov, *Bŭlgarski kulturni deitsi,* 62–70.

149. Ibid., 52. See also Vaptsarova, *Nikola Vaptsarov,* 42.

150. *Trezvenost* (Sofia), October–November 1921, 13.

151. Titko Chernokolev, "Kharakter i rolia na vŭzdŭrzhatelnoto dvizheniie," in Akhchiiski and Tosheva, *Iubileen nauchen sbornik, 1922–37,* 65.

152. *Trezvenost* (Ruse), book 7–8, April 1922, 7.

153. *Trezvenost* (Sofia), February 1924, 23.

154. *Trezvenost* (Sofia), April 1922, 14–15.

155. See, for example, *Trezvenost* (Sofia), October-November 1921, 8–9.

156. Stoianov, *Dvizheniete na tresvenost,* 31, 43. See also Petkov, *Borbata za trezvenost,* 126.

157. See, for example, their articles in Akhchiiski and Tosheva, *Iubileen nauchen sbornik, 1922–37.*

158. Stoianov, *Dvizheniete na trezvenost,* 13–14, 26, 42–43.

159. *Trezvenost* (Sofia), October–November 1921, 8.

160. *Trezvenost* (Sofia), book 2, 1924, 23.

161. *Trezvenost* (Ruse), book 7–8, 1922, 3.

162. The morality tale of the women who has fallen victim to drink and tobacco was a common trope in the abstinence literature. *Trezvenost* (Sofia), October–November, 1921, 15; TsDA, F-1027k, O-1, E-22, L-9. See also Stoianov, *Dvizheniie za trezvenost,* 26.

163. *Trezvenost* (Ruse), book 8, April 1922, 39.

164. Ianka Tosheva, "Roliata na studentkata v zhivota i v vŭzdŭrzhatelno dvizhenie," in Akhchiiski and Tosheva, *Iubileen nauchen sbornik, 1922–37,* 36.

165. Ibid., 38–40.

166. Ibid., 37.

167. TsDA, F-1027k, O-1, E-46, L-5.

168. Ibid., E-16, L-194.

169. Ibid., E-12, L-16.

170. Ibid., E-16, L-194.

171. Ibid., E-16, L-140.

172. Ibid., E-12, L-5.

173. Petkov, *Borbata za trezvenost,* 16–21.

174. TsDA, F-1027k, O-1, E-46, L-5.

175. Petkov, *Borbata za trezvenost,* 82.

176. Daskalov, *Bŭlgarsko obshtestvo,* 2:500. I have seen no evidence of this, but there are occasional articles in Bulgarian newspapers advocating abstinence from a health point of view. These openly reference the Nazi antismoking movement (more on this in chapter 5), literature, and congresses on the subject. See, for example, *Zdrave i zhivot,* 3 March 1940, 2.

177. See, for example, *Vestnik na zhenata,* 31 July 1927, 1; *Vestnik na zhenata,* 19 January 1938,

178. *Vestnik na zhenata,* 11 June 1927, 1.

179. For quote see story on kafene in *Vestnik na zhenata,*23 April 1927, 5; for a morality tale on a krŭchma see *Vestnik na zhenata,* 11 December 1936, 3.

180. See, for example, *Vestnik na zhenata,* 18 June 1927, 1.

4. The Tobacco Fortress

1. For a detailed description of the event see *Biuletin na kooperativnoto druzhestvo na sdruzhenite tiutiunoproizvoditeli ot grad Stanimaka i okoliiata,* 10 April 1922, 1. See also Angel Krŭstev, *Asenovgrad krepost: Tiutiuneva kooperatsiia Asenovgrad* (Asenovgrad: Izdatelska kŭshta belan, 1994), 51.

2. The figure of one in five men includes the immediately preceding Balkan Wars of 1912–13. See Joseph Rothschild, *East Central Europe between the Two World Wars* (Seattle: University of Washington Press, 1977), 325. See also John Bell, *Peasants in Power: Alexander Stamboliski and the Bulgarian Agrarian National Union, 1899–1923* (Princeton: Princeton University Press, 1977), 122.

3. On women rioting for food in Vienna, for example, see Maureen Healy, *Vienna and The Fall of the Habsburg Empire: Total War and Everyday Life in World War I* (Cambridge: Cambridge University Press, 2008), 32–33.

4. Todor Belchov, "Iz Borbite na tiutiunopabotnitsite v grad Plovdiv (1891–1920g.)," *Godishnik na museite v Plovdivski okrŭg* 2 (1956): 12–37, 34. While Belchov puts the numbers in the hundreds, Vangelov argues for thousands of participants. See Georgi Vangelov, *Tiutiunopabotnitsi: Spomeni iz borbite na tiutiunopabotnitsite* (Sofia: Profizdat, 1955), 99–100.

5. As a result of the incident, bread rations were raised by 125 grams, and though a few women were arrested, they were shortly released in response to sharp objections raised by other women workers. Vangelov, *Tiutiunopabotnitsi,* 100.

6. Ibid., 24.

7. For more on this late-war period see Richard Crampton, *Bulgaria* (Oxford: Oxford University press, 2007), 211–14.

8. Ibid., 215.

9. The rule of Stamboliski is extremely controversial in the historical literature because, while popular among the peasant majority, he ruled as a benevolent dictator over competing (mostly urban) interest groups. For an overview see Bell, *Peasants in Power.* For a recent Bulgarian assessment see Rumen Daskalov, *Bŭlgarsko obshtestvo, 1878–1939,* vol. 1, *Dŭrzhava, poltika, ikonomika* (Sofia: IK Gutenberg, 2005), 195.

10. Agrarian credit cooperatives actually trace back to the rural reforms of the late-Ottoman statesman Midhat Pasha in the Danube region, which were replaced with a number of native credit institutions after 1878 that aimed to secure land, seeds, and other needs for the peasantry. See Bŭlgarska Zemledelska Banka, *The Agricultural Cooperative and the Agricultural Bank of Sofia* (Sofia: National Printing Office, 1924), 4–5.

11. Krŭstev, *Asenovgrad krepost,* 23. For an overview of the historical development of cooperatives in precommunist Bulgaria see Boris Mateev, *Dvizhenieto za kooperativno zemedelie v Bŭlgariia pri usloviiata na kapitalizma* (Sofia: 1967, Izdatelstvo na Bŭlgarskata akademiia na naukite, 1967), 96–97.

12. See Rumen Avramov, *Stopanskiiat XX vek na Bŭlgariia* (Sofia: Tsentŭr za liberalni strategii, 2001), 27–28.

13. For this argument see Rumen Avramov, *Komunalniiat kapitalizŭm: Iz Bŭlgarskoto stopansko minalo, vol. 3* (Sofia: Tsentŭr za liberalni strategii, 2007). While Avramov ultimately has a rather negative view of the substance and consequences of cooperatives for the Bulgarian economy, it is by no means shared by all historians. See for example, Daskalov, *Bŭlgarsko obshtestvo,* 1:30.

14. Krŭstev, *Asenovgrad krepost,* 6.

15. Stanimaka and its surroundings, like neighboring Plovdiv, had been part of autonomous Eastern Rumelia, a province separated from the Ottomans but not given to the Bulgarians after the Russo-Turkish War of 1878. In 1885, however, Eastern Rumelia was unified with Bulgaria, where it remained after independence was declared in 1908.

16. John Lampe, *The Bulgarian Economy in the Twentieth Century* (New York: Palgrave Macmillan, 1986), 61.

17. Ibid.

18. Ibid., 89.

19. Jacques Asseoff, *Tiutiun v Bŭlgarskoto stopanstvo* (Sofia: Kooperativna pechatnitsa "napred," 1933), 202.

20. See Bŭlgarska Zemledelska Banka, *Agricultural Cooperative,* 52. See also Avramov, *Komunalniiat kapitalizŭm,* 3:43–44.

21. *Biuletin na kooperativnoto druzhestvo na sdruzhenite tiutiunoproizvoditeli ot grad Stanimaka i okoliiata,* 6 January 1922, 1.

22. Bŭlgarska Zemledelska Banka, *Agricultural Cooperative,* 53. See also Angel Timov, Georgi Lazarov, and Metodi Veselinov, *Borbi po pŭtia na nasheto tiutiunoproizvodstvo* (Plovdiv: Izdatelstvo "Khristo Danov," 1973), 55.

23. *Asenovgrad krepost,* 4 April 1926, 7.

24. Krŭstev, *Asenovgrad krepost,* 37.

25. In 1923 alone, Asenovgrad Krepost helped build 382 houses and 1,242 tobacco-drying structures, and in 1922 it supplied 5,000 lev for the rebuilding of a Turkish school. Ibid., 64.

26. Ibid., 37–42.

27. *Asenovgrad Krepost,* 24 January 1925, 5–6.

28. See, for example, *Biuletin na kooperativnoto druzhestvo na sdruzhenite tiutiuno-proizvoditeli ot grad Stanimaka i okoliiata,* 28 January 1922, and *Asenovgrad krepost,* 15 February 1926, 5.

29. *Asenovgrad krepost,* 24 January 1925, 8.

30. Here I have in mind the communist and American-funded Protestant absti-nence movements discussed in chapter 3. On Protestant efforts see James F. Clarke, *Temperance Work in Bulgaria: Its Successes* (Samokov, Bulg.: Evangelical School Press, 1909, 3). On communist abstinence movements see Kristo Stoianov, *Dvizheniie za trezvenost v Razgradski okrŭg* (Razgrad: Okrŭzhen komitet za trezvenost, 1983). See also chapter 3.

31. *Asenovgrad krepost,* 13 August 1926, 3.

32. Ibid., 24 January 1925, 8, and 23 July 1925, 8.

33. Ibid., *Asenovgrad krepost* 23 July 1926, 2, and 1 January 1925, 2.

34. Vasil Kutsoglu, a private Bulgarian merchant, was a pioneer in this respect. See a description of this period in his memoirs, Vasil Kutsolgu, *Spomeni i razmisli* (Sofia: Izdatelstvo na otechesveniia front, 1989), 14–18.

35. Krŭstev, *Asenovgrad krepost,* 43–46; see also PODA, F-1648, O-1, E-3, L-22; on trade with India via British merchants see F-96, O-1, E-93, L-23.

36. *Asenovgrad krepost,* 30 September 1926, 4.

37. See, for example, an article in the organ of tobacco merchants and factory owners *Tiutiun,* 1 June 1923, 1.

38. See, for example, *Asenovgrad krepost,* 30 June 1925, 1; 4 July 1925, 1, 8; 31 October 1925, 1, 8; and 5 December 1926.

39. See Krŭstev, *Asenovgrad krepost,* 71–73.

40. Lampe, *Bulgarian Economy,* 63.

41. *Asenovgrad krepost,* 24 January 1925, 3.

42. Ibid., 3 November 1926, 2.

43. PODA, F-85k, O-1, E-64, L-140–4.

44. *Biuletin na kooperativnoto druzhestvo na sdruzhenite tiutiunoproizvoditeli ot grad Stanimaka i okoliiata,* 28 January 1922, 1.

45. Bell, *Peasants in Power,* 235–37.

46. Krŭstev, *Asenovgrad krepost,* 72.

47. Avramov, *Komunalniiat kapitalizŭm,* 3:30.

48. Some sources seem to agree with the official assessments of Asenovgrad Kre-post as plagued by "bad governance." See, for example, ibid., 43–44.

49. See *Asenovgrad krepost,* 15 March 1925, 2.

50. Krŭstev, *Asenovgrad krepost,* 51–53.

51. *Tiutiunopabotnik,* 23 May 1919, 1.

52. See, for example, *Tiutiunopabotnik,* 28 February 1921, 3.

53. See, for example, Daskalov, *Bŭlgarskoto obshtestvo,* 1:195.

54. Boris Mateev, *Dvizhenieto za kooperativno zemedelie v Bŭlgariia pri usloviiata na kapitalisma* (Sofia: Izdatelstvo na Bŭlgarskata akademiia na naukite, 1967).

55. Stefan Abadzhiev, *Spomeni ot izminatiia pŭt* (Sofia: Profizdat, 1982), 170.

56. See, for example, Angel Ivanov, *Kogato govorekha pushkite: Spomeni* (Plovdiv: Izdatelstvo "Khristo Danov," 1984), 6.

57. Abadzhiev, *Spomeni,* 74, 99.

58. *Biuletin na kooperativnoto druzhestvo na sdruzhenite tiutiunoproizvoditeli ot grad Stanimaka i okoliiata,* 22 July 1922, 2–3.

59. See *Asenovgrad krepost,* 25 March 1927, 1, and 4 July 1925, 1.

60. Ibid., 15 May 1925, 5.

61. These numbers include the deaths by communists at the hands of IMRO paramilitaries. Tatiana Kostadinova, *Bulgaria 1879–1946: The Challenge of Choice* (Boulder, CO: East European Monographs and Columbia University Press, 1995), 62, as cited in James Frusetta, "Bulgaria's Macedonia: Nation-Building and State-Building, Centralization and Autonomy in Pirin Macedonia, 1903–1952" (PhD diss., University of Maryland, College Park, 2006), 192.

62. As cited in Abadzhiev, *Spomeni,* 117.

63. Ekaterina Ivanova, *Iz realniia sviat na romana "Tiutiun": Otlomki ot minoloto* (Sofia: Firma pandora-prim, 1994), 110.

64. PODA, F-1648, O-1, E-3, L-1. He also published articles in *Tiutiun,* the organ of tobacco merchants and factory owners. See, for example, his article on the industry in *Tiutiun,* 21 September 1921.

65. For an extensive treatment of these developments see Frusetta, "Bulgaria's Macedonia." For this exact figure see page 167.

66. TsDA, F-396k, O-2, E-17, L-162.

67. Ibid., L-48–50.

68. Ibid., L-256. See also ibid., L-26.

69. Ibid., L-258.

70. Ibid., L-181, 193.

71. Ibid., L-195.

72. Crampton, *Bulgaria,* 238.

73. TSDA, F-396k, O-2, E-39, L-124.

74. See the unpublished memoir of Kosta Kichukov, PODA, F-1943, O-2, E-1, L-19, 47; and the memoir of Ivanov, *Kogato govorekha pushkite.*

75. Ivanov, *Kogato govorekha pushkite,* 52.

76. Ibid., 36.

77. For a detailed description of these intrigues from the point of view of the Macedonian communist base in Stanimaka and Plovdiv see Kichukov, PODA, F-1943, O-2, E-1, L-31–34, 47.

78. See, for example, the unpublished memoir of Angel Dinev, TsDA, BKP-Cp-576.

79. PODA, F-1943, O-2, E-1, L-17.

80. See, for example, Ivanov, *Kogato govorekha pushkite,* 19.

81. PODA, F-1943, O-2, E-1, L-17–18.

82. Ibid., L-18–19.

83. Ibid., L- 57.

84. Ibid.

85. *Asenovgrad krepost,* 15 March 1925, 2.

86. See Avramov, *Komunalniiat kapitalizŭm,* 3:44–47.

87. Krŭstev, *Asenovgrad krepost,* 102.

88. *Asenovgrad krepost,* 22 November 1926, 4.

89. *Asenovgrad krepost,* 3 November 1926, 4.

90. While admitting some "mistakes," the AK leadership was exceedingly transparent when it came to finances, and the costs and income of the cooperative were regularly printed in the cooperative newspaper. See, for example, *Asenovgrad krepost,* 5 December 1926, 3.

91. Ibid., 1.

92. Ibid., 28 December 1926, 2.

93. Krŭstev, *Asenovgrad krepost,* 106.

94. See more on this in chapter 5.

95. Avramov, *Komunalniiat kapitalizŭm,* 3:18, 17.

96. Liapchev had initiated the creation of the Bulgarian Central Cooperative Bank, an institution for government finance and regulation of cooperatives, in 1910. Daskalov, *Bŭlgarsko obshtestvo, 1878–1939,* 1:298.

97. See, for example, Lampe, *Bulgarian Economy,* 59.

98. See Timov, Lazarov, and Veselinov, *Borbi po pŭtia,* 50–51.

99. Ibid., 54.

100. On calls for monopoly see for example the growers' newspaper, *Bŭlgarski tiutiun,* 1 May 1937, 3. See also TsDA, F-273k, O-1, E-28, L-122.

101. See Timov, Lazarov, and Veselinov, *Borbi po pŭtia,* 18.

102. Although the Library of Congress transliteration for his name would be Zhak Aseov, I use Jacques Asseoff, as that was his chosen transliteration after he emigrated to the United States in 1941.

103. For a more detailed discussion of Asseoff see chapter 5.

104. Asseoff, *Tiutiun v Bŭlgarskoto stopanstvo,* 195–96.

105. Ibid., 199.

106. Ibid., 201.

107. Ibid., 281.

108. Ibid., 163.

109. Ibid., 204.

110. Avramov, *Komunalniiat kapitalizŭm,* 3:26, 101–2.

111. On the imbedded nature of collectivism in Bulgaria see Avramov, *Stopanskiiat XX vek,* 23–27. See also all of volume 3 in Avramov, *Komunalniiat kapitalizŭm.*

112. Avramov, *Stopanskiiat XX vek,* 28.

113. Avramov, *Komunalniiat kapitalizŭm,* 3:27.

114. Vasil Kolarov, *How the Fascists "Buried" the Class Struggle* (London: Communist Party of Great Britain, 1936), 996–97.

115. Ivanov, *Kogato govorekha pushkite* 36.

116. Ibid., 996–97.

117. See, for example, Vŭlcho Bonev, *Dŭrzhavnata namesa v tiutiunevoto proizvodstvo* (Sofia: Rech iz narodo sŭbranie, 1939). See also TsDA, F-273k, O-1, E-35, L-125.

118. See Timov, Lazarov, and Veselinov, *Borbi po pŭtia,* 54.

119. See chapter 5 for more on Bulgarian-German trade relationships before and during the war.

5. From Leaf to Ash

1. Mogens Pelt, *Tobacco, Arms and Politics: Greece and Germany from World Crisis to World War 1929–41* (Copenhagen: Museum Tusculanum Press, 1998), 36.

2. Hans-Joachim Braun, *The German Economy in the Twentieth Century* (London: Taylor & Francis, 2007), 101.

3. Georgi Markov, *Bŭlgaro- Germanskite otnosheniia, 1931–39* (Sofia: Izdatelstvo nauka i izkustvo, 1984), 8.

4. Frederick B. Chary, *The Bulgarian Jews and the Final Solution, 1940–1944* (Pittsburgh: University of Pittsburgh Press, 1972), 32. See also Marshall Lee Miller, *Bulgaria during the Second World War* (Palo Alto, CA: Stanford University Press, 1975), 7.

5. See Christopher Browning, *Ordinary Men: Reserve Police Battalion 101 and the Final Solution in Poland* (New York: Harper Perennial, 1993), 65.

6. This relationship required constant and sometimes tense negotiations. According to the memoirs of the German consul, Adolph Bekerle (since July 1941), Bulgarians were often reluctant to cut German merchants in on profits on local deals but still wanted their markets and price guarantees. See Vitka Toshkova and Adolf-Heinz Bekerle, *Iz dnevnika na Bekerle: Pŭlnomoshten ministŭr na tretiia raikh v Bŭlgariia* (Sofia: Khristo Botev, 1992), 79, 85.

7. Jacques Asseoff was reported to have told Dimov's wife's friend, whom he later met in Paris, that "he was proud to have been depicted by Dimov." Neli Dospevska, *Poznat i nepoznat Dimitŭr Dimov* (Sofia, Profizdat, 1985), 196.

8. Koen is a recognizably Ashkenazic Jewish surname, though Asseoff was Sephardic, like most of his Bulgarian-Jewish compatriots.

9. On the culture of naming in Bulgaria see Mary Neuburger, *The Orient Within: Muslim Minorities and the Negotiation of Nationhood in Modern Bulgaria* (Ithaca: Cornell University Press, 2004), 142–68.

10. Beniamin Arditi, *Vidni Evrei v Bŭlgariia: Galeriia na zabravenite,* vol. 2 (Tel Aviv: 1970), 46. See also Commissariat for Jewish Affairs, Bulgaria, fond 190, file 1, p. 170, United States Holocaust Memorial Museum, Acc. 1997, A.0333.

11. Ivan Stoilov Khadzhiiski, *Sŭdbata na Evreite ot iugozapadna Bŭlgariia prez 1940–44 godina* (Sofia: Nauchna Studiia, 1998), 6.

12. Dospevska, *Poznat i nepoznat Dimitŭr Dimov,* 15.

13. See chapter 4 for more details on this period.

14. Robert Proctor, *The Nazi War on Cancer* (Princeton, NJ: Princeton University Press, 1999), 234.

15. Ekaterina Ivanova, *Iz realniia sviat na romana "Tiutiun":Otlomki ot minoloto* (Sofia: Firma pandora-prim, 1994), 124.

16. Ibid., 139.

17. Ibid., 65.

18. Ibid., 39.

19. See Nediu Nedev, *Bŭlgarskoto masonstvo (1807–2007)* (Sofia: Izdatelska Kŭshta khermes, 2009), 472–73.

20. Jacques Asseoff, *Tiutiun v Bŭlgarskoto stopanstvo* (Sofia: Kooperativna pechatnitsa napred, 1933), 195–96.

21. Ibid. 281.

22. Ibid., 163. For more details on this see chapter 4.

23. Proctor, *Nazi War on Cancer,* 234–35. See also Tino Jacobs, *Rauch und macht: Das unternehmen Reemstma 1920 bis 1961* (Göttingen: Wallstein Verlag, 2008), 133.

24. This was according to Germany's first Gestapo chief, Rudolph Diels, as cited in ibid., 235.

25. Ivanova, *Iz realniia sviat,* 56.

26. These documents are published in their entirety in Georgi Markov and Vitka Toskova, eds., *Obrecheni i spaseni: Bŭlgariia v antisemitskata programa na tretiia raikh* (Sofia: Sineva, 2007), 182–84.

27. Ibid., 184.

28. On Nazi improvisations when it came to policies in relation to Slavs, see John Connelly, "Nazis and Slavs: From Racial Theory to Racist Practice," *Central European History* 32, no. 1 (1999): 1–33.

29. Jacques Asseoff, "Za nashiiat turgovets," *Bŭlgarski tiutiun,* December 1936, 3.

30. Markov and Toskova, *Obrecheni i spaseni,* 185.

31. Ibid., 190.

32. Lampe, *Bulgarian Economy,* 88.

33. See for example *Chronica Nicotina* 4 (1940): 5–7.

34. Ivanova, *Iz realniia sviat,* 156; Dimitŭr Dimov, *Tiutiun* (Sofia: Izdatelstvo Zakharii Stoianov, 2004), 163.

35. Ivanova, *Iz realniia sviat,* 159.

36. Proctor, *Nazi War on Cancer, 201.*

37. Dimov's portrayal of Kurt Wenkel was far from flattering. Still, when he met Dimov many years later in the Russian Club in Sofia (when he resided in the city as ambassador to Bulgaria), Wenkel reportedly approached him and said, "I am your 'Von Gauer.'" Dospevska, *Poznat i nepoznat Dimitŭr Dimov,* 196.

38. Prime Minister Bogdan Filov, for example, in his diary of these years, recounts having taken a German official to a cabaret. Ilcho Dimitrov and Bogdan Filov, *Dnevik* (Sofia: Izdatelstvo na otechestveniia front, 1990), 221.

39. Ibid., 176.

40. Ibid., 11.

41. Ibid., 178. See also Sander Gilman, "Jews and Smoking," in *Smoke: A Global History of Smoking,* ed. Sander Gilman and Xhou Zun (London: Reaktion Books, 2004), 279–82.

42. Dimitrov and Filov, *Dnevik,* 231.

43. Proctor, *Nazi War on Cancer,* 207.

44. Ibid., 233.

45. See Browning, *Ordinary Men: Reserve Police Battalion 101 and the Final Solution in Poland* (New York: Harper Perennial, 1993), 65–68.

46. TsDA, F-316k, O-1, E-119, L-56.

47. See, for example, *Zdrave i zhivot,* 3 March 1940, 2.

48. See Mari Firkatian, *Diplomats and Dreamers: The Stancioff Family in Bulgarian History* (Landam, MD: University Press of America, 2008).

49. Richard Crampton, *Bulgaria* (New York: Oxford University Press, 2009), 253.

50. According to Khaim Oliver, Ratnik was purportedly funded by Bulgarian tobacco manufacturers and exporters. See Khaim Oliver, *We Were Saved: How the Jews in Bulgaria Were Kept from the Death Camps* (Sofia: Sofia Press, 1978), 28.

51. Michael Bar-Zohar, *Beyond Hitler's Grasp: The Heroic Rescue of Bulgaria's Jews* (Holbrook, NJ: Adams Media Corp., 1998), 27.

52. Miller, *Bulgaria during the Second World War,* 95.

53. See, for example, Markov and Toskova, *Obrecheni i spaseni*; David Koen, ed. *Otseliavaneto 1940–44: Sbornik ot dokumenti* (Sofia: Izdatelski tsentŭr shalom, 1995);

and Natan Grinberg, *Dokumenti* (Sofia: Izdavane na tsentŭr na tsentralnata konsistoria na Evreite v Bŭlgariia, 1945).

54. Voin Bozhinov, ed. *Borbata na Bŭlgarskata narod za zashtita i spasiavane na Evreite v Bŭlgariia prez vtorata svetovna voina* (Sofia: Izdatelstvo na Bŭlgarskata akademiia na naukite, 1978), 57.

55. Ibid., 20.

56. Koen, *Otseliavaneto,* 18.

57. Ibid., 63.

58. Alexander Matkovski, *A History of Jews in Macedonia* (Skopje: Macedonian Review Editions, 1982), 119.

59. Vicki Tamir, *Bulgaria and Her Jews: The History of a Dubious Symbiosis* (New York: Yeshiva University Press, 1979). 167.

60. There is at least a partial consensus among historians—Bulgarian, Jewish, and Western—about the relative lack of popular anti-Semitism in Bulgaria in this period as previously. See Chary, *Bulgarian Jews,* 36.

61. See the transcripts of parliamentary debates in *Stenografski dnevnitsi na XXV-to obiknoveno narodno sŭbranie: Vtora redovna sesiia,* vol. 1 (Sofia: Narodno sŭbranie, 1940), 694.

62. Chary, *Bulgarian Jews,* 82.

63. *Stenografski dnevnitsi,* 1:218.

64. Miller, *Bulgaria during the Second World War,* 94.

65. Trial of Dimo Kazasov, reel 1, tom 3, p. 183, Archives of the Ministry of the Interior, 1938–48, Bulgaria, fond 190, file 1, p. 170, United States Holocaust Memorial Museum, Acc. 1997, A.0333.

66. Ibid., pp. 187–89.

67. *Stenografski dnevnitsi,* 1:698.

68. Chary, *Bulgarian Jews,* 57.

69. Ibid., 42.

70. Khadzhiicki, *Sŭdbata na Evreite.* 9.

71. For estimated figures on confiscations see Chary, *Bulgarian Jews,* 58.

72. Deposition of Isak Frantsez, reel 1, tom 3, p. 38, Archives of the Ministry of the Interior, 1938–48, Bulgaria, fond 190, file 1, p. 170, United States Holocaust Memorial Museum, Acc. 1997, A.0333.

73. Commissariat for Jewish Affairs, Bulgaria, fond 190, file 1, pp. 10–14, United States Holocaust Memorial Museum, Acc. 1997, A.0333.

74. Ibid., pp. 13, 60.

75. Matkovski, *A History of Jews,* 103.

76. On the German occupation of Salonika see Mark Mazower, *Inside Hitler's Greece: The Experience of Occupation, 1941–44* (New Haven, CT: Yale University Press, 1995).

77. TsDA, F-264k, O-1, E-176, L-1.

78. Ibid., E-143, L-124.

79. Turkey still had tobacco-growing regions on the Black Sea coast, but it had lost the best ones, Thrace and Macedonia, in the 1912–13 Balkan Wars. Al. Krekmanov, *Zlatoto na Bŭlgariia: Tiutiunoproizvodstvo v raiona na kamarata* (Sofia: Sofiiska zemedelska Kamara, 1942), 35.

80. Krekmanov, *Zlatoto,* 55.

81. Koitcho Belchev, *Tobacco in Bulgaria* (Durham, NC: Duke University Press, 1950), 70.

82. The Germans did raise prices paid to growers—by 60 percent in 1943, for example—out of fear that peasants would stop cultivating tobacco and switch to potatoes or some other subsistence crop. This, however, was not enough to keep up with the steep inflation in Bulgaria during the war. Ivanova, *Iz realniia sviat,* 59.

83. Ivanova, *Iz realniia sviat,* 53.

84. Joshua Eli Plaut, *Greek Jewry in the Twentieth Century 1918–1983: Patterns of Survival in the Greek Provinces before and after the Holocaust* (Madison, NJ: Fairleigh Dickinson University Press, 2000), 43.

85. *Tiutiunoproizvoditel,* 25 November 25 1941, 1.

86. *Tiutiunev pregled,* 12 January 1942, 23.

87. Ibid., 30.

88. For details on supplying German troops see TsDA, F-1471k, O-1, E-333, L-4–5.

89. TsDA, F-1341k, O-1, E-95, L-59; F-1341k, O-1, E-93, L-233.

90. Belchev, *Tobacco in Bulgaria,* 70.

91. See also chapter 4.

92. On the effect of this on growers' associations see Georgi Lazarov, *Borbite na tiutiunoproizvoditelite* (Sofia: Zemizdat, 1967), 65-8.

93. Angel Ivanov, *Kogato govorekha pushkite: Spomeni* (Plovdiv: Izdatelstvo Khristo G. Danov, 1984), 145.

94. Ibid., 48.

95. Chary, *Bulgarian Jews,* 139.

96. Gila Hadar, "Jewish Tobacco Workers in Salonika: Gender and Family in the Context of Social and Ethnic Strife," in *Women in the Ottoman Balkans,* ed. Amila Buturovic and Irvin Cemil Schick (London: I.B. Tauris, 2007), 128.

97. Chary, *Bulgarian Jews,* 48. On Jews in the Macedonian resistance, see also Matkovski, *History of Jews,* 103.

98. Bar-Zohar, *Beyond Hitler's Grasp,* 66.

99. TsDA, F-656k, O-1, E-1, L-6–8.

100. Ibid., E-4, L-1–3, 8–9.

101. Bar-Zohar, *Beyond Hitler's Grasp,* 89.

102. Khadzhiicki, *Sŭdbata na Evreite,* 10–11.

103. Bar-Zohar, *Beyond Hitler's Grasp,* 89.

104. Trial of Ivan Popov, reel 1, tom 2, pp. 82–84, Archives of the Ministry of the Interior, 1938–48, Bulgaria, fond 190, file 1, United States Holocaust Memorial Museum, Acc. 1997, A.0333.

105. Khadzhiicki, *Sŭdbata na Evreite,* 11.

106. Chary, *The Bulgarian Jews,* 149.

107. Khristo Boiadzhiev, *Saving the Bulgarian Jews in World War II* (Ottawa: Free Bulgaria Center, 1989), 61.

108. For a detailed account of Asseoff's activities see Buko Piti, *Te, spasiteli* (Tel Aviv, 1969), 81–84.

109. Ibid., 82–83.

110. On the experience of Jews in the tobacco warehouses, see also Matkovski, *History of Jews,* 139–40.

111. Bar-Zohar, *Beyond Hitler's Grasp,* 135.

112. Tamir, *Bulgaria and Her Jews,* 195.

113. Deposition of Avram Tadzher, reel 1, tom 3, p. 46, Archives of the Ministry of the Interior, 1938–48, Bulgaria, fond 190, file 1, United States Holocaust Memorial Museum, Acc. 1997, A.0333.

114. Tamir, *Bulgaria and Her Jews,* 195.

115. Bar-Zohar, *Beyond Hitler's Grasp,* 202.

116. Nir Baruch, *Otkupŭt: Tsar Boris i sŭdbata na Bŭlgarskite Evrei* (Sofia: Universitetsko izdatelstvo "Sv. Kliment Okhridski," 1991), 60.

117. Miller, *Bulgaria during the Second World War,* 63.

118. TsDA, F-656k, O-1, E-2, L-8–9. See also Chary, *Bulgarian Jews,* 85. See also Matkovski, *History of Jews,* 137.

119. Tadzher deposition, 27, 33–35.

120. Trial of Peiu Peev, reel 1, tom 2, 31, Archives of the Ministry of the Interior, 1938–48, Bulgaria, fond 190, file 1, United States Holocaust Memorial Museum, Acc. 1997, A.0333.

121. Iain Gately, *Tobacco: A Cultural History of How an Exotic Plant Seduced Civilization* (New York: Grove Press, 2003), 262. See also, Mazower, *Hitler's Greece,* 65.

122. Rumen Avramov also discusses the LDN and wartime measures in terms of Bulgarianization of the economy and cites the Asseoff case as a prime example. See Rumen Avramov, *Komunalniiat kapitalizŭm: Iz Bŭlgarskoto stopansko minalo* (Sofia: Tsentŭr za liberalni strategii, 2007), volume 3, 267.

123. Miller, *Bulgaria during the Second World War,* 125.

124. Ibid., 198.

125. Lazarov, *Borbite na tiutiunoproizvoditeli,* 9.

126. Ibid., 10.

127. Dospevska, *Poznat i nepoznat Dimitŭr Dimov,* 205.

128. Miller, *Bulgaria during the Second World War,* 217. The Bulgarian government recorded almost twelve thousand trials, but unofficial estimates are as high as thirty to a hundred thousand. Crampton, *Bulgaria,* 149. See also Tamir, *Bulgaria and Her Jews,* 223.

129. Ivanova, *Iz realniia sviat,* 100. See also Petŭr Semerdzhiev, *Narodniiat sŭd v Bŭlgariia, 1944–45: Komu i zasto e bil neobkhodimo* (Sofia: Makedoniia Press, 1997), 362.

130. Stefane Groueff, *My Odyssey* (Bloomington, IN: I Universe, 2003) 142–43.

131. Tamir, *Bulgaria and Her Jews,* 222.

132. See Jan Gross, *Fear: Anti-Semitism in Poland after Auschwitz* (New York: Random House, 2006).

133. See, for example, Donald Bloxham, *Genocide on Trial: War Crimes Tribunals and the Formation of Holocaust History* (Oxford: Oxford University Press, 2003), 99–101.

134. On Poland, see Jan Gross, *Neighbors* (New York: Penguin, 2002). On the Soviet Union see Lucjan Dobroszycki, *The Holocaust in the Soviet Union: Studies and Sources on the Destruction of the Jews in the Nazi-Occupied Territories of the USSR, 1941–1945* (New York: M.E. Sharpe, 1993), 149.

135. Archives of the Ministry of the Interior, 1938–48, Bulgaria, fond 190, file 1, United States Holocaust Memorial Museum, Acc. 1997, A.0333.

136. While most were under the assumption that Belev was trying to get papers to prove he was Aryan, most also rightly assumed that such papers would never actu-

ally materialize. See, for example, the trial of Khristo Stomaniakov, reel 1, tom 1, p. 175, ibid. See also the trial of Liliana Panitsa, reel 1, tom 2, p. 128, ibid.

137. See for example, the Panitsa trial, 115; trial of Maria Pavlova, reel 1, tom 2, p. 118, Archives of the Ministry of the Interior, 1938–48, Bulgaria, fond 190, file 1, United States Holocaust Memorial Museum, Acc. 1997, A..033; Frantsez deposition, 38.

138. See trial of Nikolai Rashkov, reel 1, tom 2, p. 33, Archives of the Ministry of the Interior, 1938–48, Bulgaria, fond 190, file 1, United States Holocaust Memorial Museum, Acc. 1997, A.0333.

139. See the trial of Aleksandŭr Pudrev, reel 1, tom 2, p. 31, ibid.

140. For example, at his trial Iordan Iontsev agreed that he had always assumed that the social question in Bulgaria was not going to be solved by the elimination of Jews. The trial of Iordan Iontsev, reel 1, tom 1, p. 199, ibid.

141. The trial of Asen Paitashev, reel 1, tom 1, pp. 218–19, ibid.

142. See, for example, the trial of Ivan Mitsev, reel 1, tom 1, 183, ibid. For other examples in which offers of cigarettes to Jews were brought up in a trial, see trial of Todor Kolibarov, reel 1, tom 2, 182; and the trial of Aleksi Shonkin, reel 1, tom 2, 35, both in ibid.

143. See, for example, the trial of Iaroslav Kalitsin, reel 1, tom 1, 313, ibid. See also rial of Iliev Dobrevski, reel 1, tom 2, 51, ibid.

144. See, for example, Kalitsin trial, 313.

145. See, for example, ibid., 315.

146. Semerdzhiev, *Narodniiat sŭd v Bŭlgariia,* 296. On Belev see Bar-Zohar, *Beyond Hitler's Grasp,* 250.

147. Bar-Zohar, *Beyond Hitler's Grasp,* 53.

148. Khadzhiicki, *Sŭdbata na Evreite,* 28.

149. Ibid., 38.

150. Tamir, *Bulgaria and Her Jews,* 224. He was later given a pension by the Israeli government and was recognized as a "righteous gentile" by Vad Yashem.

151. Esther Benbassa and Aron Rodrigue, *Sephardi Jewry: A History of the Judeo-Spanish Community, 14–20th Centuries* (Berkeley: University of California Press, 2000), 190.

6. Smoke-Filled Rooms

1. *Turist,* August 1969, 16–17.

2. The term "Red Riviera" can be found in Western sources from the 1930s in reference to Yalta and the Soviet Black Sea coast. By the 1960s it was also applied to the Bulgarian Black Sea coast. See, for example, Edouard Calic, *Life in Bulgaria as Seen by Edouard Calic* (Sofia: Foreign Languages Press, 1964), 160. It was also used as the title of a more recent and insightful study. See Kristen Ghodsee, *The Red Riviera: Gender, Tourism, and Postsocialism on the Black Sea* (Durham: Duke University Press, 2005).

3. The study of leisure and consumption during the period of the "thaw" is still in its infancy. For some beginnings in this direction see David Crowley and Susan Reid, eds., *Style and Socialism: Modernity and Material Culture in Post-War Eastern Europe* (Oxford: Berg, 2000), and David Crew, ed., *Consuming Germany in the Cold War* (Oxford, Berg, 2003). On tourism see Anne E. Gorsuch and Diane Koenker, eds., *Turizm: The Russian and East European Tourist under Capitalism and Socialism* (Ithaca: Cornell University Press, 2006).

4. Though it was conceived in an entirely different context, I am referring here to Foucault's influential notion of how the masses, or the "crowd," become entwined in state power structures through "self-regulation," a powerful tool for the exercise of social control. See Michel Foucault, *Discipline and Punish: The Birth of the Prison* (London: Penguin, 1977), 63.

5. Anne White argues that in the post-Stalinist era the state relinquished much of its control over leisure, at least in the Soviet, Polish, and Hungarian cases. She also seems to present evidence for increased surveillance and attempts to direct leisure pursuits after Stalin. White, *Destalinization and the House of Culture* (London: Routledge, 1990), 21, 38.

6. Atanas Liutov, Boris Atanasov, Violeta Samardzhieva, and Katia Stoianova, *Upravlenie na narodnoto potreblenie* (Sofia: Izdatelstvo na Bŭlgarskata akademiia na naukite—ikonomicheski institut, 1984), 86. See also Veselina Vlakhova-Nikolova, *Problemi na tiutiunopusheneto i alkokholnata upotreba sred mladezhta* (Plovdiv: Nauchnoizsledovatelska laboratoriia za mladezhdta, 1983), 154.

7. As Susan Reid has noted, women and children in the Soviet context were most likely to be targeted as "irrational consumers." Reid, "Cold War in the Kitchen: Gender and the De-Stalinization of Consumer Taste in the Soviet Union under Khrushchev," *Slavic Review* 61 (2008): 219.

8. On alcohol and temperance in the Soviet Union, see Laura Phillips, *Bolsheviks and the Bottle: Drink and Worker Culture in St. Petersburg, 1900–1929* (DeKalb: Northern Illinois University Press, 2000); see also Kate Transchel, *Under the Influence: Working-Class Drinking, Temperance, and Cultural Revolution in Russia, 1895–1932* (Pittsburgh: University of Pittsburgh Press, 2006).

9. For more on the party and abstinence in the interwar period see chapter 3.

10. Pavel Petkov, *Borbata za trezvenost vŭv Vrachanski okrŭg, 1920–1980* (Sofia: Izdatelstvo na otechestveniia front, 1982), 134.

11. This is how Khristo Stoianov, a participant in early organizational efforts, refers to the 1944–48 period. Stoianov, *Dvizheniie za trezvenost v Razgradski okrŭg* (Razgrad: Okrŭzhen komitet za trezvenost, 1983), 56.

12. Petkov, *Borbata za trezvenost,* 128.

13. On the krŭchmars see Ivailo Znepolski, *Bŭlgarskiiat komunizŭm: Sotsiokulturni cherti i vlastova traektoriia* (Sofia: Ciela Press, 2008), 121.

14. In the interwar abstinence journal *Trezvenost,* January–February 1922, 6–7, one article estimated that there was one krŭchma for every 245 Bulgarians. To achieve this number, however, they had taken out women, children, and Turks, who they assumed did not go to krŭchmas.

15. Petkov gives examples of towns such as Kozlodui and Plachene where all taverns were closed. See *Borbata za trezvenost,* 140.

16. Stoianov, *Dvizheniie za trezvenost,* 56.

17. Lora Shumkova, "Mechtaniia za kafene Sredets," in *Kafeneto kato diskurs,* ed. Georg Kraev (Sofia: Nov Bŭlgarski Universitet, 2005), 71.

18. See, for example, Irina Gigova, "The Feminisation of Bulgarian Literature and the Club of Bulgarian Women Writers," *Aspasia* 2 (2008): 105.

19. Paun Genov, *S fakela na trezvenostta: Momenti ot borbata protiv pianstvoto i tiutiunopusheneto pres 1300-godishnata istoriia na Bŭlgariia* (Sofia: Meditsina i fizkultura, 1980), 43.

20. Nauchnoizsledovatelska laboratoriia za mladezhdta kŭm HIIM pri TsK na DKMS, *Problemi na tiutiunopusheneto i alkokholnata upotreba sred mladezhta* (Plovdiv: Izdatesltvo na Bŭlgarskata akademiia na naukite, 1983), 8.

21. On the Bulgarian thaw see Richard Crampton, *Bulgaria* (Oxford: Oxford University Press, 2008), 347–49. The eruption of mass discontent in the midst of this de-Stalinization—namely, East Germany and Poland in 1953 (and on a smaller scale Bulgaria and Romania) and Hungary in 1956—is often cited as a major factor in the decision by socialist regimes to stabilize their regimes through expanded offerings in consumer goods. See, for example, David Crowley and Susan Reid, eds., *Pleasures in Socialism: Leisure and Luxury in the Bloc* (Evanston, IL: Northwestern University Press, 2010), 8. See also Ferenc Fehér, Ágnes Heller, and György Márkus, *Dictatorship over Needs* (New York: St. Martin's, 1983), 98.

22. Crowley and Reid, *Style and Socialism,* 10–12.

23. See, for example, ibid., 14–15; Crowley and Reid, *Pleasures in Socialism;* and Karin Taylor, *Let's Twist Again: Youth and Leisure in Socialist Bulgaria* (Berlin: Lit Verlag, 2008).

24. Genov, *S fakela na trezvenostta,* 14.

25. See Georgi Bokov, *Modern Bulgaria: History, Policy, Economy, Culture* (Sofia: Sofia Press, 1981), 119. See White, *Destalinization,* 14. See also Paul Byton, *Time, Work, and Organization* (New York: Routledge, 2001), 111. On East Germany's reducing the workweek to forty-five hours see Sheldon Anderson, *A Cold War in the Eastern Bloc: Polish-East German Relations, 1945–62* (Boulder, CO: Westview, 1989), 161.

26. There is a disagreement on this point in the literature between Fitzpatrick, who argues that the Soviet state responded to consumer needs, and Gronow and Verdery, who argue that the state "dictated" such needs. Sheila Fitzpatrick, *Everyday Stalinism: Ordinary Life in Extraordinary Times, Soviet Russia in the 1930's* (New York: Oxford University Press, 1999), 91; Jukka Gronow, *Caviar with Champagne: Common Luxury and the Ideals of the Good Life in Stalin's Russia* (Oxford: Berg, 2003), 8; and Katherine Verdery, *What Was Socialism and What Comes Next* (Princeton: Princeton University Press, 1996), 28. In the Bulgarian case, certain state agencies were definitely responding to needs, although others were trying to direct them, so I see neither argument as mutually exclusive.

27. See Petko Takov, *Nov etap v razvitieto na turizma v NRP* (Sofia: Meditsina i fizkultura, 1976), 5–7.

28. Ghodsee, *Red Riviera,* 82–83.

29. Ibid., 20.

30. *Turist,* June 1964, 29.

31. See, for example, Ivan Vazov, *Pŭtepisi* (Sofia: Bŭlgarski pisatel, 1974); Ivan Vazov, *Velika Rilska Gora* (Sofia: Dimitŭr Blagoev, 1954).

32. See chapter 7 for details on tobacco production in this period.

33. Todor Iordanov, *Materialnoto-tekhnicheska basa na razvitoto sotsialistichesko obshtestvo* (Sofia: Partizdat, 1973), 7.

34. *Bŭlgarski tiutiun,* no. 1 (1961): 26; and ibid., no. 9 (1962): 32.

35. Ibid., no. 26 (1961): 26.

36. Ibid., 57.

37. TsDA, F-347, O-18, E-147, L-1.

38. The advertisements noted here were from the back pages of *Bŭlgarski tiutiun,* particularly throughout the 1970s.

39. See, for example, Tsentralno statistichesko upravlenie pri ministerskiia sŭvet, *Mezhdunaroden i vŭtreshen turizŭm, 1960–1967* (Sofia: Tsentralno statistichesko upravlenie, 1968), 70, 141.

40. Takov, *Nov etap,* 27–28.

41. *Plovdivski panair,* September 1956, 32.

42. Emil Giatzidis, *An Introduction to Post-Communist Bulgaria: Political Economic and Social Transformation* (Manchester, UK: Manchester University Press, 2002), 27.

43. Vicho Sŭbev, *90 godini organizirano turistichesko dvizheniie v Bŭlgariia* (Sofia: Meditsina i fizkultura, 1986), 11.

44. David Turncock, *East European Economy in Context: Communism and Transition* (Routledge: New York, 1997), 45.

45. For this figure on Bulgaria see Derek Hall, Melanie Smith, and Barabara Marcisewska, eds. *Tourism in the New Europe: The Challenges and Opportunities of EU Enlargement* (Oxfordshire, UK: Cabi Publishing, 2006), 251.

46. For Soviet travelers to Bulgaria and elsewhere in Eastern Europe as "demi-other" see Anne Gorsuch, "Time Travelers: Soviet Tourists to Eastern Europe," in Gorsuch and Koenker, *Turizm,* 205–26.

47. Edouard Calic, *Life in Bulgaria,* 173.

48. On the Soviet example see Shawn Salmon, "Marketing Socialism: Inturist in the Late 1950s and Early 1960s," in Gorsuch and Koenker, *Turizm,* 186–204.

49. Calic, *Life in Bulgaria,* 160.

50. *Plovdivski Panair,* September 1960, 3; PODA, F-1812k, O-1, E-70, L-1.

51. Calic, *Life in Bulgaria,* 161.

52. For images of this see Strashimir Rashev and Boyan Bolgar, *Bulgarian Black Sea Coast* (Sofia: Sofia Press, 1968), 41, 65.

53. See, for example, Arthur Eperson, "Tourism Opens Frontiers in Bulgaria," *New York Times,* 2 March 1969; Eperson, "Following a New Road," *New York Times,* 26 February 1967, and "The Lure of Inland Bulgaria" *New York Times,* 25 February 1968.

54. Denise Kalette, "After Sofia, The Sophisticated Seaside," *New York Times,* 8 March 1970.

55. See Paul Hoffman, "Bulgarians Relish Yogurt, Wink at Nudism," *New York Times,* 28 February 1970, and ibid., C. L. Sulzberger, "Foreign Affairs: The Coexistence Bazaar," 17 October 1965.

56. Leslie Gardiner, *Curtain Calls: Travels in Albania, Romania and Bulgaria* (London: Duckworth Press, 1976), 163.

57. For some discussion of this phenomenon see Ghodsee, *Red Riviera,* 92–95.

58. Calic, *Life in Bulgaria,* 157.

59. Ibid.

60. Ibid., 156.

61. On the role of tourism in Cold War rivalry see Anne Gorsuch and Diane Koenker, introduction to Gorsuch and Koenker, *Turizm,* 11–12.

62. Stoianov, *Dvizheniie za trezvenost,* 67–68.

63. Vlakhova–Nikolova, *Problemi na tiutiunopusheneto,* 9.

64. Vasil Tsonchev, ed., *Tiutiunopushene i zdrave: Sbornik tezisi za lektsii* (Sofia: Ministerstvo na narodnoto zdrave, 1979), 44.

65. Ministerstvo na Zdravookhraneniia—NR Bŭlgariia, *Shestoi simposium institutov sanitarnovo prosveshteniia sotsialisticheskikh stran* (Sofia: Institut Sanitarnovo Prosveshteniia, 1982), 89.

66. Liutov et al., *Upravlenie,* 90.

67. On how the industry was brought to its knees by lawsuits in the United States see Allan Brandt, *The Cigarette Century: The Rise, Fall and Deadly Persistence of the Product That Defined America* (New York: Basic Books, 2007), 319–448.

68. For more on the use of higher nicotine blends in this period see chapter 7.

69. Tsonchev, *Tiutuinopushene i zdrave,* 47.

70. Atanas Liutov, Boris Atanasov, and Kapka Stoianova, *Razvitie na narodnoto potreblenie* (Sofia: Izdatelstvo na Bŭlgarskata akademiia na naukite, 1982), 110.

71. Bulgaria signed licensing and trade agreements with both R.J. Reynolds and Philip Morris in 1975, which allowed it to locally produce, package, and sell Winston (R.J. Reynolds) and Marlboro (Philip Morris) cigarettes. The timing of such agreements coincided with the United States' granting Bulgaria most-favored-nation status in 1975. *Tobacco Reporter,* January 1976, 47. For more on this see chapter 7.

72. *Tobacco Reporter,* April 1976, 80.

73. See, for example, *Bŭlgarski tiutiun,* no. 3 (1965), 3–4.

74. Natsionalen Komitet za Trezvenost, *Besedi za vredata ot tiuntiunopusheneto* (Sofia: Institut za Zdravna Prosveta, 1976), 13.

75. Liutov, Atanasov, and Stoianova, *Razvitie na narodnoto potreblenie,* 116.

76. See, for example, Zakhari Staikov, *Biudzhet na vremeto na trudeshtite se v NRB* (Sofia: Dŭrzhavno izdatelstvo nauka i izkustvo, 1964), 55–105.

77. Geno Tsonkov, *Trezvenostta, svobodno vreme i vsestrannoto razvitie na lichnostta* (Sofia: Meditsina i fizkultura, 1980), 14.

78. Ibid., 16.

79. Dobrinka Atanasova, *Tiutiun, sŭrtse, pol* (Plovdiv: Izdatelstvo Khristo G. Danov, 1977), 16.

80. *Otechestven front,* July 1976, 4.

81. Nikolai Sikulnov, *Za da ne propushat nashite detsa* (Sofia: Meditsina i fizkultura, 1980), 3.

82. Geno Tsonkov, *Sotsialisticheski nachin na zhivot i trezvenost* (Sofia: Meditsina i fizkultura, 1978), 32.

83. Atanasova, *Tiutiun, sŭrtse, pol,* 104.

84. Ibid., 132.

85. Tsonchev, ed., *Tiutiunopushene,* 44.

86. *Turist,* August 1964, 15.

87. *Trezvenost,* 4 August 1972, 4.

88. Ibid., 1 January 1975, 4.

89. *Turist,* June 1964, 29.

90. Significantly, Shtastlivets means the "happy one" in Bulgarian and was also the well-known pen name of the aforementioned writer and "tourist," Aleko Konstantinov.

91. *Turist,* November 1974, 30.

92. Ibid., February 1974, 6–7.

93. Liutov et al., 117.

94. Vlakhova-Nikolova, *Problemi na tiutiunopusheneto,* 26.

95. Ibid., 154.

96. *Trezvenost,* 21 July 1972, 2. For another example see ibid., 18 August 1972, 1.

97. Ibid., 10 January 1975, 2.

98. Ibid., 1 July 1972, 4.

99. Ibid., 18 February 1972, 2.

100. See, for example, Mila Miladinova, *Esteticheska kultura i trezvenost* (Sofia: Meditsina i fizkultura, 1979), 17.

101. Ibid., 22–23.

102. Natsionalen Komitet za Trezvenost, *Besedi,* 34.

103. *Zdrave,* July 1966, 11.

104. For a wider discussion of the citizen consumer see Katherine Pence, "'A World in Miniature': The Leipzig Trade Fairs in the 1950s and East German Consumer Citizenship," in Crew, *Consuming Germany in the Cold War,* 21–50. See also Crowley and Reid, *Pleasures in Socialism,* 7.

105. This was true for any number of avenues of consumption and material culture. On the special place of Muslim women in Bulgaria as visible consumers of modernity see Mary Neuburger, "Pants, Veils, and Matters of Dress: Unraveling the Fabric of Women's Lives in Communist Bulgaria," in Crowley and Reid, *Style and Socialism,* 169–87.

106. *Bŭlgarski tiutiun,* no. 9 (1971): 18.

107. Ibid., no. 7 (1980): 43.

108. Vlakhova-Nikolova, *Problemi na tiutiunopusheneto,* 6.

109. Natsionalen Komitet za Trezvenost, *Besedi,* 29.

110. Ibid., 26.

111. Tsonchev, *Tiutiunopushene,* 32, and Natsionalen Komitet za Trezvenost, *Besedi,* 26.

112. *Trezvenost,* 19 January 1973, 2.

113. Tsonchev, *Tiutiunopushene,* 9, 40.

114. Ibid., 32.

115. Ibid., 40.

116. Natsionalen Komitet za Trezvenost, *Besedi,* 29.

117. See, for example, *Trezvenost,* 14 April 1972, 7; ibid., 10 November 1972, 2; and ibid., 16 February 1973, 2.

118. Ibid., 23 June 1972, 2.

119. Ibid., 24 November 1972, 4.

120. See Nauchnoizsledovatelska laboratoriia za mladezhdta, *Problemi na tiutiunopusheneto,* 59, 83.

121. Ibid.

122. Liutov et al., *Upravlenie,* 116.

7. Smokes for Big Brother

1. Dimitŭr Iadkov, *Bulgartabak: Spomeni* (Sofia: Izdateslvo Sibia 34, 2003), 35.

2. *Bŭlgarski tiutiun,* no. 2 (1966): 1, see also *Tobacco Reporter,* March 1974, 17.

3. *Tobacco,* 23 July 1971, 23–26.

4. Iadkov, *Bulgartabak,* 167.

5. I am well aware of the debates surrounding the term "Pomak," which has become politically incorrect in historical and contemporary Bulgarian academic parlance for various reasons. I use the term here for the sake of simplicity.

6. According to Iadkov, Nazi Germany made its last purchase of 22,000 tons of tobacco in the spring of 1944. Iadkov, *Bulgartabak,* 170–71.

7. Most factories supplied about three to four times more tobacco to the Red Army than to the Bulgarian troops and about two times more than to the Bulgarian population at large. TsDA, F-1471k, O-1, E-337, L-180–2.

8. Iadkov, *Bulgartabak,* 23.

9. Officially almost twelve thousand trials were reported, but unofficial estimates are as high as thirty to one hundred thousand. Marshall Miller, *Bulgaria during the Second World War* (Palo Alto, CA: Stanford University Press, 1975), 217.

10. Arkhiv na Ministertsvo na Vŭtreshni Raboti (hereafter AMVR), Naroden Sŭd Deseti Sustav, op. 240, tom 2, p. 8.

11. Ibid.

12. Ekaterina Ivanova, *Iz realniia sviat na romana "Tiutiun": Otlomki ot minoloto* (Sofia: Firma Pandora-Prim, 1994), 100. See also Petŭr Semerdzhiev, *Narodniat sŭd v Bŭlgariia, 1944–45: Komu i zashto e bil neobkhodimo* (Sofia: Makedoniia Press, 1997), 362.

13. MVR, Naroden Sŭd, Deseti Sustav, fond 239, tom 2, 96.

14. Ibid., fond 243, tom 5, 251.

15. Ibid., fond 240, tom 2, 119.

16. For a personal account of the lives of several Bulgarian tobacco merchant families in exile in Western Europe see Stefane Groueff, *My Odyssey* (Bloomington, IN: I Universe, 2003), 74, and 143.

17. P. Penchev and Ct. Banov, *Tiutiun i tsigari* (Sofia: 1961), 138.

18. Iadkov, *Bulgartabak,* 91.

19. PODA, F-1812k, O-1, E-16, L-38.

20. Kostov had dealings with the now wholly demonized Yugoslavs (since 1948) and other foreign trade ministries, Anton Koev, ed. *The Trial of Traicho Kostov and His Group* (Sofia: Press Department, 1949), 233.

21. George Hodos, *Show Trials: Stalinist Purges in Eastern Europe, 1948–1954* (Santa Barbara, CA: Praeger, 2003), 16.

22. Iadkov, *Bulgartabak,* 95.

23. Ibid., 10.

24. Ivan Pitekov, *S aromata na tiutiun: Stati, razkazi, pŭtepisi* (Sofia: Kompiutŭr art media, 2009), 17.

25. Iadkov, *Bulgartabak,* 89.

26. Ibid., 91.

27. HODA, F-1, O-25, E-103, L-21, 34.

28. TsDA, F-1B, O-12, E-222, L-53:1946; TsDA, F-1B, O-12, E-222, L-53:1946.

29. Ibid., F-214B, O-1, E-716, L-58:1947.

30. Gulbrand Alhaug and Yulian Konstantinov, *Names, Ethnicity and Politics: Islamic Names in Bulgaria 1912–1992* (Oslo: Novus Press, 1995), 27.

31. E. Misirkova, *Turetskoe menshinstvo v narodnoi respublike Bolgarii* (Sofia: Stopancko rasvitie, 1951), 56.

32. TsDA, F-142, O-5, E-67, L-6:1948.

33. John Lampe, *The Bulgarian Economy in the Twentieth Century* (London: Croom Helm, 1986), 146.

34. TsDA, F-28, O-1, E-268, L-9:1945.

35. While encouraging rapid emigration of Turks (and Muslim Gypsies), the Bulgarian government categorically refused exit visas to Pomaks because they were considered Bulgarian. See TsDA, F-136, O-1A, E-1558, L-42:1950. For more on this issue see ibid., E-1557, L-9, 14:1950) and ibid., E-1558, L-15, 43, 49:1950.

36. The greatest annual increase in the Bulgarian collectivization campaign occurred in 1950, when the percentage of arable land collectivized jumped from 11.3 percent to 44.2 percent. Huey Kostanick, *Turkish Resettlement of Bulgarian Turks: 1950–1953* (Berkeley: University of California Press, 1957), 82–84.

37. TsDA, F-1b, O-22, E-578, L-1:1949.

38. Ibid., L-4, 8:1949.

39. Vasil Giuzelev et al., *"Văzroditelniia protses," Bŭlgarskata dŭrzhava i Bŭlgarskite Tiurtsi, sredata na 30-te–nachaloto na 90-te godini na XX vek,* vol. 1 (Sofia: Dŭrzhavna agentsia arkhivi, 2009), 51.

40. *New Yorker,* September 1954, 264.

41. *Tobacco News,* September 1960, 4.

42. Iadkov, *Bulgartabak,* 96.

43. *Bŭlgarski tiutiun,* no. 2 (1966):, 1.

44. Iadkov, *Bulgartabak,* 8.

45. *Washington Evening Star,* 12 October 1965.

46. Allan Brandt, *The Cigarette Century: The Rise, Fall and Deadly Persistence of the Product That Defined America* (New York: Basic Books, 2007), 54–55.

47. TsDA, F-347, O-14, E-3, L-3:1966.

48. Justus Heymans, "Report Visit to Moscow—Justus Heymans 640626–640706," 26 June 1964, Philip Morris Collection, http://tobaccodocuments.org/pm/2012582923-2927.html, 2.

49. Penchev and Banov, *Tiutiun i tsigari,* 149.

50. Ibid., 151.

51. *Bŭlgarski tiutiun,* no. 4 (1961): 28.

52. Justus Heymans, "Letter No. 9 Rumania and Bulgaria," 28 July 1964, Philip Morris Collection, http://tobaccodocuments.org/pm/2012582864-2865.html, 3.

53. Twenty-eight countries were in attendance: the USSR, East and West Germany, the United Kingdom, the United States, France, Yugoslavia, Italy, Belgium, Holland, Poland, Czechoslovakia, Austria, Hungary, Rumania, Yugoslavia, Greece, Portugal, Switzerland, China, Vietnam, Cuba, Lebanon, Egypt, Korea, Turkey, Israel, and Somalia. *The First Tobacco Symposium, Plovdiv Bulgaria* (Plovdiv: Conference Publication, 1965), 10.

54. United States Department of Agriculture, Foreign Agricultural Service, "Foreign Agriculture Circular Tobacco," October 1966, Philip Morris Collection, http://tobaccodocuments.org/pm/2024998585-8592.html, 1–4.

55. Letter from Helmut Wakeham to Albert E. Bellot, 1967 (est.), Philip Morris Collection, http://tobaccodocuments.org/pm/1000322484-2486.html, 1–2.

56. *First Tobacco Symposium,* 8.

57. Ibid., 67–70.

58. TsDA, F-347, O-14, E-2, L-213:1965.

59. Ibid., E-3, L-183:1966.

60. *First Tobacco Symposium,* 4–5.

61. TsDA, F-347, O-14, E-3, L-3:1966.

62. Ibid., L-4:1966.

63. Philip Morris also concluded licensing agreements with the USSR in 1975 and with Poland in 1973. TsDA, F-347, O-14, E-3, L-5:1966.

64. In anonymous taste tests conducted in Bulgaria in 1969, 99 percent of participants reportedly picked an American blend as their first choice. TsDA, F-347, O-14, E-148, L-7:1969.

65. Ibid., E-131, L-103:1968–69.

66. Ibid., E-133, L-2:1968.

67. Ibid., E-3, L-16:1966. Eastman Kodak was apparently paid one cent for every six thousand cigarettes.

68. Ibid., E-130, L-33:1968.

69. Ibid., O-16, E-6, L-1:1968.

70. For a detailed description of a taste test in Prague in 1981 see Iadkov, *Bulgartabak,* 169.

71. Letter from I. J. Beffinger, Investigaciones Del Humo Del Tabaco (Tobacco Smoking Research), to D. V. Bates, 21 September 1967, Philip Morris Collection, http://tobaccodocuments.org/pm/2025041470-1473.html, 3.

72. See chapter 6 for more on this. Nauchnoizsledovatelska laboratoriia za mladezhdta kŭm HIIM pri TsK na DKMS, *Problemi na tiutiunopusheneto i alkokholnata upotreba sred mladezhta* (Plovdiv: BAN, 1983), 59, 83.

73. Pitekov, *S aromata na tiutiun,* 10.

74. *Bŭlgarski tiutiun,* no. 7 (1977), 7.

75. Ibid., no. 5 (1972): 38, and no. 3 (1971): 20.

76. Ibid., no. 12 (1972): 4.

77. Ibid., no. 3 (1971):18.

78. There was also a rare mention of Roma women, such as Filka Micheva, a factory worker whose dark past under capitalism was likened to that of Carmen, the famous "Gypsy tobacco worker" in Bizet's opera. Ibid., no. 4 (1961): 44.

79. Ibid., no. 11 (1962): 42.

80. Iadkov, *Bulgartabak,* 19.

81. For a detailed study of these campaigns see Mary Neuburger, *The Orient Within: Muslim Minorities and the Negotiation of Nationhood in Modern Bulgaria* (Ithaca: Cornell University Press, 2004), 142–68.

82. TsDA, F-417, O-4, E-34, L-6:1972.

83. *Bŭlgarski tiutiun,* no. 1 (1975), back cover.

84. Iadkov, *Bulgartabak,* 11.

85. Ibid., 13.

86. Ibid., 8.

87. Ibid., 188.

88. Ibid., 21.

89. Ibid., 30–31.

90. Ibid., 31–32.

91. Ibid., 36.

92. Ibid., 36.

93. Letter from Hugh Cullman to Andreas Gembler, 7 May 1974, Philip Morris Collection, http://tobaccodocuments.org/pm/1000272443-2445.html, 1–3.

94. Iadkov, *Bulgartabak,* 43, 58, 57.

95. Ibid., 58.

96. Ibid., 138.

97. Ibid., 163.

98. Ibid., 226.

99. Ibid., 143.

100. Ibid., 220.

101. Ibid., 188–90.

102. Ibid., 216.

103. TsDA, F-1-B, O-64, E-478, L-1.

104. Iadkov, *Bulgartabak,* 311–12.

105. Ibid., 192–93.

106. TsDA, F-347, O-20, A-75, L-7:1984.

107. Ibid., A-85, L-3:1985.

108. Ibid., F-1B, O-39, E-522, L-187:1970. Giuzelev et al., *"Vŭzroditelniia protses,"* 1:77.

109. TsDA, F-1B, O-39, E-522, L-186:1970.

110. Giuzelev et al., *"Vŭzroditelniia protses,"* 1:93.

111. Ibid., 1:295–96.

112. Iadkov, *Bulgartabak,* 353.

113. Giuzelev et al., *"Vŭzroditelniia protses,"* 1:532–33, 563.

114. Ibid., 1:564.

115. Ibid., 2:677–78.

116. Iadkov, *Bulgartabak,* 370–71.

Conclusion

1. Ivan Pitekov, *S aromata na tiutiun: Stati, razkazi, pŭtepisi* (Sofia: Kompiutŭr art media, 2009), 21.

2. 39 percent of the population of Bulgaria currently smokes, http://www.euronews.net/tag/world-no-tobacco-day.

3. See http://sofiaecho.com/2010/04/16/888409_debate-on-easing-smoking-ban-postponed-by-a-week.

4. Nikolai Genov and Anna Krasteva, *Recent Social Trends in Bulgaria, 1960–1995* (Montreal: McGill-Queens University Press, 2001), 367, 413.

5. Kristen Ghodsee, "Potions, Lotions and Lipstick: The Gendered Consumption of Cosmetics and Perfumery in Socialist and Post-Socialist Urban Bulgaria," *Women's Studies International Forum* 30 (2007): 31.

BIBLIOGRAPHY

Archival Sources

TsDA (Tsentralen Dŭrzhaven Arkhiv): Central State Archive, Sofia, Bulgaria

Pre-1944 Government Collection

Fond 264k—Ministry of Internal Affairs and National Health
Fond 273k—Union of Tobacco Cooperatives in Bulgaria
Fond 316k—Bulgarian Embassy in Berlin
Fond 396k—Macedonian Internal Revolutionary Organization (IMRO)
Fond 656k—Police Files, Drama 1943–44
Fond 1027k—Bulgarian Evangelical Temperance Union
Fond 1341k—State Tobacco Factory Pobeda, Kavala, 1941–45

Post-1944 Government Collection

Fond 28—National Committee of the Fatherland Front
Fond 142—Ministry of Education
Fond 136—Ministry of Internal Affairs and National Health
Fond 347—State Tobacco Monopoly, Bulgartabak
Fond 417—Committee of Bulgarian Women

Bulgarian Communist Party Collection

Fond 1B—Central Committee of the Communist Party
Cp-576—Angel Dinev

PODA (Plovdiv Okrŭzhen Dŭrzhaven Arkhiv): Plovdiv Regional Government Archive, Plovdiv, Bulgaria

HODA (Haskovo Okrŭzhen Dŭrzhaven Arkhiv): Haskovo Regional Government Archive, Haskovo, Bulgaria

AMVR (Arkhiv na Ministertsvo na Vŭtreshni Raboti): Archive of the Ministry of Internal Affairs, Sofia, Bulgaria

American Tobacco Industry Documents

Philip Morris collection, http://tobaccodocuments.org/pm/

United States Holocaust Memorial Museum

Commissariat for Jewish Affairs, Bulgaria, fond 190.

Bulgarian Newspapers and Periodicals

Asenovgrad krepost
*Biuletin na kooperativnoto druzhestvo na sdruzhenite tiutiunoproizvoditeli ot grad Stanimaka
    i okoliiata*
Bŭlgarski tiutiun
Nasheto pŭrvo izlozhenie
Otechestven front
Plovdivski panair
Rodopa
Rabotnicheska borba
Rabotnicheski vestnik
Tiutiunev pregled
Tiutiunopabotnik
Tiutiunopabotnik zashtitnik
Tiutiunoproizboditel
Turist
Trezvenost (Ruse)
Trezvenost (Sofia)
Vestnik na zhenata
Zdrave
Zdrave i zhivot

English-Language Newspapers and Periodicals

The New Yorker
New York Times
Tobacco
Tobacco News
Tobacco Reporter
Washington Evening Star

Secondary Sources

Abadzhiev, Liuben. *Psikhologiata na nachunaishtia pushach*. Sofia: Pechatnitsa khudozh-
    nik, 1933.
Abadzhiev, Stefan. *Spomeni ot izminatiia pŭt*. Sofia: Profizdat, 1982.
Alhaug, Gulbrand, and Yulian Konstantinov. *Names, Ethnicity and Politics: Islamic
    Names in Bulgaria 1912–1992*. Oslo: Novus Press, 1995.
Allcock, John. "Constructing the Balkans." In *Black Lambs and Grey Falcons: Women
    Travelling in the Balkans*, edited by John Allcock and Antonia Young, 170–91.
    New York: Berghahn Books, 2000.
Allcock, John, and Antonia Young, eds. *Black Lambs and Grey Falcons: Women Travel-
    ling in the Balkans*. New York: Berghahn Books, 2000.
Alloula, Malek. *The Colonial Harem*. Minneapolis: University of Minnesota Press, 1986.
Alvadzhiev, Nikola. *Plovdivska khronika*. Plovdiv: Izdatelstvo na Khristo G.
    Danov, 1971.
American Tobacco Company. *"Sold American!" The First Fifty Years, 1904–1954*.
    New York, 1954.

Anderson, Sheldon. *A Cold War in the Eastern Bloc: Polish-East German Relations, 1945–62*. Boulder, CO: Westview, 1989.

Andonov, Ivan. *Iz spomenite mi ot Tursko vreme: Sŭedinenieto, volumes 1 and 2*. Sofia: Akademichno izdatelstvo, Marin Drinov, 1995.

Andonov-Poljanski, Hristo. *Documents on the Struggle of the Macedonian People for Independence and a Nation-state*. Skopje: Kultura, 1985.

Appadurai, Arjun. "Introduction: Commodities and the Politics of Value." In *The Social Life of Things: Commodities in Cultural Perspective*, edited by Arjun Appadurai, 3–63. Cambridge: Cambridge University Press, 1986.

Arditi, Beniamin. *Vidni Evrei v Bŭlgariia: Galeriia na zabravenite*. Vol. 2. Tel Aviv: 1970.

Asseoff, Jacques. *Tiutiun v Bŭlgarskoto stopanstvo*. Sofia: Kooperativna pechatnitsa napred, 1933.

Atanasova, Dobrinka. *Tiutiun, sŭrtse, pol*. Plovdiv: Izdatelstvo na Khristo G. Danov, 1977.

Avramov, Rumen. *Komunalniiat kapitalizŭm: Iz Bŭlgarskoto stopansko minalo*. Volume 1–3. Sofia: Tsentŭr za liberalni strategii, 2007.

———. *Stopanskiiat XX vek na Bŭlgariia*. Sofia: Tsentŭr za liberalni strategii, 2001.

Bakić-Hayden, Milica. "Nesting Orientalisms: The Case of Former Yugoslavia." *Slavic Review* 54 (1995): 917–31.

Barth, Ilene. *The Smoking Life*. Columbus, MS: Genesis Press, 1997.

Baruch, Nir. *Otkupŭt: Tsar Boris i sŭdbata na Bŭlgarskite Evrei*. Sofia: Universitetsko izdatelstvo Sv. Kliment Okhridski, 1991.

Bar-Zohar, Michael. *Beyond Hitler's Grasp; The Heroic Rescue of Bulgaria's Jews*. Holbrook, NJ: Adams Media Corp., 1998.

Bekhar, Alfred. *Tiutiun v Bŭlgariia*. Sofia, 1927.

Belchev, Koitcho. *Tobacco in Bulgaria*. Durham, NC: Duke University Press, 1950.

Belchov, Todor. "Iz borbite na tiutiunopabotnitsite v grad Plovdiv (1891–1920g.)." *Godishnik na museite v Plovdivski okrŭg* 2 (1956): 12–37.

Bell, John. *Peasants in Power: Alexander Stamboliski and the Bulgarian Agrarian National Union, 1899–1923*. Princeton: Princeton University Press, 1977.

Benbassa, Esther, and Aron Rodrigue. *Sephardi Jewry: A History of the Judeo-Spanish Community, 14–20th Centuries*. Berkeley: University of California Press, 2000.

Bichev, Milko. *Architecture in Bulgaria: From Ancient Times to the Late Nineteenth Century*. Sofia: Foreign Language Press, 1961.

———. *Bŭlgarski barok: Prinos kŭm problemite na Bŭlgarskoto izkustvo prez epokhata na vŭzrazhdaneto*. Sofia: Nauka i izkustvo, 1954.

Bierman, Irene, Rifa'at Abou-El-Haj, and Donald Preziosi, eds. *The Ottoman City: Urban Structure and Its Parts*. New Rochelle, NY: A.D. Caratzas, 1991.

Blunt, Fanny. *My Reminiscences*. London: Murray, 1918.

Bloomer, D.C. *The Life and Writings of Amelia Bloomer*. New York: Schocken Books, 1975.

Bloxham, Donald. *Genocide on Trial: War Crimes Tribunals and the Formation of Holocaust History*. Oxford: Oxford University Press, 2003.

Bogatinova, Dona. *Trudno i slavno minalo*. Sofia: Partizdat, 1973.

Bogdanova, Elena. *Vela Blagoeva: Biografichen ocherk*. Sofia: Izdatelstvo na BKP, 1969.

Boiadzhiev, Khristo. *Saving the Bulgarian Jews in World War II*. Ottawa: Free Bulgaria Center, 1989.

Bokov, Georgi. *Modern Bulgaria: History, Policy, Economy, Culture.* Sofia: Sofia Press, 1981.

Bonev, Vŭlcho. *Dŭrzhavnata namesa v Tiutiunevoto proizvodstvo.* Sofia: Rech iz narodo sŭbranie, 1939.

Bozhinov, Voin, ed. *Borbata na Bŭlgarskata narod za zashtita i spasiavane na Evreite v Bŭlgariia prez vtorata svetovna voina.* Sofia: Izdatelstvo na Bŭlgarskata akademiia na naukite, 1978.

Bozhinov, Voin, and Dimitur Kosev, eds. *Macedonia: Documents and Material.* Sofia: Bulgarian Academy of Sciences, 1978.

Brailsford, H. N. *Macedonia: Its Races and Their Future.* London: Methuen, 1906.

Brandt, Allan. *The Cigarette Century: The Rise, Fall and Deadly Persistence of the Product That Defined America.* New York: Basic Books, 2007.

Braun, Hans-Joachim. *The German Economy in the Twentieth Century.* London: Taylor & Francis, 2007.

Bren, Paulina and Mary Neuburger, eds. *Communism Unwrapped: Consumption in Cold War Eastern Europe.* New York: Oxford University Press, 2012.

Brown, Keith. *The Past in Question: Modern Macedonia and the Uncertainties of Nation.* Princeton: Princeton University Press, 2003.

Browning, Christopher. *Ordinary Men: Reserve Police Battalion 101 and the Final Solution in Poland.* New York: Harper Perennial, 1993.

Brŭzitsov, Khristo. *Niakoga v Sofiia: Spomeni 1913–1944.* Sofia: Bŭlgarski pisatel, 1970.

———. *Niakoga v Tsarigrad.* Varna: Dŭrzhavno izdatelstvo, 1966.

Bŭlgarska Zemledelska Banka. *The Agricultural Cooperative and the Agricultural Bank of Sofia.* Sofia: National Printing Office, 1924.

Byton, Paul. *Time, Work, and Organization.* New York: Routledge, 2001.

Calic, Edouard. *Life in Bulgaria as Seen by Edouard Calic.* Sofia: Foreign Language Press, 1964.

Carrier, James, ed. *Occidentalism: Images of the West.* Oxford, Oxford University Press, 1995.

Çelik, Zeynep. *The Remaking of Istanbul: Portrait of an Ottoman City in the Nineteenth Century.* Berkeley: University of California Press, 1993.

Chary, Frederick. *The Bulgarian Jews and the Final Solution, 1940–1944.* Pittsburgh: University of Pittsburgh Press, 1972.

Chernokolev, Titko. "Kharakter i rolia na vŭzdŭrzhatelnoto dvizheniie." In *Iubileen nauchen sbornik, 1922–37,* edited by Krum Akhchiiski and Ianka Tosheva, 65–70. Sofia: Studentska vŭzdŭrzhatelno druzhestvo, 1937.

Cholakof, Stefan. "U.N.V.S.—Shkola na podvig i samozhertva." In *Iubileen nauchen sbornik, 1922–37,* edited by Krum Akhchiiski and Ianka Tosheva, 17–21. Sofia: Studentska vŭzdŭrzhatelno druzhestvo, 1937.

Chrissidis, Nikolaos. "Sex, Drink, and Drugs: Tobacco in Early Modern Russia." In *Tobacco in Russian History and Culture,* edited by Matthew Romaniello and Tricia Starks, 26–44. New York: Routledge, 2009.

Clarke, James. *Bible Societies, American Missionaries, and the National Revival of Bulgaria.* New York: Arno Press: 1971.

———. *Bulgaria and Salonica in Macedonia.* Boston: American Board of Commissioners for Foreign Missionaries, 1885.

———. *Sketch of the European Turkey Mission of the American Board.* Boston: American Board of Commissioners for Foreign Missionaries Congregational House, 1901.

———. *Temperance Work in Bulgaria: Its Successes.* Samokov, Bulg.: Evangelical School Press, 1909.

Connelly, John. "Nazis and Slavs: From Racial Theory to Racist Practice." *Central European History* 32 (1999): 1–33.

Cooper, Fredrick. *Colonialism in Question: Theory, Knowledge, History.* Berkeley: University of California Press, 2005.

Courtright, David. *Forces of Habit: Drugs and the Making of the Modern World* (Cambridge, MA: Harvard University Press.

Cowan, Brian. *The Social Life of Coffee: The Emergence of the British Coffeehouse.* New Haven: Yale University Press, 2005.

Cox, Howard. *The Global Cigarette: Origins and Evolution of British American Tobacco.* Oxford: Oxford University Press, 2000.

Crampton, Richard. *Bulgaria.* Oxford: Oxford University Press, 2008.

———. "The Turks in Bulgaria, 1878–1944." In *The Turks of Bulgaria: The History and Fate of a Minority,* edited by Kemal Karpat, 43–78. Istanbul: ISIS Press, 1990.

Crew, David, ed. *Consuming Germany in the Cold War.* Oxford, Berg, 2003.

Crowley, David, and Susan Reid, eds. *Pleasures in Socialism: Leisure and Luxury in the Bloc.* Evanston, IL: Northwestern University Press, 2012.

———, eds. *Style and Socialism: Modernity and Material Culture in Post-War Eastern Europe.* Oxford: Berg, 2000.

Curtis, William. *The Turk and His Lost Provinces: Greece, Bulgaria, Servia, Bosnia.* Chicago: Fleming and H. Revell, 1903.

Dabrowski, Patrice. *Commemorations and the Making of Modern Poland.* Bloomington: University of Indiana Press, 2004.

Dakov, Vasil. *Reka Dunav i neinoto stopansko znachenie za Bŭlgariia.* Sofia: Nauka i izkustvo, 1964.

Danov, Khristo. *Za teb mili rode.* Plovdiv: Izdatelstvo na Khristo G. Danov, 1978.

Daskalov, Rumen. *Bŭlgarskoto obshtestvo.* Vol. 1, *Dŭrzhava, politika, ikonomika, 1878–1939,* and vol. 2, *Naselenie, obshtestvo, kultura.* Sofia: IK Gutenberg, 2005.

———. "Images of Europe: A Glance from the Periphery." Working Paper SPS No. 94/8, European University Institute, Florence, 1996.

———. *Mezhdu iztoka i zapada: Bŭlgarski kulturni dilemi.* Sofia: Lik, 1998.

Daunton, Martin, and Mathew Hilton, eds. *The Politics of Consumption: Material Culture and Citizenship in Europe and America.* New York: Berg, 2001.

Davenport-Hines, Richard. *The Pursuit of Oblivion: A Global History of Narcotics.* New York, W.W. Norton.

de Grazia, Victoria, and Ellen Furlough, eds. *The Sex of Things: Gender and Consumption in Historical Perspective.* Berkeley: University of California Press, 1996.

Destani, Bejtullah, ed. *Ethnic Minorities in the Balkan States.* Vol. 2, *1888–1914.* London: Archive Editions Limited, 2003.

Dimchev, Khristo. "Pŭrvi Iskri." In *Iubileen nauchen sbornik, 1922–37,* edited by Krum Akhchiiski and Ianka Tosheva, 9–16. Sofia: Studentska vŭzdŭrzhatelno druzhestvo, 1937.

Dimitrov, Ilcho, and Bogdan Filov. *Dnevik.* Sofia: Izdatelstvo na otechestveniia front, 1990.

Dimitrova, Blaga, and Iordan Vasilev, eds. *Mladostta na Bagriana i neinite sputnitsi.* Plovdiv: Izdatelstvo na Khristo G. Danov, 1976.

Dimov, Dimitŭr. *Tiutiun.* Sofia: Izdatelstvo Zakharii Stoianov, 2004.

Direktsia na Statistika, *Vŭnshnata tŭrgovia na Bŭlgaria prez godinite 1897–190.* Sofia: Pechatnitsa na P.M. Buzaitov, 1905.

Dobrinov, Aleksandŭr. and Adelina Fileva. *Alexander Dobrinov, 1898–1958.* Sofia: Sofia Municipal Art Gallery, 1998.

Dobroszycki, Lucjan. *The Holocaust in the Soviet Union: Studies and Sources on the Destruction of the Jews in the Nazi-Occupied Territories of the USSR, 1941–1945.* New York: M.E. Sharpe, 1993.

Dospevska, Neli, *Poznat i nepoznat Dimitŭr Dimov.* Sofia: Profizdat, 1985.

Dragoicheva, Tsola. *Poveliia na dŭlga.* Vol. 1, *Spomeni razmisli,* and vol. 2, *Shturmŭt,* Sofia: Profizdat, 1975.

Dragostinova, Theodora. *Between Two Motherlands: Nationality and Emigration among the Greeks of Bulgaria, 1900–1949.* Ithaca: Cornell University Press, 2011.

Dufev, Konstantin. *Tam gore na trikhŭlmieto: Kniga za rodoliubitsi.* Plovdiv: Telerpres, 1993.

Duravenski, V. N. *Dunavskata problema.* Sofia: Izdatelstvo na Bŭlgarskata rabotnicheskata partia, 1947.

Eldem, Edhem, Daniel Goffman, and Bruce Masters. *The Ottoman City between East and West: Aleppo, Izmir, and Istanbul.* New York: Cambridge University Press, 1999.

Doinov, Plamen. "Kafene, meniu, literatura: Tekst i literaturen protocol v Evropeĭski i Bŭlgarksi kafeneta." In *Kafene Evropa,* edited by Raia Zaimova, 166–70. Sofia: Izdatelstvo Damian Iakov, 2007.

Ellis, Markman. *The Coffee-House: A Cultural History.* London: Weidenfeld and Nicholson, 2004.

Faroqhi, Suraiya. *Subjects of the Sultan: Culture and Daily Life in the Ottoman Empire.* London: I.B. Tauris, 2005.

Fehér, Ferenc, Ágnes Heller, and György Márkus. *Dictatorship over Needs.* New York: St. Martin's, 1983.

Firkatian, Mari. *Diplomats and Dreamers: The Stancioff Family in Bulgarian History.* Lanham, MD: University Press of America, 2008.

The First Tobacco Symposium, Plovdiv Bulgaria. Plovdiv: Conference Publication, 1965.

Fitzpatrick, Sheila. *Everyday Stalinism: Ordinary Life in Extraordinary Times, Soviet Russia in the 1930's.* New York: Oxford University Press, 1999.

Foucault, Michel. *Discipline and Punishment: The Birth of the Prison.* London: Penguin, 1977.

Frank, Alison. *Oil Empire: Visions of Prosperity in Habsburg Galicia.* Cambridge, MA: Harvard University Press, 2005.

Fraser, John. *Pictures from the Balkans.* London: Cassell, 1912.

Fraser, Nancy. "Rethinking the Public Sphere: A Contribution to the Critique of Actually Existing Democracy." In *Habermas and the Public Sphere,* edited by Craig Calhoun, 109–42. Cambridge, MA: MIT Press, 1992.

Freifeld, Alice. *Nationalism and the Crowd in Liberal Hungary, 1848–1914.* Baltimore: Woodrow Wilson Center Press, 2000.

Frusetta, James. "Bulgaria's Macedonia: Nation-Building and State-Building, Centralization and Autonomy in Pirin Macedonia, 1903–1952." PhD diss., University of Maryland, College Park, 2006.

Fuhrman, Malte. "Cosmopolitan Imperialists and the Ottoman Port Cities: Conflict-ing Logics in the Urban Social Fabric." *Du Cosmopolitisme en Méditerrannée* 67 (2007): 1–50.

Ganchev, Khristo, Grigor Doinchev, and Ivana Stoianova. *Bŭlgariia 1900: Evropeĭskata vliianiia v Bŭlgarskoto gradoustroĭstvo, arkitektura, parkove, i gradini, 1878–1918.* Sofia: Izkustvo i arkitektura, 2002.

Gardiner, Leslie. *Curtain Calls: Travels in Albania, Romania and Bulgaria.* London: Duckworth Press, 1976.

Gately, Iain. *Tobacco: A Cultural History of How an Exotic Plant Seduced Civilization.* New York: Grove Press, 2003.

Gavrilova, Raina. *Bulgarian Urban Culture in the Eighteenth and Nineteenth Centuries.* London: Associated University Press, 1999.

———. *Kolelota na Zhivota: Vsekidnevieto na Bŭlgarskiia vŭzrozhdenski grad.* Sofia: Uni-versitetsko izdatelstvo Sv. Kliment Okhridski, 1999.

Genov, Paun. *S Fakela na trezvenostta: Momenti ot borbata protiv pianstvoto i tiutiuno-pusheneto pres 1300-godishnata istoriia na Bŭlgariia.* Sofia: Meditsina i fizkul-tura, 1980.

Georgiev, Georgi. *Sofiia i Sofiiantsi, 1878–1944.* Sofia: Nauka i izkustvo, 1983.

Georgieva, Milena. "Kafeneto kato atelie, ili na bohemstvo kato nachin na zhivot v Bŭlgarskoto izkustvo prez pŭrvata polovina na XX vek." In *Kafene Evropa*, edited by Raia Zaimova, 197–208. Sofia: Izdatelstvo Damian Iakov, 2007.

Georgieva, Nikola. *Imeto na rozata i na tuituina.* Sofia: Izdatelstvo na Bŭlgarskata aka-demiia na naukite, 1992.

Ghodsee, Kristen. *The Red Riviera: Gender, Tourism, and Postsocialism on the Black Sea.* Durham, NC: Duke University Press, 2005.

Giatzidis, Emil. *An Introduction to Post-Communist Bulgaria: Political Economic and Social Transformation.* Manchester, UK: Manchester University Press, 2002.

Giddens, Anthony. "The Nature of Modernity." In *The Giddens Reader,* edited by Phillip Cassel and Anthony Giddens, 284–316. Palo Alto, CA: Stanford Uni-versity Press, 1993.

Gigova, Irina. "The Feminisation of Bulgarian Literature and the Club of Bulgarian Women Writers." *Aspasia* 2 (2008): 91–108.

———. "Writers of the Nation: Intellectual Identity in Bulgaria, 1939—1953." PhD diss., University of Illinois at Urbana-Champaign, 2005.

Gilman, Sander. "Jews and Smoking." In *Smoke: A Global History of Smoking,* edited by Sander Gilman and Xhou Zun, 278–86. London: Reaktion Books, 2004.

Giustino, Cathleen. *Tearing Down Prague's Jewish Town: Ghetto Clearance and the Legacy of Middle-Class Ethnic Politics around 1900.* Boulder, CO: East European Mono-graphs, 2003.

Giuzelev, Vasil et al. *"Vŭzroditelniia Protses": Bŭlgarskata dŭrzhava i Bŭlgarskite Turtsi (sredata na 30-te–nachaloto na 90-te godini na XX vek),* Vols. 1 and 2. Sofia: Dŭrzhavna agentsia arkhivi, 2009.

Gocheva, Rositsa. *Rasvitie na materialnoto blagosŭstoianie na Bŭlgarskiia narod.* Sofia: Izdatelstvo na Bŭlgarskata komunisticheska partiia, 1965.

Goodman, Jordan. *Tobacco in History: The Cultures of Dependence.* London: Rout-ledge, 1993.

Gorsuch, Anne. "Time Travelers: Soviet Tourists to Eastern Europe." In *Turizm: The Russian and East European Tourist under Capitalism and Socialism,* edited by Anne Gorsuch and Diane Koenker, 205–26. Ithaca: Cornell University Press, 2006.

Gorsuch, Anne, and Diane Koenker, eds. *Turizm: The Russian and East European Tourist under Capitalism and Socialism.* Ithaca: Cornell University Press, 2006.

Gospodinov, Nikola. *Zhiznen pŭt: Publististika, dokumenti, spomeni.* Sofia: Profizdat, 1977.

Gounaris, Basil, ed. *The Events of 1903 in Macedonia as Presented in European Diplomatic Correspondence.* Thessaloniki: Museum of the Macedonian Struggle, 1993.

Grabill, Joseph. *Protestant Diplomacy and the Near East: Missionary Influence on American policy, 1810–1927.* Minneapolis: University of Minnesota Press, 1971.

Grehan, James. "Smoking and 'Early Modern' Sociability: The Great Tobacco Debate in the Ottoman Middle East (Seventeenth to Eighteenth Centuries)." *American Historical Review* 111 (2006): 1352–76.

Grinberg, Natan. *Dokumenti.* Sofia: Izdavane na tsentŭr na tsentralnata konsistoria na Evreite v Bŭlgariia, 1945.

Gronow, Jukka. *Caviar with Champagne: Common Luxury and the Ideals of the Good Life in Stalin's Russia.* Oxford: Berg, 2003.

Gross, Jan. *Fear: Anti-Semitism in Poland after Auschwitz.* New York: Random House, 2006.

———. *Neighbors.* New York: Penguin, 2002.

Groueff, Stefane. *My Odyssey.* Bloomington, IN: I Universe, 2003.

Grŭncharov, Mikhail. *Chorbadzhiistvoto i Bŭlgarskoto obshtestvo prez vŭzrazhdaneto.* Sofia: Universitetsko izdatelstvo Sveti Kliment Okhridski, 1999.

Gulubov, Konstantin. *Spomeni veseli i neveseli za bŭlgarski pisateli.* Sofia: Bŭlgarski pisatel, 1959.

Habermas, Jürgen. *The Structural Transformation of the Public Sphere: An Inquiry into a Category of Bourgeois Society.* Cambridge, MA: MIT Press, 1992.

Hadar, Gila. "Jewish Tobacco Workers in Salonika: Gender and Family in the Context of Social and Ethnic Strife." In *Women in the Ottoman Balkans,* edited by Amila Buturović; and Irvin Cemil Schick, 127–52. London: I.B. Tauris, 2007.

Haine, Scott, *The World of the Paris Café: Sociability among the French Working Classes, 1789–1914.* Baltimore: Johns Hopkins University Press, 1996.

Hall, Derek, Melanie Smith, and Barabara Marcisewska, eds. *Tourism in the New Europe: The Challenges and Opportunities of EU Enlargement.* Oxfordshire, UK: Cabi Publishing, 2006.

Hall, Richard. *The Balkan Wars 1912–3: Prelude to World War One.* New York: Routledge, 2000.

Hamlin, Cyrus. *My Life and Times.* Boston: Congregational Sunday School and Publishing Society, 1893.

Harlaftis, Gelina. *A History of Greek-Owned Shipping: The Making of an International Tramp Fleet, 1830 to the Present Day.* New York: Routledge, 1996.

Harvey, David. *Paris: Capital of Modernity.* New York: Routledge, 2005.

Hattox, Ralph. *Coffee and Coffeehouses: The Origins of a Social Beverage in the Medieval Near East.* Seattle: University of Washington Press, 1985.

Healy, Maureen. *Vienna and the Fall of the Habsburg Empire: Total War and Everyday Life in World War I.* Cambridge: Cambridge University Press, 2004.

Hilendarski, Paisii. *Slavianobŭlgarska istoriia.* Sofia: Bŭlgarski pisatel, 1963.

Hixson, Walter. *Parting the Curtain: Propaganda, Culture, and the Cold War, 1945–1961.* New York: Palgrave Macmillan, 1997.

Hodos, George. *Show Trials: Stalinist Purges in Eastern Europe, 1948–1954.* Santa Barbara, CA: Praeger, 2003.

Iadkov, Dimitŭr. *Bulgartabak: Spomeni.* Sofia: Izdatelstvo Sibia 34, 2003.

Iankovo, Ivanka, and Mincho Semov. *Bŭlgarskite gradove prez vŭzrazhdaneto: Istorichesko, sotsiologichesko i politichesko izsledvane,* Vol. 1, Sofia: Universitetsko izdatelstvo Sveti Kliment Okhridski, 2004.

Ilchev, Ivan, and Plamen Mitev, eds. *Bŭlgaro-Amerikanski kulturni i politicheski vrŭzki prez XIX–pŭrvata polovina na XX v.* Sofia: Universitetsko izdatelstvo Sveti Kliment Okhridski, 2004.

Iordanov, Iordan. *Istoriia na Bŭlgarskata tŭrgoviia do osvobozhdenieto: Kratŭk ocherk.* Sofia: Pechatnitsa S.M. Staikov, 1938.

Iordanov, Todor. *Materialnoto-tekhnicheska basa na razvitoto sotsialistichesko obshtestvo.* Sofia: Partizdat, 1973.

Ivanov, Angel. *Kogato govorekha pushkite: Spomeni.* Plovdiv: Izdatelstvo na Khristo G. Danov, 1984.

Ivanova, Ekaterina. *Iz realniia sviat na romana "Tiutiun": Otlomki ot minoloto.* Sofia: Firma Pandora-Prim, 1994.

Jacobs, Tino. *Rauch und Macht: Das Unternehmen Reemstma 1920 bis 1961.* Göttingen: Wallstein Verlag, 2008.

Jezernik, Bozhidar. *Wild Europe: The Balkans in the Gaze of Western Travelers.* London: Saqi Books, 2004.

Jochmus, A. "Notes on a Journey into the Balkan, or Mount Haemus in 1847." *Journal of the Royal Geographic Society of London,* no. 24 (1854): 36–85.

Karaivanov, Petŭr. *Vasil Levski po spomeni na Vasil Karaivanov.* Sofia: Izdatelstvo na otechestveniia front, 1987.

Karakasidou, Anastasia. *Fields of Wheat, Hills of Blood: Passages to Nationhood in Greek Macedonia, 1870–1990.* Chicago: University of Chicago Press, 1997.

Karakostov, Stefan. "*Chitalishte i vŭzdŭrzhatelno dvizhenie.*" In *Iubileen nauchen sbornik, 1922–37,* edited by Krum Akhchiiski and Ianka Tosheva, 57–59. Sofia: Studentska vŭzdŭrzhatelno druzhestvo, 1937.

Karpat, Kemal. *Studies on Ottoman Social and Political History.* London: Brill, 2002.

Kazasov, Dimo. *Vidiano i prezhiviano, 1891–1944.* Sofia: Otechestven front, 1969.

Keiger, John, ed. *British Documents on Foreign Affairs: Reports and Papers from the Foreign Office Confidential Print: Part 1, Series F, Volume 15.* London: Great Britain Foreign Office, 1952.

Kennan, George, ed. *The Other Balkan Wars: A 1913 Carnegie Endowment Inquiry in Retrospect.* Washington, DC: Carnegie Endowment for International Peace, Brookings Institution Publications, 1993.

Khadzhiiski, Ivan. *Sŭdbata na Evreite ot iugozapadna Bŭlgariia prez 1940–44 godina.* Sofia: Nauchna studiia, 1998.

Kirli, Cengiz. "Coffeehouses: Public Opinion in the Nineteenth Century Ottoman Empire." In *Public Islam and the Common Good,* edited by Armando Salvatore and Dale F. Eickelman, 75–97. Boston: Brill Academic Publishers, 2004.

———. "The Struggle over Space: Coffeehouses of Ottoman Istanbul, 1780–1845." PhD diss., State University of New York, Binghamton, 2001.

Kirova, Lilia. "Razmisli za neprekhodeniia char na Balkanskite kafeneta." In *Kafene Evropa,* edited by Raia Zaimova, 25–34. Sofia: Izdatelstvo Damian Iakov, 2007.

Klein, Richard. *Cigarettes Are Sublime.* Durham, NC: Duke University Press, 1993.

Koen, David, ed. *Otseliavaneto 1940–44: Sbornik ot dokumenti.* Sofia: Izdatelski tsentŭr shalom, 1995.

Koev, Anton, ed. *The Trial of Traicho Kostov and His Group.* Sofia: Press Department, 1949.

Kolarov, Vasil. *How the Fascists "Buried" the Class Struggle.* London: Communist Party of Great Britain, 1936.

Konstantinov, Aleko. *Razkazi i feiletoni.* Sofia: Knigoizdatesltvo Fakel, 1937.

Konstantinov, Konstantin. *Pŭtuvane kŭm vŭrkhovete: Portreti, spomeni, eseta.* Varna: Knigoizdatelstvo Georgi Bakalov, 1976.

Kostadinova, Tatiana. *Bulgaria 1879–1946: The Challenge of Choice.* Boulder, CO: East European Monographs and Columbia University Press, 1995.

Kostanick, Huey. *Turkish Resettlement of Bulgarian Turks: 1950–1953.* Berkeley: University of California Press, 1957.

Kostentseva, Raina. *Moiat roden grad Sofiia v kraia na XIX–nachalo na XX vek i sled tova.* Sofia: Riva, 2008.

Kozhukharov, Georgi. *Bŭlgarskata kŭshta prez pet stoletie: Kraia na XIV Vek–kraia na XIX vek.* Sofia: Bŭlgarskata akademiia na naukite, 1967.

Kraev, Georg, ed., *Kafeneto kato diskurs.* Sofia: Nov Bŭlgarski Universitet, 2005.

Krekmanov, Al. *Zlatoto na Bŭlgariia: Tiutiunoproizvodstvo v raiona na kamarata.* Sofia: Sofiiska zemedelska kamara, 1942.

Krustev, Angel. *Asenovgrad krepost: Tiutiuneva kooperatsiia Asenovgrad.* Asenovgrad: Izdatelska kŭshta belan, 1994.

——. *Tiutiuneva promishlenost v Asenovgrad, 1948–1999g.* Asenovgrad: Izdatelska Kŭshta Belan, 2000.

Kulichev, Khristo. *Zaslugi na Protestantite za Bŭlgarskiia narod.* Sofia: Universitetsko izdatelstvo Sveti Kliment Okhridski, 2008.

Kutsoglu, Vasil. *Spomeni i razmisli.* Sofia: Izdatelstvo na otechestveniia front, 1989.

Kuzmova-Zografa, Katiia. "Ot imaniarski legendi do mornata utopia 'Viensko kafene.'" In *Kafene Evropa,* edited by Raia Zaimova, 157–67. Sofia: Izdatelstvo Damian Iakov, 2007.

Lampe, John. *The Bulgarian Economy in the Twentieth Century.* London: Croom Helm, 1986.

——. "Imperial Borderlands or Capitalist Periphery? Redefining Balkan Backwardness, 1520–1914." In *The Origins of Backwardness in Eastern Europe: Economics and Politics from the Middle Ages until the Early Twentieth Century,* edited by Daniel Chirot, 177–209. Berkeley: University of California Press, 1989.

Lampe, John, and Marvin Jackson. *Balkan Economic History, 1550–1950: From Imperial Borderlands to Developing Nations.* Bloomington: Indiana University Press, 1982.

Lazarov, Georgi. *Borbite na tiutiunoproizvoditelite.* Sofia: Zemizdat, 1967.

Leslie, Henrietta. *Where East Is West: Life in Bulgaria.* Boston: Houghton Mifflin, 1933.

Liutov, Atanas, Boris Atanasov, Violeta Samardzhieva, and Katia Stoianova. *Upravlenie na narodnoto potreblenie.* Sofia: Izdatelstvo na Bŭlgarskata akademiia na naukite—ikonomicheski institut, 1984.

MacDermott, Mercia. *Apostle of Freedom: A Portrait of Vasil Levsky against a Background of Nineteenth Century Bulgaria.* South Brunswick, N.J.: A.S. Barnes, 1969.

——. *For Freedom and Perfection: The Life of Yane Sandansky.* London: Journeyman Press, 1988.

Mandel, Ruth. "Cigarettes in Soviet and Post-Soviet Central Asia." In *Smoke,* edited by Sander Gilman and Xhou Zun, 180–89. London: Reaktion Books, 2004.

Manning, Clarence. *The History of Modern Bulgarian Literature.* New York: Bookman Associates, 1960.

Marinov, Khristo. "Ivan Pavlov." In *Iubileen nauchen sbornik, 1922–37,* edited by Krum Akhchiiski and Ianka Tosheva, 34–36. Sofia: Studentska vŭzdŭrzhatelno druzhestvo, 1937.

Markov, Georgi. *Bŭlgaro-Germanskite otnosheniia, 1931–39.* Sofia: Nauka i izkustvo, 1984.

Markov Georgi, and Vitka Toskova, eds. *Obrecheni i spaseni: Bŭlgariia v antisemitskata programa na tretiia raikh.* Sofia: Sineva, 2007.

Mateev, Boris. *Dvizhenieto za kooperativno zemedelie v Bŭlgariia pri usloviiata na kapitalizma.* Sofia: Izdatelstvo na Bŭlgarskata akademiia na naukite, 1967.

Mateev, Matei. *Stara arkhitektura v Plovdiv.* Sofia: Izdatelstvo Septemvri, 1976.

Matkovski, Alexander. *A History of Jews in Macedonia.* Skopje: Macedonian Review Editions, 1982.

Mazower, Mark. *Inside Hitler's Greece: The Experience of Occupation, 1941–44.* New Haven, CT: Yale University Press, 1995

——. *Salonica, City of Ghosts: Christians, Muslims, and Jews 1430–1950.* New York: Vintage, 2006.

McCarthy, Justin. *Death and Exile: The Ethnic Cleansing of Ottoman Muslims, 1821–1922.* Princeton, NJ: Darwin Press, 1996.

Mevsim, Hüseyin. "'Balkapan han' as Social and Private Place of Bulgarians in Istanbul in the Nineteenth Century." *Balkanistic Forum* 9 (2006): 61–66.

Miladinova, Mila. *Esteticheska kultura i trezvenost.* Sofia: Meditsina i fizkultura, 1979.

Miller, Marshall. *Bulgaria during the Second World War.* Palo Alto, CA: Stanford University Press, 1975.

Miller, William. *Travels and Politics in the Near East.* New York: Arno Press, 1971.

Mills, Mary. *Under Five Sultans.* London: Century Co., 1929.

Ministerstvo na Zdravookhraneniia, NR Bŭlgariia. *Shestoi simposium institutov sanitarnovo prosveshteniia sotsialisticheskikh stran.* Sofia: Institut sanitarnovo prosveshteniia, 1982.

Mirchev, Petŭr. *Sofiia tŭzhna i vesela: Spomeni na edno Sofiianche.* Sofia: Otechestvo, 1978.

Misirkova, E. *Turetskoe menshinstvo v narodnoi respublike Bolgarii.* Sofia: Stopancko rasvitie, 1951.

Montagu, Mary Wortley. *Turkish Embassy Letters.* Athens: University of Georgia Press, 1993.

Moore, Fredrick. *The Balkan Trail.* New York: Macmillan, 1906.

Müller, Karl. *Proizvodstvo, obrabotvane i tŭrgovie c tiutiuna v Evropeĭska Turtsia, a sega nova Bŭlgariia.* Sofia: Dŭrzhavna pechatnitsa, 1916.

Nachev, Ivan. "Politicheski aspekti na vŭzrozhdenskoto kafene." In *Kafeneto kato diskurs,* edited by Georg Kraev, 28–33. Sofia: Nov Bŭlgarski Universitet, 2005.

Nachov, Naiden. *Sbornik na Bŭlgarskata akademiia na naukite,* Vol. 19. Sofia: Pechatnitsa P. Glushkov, 1925.

Nachovich, Georgi. *Tiutiuneva industriia v Bŭlgarskoto kniazhestvo.* Sofia: Pechatnitsa na Bŭlgarski glas, 1883.

Natsionalen komitet za trezvenost, *Besedi za vredata ot tiutiunopusheneto.* Sofia: Institut za zdravna prosveta, 1976.

Nauchnoizsledovatelska laboratoriia za mladezhdta kŭm HIIM pri TsK na DKMS, *Problemi na tiutiunopusheneto i alkokholnata upotreba sred mladezhta.* Plovdiv: Izdatesltvo na Bŭlgarskata akademiia na naukite, 1983.

Nedialkov, Khristo. *Bŭlgarski kulturni deitsi za trezvenostta.* Sofia: Meditsina i fizkultura, 1977.

Nedev, Nediu. *Bŭlgarskoto masonstvo (1807–2007).* Sofia: Izdatelska kŭshta khermes, 2009.

Neikov, Petŭr. *Tekhnite obrazi: Spomeni.* Sofia: Bŭlgarski pisatel, 1956.

Nemeth, Robert. *The Once and Future Budapest.* Dekalb: Northern Illinois University Press, 2005.

Neuburger, Mary. *The Orient Within: Muslim Minorities and the Negotiation of Nationhood in Modern Bulgaria.* Ithaca: Cornell University Press, 2004.

——. "Pants, Veils, and Matters of Dress: Unraveling the Fabric of Women's Lives in Communist Bulgaria." In *Style and Socialism: Modernity and Material Culture in Post-War Eastern Europe,* edited by David Crowley and Susan Reid, 169–88. Oxford: Berg, 2000.

——. "To Chicago and Back: Aleko Konstantinov, Rose Oil, and the Smell of Modernity." *Slavic Review* 65 (2006): 427–45.

——. "Fair Encounters: Bulgaria and the 'West' at International Exhibitions from Plovdiv (1892) to Chicago (1893) to St. Louis (1904)." *Slavic Review* 69, no. 3 (2010): 547–70.

Newton, Charles. *Images of the Ottoman Empire.* London: Victoria and Albert Publications, 2007.

Norton, Marcy. *Sacred Gifts, Profane Pleasures: A History of Tobacco and Chocolate in the Atlantic World.* Ithaca: Cornell University Press, 2008.

Oliver, Khaim. *We Were Saved: How the Jews in Bulgaria Were Kept from the Death Camps.* Sofia: Sofia Press, 1978.

Özendes, Engin. *Photography in the Ottoman Empire, 1839–1919.* Istanbul: Haset Kitabevi, 1987.

Özkoçak, Selma. "Coffee Houses: Rethinking the Public and Private in Early Modern Istanbul." *Journal of Urban History* 33 (2007): 965–86.

Palairet, Michael. *The Balkan Economies c. 1800–1914: Evolution without Development.* Cambridge: Cambridge University Press, 2003.

Pamuk, Şevket. "The Ottoman Empire in the 'Great Depression' of 1873–1896." *Journal of Economic History* 44 (1984): 107–18.

Pamuk, Şevket, and Jeffrey Williamson. *The Mediterranean Response to Globalization Before 1950.* New York: Routledge, 2000.

Panova, Snezhka. *Bu˘lgarskite tu˘rgovtsi prez XVII vek: Izsledvane.* Sofia: Nauka i izkustvo, 1980.

Parusehva, Dobrinka. "Politicheska kultura na kafeneta." In *Kafene Evropa,* edited by Raia Zaimova, 80–87. Sofia: Izdatelstvo Damian Iakov, 2007.

Pashaliiska, Rumiana. "Santimentalna razkhodi iz literaturnite kŭtcheta na Sofiiska khudozhestvena bokhema." In *Kafene Evropa,* edited by Raia Zaimova, 148–56. Sofia: Izdatelstvo Damian Iakov, 2007.

Peev, Khristo. *Plovdivskata kŭshta prez epokhata na vŭzrazhdaneto.* Sofia: Tekhnika, 1960.

Pelt, Mogens. *Tobacco, Arms and Politics: Greece and Germany from World Crisis to World War 1929–41.* Copenhagen: Museum Tusculanum Press, 1998.

Pence, Katherine. "'A World in Miniature': The Leipzig Trade Fairs in the 1950s and East German Consumer Citizenship." In *Consuming Germany in the Cold War,* edited by David Crew, 21–50. Oxford: Berg, 2003.

Penchev, P., and Ct. Banov, *Tiutiun i tsigari.* Sofia, 1961.

Penev, Boian. "Uvod v Bŭlgarskata literatura sled osvobozhdenieto." In *Zasto sme takiva?V tŭrsene na Bŭlgarskata kulturna identichnost,* edited by Rumen Daskalov and Ivan Elenkov, 144–62. Sofia: Prosveta, 1994.

Perry, Duncan. *The Politics of Terror: The Macedonian Revolutionary Movements, 1893–1903* (Durham, NC: Duke University Press, 1988.

———. *Stefan Stambolov and the Emergence of Modern Bulgaria, 1870–1895.* Durham, NC: Duke University Press, 1993.

Petkov, Pavel. *Borbata za trezvenost vŭv Vrachanski okrŭg, 1920–1980.* Sofia: Izdatelstvo na otechestveniia front, 1982.

Petkov, Tzetko. "Vŭzdŭrzhane i intelligentsia." In *Iubileen nauchen sbornik, 1922–37,* edited by Krum Akhchiiski and Ianka Tosheva, 250–53. Sofia: Studentska vŭzdŭrzhatelno druzhestvo, 1937.

Phillips, Laura. *Bolsheviks and the Bottle: Drink and Worker Culture in St. Petersburg, 1900–1929.* DeKalb: Northern Illinois University Press, 2000.

Pitekov, Ivan. *S aromata na tiutiun: Stati, razkazi, pŭtepisi.* Sofia: Kompiutŭr art media, 2009.

Piti, Buko. *Te, spasiteli.* Tel Aviv: 1969.

Plaut, Joshua. *Greek Jewry in the Twentieth Century 1918–1983: Patterns of Survival in the Greek Provinces before and after the Holocaust.* Madison, NJ: Fairleigh Dickinson University Press, 2000.

Proctor, Robert. *The Nazi War on Cancer.* Princeton, NJ: Princeton University Press, 1999.

Quataert, Donald, ed. *Consumption Studies and the History of the Ottoman Empire, 1550–1922.* Albany: State University of New York Press, 2000.

———. Ottoman Manufacturing in the Nineteenth Century." In *Manufacturing in the Ottoman Empire and Turkey, 1500–1950,* edited by Donald Quataert, 87–122. Albany: State University Press of New York Press, 1994.

Radoslavov, Ivan, Lilia Radoslavova Popova, and Ivan Sestrimski. *Spomeni, dnevnitsi, pisma.* Sofia: Bŭlgarski pisatel, 1983.

Rashev, Strashimir, and Boyan Bolgar. *Bulgarian Black Sea Coast.* Sofia: Sofia Press, 1968.

Reato, Danilo. *The Coffee-house: Venetian Coffee-houses from 18th to 20th century.* Venice: Arsenale, 1991.

Reid, Susan. "Cold War in the Kitchen: Gender and the De-Stalinization of Consumer Taste in the Soviet Union under Khrushchev." *Slavic Review* 61 (2008): 211–52.

Roche, Daniel. *A History of Everyday Things: The Birth of Consumption in France, 1600–1800.* Cambridge: Cambridge University Press, 2000.

Rothschild, Joseph. *East Central Europe between the Two World Wars.* Seattle: University of Washington Press, 1977.

Rowe, William. "The Public Sphere in Modern China." *Modern China* 16 (1990): 309–29.

Roy, Srirupa. "Seeing a State: National Commemorations and the Public Sphere in India and Turkey." *Comparative Studies in Society and History* 48 (2006): 200–232.

Said, Edward. *Orientalism*. New York: Vintage, 1979.

Salmon, Shawn. "Marketing Socialism: Inturist in the Late 1950s and Early 1960s." In *Turizm: The Russian and East European Tourist under Capitalism and Socialism*, edited by Anne Gorsuch and Diane Koenker, 186–204. Ithaca: Cornell University Press, 2006.

Sarandev, Ivan. *Dora Gabe*. Sofia: Nauka i izkustvo, 1986.

Schivelbusch, Wolfgang. *Tastes of Paradise: A Social History of Spices, Stimulants, and Intoxicants.* New York: Vintage Books, 1992.

Semerdzhiev, Petŭr. *Narodniit sŭd v Bŭlgariia, 1944–45: Komu i zasto e bil neobkhodimo.* Sofia: Makedoniia Press, 1997.

Sergeeva, Boriana. "Kafeto—Luks, koito vseki mozhe da si pozvoli." In *Kafeneto kato diskurs,* edited by Georg Kraev, 96–97. Sofia: Nov Bŭlgarski universitet, 2005.

Shaw, Stanford, and Ezel Shaw. *The History of the Ottoman Empire and Turkey.* Vol. 2, *Reform, Revolution, and Republic.* Cambridge: Cambridge University Press, 1977.

Shechter, Relli. *Smoking, Culture and Economy in the Middle East: The Egyptian Tobacco Market 1850–2000.* New York: I.B. Tauris, 2006.

Shumkova, Lora. "Mechtaniia za kafene sredets." In *Kafeneto kato diskurs,* edited by Georg Kraev, 66–75. Sofia: Nov Bŭlgarski Universitet, 2005.

Sheimanov, Naiden. "Preobrazhenie na Bŭlgariia." In *Zasto sme takiva: V tursene na Bŭlgarskata idenitichnost,* edited by Rumen Daskalov and Ivan Elenkov, 266–69. Sofia: Izdatelstvo prosveta, 1994.

Sikulnov, Nikolai. *Za da ne propushat nashite detsa.* Sofia: Meditsina i fizkultura, 1980.

Şimşir, Bilal. *Bulgarian Turks: 1878–1895.* London: K. Rustem, 1988.

Slater, Don. *Consumer Culture and Modernity, Polity.* Cambridge: Polity Press, 1999.

Smith, Anthony. *The Ethnic Origins of Nations.* Oxford: Blackwell, 1986.

Smith, Woodruff. *Consumption and the Making of Respectability, 1600–1800.* New York: Routledge, 2002.

Spasov, Malamar. "Balkanski mekhani-zmi." In *Kafene Evropa,* edited by Raia Zaimova, 110–16. Sofia: Izdatelstvo Damian Iakov, 2007.

Staikov, Zakhari. *Biudzhet na vremeto na trudeshtite se v NRB.* Sofia: Nauka i izkustvo, 1964.

Starks, Tricia. "Papirosy, Smoking, and the Anti-Cigarette Movement." In *Tobacco in Russian History and Culture: From the Seventeenth Century to the Present,* edited by Matthew Romaniello and Tricia Starks, 132–47. New York: Routledge, 2009.

St. Clair, Stanislas, and Charles Brophy. *Residence in Bulgaria: or, Notes on the Resources and Administration of Turkey: The Condition and Character, Manners, Customs, and Language of the Christian and Musselman Populations, with Reference to the Eastern Question.* London: J. Murray, 1869.

Stenografski dnevnitsi na XXV-to obiknoveno narodno sŭbranie: Vtora redovna sesiia. Vol. 1. Sofia: Narodno sŭbranie, 1940.

Sterns, Peter. *Consumerism in World History: The Global Transformation of Desire.* New York: Routledge, 2006.

Stoianov, Kristo. *Dvizheniie za trezvenost v Razgradski okrŭg.* Razgrad: Okrŭzhen komitet za trezvenost, 1983.

Stoianovich, Traian. "The Conquering Balkan Orthodox Merchant." *Journal of Economic History* 20 (1960): 234–313.

Stoyanov, Zahari. *Extracts from Notes on the Bulgarian Uprisings.* Sofia: Sofia Press, 1976.

Strashimirov, Anton. *Zheni i muzhe v zhivota i v literaturata.* Sofia: S.M. Staikov, 1930.

Sŭbev, Vicho. *90 godini organizirano turistichesko dvizheniie v Bŭlgariia.* Sofia: Meditsina i fizkultura, 1986.

Takhov, Rosen. *Golemite Bŭlgarski senzatsii.* Sofia: Izdatelstvo iztok-zapad, 2005.

Takov, Petko. *Nov etap v razvitieto na turizma v NRP.* Sofia: Meditsina i fizkultura, 1976.

Tamir, Vicki. *Bulgaria and Her Jews: The History of a Dubious Symbiosis.* New York: Yeshiva University Press, 1979.

Tashev, Petŭr. Sofiia; arkhitekturno gradoustroistveno razvitie: Etapi, postizheniia i problemi. Sofia: Tekhnika, 1972.

Taylor, Karin. *Let's Twist Again: Youth and Leisure in Socialist Bulgaria.* Berlin: Lit Verlag, 2008.

Tileva, Viktoria. *Bŭlgarsko pechatarsko druzhestvo 'promishlenie' v Tsarigrad, 1870–85.* Sofia: Narodna biblioteka Kiril i Metodi, 1985.

Timov, Angel, Georgi Lazarov, and Metodi Veselinov. *Borbi po pŭtia na nasheto tiutiunoproizvodstvo.* Plovdiv: Izdatelstvo na Khristo G. Danov, 1973.

Todorov, Georgi. "Deinostta na vremenoto Rusko upravlenie v Bŭlgariia po urezhdane na agrarniia i bezhanskiia vŭpros prez 1877–1879 g." *Istoricheski Pregled* 6 (1955): 36–48.

Todorova, Maria. *Imagining the Balkans.* Oxford: Oxford University Press, 1997.

Todorova, Tsvetana, ed. *Bŭlgariia v pŭrvata svetovna voina: Germanski diplomatichecki dokumenti.* Sofia: Glavno upravlaniie na arkhivite pri ministerkiia suvet, 2005.

Toshev, Biser. "Kafeneta. Galeriia ot tipove i nravi Bŭlgarski v tursko vreme." In *Kafeneto kato diskurs,* edited by Georg Kraev, 25–28. Sofia: Nov Bŭlgarski Universitet, 2005.

Tosheva, Ianka. "Roliata na studentkata v vŭzdŭrzhatelno dvizhenie." In *Iubileen nauchen sbornik, 1922–37,* edited by Krum Akhchiiski and Ianka Tosheva, 36–42. Sofia: Studentska vŭzdŭrzhatelno druzhestvo, 1937.

Toshkova, Vitka, and Adolf-Heinz Bekerle. *Iz dnevnika na Bekerle: Pŭlnomoshten ministur na tretiia raikh v Bŭlgariia.* Sofia: Khristo Botev, 1992.

Traichev, Georgi. *Grad Prilep: Istoriko-geografsko i stopansko pregled.* Sofia: Pechatnitsa Fotinov, 1925.

Transchel, Kate. *Under the Influence: Working-Class Drinking, Temperance, and Cultural Revolution in Russia, 1895–1932.* Pittsburgh: University of Pittsburgh Press, 2006.

Trotsky, Leon. *The Balkan Wars: 1912–3.* New York: Monad Press, 1980.

Tsanev, Georgi. *Sreshta s minaloto: Spomeni.* Sofia: Bŭlgarski pisatel, 1977.

Tsentralno statistichesko upravlenie pri ministerskiia sŭvet. *Mezhdunaroden i vŭtreshen turizŭm, 1960–1967.* Sofia: Tsentralno statistichesko upravlenie, 1968.

Tsonchev, Vasil, ed. *Tiutiunopushene i zdrave: Sbornik tezisi za lektsii.* Sofia: Ministerstvo na narodnoto zdrave, 1979.

Tsonkov, Geno. *Sotsialisticheski nachin na zhivot i trezvenost.* Sofia: Meditsina i fizkultura, 1978.

——. *Trezvenostta, svobodno vreme i vsestrannoto razvitie na lichnostta.* Sofia: Meditsina i fizkultura, 1980.

Tunçay, Mete, and Erik Jan Zürcher, eds. *Socialism and Nationalism in the Ottoman Empire, 1876–1923.* London: Palgrave Macmillan, 1994.

Turncock, David. *East European Economy in Context: Communism and Transition.* Routledge: New York, 1997.

Uzunska, Elena. "Plovdiv v navecheriia na osvoboditelna voina." In *Plovdiv, 1878–1968: 90 godini ot osvobozhdeniie na grada i Plovdivskiia krai,* edited by Ivan Undzhiev, Plovdiv: Izdatelstvo na Khristo G. Danov, 1968.

Vangelov, Georgi. *Tiutiunopabotnitsi: Spomeni iz borbite na tiutiunopabotnitsite.* Sofia: Profizdat, 1955.

Vaptsarova, Boika. *Nikola Vaptsarov: Letopis za zhivota i tvorchestvoto mu.* Sofia: BAN, 1978.

Vazov, Ivan. *Chichovtsi: Galeriia ot tipove i nravi Bŭlgarski v Tursko vreme.* Plovdiv: Izdatelstvo na Khristo G. Danov, 1983.

——. *Pŭtepisi.* Sofia: Bŭlgarski Pisatel, 1974.

——. *Under the Yoke.* New York: Twayne Publishers, Inc., 1971.

——. *Velika Rilska Gora.* Sofia: Dimitur Blagoev, 1954.

Velchev, Koitcho. *Tobacco in Bulgaria.* Sofia: Marco Beltchev and Sons.

Verdery, Katherine. *What Was Socialism and What Comes Next.* Princeton: Princeton University Press, 1996.

Villari, Luigi, ed. *The Balkan Question: The Present Condition of the Balkans and of European Responsibilities by Various Writers.* London: John and Murray, 1905.

Vlakhov, Dimitŭr. *Rezhima na tiuiutna v nova i stara Bŭlgariia.* Burgas: Pechatnitsa N. V. Velchev, 1914.

Vlakhova-Nikolova, Veselina. *Problemi na tiutiunopusheneto i alkokholnata upotreba sred mladezhta.* Plovdiv: Nauchnoizsledovatelska laboratoriia za mladezhdta, 1983.

Washburn, George. *Fifty Years in Constantinople and Recollections of Robert College.* New York: Houghton Mifflin, 1909.

Webster, William. *Puritans in the Balkans: The American Board Mission in Bulgaria, 1878–1918, A Study in Purpose and Procedure.* Sofia: Studia Historico-Philologica Serdicensia, 1938.

Weinbaum, Alys Eve et al., eds. *The Modern Girl around the World: Consumption, Modernity, Globalization.* Durham, NC: Duke University Press, 2008.

Weinberg, Alan, and Bonnie Bealer, *The World of Caffeine: The Science and Culture of the World's Most Popular Drug.* New York: Routledge, 2002.

White, Anne. *Destalinization and the House of Culture.* London: Routledge, 1990.

Wilkinson, Henry. *Maps and Politics: A Review of the Ethnographic Cartography of Macedonia.* Liverpool: Liverpool University Press, 1951.

Wills, Martin. *A Captive of the Bulgarian Brigands: Englishman's Terrible Experiences in Macedonia.* London: EDE, Allom, and Townsend, 1906.

Wolff, Larry. *Inventing Eastern Europe: The Map of Civilization on the Mind of the Enlightenment.* Palo Alto, CA: Stanford University Press, 1994.

Zahra, Tara. *Kidnapped Souls: National Indifference and the Battle for Children in the Bohemian Lands, 1900–1948.* Ithaca: Cornell University Press, 2008.

Zaimes, Theodoros. *The Crimes of Bulgaria in Macedonia: An Authentic Document, Based on Facts and Records.* Washington, DC: University of Athens, 1914.

Zaimova, Raia. ed. *Kafene Evropa*. Sofia: Izdatelstvo Damian Iakov, 2007.

Zhelova, Neli. "Kafenetata na stariia Shumen." In *Kafeneto kato diskurs,* edited by Georg Kraev, 45–52. Sofia: Nov Bŭlgarski Universitet, 2005.

Znepolski, Ivailo. Bŭlgarskiiat komunizŭm: Sotsiokulturni cherti i vlastova traektoriia. Sofia: Ciela Press, 2008.

INDEX

Numbers in italics refer to illustrations and photographs.

Sokotab (Oriental tobacco buyer), 221
Soviet Union, 163, 174, 278n63
  abstinence movement and, 98, 170,
    255n25
  tobacco market, 200, 202
Sredets *(kafene),* 89, 93, 173
St. Clair, Stanislas, 15–16, 18–19
Stalin, Joseph, 98, 170, 174
Stamatov (tobacco factory owner), 68
Stamboliski, Alexander, 83, 111–112, 120,
    123, 128, 261n9
  support for agricultural cooperatives,
    114, 115
Stambolov, Stefan, 45, 247n12
Stamov, Stavri, 52
Stanimaka, 108, 113, 121
  Cherveni Kvartal (Red Quarter),
    125, 126
State Council of Bulgaria, 186
Stavrides, Dimitŭr, 44, 51, 63, 68, 248n36
Stoianov, Khristo, 172, 244n106
Stoianov, Kosta, 90
Stomaniakov, Khristo, 160
Stone, Ellen, 61
Storm brand cigarettes, 140
Strashimirov, Anton, 101
"Strast" (Konstantinov), 38
Sufism, 20

Tadzher, Avram, 158
Tadzher, Leon, 154
Takvorian, Takvor, 139, 142, 162
temperance movement. *See* abstinence
    movement
textile industry, 6, 49, 244n99
Thrace, 44, 46, 49, 55, 145
  deportation of Jews, 155–157
  ethnic tensions within, 71
  Slavic refugees to Bulgaria, 59,
    251n100
  World War II occupation, 151–153
Timov, Angel, 205
Tir brand cigarettes, 223–224
Tiutiun (Dimov), 137, 143, 161
*Tiutiunopabotnik zashitnik/Tobacco-Worker
    Protector* (Narrows publication), 65, 66,
    68, 69
tobacco, 3–4
  economic importance to Bulgaria,
    44–45, 46, 58–59, 114
  as literary muse, 88–89
  Muslim religious elites, objection
    to, 20–21
  processing needs, *50,* 51, *52,* 113–114

  World War I rise in production and
    consumption, 69–70
  World War II demand, 135–136
  See also smoking; *specific* tobaccos
Tobacco and Cigarettes, 210
tobacco cooperatives, 114, 115, 123–124,
    128–129, 132, 146–147
  See also Asenovgrad Krepost
tobacco export trade, 57–58
tobacco factory owners, 67–68
tobacco industry, American
  Eastern Bloc focus, 211–213
tobacco industry, Bulgarian, 2, *47,* 55,
    194, 204
  Balkan Wars as boon to, 72–73
  early prominent tobacconists, 50–53
  exports to Nazi Germany, 142, 202,
    250n68
  protectionism and, 59
  workforce, 68–69, 73, 75, 120,
    218–219
  working conditions, 120, 153–154
  World War I and, 74–75
  See also Bulgartabak; labor movement
Tobacco Institute (Plovdiv), 216
Tobacco in the Bulgarian Economy
    (Asseoff), 129–130
tobacco smuggling, 56–57
tobacco workers, 68–69, 73, 75, 120, 218–219
  communism as boon to, 201
  support for Fatherland Front, 205, 206
Todorova, Maria, 238n9, 239n23
Tolstoy, Lev, 97
Tolstoyanism, 97
Tomasian, Magurdich, 50–51, 68
Tomasian and Sons Inc., 50
Tosheva, Ianka, 102, 104
tourism industry, 168, 179–180
  foreign visitors, 180–182
  proliferation of leisure sites, 168–169,
    176–178
  state promotion of, 167–168
tourist movement, 38–39, 175
Treaty of Berlin (1878), 49, 245n131
Treaty of Bucharest (1913), 73
Treaty of Niš (1923), 118–119
Trezva borba/Abstinence Struggle (newspaper),
    171
Trezvenost (abstinence newspaper), 80, 82,
    103, 189, 192, 194, 271n14
  depictions of smoking women,
    196–197
  revival of, 183
Triest, Fred, 212

CPSIA information can be obtained
at www.ICGtesting.com
Printed in the USA
LVHW091513060222
710388LV00007B/1136